To MY DEAR SON A

MW01490384

DAD/Tom

My Mouth Will Speak
in Praise of the Lord

To my precious children, grandchildren and their children:
may these words speak to them.

My Mouth Will Speak
in Praise of the Lord

Psalm 145.21

Thomas A. Kuster

First Printing: 2020

ISBN 978-1-71681-991-9

Thomas A. Kuster
1018 S. Payne St.
New Ulm, Minnesota, USA 56073

Cover pictures: Locations where most of these sermons were presented.

Front: Altar area of Trinity Chapel, Bethany Lutheran College, Mankato, Minnesota, USA.
    Triptych painted by William Bukowski.

Back: Window in the Good Shepherd Chapel, Bethany Lutheran Theological Seminary,
    Mankato, Minnesota, USA.

Images used by permission.

This is a Lulu publication. https://www.lulu.com

Contents

Foreword

The title of this collection of "chapel talks" and sermons is taken from Psalm 145. It was the motto of the Bethany Lutheran College Speech Team for the years I had the honor of coaching. I hope too it was the overriding spirit of all the preaching I was privileged to do throughout my ministry.

This collection represents my preaching over the twenty-five or so years of my service at Bethany which began full-time in 1991. Every faithful and experienced pastor has a trove of sermons preached over many decades, each of them the result of painstaking study of a scriptural text and his best effort at that time of discerning and presenting to his flock the message of God to his people. Each of those sermons deserves placement and preservation in a book. There is nothing special about these ten-dozen or so short "chapel talks," most of them prepared for the students gathered in Trinity Chapel at Bethany Lutheran College in Mankato, Minnesota.[1] I have reconstructed them from my preaching notes and gathered them here primarily for my family.

I've found great comfort in reviewing these works of years ago, writing now at the time when the COVID-19 virus spreads rapidly and finding myself by virtue of my age [80] among the "vulnerable" population. To paraphrase Samuel Johnson, the realization that one might be on a respirator in three days and dead in six "concentrates the mind." But then, that is an attitude that becomes Christians at any age and enhances their commitment to trust the Lord's plan in all things. We have prayed all of our lives, "Thy will be done on earth as it is in Heaven" and concluded with "Amen" which means "I am confident it will be so." Meanwhile Judy and I will follow Martin Luther's advice as he dealt with the black plague: pray for God's protection, then be as careful as possible to protect ourselves and others.[2] Our plan is not to get it. Plan B is if we get it, to get well. If God has another plan, it will by God's grace

---

[1] Those not presented in Trinity Chapel at Bethany are noted in the headings.

[2] "I shall ask God mercifully to protect us. Then I shall fumigate, help purify the air, administer medicine, and take it. I shall avoid places and persons where my presence is not needed in order to not become contaminated and thus perchance infect and pollute others, and so cause their death as a result of my negligence. If God should wish to take me, he will surely find me, and I have done what he has expected of me and so I am not responsible for either my own death or the death of others. If my neighbor needs me, however, I shall not avoid place or person but will go freely, as stated above. See, this is such a God-fearing faith because it is neither brash nor foolhardy and does not tempt God." Letter to Rev. Dr. Johann Hess (1527), "Whether one may flee from a deadly plague," *Luther's Works*, Vol. 43, p.132.

be a better one and we will manage according to the title of my earlier sermon collection: *With the Strength God Gives Me.*

Sermons, even shorter chapel talks like most of these, with few exceptions don't come easily for any pastor. They are typically hard, even agonizing work especially given the obligation to be a faithful spokesperson for God. Judy well knows how to recognize from my withdrawn demeanor that I have a sermon coming up in a few days. But the reward is great. It is profoundly and personally enriching to dig deeply into the Word, discern God's message for the particular audience he has placed before me, find the words to present it as clearly as I can so it will be attended to, and then leave the effect to the Holy Spirit.

Anyone who chooses to read much of this book will notice that some themes recur, reworked for various texts, such as the basketball on the rim and the dangers of visiting Israel these days. These were presented several years apart and each time for a new audience. In college the major part of the audience changes entirely in four years and the part that doesn't, the faculty and staff, might not remember something they heard a half-decade before.

One theme, however, that appears repeatedly is the Gospel, the good news of what God in his love for us has done to rescue us from our sin, the narrative of how the life, death and resurrection of his Son Jesus, the promised Messiah (in Greek, the Christ), paid for all of our sins and restored us to God. This message of the forgiveness of our sins, a gift of God's pure and undeserved grace that we receive by faith, appears in some fashion in every item in this book. Is the Gospel message repetitive here? I hope so. There should be Gospel, the proclamation of the forgiveness of sins, in every sermon. I myself need to hear it every Sunday and to be assured of it when remembering my Baptism every day. If your preacher omits preaching the forgiveness of sins once in a while, forgive him. If it's missing all the time, switch churches.

What follows is an abridgement of the *Foreword* of my previous sermon collection, *With the Strength God Gives Me*, which I include here because it applies to this collection as well.

Thomas A. Kuster
May 2020

From the Foreword to Previous Collection

This book does not contain great sermons. I hear better ones every week at my home church, and I hope you do too at yours. But I've compiled this collection as a gift to my family, in the hope that it will further stir up the faith that is already in them, and reinforce their commitment to pass on to the next generations the inestimable treasure that is the Gospel of Jesus Christ, and in particular, the Bible-centered Lutheran understanding of it which is the essence of Christianity.

It's a test of trust in God's wisdom that he chooses to call on frail human beings to **preach his Word**. Why doesn't he just ask us to go about handing out copies of the Bible? My understanding of God's plan goes to the heart of my academic specialty, Rhetoric, in which the concept of "audience" is paramount. God's Word is true and a reliable guide to doctrine and life for all people of all times and it never changes. But people and times do change. So God calls on preachers to consider the truths of his Word, then bring them to people, individually and in groups, in a way that enables them to understand how the Word speaks to them in their particular situations and needs – and through that preaching God the Holy Spirit works to produce saving faith in the hearts of listeners.

While my preaching style may have evolved over the decades, I'm satisfied to note, looking back over these sermons, that the Gospel was always there – not always as clearly and powerfully as it should have been, perhaps, but there was always the message that, because of the life, death, and resurrection of our Lord Jesus Christ, our sins are forgiven, and God's strength and the sure promise of eternal life belong to all who trust in him. I hope the reader can look past the peculiarities and imperfections of these sermons and see that central message.

A few notes about sermons in print. I hope it doesn't bother you that I do not follow the older tradition of capitalizing pronouns referring to God and Jesus, a tradition that has passed away. The word "Heaven" is capitalized because it is a real place; hell is also a real place but is not capitalized because it doesn't deserve the respect. On my sermon notes "INI" always appears at the top; it stands for the Latin phrase *in nomine Iesu* ("in Jesus' name"), a reminder to the preacher that he is to say no more and no less than is found in the portion of Scripture before him, and that he is speaking not his own opinions, but as a representative of our Lord. At the end of all my sermon notes appears "SDG," a notation used by Bach, Handel and others; it stands for *soli deo Gloria*, "to God alone the glory," reminding the preacher that it is only by God's grace and strength that he is able to be such a spokesperson for God. That's why, before and after every time I spoke in church or chapel, I said a prayer of thanks for that great gift and honor. And it underlies the title of this book.

Those, however, are all matters of print – they don't show up as a sermon is preached. And sermons are meant to be preached, not read. I'm afraid the reader of those in this book may miss the aspects of these sermons that are conveyed by eye contact, gesture, and vocal emphasis. Reading devotional materials is useful, but I believe there is profound meaning in the Bible's phrase, "Faith comes by **hearing**..." Romans 10.17

An exercise in looking back, as this has been for me, cannot but revive all the memories of the times I've failed, that I haven't been clear, or even haven't been ready to "give an answer to everyone who asks a reason for the hope that is in you." 1 Peter 3.15 Each of those times still troubles me – and there may be others of which I don't even know. But I take refuge in the assurance that even these sins have been fully paid for by my Lord Jesus on the cross, and that at the Judgment God will look at me wearing the white robe of perfect preaching and witnessing carried out by Jesus and graciously transferred to me. Whatever good I have done has been, as the title gratefully proclaims, with the strength God gives me.

Sunday worship among Norwegian Lutherans traditionally ended with the pastor kneeling at the altar and, on behalf of the congregation, speaking this closing prayer:

> *"O Lord! We render unto Thee our heartfelt thanks that Thou hast taught us what Thou wouldst have us believe and do. Help us, O God, by Thy Holy Spirit, for the sake of Jesus Christ, to keep Thy Word in pure hearts, that we thereby may be strengthened in faith, perfected in holiness, and comforted in life and in death. Amen."*

May this be the prayer of all of our children and grandchildren and others who follow. To them this book is dedicated.

Thomas A. Kuster
May 2017

January 24, 1996

A Dramatic Conversion

INI

[With the help of the Bethany Speech Team, this chapel service featured an unique way of presenting the Scripture reading assigned for this day.]

N1 (m) and N2 (m) are narrators, located front and center.
J is the voice of Jesus (2 or 3 persons (1or 2 m 1 f), in balcony)
S is Saul, located in front stage-left corner
A is Ananias, located in front stage-right corner
P1 (f) and P2 (m) are people of Damascus, located front stage-right side

N1: Meanwhile, Saul was still breathing out murderous threats against the Lord's disciples. He went to the high priest and asked him for letters to the synagogues in Damascus,

N2: so that if he found any there who belonged to the Way, whether men or women, he might take them as prisoners to Jerusalem.

N1: As he neared Damascus on his journey, suddenly a light from heaven flashed around him. He fell to the ground and heard a voice say to him,

J: "Saul, Saul, why do you persecute me?"

S: "Who are you, Lord?"

J: "I am Jesus, whom you are persecuting. Now get up and go into the city, and you will be told what you must do."

N1: The men traveling with Saul stood there speechless;

N2: they heard the sound but did not see anyone.

N1: Saul got up from the ground, but when he opened his eyes he could see nothing.

N2: So they led him by the hand into Damascus.

N1: For three days he was blind and did not eat or drink anything.

N2: In Damascus there was a disciple named Ananias. The Lord called to him in a vision,

J: "Ananias!"

A: "Yes, Lord,"

J: "Go to the house of Judas on Straight Street and ask for a man from Tarsus named Saul, for he is praying. In a vision he has seen a man named Ananias come and place his hands on him to restore his sight."

A: "Lord, I have heard many reports about this man and all the harm he has done to your saints in Jerusalem. And he has come here with authority from the chief priests to arrest all who call on your name."

J: "Go! This man is my chosen instrument to carry my name before the Gentiles and their kings and before the people of Israel. I will show him how much he must suffer for my name."

N1:   Then Ananias went to the house and entered it. Placing his hands on Saul, he said,

A: "Brother Saul, the Lord – Jesus, who appeared to you on the road as you were coming here – has sent me so that you may see again and be filled with the Holy Spirit."

N2:   Immediately, something like scales fell from Saul's eyes, and he could see again.

N1:   He got up and was baptized, and after taking some food, he regained his strength.

N2:   Saul spent several days with the disciples in Damascus. At once he began to preach in the synagogues that Jesus is the Son of God.

N1:   All those who heard him were astonished and asked,

P1:   "Isn't he the man who raised havoc in Jerusalem among those who call on this name?

P2:   And hasn't he come here to take them as prisoners to the chief priests?"

N1:   Yet Saul grew more and more powerful and baffled the Jews living in Damascus by proving that Jesus is the Christ.   Acts 9.1ff

John Lennon, we are told, is the one who said, "Life is what happens while you are making other plans." Could a thought like that have passed through the mind of the Apostle Paul as, later in life, he reflected back on the happening we just heard?

More likely, in his more serious moments, his thoughts about this event echoed the traditional prayer of the believing church through the ages: ***converte me, domine, ad te***. That is, "Turn me around, O Lord, toward you."

It's a marvelous prayer, one that I recommend this morning should become your daily prayer, because it's a prayer that reflects deepest Christian faith. It's a prayer by which we put all our trust in God. This prayer recognizes that in our natural condition of unbelief we can do nothing, that it takes action by God to turn us around from our sinful condition. There was nothing we did do or could do to turn ourselves toward God. That's why God, moved by his love to save us, took action, and sent Jesus to do all that was needed to satisfy God's demands on our behalf.

Then God also sends us his Holy Spirit to seize our hearts and turn them into believing hearts that put on, like a white robe, the righteousness that Christ has won for us. That's all God's work, not ours – he turns us toward himself by giving us the gift of faith.

But even after that happens, God is not done turning us, and the **believer** is not done praying: *converte me domine ad te.* Even as believers our direction is so often wrong. Saul was no unbeliever. He was a believer. He believed fervently in God, but he did not believe as God wanted him to. In persecuting the followers of Jesus, he thought he was right. He thought he was serving God. But in persecuting them he was persecuting his Savior Jesus and didn't even realize it.

Now, we always think we are right, don't we? It was someone named Ashleigh Brilliant who said, "My opinions may have changed, but not the fact that I am right." Isn't that how it is with us? We always think we are right even though we are not – yesterday I thought I was right, then I changed my mind, and now I think more than ever I am right!

No, we continually need God's help to be on the right track. We constantly need to be turned toward God. We constantly need to be surprised, as Saul was, perhaps stricken with blindness, without a clue about why this is happening to us, and confronted with words like those he heard: "Get up, go into city, you will be told what you must do."

God still is the one who turns us, who stops us on our way, who then speaks to us through his Ananiases, his messengers who bring us his **Word** to direct us. And by that Word we are turned around again toward God. It's not always a way we would have chosen; as the Lord said about Saul, he would show him how much he must suffer.

So the next time you are surprised, the next time your life takes a new route while you are making other plans, the next time you are turned around, remember that it is in response to our prayer: turn me around, O Lord, toward you. Lord, I know and believe your promise, that all things work together for good to them that love God. And I remember and cling to those verses from Romans chapter 8 that many of us heard again as the sermon text last Monday morning, that nothing can separate us from the love of God. Romans 8.39

And with that awareness we can be content. In fact, we can be emboldened, no matter what happens, no matter how things seem to be against us, no matter how much our plans are forced to change, we can face our new, unplanned future with no regrets, no whining. Saul never said after his life was changed, "Oh nuts, I still wish I could persecute at least a couple of Christians." No, no regrets at all, for we recognize the hand of God in even the unhappy twists of life. We let God turn us, knowing that even the happenings beyond our control – maybe **especially** the happenings beyond our control, somehow have in them the answer to our prayer of faith: *converte me domine ad te.*   †

January 11, 1999

In View of God's Mercy

INI

Did you enjoy Christmas? Did you talk with your folks about your plans? Maybe you came back to school with new plans about class work, extracurriculars, life with your friends, what you'll be doing next year. For some of you this is your last semester at Bethany.[1] It's plan-making time; you can't put it off anymore.

Your plan-making – that's what I want to talk with you about this morning. This message from the Word of God gives you some important factors to take into account when you plan, if you want your plans to be God-pleasing and successful. This message is only for those who enjoyed Christmas. If you didn't enjoy Christmas, if you missed Christmas, I'm not talking to you this morning. I'm not talking about the vacation part, I'm talking about what Christmas really is, because Christmas – what Christmas really is – will have a huge effect on your planning.

Enjoying Christmas starts with listening to the Word of God and learning about the death sentence hanging over us. When we compare ourselves to the standard set by our Creator and see how far short we've fallen, we know the condemnation we deserve. It's as if we are on death row, just counting down the days until ushered into the execution chamber. Not a happy thought, to be sure, but we have to know sin or we won't enjoy Christmas. That's because in Christmas we see the mercy of God. Christmas was when, according to his promise, God began to bring about our rescue from death row. At Christmas God sent his Son Jesus to become human. He came to live without sin. He came to die, punished for sin – not his, but mine and yours. He came to fulfill our death sentence for us and left us with **life.** That's why we enjoy Christmas: it displays the mercy of God to you and me.

Now, what does that have to do with your planning? Consider these words: "In view of God's mercy." I said this Word of God is about planning, and it is only for those who enjoyed Christmas. I know that because these words open the reading: "in view of God's mercy." God is urging us here, through his apostle, to make our plans "in view of God's mercy." Will that make a difference? Listen carefully:

> Therefore, I urge you, **in view of God's mercy**, to offer your bodies as living sacrifices, holy and pleasing to God — this is your spiritual

---

[1] Bethany still had a strong A.A. degree program at this time; only a minority of sophomores would continue in the four-year-degree program. Bethany's first B.A. degrees were issued in 2001.

act of worship. **Do not conform any longer to the pattern of this world** but be transformed by the renewing of your mind. Then you will be able to test and approve what God's will is – his good, pleasing and perfect will. For by the grace given me I say to every one of you: Do not think of yourself more highly than you ought, but rather think of yourself with sober judgment, in accordance with the measure of faith God has given you. Just as each of us has one body with many members, and these members do not all have the same function, so in Christ we who are many form one body, and each member belongs to all the others. Romans 12.1-5

That's the reading. Now consider: How will you make plans in view of God's mercy? How will you plan **classwork** in view of God's mercy? We read, "offer your bodies as living sacrifices." How will you plan **life with friends** in view of God's mercy? We read, "Don't conform to the pattern of this world." How will you plan **extracurriculars** in view of God's mercy? We read, "Be transformed by the renewing of you mind." How will you plan your choice of a **major** in view of God's mercy? We read, "Test and approve what God's will is." How will you plan your **life** in view of God's mercy? We read, "We who are many form one body, and each member belongs to all the others."

You've enjoyed Christmas – you know God's mercy. Consider how will you make your plans in view of God's mercy?

†

February 1, 1999

The Answer is Yes

INI

Have you ever visited Jerusalem? Of course the answer for most of us here must be – yes.

Did you ever authorize the killing of two pigeons? Again the answer is the same for all of us – yes.

Did you ever love someone perfectly, constantly, without wavering and without ever a selfish thought? Yes.

Have you loved God perfectly, acting always in complete and willing harmony with God's will? Once more the answer is, yes, of course.

I don't know which of these answers struck you as most strange – in fact, most false. I know that most of us here have never been in Jerusalem. Certainly none of us, not one, loves God perfectly. So the real answers are just the opposite of what I first gave. We never were in Jerusalem, never had pigeons killed, never loved anyone perfectly, never loved God perfectly. All this becomes quite important, especially important if you were to hear that all these are things God expects, even commands us to do.

That's the point of those questions, really. They highlight our failures. Even the best of our attempts to love each other, even those we choose to love the most are tainted with selfish lapses where we hurt instead of love. As for loving God perfectly in full harmony with his will? Not – even – close.

Yet while all of our answers to these questions – have we obeyed God in this or that – must be **no,** still I'll cling to the answers I first gave: the answer is **yes.** Because Jesus did it on our behalf. We hear often of how Jesus bore our sins and paid for them on the cross. We can never overstate the importance of that to us. Because of Jesus' death on the cross our sins are forgiven. But this is equally important: Jesus fulfilled all of God's demands for us, in our place. To die for **our** sins, Jesus had to be himself sinless. Before giving his life to pay our debt of sin he lived his life free of sin on our behalf. Our sin was loaded on him and his sinless life was credited to us.

So we can, in Christ, answer all those questions **yes**. Did you ever visit Jerusalem as God had commanded all firstborn males to do? In Christ we answer yes, we fulfilled that law of God. Did you ever authorize the killing of two pigeons, the sacrifice God ordered for that occasion? In Christ we answer yes, we fulfilled that law of God. Did you ever love someone perfectly, constantly, without wavering, and without a selfish thought? In Christ, only in Christ, we answer yes, we fulfilled that law of God. Have you loved God perfectly, always in complete and willing harmony with God's will? Thank you, Lord Jesus, for in you we can answer this question too: **yes**.

Listen now, as we read the Evangelist Luke's account of how Jesus began to fulfill all of God's Law for us and of the wondrous events that happened on his – may I say **our** trip to Jerusalem?

> When the time of their purification according to the Law of Moses had been completed, Joseph and Mary took him to Jerusalem to present him to the Lord, (as it is written in the Law of the Lord, "Every firstborn male is to be consecrated to the Lord"), and to offer a sacrifice in keeping with what is said in the Law of the Lord: "a pair of doves or two young pigeons." Now there was a man in Jerusalem called Simeon, who was righteous and devout. He was waiting for the consolation of Israel, and the Holy Spirit was upon him. It had been revealed to him by the Holy Spirit that he would not die before he had seen the Lord's Christ. Moved by the Spirit, he went into the temple courts. When the parents brought in the child Jesus to do for him what the custom of the Law required, Simeon took him in his arms and praised God, saying, "Sovereign Lord, as you have promised you now dismiss your servant in peace. For my eyes have seen your salvation, which you have prepared in the sight of all people, a light for revelation to the Gentiles and for glory to your people Israel." The child's father and mother marveled at what was said about him. Then Simeon blessed them and said to Mary, his mother: "This child is destined to cause the falling and rising of many in Israel, and to be a sign that will be spoken against, so that the thought of many hearts will be revealed. And a sword will pierce your own soul too." There was also a prophetess, Anna, the daughter of Phanuel, of the tribe of Asher. She was very old; she had lived with her husband seven years after her marriage, and then was a widow until she was eighty-four. She never left the temple but worshiped night and day, fasting and praying. Coming up to them at that very moment, she gave thanks to God and spoke about the child to all who were looking forward to the redemption of Jerusalem. When Joseph and Mary had done everything required by the Law of the Lord, they returned to Galilee to their own town of Nazareth. And the child grew and became strong; he was filled with wisdom, and the grace of God was upon him. Luke 2.22-40

✝

February 10, 1999

Lifeline

INI

Judah [is] a lion's whelp; from the prey, my son, you have gone up. He bows down, he lies down as a lion; and as a lion, who shall rouse him? The scepter shall not depart from Judah, nor a lawgiver from between his feet, until Shiloh comes; and to him [shall be] the obedience of the people. Binding his donkey to the vine, and his donkey's colt to the choice vine, he washed his garments in wine, and his clothes in the blood of grapes. his eyes [are] darker than wine, And his teeth whiter than milk. Genesis 49.9-12

Perhaps it's too much like a bad dream if I'd ask you to imagine being caught in a flood of rushing water like that below a dam, being pushed this way and that by swirling water but held fast by a lifeline tight around your waist and slowly being pulled to safety.

It's not a bad analogy for life, though usually not so dramatic. We do often feel pilled this way, pushed that way seemingly by forces beyond our control. Maybe we're not in great danger, always, but we are frequently surprised, aren't we, at where we are at any given moment.

Haven't you expressed the thought – or you will: "I never expected I'd be doing…" or "If you had predicted ten years ago… I wouldn't have believed it." The uncertainty of our lives is getting worse. Consider the statistics which show that the average person changes careers four or more times over a lifetime. We make plans and decisions, sometimes agonizing over them, then finding ourselves doing something completely different.

In the reading before us we drop in on Jacob at end of his life as he talks with his sons. It wasn't an era, perhaps, of such blindingly fast change as ours, but a time of uncertainty to be sure. He is assuring them with prophecy, lending some certainty to their lives. In his words to Judah he gives his sons their lifeline; he tells them of the Messiah, the coming Savior. "The scepter shall not depart from Judah, nor a lawgiver from between his feet, until Shiloh comes; and to him [shall be] the obedience of the people."

Jacob knew about uncertainty and surprises. His life was full of "I never would have predicteds," not least of them the matter of a birthright which included who should carry the promise. Should Jacob himself have carried it? He did, though it wasn't his at first. He wasn't the firstborn to whom it ordinarily went, so he had to steal it by deception. To whom should he pass it on? To his eldest, Reuben? No. To his favorite, Joseph? No. To the most deserving? Out of the unruly rabble his sons had been, Judah was far from most worthy – read his history! No one would have predicted it but he was the one chosen. By now Jacob had learned to follow God's direction; he named Judah as the one to carry on the line that would eventually give birth to the Savior.

Here almost hidden in the middle of his prophecy to Judah comes the promise that ran like a thread – no, like a lifeline through Abraham, Isaac, now Judah and all the Old Testament. No matter what surprises, uncertainties, even tragedies lay in store for God's people, that lifeline, the promise of a Savior, would hold fast.

We make plans with due care, but confident not that our plans will come to pass but confident that whatever way life tosses and pulls us, the lifeline of God's promise, now fulfilled in Jesus Christ, holds us fast and draws us slowly, surely to God's loving destiny for us.

†

March 2, 1999

Jesus Looks at Us

INI

There are defining moments in life. Most of our dealings are not that way; we make decisions, then change our minds. We do poorly on a test but make it up later. Most of the time what happens doesn't matter forever. But once in a while it does.

I recall it clearly – a basketball teetering on a rim. Will it fall in, or will it go out? Certainly a little thing to be decided by a spin of the ball or even a breeze from the ventilating system. And yet, occurring as it did in the closing seconds of overtime in a sectional tournament game, this little thing would determine whether my son's team would get into the state tournament. And while people may differ on how important any sports contest is in the grand scheme of things, those state tournament experiences still remain among the fondest in my memory and that of many others.

Once in a while something happens, perhaps only a little thing, that changes the future in big ways, maybe for good. Those are "defining moments." We hear of one, much bigger than the one I just told you of in this incident from Scripture.

> Then seizing Jesus, they led him away and took him into the house of the high priest. Peter followed at a distance. But when they had kindled a fire in the middle of the courtyard and had sat down together, Peter sat down with them. A servant girl saw him seated there in the firelight. She looked closely at him and said, "this man was with him." But he denied it. "Woman, I don't know him," he said. A little later someone else saw him and said, "You also are one of them." "Man, I am not!" Peter replied. About an hour later another asserted, "Certainly this fellow was with him, for he is a Galilean." Peter replied, "Man, I don't know what you're talking about!" Just as he was speaking, the rooster crowed. The Lord turned and looked straight at Peter. Then Peter remembered the word the Lord had spoken to him: "Before the rooster crows today, you will disown me three times." And he went outside and wept bitterly. Luke 22.54-62

Down the street, at the seminary and synod office building for Lent they've erected a cross in the lobby. It stands 7-8 feet tall, draped with a cloth of purple, the penitential color of Lent and it's adorned with a thorny wreath representing the crown of thorns pressed on our Savior's brow as he died there. I walked over, along with the seminary student who made the crown, to take a closeup look, to see how it was woven together. I asked him where he had found the thorns, vines with sharp nearly inch-long spikes. Did he have to go out and order them specially? No, he said, they were nearby. He just rummaged around in the bushes below the hilltop. I said, as I examined it, that's interesting. I've never made a crown of thorns.

And as soon as I said it I realized it's not true. I do it all the time. Every sin I commit is a crown of thorns. The thorns aren't hard to find either; they are always right nearby in the bushes beneath the surface of my life adding to my Savior's suffering as he bears each of my sins on the cross.

Peter denied his Lord three times even as his Lord was in the process of going to his death on Peter's behalf. We recognize that's terrible. But can't we all look on each and every sin we commit in the same way? Each sin says I don't know Jesus. Each sin is a rejection of his Spirit in us. Each of them is another thorny crown which we add to our Savior's burden of suffering even as he bears our sins for us.

But thankfully the sins are not the defining moment of which I spoke before. While our sins should be what makes all the difference for our future, our Lord changed that for us too. The defining moment in this incident is his look: "The Lord turned and looked straight at Peter." Despite the shameful cowardly sin Peter was committing Jesus did not turn away, did not discard Peter but he turned and he looked straight at Peter.

What a look that must have been! It spun Peter around, smote his conscience and began the process of restoring him which culminated in a conversation on the lakeshore some weeks later where Jesus confirmed for Peter that his sin was forgiven. That transformed him into one of the greatest men of God.

The Lord turned and looked straight at Peter. What a look that must have been! Can you see it? I hope you can because it wasn't just at Peter, it was also at us who sin against our Lord even as he dies for us. It's a look that says, "I'm sad, terribly disappointed in you because I know your failures, every one of them." But it's a look that also says, "I care. And while your devotion to me is weak, my devotion to you is strong. While your love for me wavers, my love for you is constant and I am carrying on my task, continuing to my death so that you might be saved. I'm carrying even this sin to the cross so that its punishment will never touch you. Because my goal," says Jesus, "is to restore you as I did Peter. My goal is to make you a useful, profitable woman or man of God, serving my lambs, serving my sheep. That I will do. You can count on it," says Jesus as he proceeds to the cross.

†

April 6, 1999, revised from 1991

Without Life

INI

> Moreover, brethren, I declare to you the gospel which I preached to you, which also you received and in which you stand, by which also you are saved, if you hold fast that word which I preached to you – unless you believed in vain. For I delivered to you first of all that which I also received: that Christ died for our sins according to the Scriptures, and that he was buried, and that he rose again the third day according to the Scriptures, and that he was seen by Cephas, then by the twelve. After that he was seen by over five hundred brethren at once, of whom the greater part remain to the present, but some have fallen asleep. After that he was seen by James, then by all the apostles. Then last of all he was seen by me also... Now if Christ is preached that he has been raised from the dead, how do some among you say that there is no resurrection of the dead? But if there is no resurrection of the dead, then Christ is not risen. And if Christ is not risen, then our preaching [is] empty and your faith [is] also empty. Yes, and we are found false witnesses of God, because we have testified of God that he raised up Christ, whom he did not raise up – if in fact the dead do not rise. For if [the] dead do not rise, then Christ is not risen. And if Christ is not risen, your faith [is] futile; you are still in your sins! Then also those who have fallen asleep in Christ have perished. If in this life only we have hope in Christ, we are of all men the most pitiable. But now Christ is risen from the dead, [and] has become the firstfruits of those who have fallen asleep. 1 Corinthians 15.1-21

How can I impress on you again the importance of Easter? Paul does it well, here, by inviting us to consider what we would be like if left wallowing hopelessly in our many sins. Let me try, more haltingly, to give you a mirror-image of that invitation. Consider what we would be like without what is best in our lives.

Can I ask you to think back into your childhood, to think of some happy moment – perhaps a special place only you know about, where you could go to enjoy being alone? Or perhaps the feeling you had when you arrived at your grandparents' house? Reach back into your childhood and pull from your memory something happy. That memory is precious and good, something you can treasure forever.

Unless – everything ends in death. If when death comes it means you are gone, what happens to that private precious memory? It disappears. When you are gone, it becomes *nothing*.

Now think of some achievement of yours, some recognition you received.

Your parents, family, and friends noticed and were proud of you. That was good for you. Oh, it isn't something you dwell on much anymore; you've gone beyond that to new goals and challenges. But once in a while it moves back into your mind, and you recognize that it was an important step in your life. It meant something, and it always will.

Unless – everything ends in death. If when death comes it means you are gone, what happens to that achievement? It disappears. When you are gone, it becomes *nothing*.

Think of your career plans. You work hard on those plans, think about them a lot, talk and write to people about them. You study hard working toward career goals, and you do it to make a mark, to do something of value with your life. And that will happen. It will all be worthwhile.

Unless – everything ends in death. If when death comes it means you are gone, what happens to that valuable career? It disappears. When you are gone, it becomes *nothing*.

Think of a special relationship you once enjoyed, or do now, or perhaps will in the future, a relationship in which there is a genuine expression of love. If that expression of love is true and deep, it can last forever.

Unless – everything ends in death. If when death comes it means you are gone, what happens to that precious love? It disappears. When you are gone, it becomes *nothing*.

There is just one reason that anything we do has worth or value. That reason is stated at the end of the reading a moment ago: "But now is Christ risen from the dead." In fact, these words underlie God's universal plan. Creation was not made for death, but for life.

We often think of the benefits of Christ's resurrection coming to us at **our** resurrection, after our death. And of course, how important that is we will fully appreciate only when it happens. But let's not forget that Christ's resurrection benefits us now, by giving eternal significance to all we do. Without life, the eternal life which Christ provides as a gift, everything just snuffs out, it becomes nothing. Worse than that, those moments of pleasure, satisfaction, and accomplishment just mock us as we suffer the eternal punishment for our many sins.

Without life there is no **significance**. Without life there is no **meaning**. Without life there is no **good**. Without life there is no **happiness**. Without life there is no **truth**. Without life there is no **beauty**. Without life there is no **love**. Without Christ there is no life. Without the resurrection, there is no Christ.

"But now is Christ risen from the dead!" Celebrate Easter!   †

September 13, 1999

Who Is Your Leader?

INI

In a pizza joint near our home is a vending machine. Put in three quarters and out comes not gum, not candy, but collectable trading cards – not wholesome baseball cards, or even football cards. These cards feature pro wrestlers. I'll ask you only to imagine the poses and facial expressions on these brutes. You wouldn't want to see me try to imitate them. Enough to say they are the sort that worry most parents with fear that kids might choose these guys as heroes and models and start to imitate them. Kids like these cards, maybe because it makes their parents worry.

Who are your heroes? Your leaders? The ones you imitate, your models? The Bible writer urges us:

> Remember your leaders, who spoke the word of God to you. Consider the outcome of their way of life and imitate their faith. Hebrews 13.7

These two sentences from God make two points: 1. We have leaders who are spiritual; 2. Consider their way of life and its outcome and Imitate it. Look at each please.

First, we have leaders who are spiritual. I'm not suggesting Preacher Trading Cards – I'll give you two Moldstads for one Teigen. No, God is reminding us that we learned the Gospel from someone. "Remember your leaders who spoke the Word of God to you." Who taught you the Gospel? It might have been several people but narrow in on one if you can. From whom did you learn that Jesus loves you, that he found you lost in your sin, that he shed his blood on the cross to pay your penalty to God, that he in this way turned you into a Child of God, bound for Heaven. Who was it that helped you understand this beautiful, pure, Gospel? Who is it that keeps reminding you of it?

God says these are your spiritual leaders. They are important to you; they've played a central role in your life. Remember them, bring them to mind, and then:

Second, consider their way of life and its outcome and imitate it. I wonder how many kids have studied Michael Jordan's jump shot and tried to shoot just like Mike, or studied Mark McGwire's home run swing and tried to swing that way, or right now are studying Venus Williams' serve and are trying to imitate it. God says do that with your spiritual leaders.

Have you ever thought carefully about how that person you have in mind lives? God says, make her or him your study and your model. Consider how they live – the vocations they choose, consider the projects they undertake, consider the service they provide, consider the love they show. Consider their assurance. Consider how they know where they are heading; as forgiven children of God they are heading for Heaven. Consider how they do all these things and then try to live that way too.

Do you know what will happen then? You'll be a **spiritual leader for others**. No, change the verb tense: you **are** a spiritual leader for others. I'm not just addressing us older folk now. All of you are, for someone, already a spiritual leader. There is someone now in your life who is ready to watch you. You are the one whose Christian life they will notice, remember, study, and imitate.

Is that a heavy burden? A big responsibility? Yes, but since it's God's plan and it's at his urging that we "remember our leaders, who spoke the word of God to us. Consider the outcome of their way of life and imitate their faith," then it's also a blessed privilege, one for which he empowers us when he comes to us with the Holy Spirit through his Word and Sacraments. It's a joy. Step willingly into the cycle. Find a Christian model to imitate so you can **be** a Christian model to imitate.

Do it for Jesus' sake.

†

October 1999

Awesome!

INI

First, clarify: that wasn't me yesterday speaking to you from here. It was Pastor Bryant.[1] I wish it had been me; it was a very good sermon. In fact it was awesome.

And the weather today – isn't it awesome? Did you see the football game Sunday? Randy Moss is awesome! The week before that, Bret Favre was... in fact, everyone, everything these days is awesome!

I typed the word into Lycos, the internet search engine.[2] The first page of sites returned told me the following were awesome: video games, a clip art collection, travel through Alberta, an online shopping site, an online gambling site, some email greeting cards, music from the 80's, and both John's and Peter's home pages, all self-proclaimed "awesome." The Oxford English Dictionary, the great solemn record of the English tongue in a dozen volumes, provides examples of words in actual sentences. Here is a sentence from the OED illustrating this word: "It's so awesome, I mean, fer shurr, toadly toe-dully!"

So what are we to think when the worship folder says this morning's theme is: **God does awesome things?** Well, we look at the reading for this morning. The children of Israel and we are urged by the prophet,

> Fear the Lord your God and serve him. Hold fast to him and take your oaths in his name. He is your praise; he is your God, who performed for you those great and awesome wonders you saw with your own eyes. Deuteronomy 10. 20-21

Why must God remind us of that? Why must he seem to **beg** us to realize fully who he is, what he has done? Because just as the word **awesome** is **devalued** by careless use, our very **awe** at God's works is **devalued** by familiarity.

Consider our attitudes toward chapel – ho hum – at least we go to chapel, most days. Church attendance on Sunday? Maybe, maybe not. Religion class – do we have to study this stuff? Bible study? Who has time for it. We know all those stories anyway. Our puny prayer life – yawn.

---

[1] The worship folder for the week had switched the chapel preachers' names.
[2] This old search engine from Carnegie Mellon University is still around but since Google probably few people use it anymore. www.lycos.com

But those are the places we meet God in his Word! And God and his works are awesome!

So God urges us, get back to his word and **let's become children again,** see a Christmas tree as if for first time through bright eyes, realize God as if we'd never met Him before! Let God's works stun us, stagger us, fill our minds with wonder, our hearts with the tinge of fear. Let's be stirred to profound reverence in the presence **of the beauty, majesty, sublimity, power, love** of God.

That's what awesome means.

In contrast to the list from the internet consider just a short list like this from God's Word:

- God created all things;
- By calling light out of darkness he established all the laws of physics, chemistry, science;
- He invented living things in all their complexity;
- This God we can meet;
- To this God we can talk;
- This God has made you and me his children;
- This God worked out a cosmic salvation plan;
- The infinite God who transcends time and space became a human baby;
- God died on the cross;
- Our every wrongful deed and thought was paid for there; our sins are forgiven;
- The One who was dead came back to life again;
- There is a Heaven, of unsurpassed unimaginable peace and beauty;
- There is a place there waiting for you and me.

These are just words on a list, so inadequate. Look behind each of them. Go to the Word! See what God in love has done for you.

Rekindle the awe!

†

October 25, 1999

With You Always

INI

Hear Jesus' words of promise:

And surely I am with you always, to the very end of the age. Matthew 28.20

It's remarkable, what some people will do to avoid being alone. They turn on the radio or TV in the background, providing the illusion of companionship. During a long weekend at college, when all your friends are gone, you might even hang out with someone you never hang out with. Some people even get married. We fight loneliness. That reflects a deep human need. Thomas Wolfe wrote, "The whole conviction of my life rests upon the belief that loneliness, far from being a rare and curious phenomenon, peculiar to myself and to a few other solitary men, is the central and inevitable fact of human existence." That leads to this contradiction: if you feel lonely, you are not alone.

There is a theological loneliness too. It might be basis for all the others. The basic theological question, everyone's starting point, is "What is my relationship with God?" Because of sin, the answer to that question seems to be that we have no relationship with God at all. We are alone.

Consider how sin works in your own life. Isn't it always an act of pushing God away? We don't want God there when we sin. Those are moments we pretend God doesn't exist. In fact, those are moments we **believe** God doesn't exist. When we sin, and push God away, we are truly alone and lonely. Joseph F. Newton said, "People are lonely because they build walls instead of bridges." That's true on both the human and divine level. We are lonely because by our sins we build walls between us and God.

Then came Immanuel. That's a name the Old Testament gave to Jesus. Isaiah 7.14 The Hebrew word means "God With Us." We push God away, then God became human and lived among us, took on our flesh, our feelings, our sorrows, became our brother. Then he also took on himself our sins, our death, our separation from God. On the cross suffering the depths of hell he cried out, "O God why have you left me all alone?" Mark 15.34 He was truly "on our side" of the God-human divide. He was "with us." That act of joining us broke the wall. It was a bridge, one God built to us, so we can cross it to him.

It's significant that Jesus said "I will be with you always" just as he visibly left, leaving his disciples a huge, seemingly impossible task. It reminds us that these situations are when he is with us most. When he seems to have gone, when the tasks seem most difficult, there especially he wants us to hear his word: "I am with you always." Jesus is Immanuel forever, always with us, so we can be always with him.   †

November 1999

Promise of Success

INI

When you're in college you're living in achievement-oriented world. You work hard, the faculty works hard so you can achieve and succeed. We measure with tests and grades to see if you are doing so. That gives rise to stress, tension, and worry. I want to assure you this morning on the basis of God's Word that achievement there will be! You have the encouragement and promise from God: you will succeed.

You all know most famous episode of Joshua's life. It happened at Jericho. Before Moses died, he appointed Joshua to lead Israel into the promised land. His first obstacle was the city of Jericho. You know how the history turned out: the walls of Jericho fell. In fact, Joshua's leadership in conquering the land was a great achievement.

But the night before Jericho, before he knew how it would turn out, Joshua went outside the camp to look at the city and there we read of this strange encounter.

> And it came to pass, when Joshua was by Jericho, that he lifted his eyes and looked, and behold, a Man stood opposite him with His sword drawn in His hand. And Joshua went to Him and said to Him, "Are You for us or for our enemies?" "Neither," he replied, "but as Commander of the army of the LORD I have now come." Then Joshua fell face down to the ground in reverence, and asked Him, "What message does my Lord have for His servant?" The Commander of the LORD's army replied, "Take off your sandals, for the place where you are standing is holy." And Joshua did so. Joshua 5.13-15

That's the story. Can you imagine the encouragement and comfort Joshua felt to know that the Lord himself was leader of his army? What a great promise of achievement and success! And at the same time a humbling reminder – the Lord reminded Joshua: off with your shoes, show me reverence! Achievement comes, but it is not ours; it is the Lord's.

That's how Joshua succeeded. That's how Joshua stayed a humble servant of God in success. He recognized that it wasn't his achievement, it was Lord's. Notice he wasn't given a promise of ease. He faced great struggles but he could do it with confidence of success.

That's how the Lord works. He put each of us here to accomplish something and achievement there will be! In that which matches God's will for us – that is, that which in his love he knows is good for us – you will achieve. He does not promise it will be easy but when you do achieve, take off your sandals – stay humble, revere Jesus. It's his doing.

That's true especially in our greatest challenge, the battle each of us must wage against sin and death. That too is not an easy struggle. For Jesus himself it was not an easy struggle as he led the once-for-all battle and conquered death by breaking its shackles when he rose from dead on Easter. That victory he gives to us. We know it's God's will that we win this victory and so we will succeed because the commander of Lord's army has gone ahead of us, has done it for us. Our sins are forgiven, and he gives us the victory. For that we take off our shoes and revere Jesus. The achievement of victory, eternal life and Heaven is ours, but it's all his doing.

†

December 1999

Christmas with the Assyrians

INI

Are you in the Christmas mood yet? Christmas can be disappointing if we don't catch the spirit of the season. This verse from the Bible assigned to us today might help:

> That night the angel of the LORD went out and put to death a hundred and eighty-five thousand men in the Assyrian camp. When the people got up the next morning there were all the dead bodies! 2 Kings 19.35

Well, merry Christmas to you too. Quite a Bible verse for starting Christmas week. But it fits. Let me show you how. It's a tale of two times but one place.

The verse I just read ends the history of the Assyrian invasion of Judea under Sennacherib. The Assyrian army had swept away all resistance, even had taken the Judean southern fortresses. Sennacherib had set up headquarters in Lachish southwest of Jerusalem and had sent troops up to the city from the south and messengers ahead of them with an ultimatum to King Hezekiah: "Don't count on God to save you. Give up." Hezekiah, who had been a faithful godly king, turned to the Lord. The prophet Isaiah replied to the King with words of encouragement from the Lord and the story ends with the verse I read.

Sennacherib forgot about the power of God and the righteousness of God, about how a righteous God uses his power to punish sin. If it's startling to contemplate God wiping out so many people in one night let it just remind us of how much we, by our many sins, deserve the same from a holy God.

Let's go back to that region south of Jerusalem, probably not the same field but it could have been.

South of Jerusalem lies Bethlehem and near Bethlehem one night some 700 years after the story we just recalled, an angel of the Lord appeared again, this time not to destroy, but just the opposite: to proclaim *"Don't be afraid, I have good news: a Savior is born for you, Christ the Lord."* Luke 2.10f.

I expect we'll hear more about that angel tomorrow. For now, ponder the contrast which illustrates the two great doctrines of the Bible: Law and Gospel. The Law teaches us – as angel number 1 on that field south of Jerusalem shows us – that God punishes sin. The punishment for sin is death and sin will not be overlooked; it will be punished.

But the Gospel teaches us – as angel number 2 on the field south of Jerusalem proclaims – that a Savior has come to make peace on earth between God and us sinners. If that seems a contradiction, that the same God who can kill three football stadiums full of people can also be loving and forgiving, the resolution is found in that manger in Bethlehem where there is a Baby, God's own Son who has come to die bearing our sins. In Him our sins were punished with the death we deserved, so that God can, and actually does forgive us. We're not going to fully appreciate message of angel 2 unless we appreciate the mission of angel 1.

Want a really good satisfying Christmas this year? Think hard about your sins, then think hard about your Savior.

✝

September 2000

The Ten Words

INI

Turn to the list of Commandments on page 31 in the front of the Hymnary. Let's see now, one at a time:

1. I've never bowed down to a stone idol, I'm OK there;
2. I don't swear much;
3. I'm a regular church goer, and I'm here in chapel;
4. I'm on good terms with my parents;
5. I never shot or stabbed anybody;
6. I never broke a marriage vow, I'm not even married;
7. I never stole anything worth much;
8. I never told a lie under oath;
9. I never obsessed to have anybody's house, and
10. I never wanted anybody's cow.

Surely none of us here would ever treat the Ten Commandments so cavalierly as that. We've moved beyond the superficial in our spiritual lives. May I review with you the spiritual stages we've moved through? I feel compelled to when we read God's introduction to the Commandments.

> And God spake all these words, saying, I am the LORD thy God, which have brought thee out of the land of Egypt, out of the house of bondage. Thou shalt have no other gods before me. Thou shalt not make unto thee any graven image, or any likeness of any thing that is in heaven above, or that is in the earth beneath, or that is in the water under the earth. Thou shalt not bow down thyself to them, nor serve them: for I the LORD thy God am a jealous God, visiting the iniquity of the fathers upon the children unto the third and fourth generation of them that hate me; And shewing mercy unto thousands of them that love me, and keep my commandments. [then follow the rest of Ten Commandments] Exodus 20.1f

We can't be superficial about the Ten Commandments when clearly God is serious about them. He rewards those who keep the Commandments. He punishes those who don't, and their children and their grandchildren. So then as we become more familiar with God's word, we learn God's intent for us in the Commandments. They are not there to annoy or limit us or to hedge us in but to show His love for us by protecting, by fencing off against violation the most precious aspects of our lives. Each one protects something of great value in our lives. What would our lives be without them?

1. The First protects God's own pre-eminence – God is, and rules all creation;
2. The Second protects truth, especially truth about God, his Word;
3. Number Three protects worship, the most direct relationship between God and us;
4. The Fourth protects authority;
5. The Fifth protects life;
6. The Sixth protects marriage – those who sin diminish their own marriage;
7. The Seventh protects property;
8. The Eighth protects reputation;
9. The Ninth protects potential, freedom to have a place to live, grow, and become all we can be;
10. The Tenth protects the value of work, an honest day's labor for an honest day's pay. [1]

By now, we've begun to see and come to realize we're not so OK; we all sin more than we think we do. Review the Commandments once more, this time backwards. Come to realize that, if you have loafed on your job and taken pay anyway you've broken number 10. If you've cut line or tossed trash out your car window you've broken number 9. If you've held anyone or any group in contempt no matter how much their lifestyle deserves it you've broken number 8. If you've taken someone else's answer or included a paragraph without citing it you've broken number 7. There are so many temptations to sexual sin in deed, word and thought, it's impossible to imagine anyone claiming innocence for number 6. To break 5 just rejoice in the bad fortune of a rival. Count 4 if you broke a rule at home or school, 3 if you've ever been reluctant about going to worship, 2 if you forget to pray, and 1 any time you or I sin since that's acting as if God isn't there. If we really believed in God we wouldn't dare to disobey Him. Sin is exalting over God something else that at the moment seems a pleasure or profit or advantage.

We all sin more than we think we do, these ways and many more. When the Holy Spirit works on us through the Ten Commandments we know we are guilty before God, who is "jealous," who **will punish** sin, who **must** punish sin in order to be God. The 10 Words show us we deserve the payment for sin: death, total separation from God and all that's good, all that's love now and forever. Then the Ten Commandments have had their proper effect: they have driven us to know our need and opened us up to hear with eager hearts the refreshing comforting soothing Gospel.

---

[1] For a deeper understanding of the Ninth and Tenth Commandments, see "The Final Fifth of God's Will" in my earlier book, *A3 The Early Years.*

We look with wonder on the life of Jesus who "went about doing good," how his behavior and words and thought patterns were in exact harmony with God's will. We realize that in the case of each of those ten commands (which are such a snare for us) Jesus not only avoided the sin but fully and positively carried out each command's full intent. He **pleased** God, as we did not. And as he did that, he had you and me in mind because he did it for us. Exactly where we failed, Jesus succeeded on our behalf.

And so he came to the end of his life the only person in all time to **not** deserve punishment from God for a single sin. What a triumph! He didn't deserve to die.

And then he did. He died an agonizing, humiliating death, punished for sins, for the worst violations of God's commandments – not his own sins, but yours and mine. They need to go together: the Ten Commandments and Jesus, the Commandments convicting our hearts, and driving us to Jesus, the Commandments showing us our sins and pushing us to remember how in Baptism Jesus washes those sins away and impelling us to Lord's table where in his body and blood we find forgiveness absolutely full and absolutely free.

There's a movement out there that advocates posting the Ten Commandments on schoolroom walls. Wherever the Ten Commandments are posted, a picture of Jesus should be posted beside them. They are not complete without him. Try that on your room wall: the Ten Commandments and Jesus. It might change the look of your wall. Even better: post them again on your heart: the Ten Commandments and Jesus. See how it continues changing your life.

✝

September 24, 2000

Dedication of the Communication Center
(formerly the Seminary, remodeled with new Media Studio added)

Service held in Trinity Chapel prior to a march to the CC

INI

My mouth will speak in praise of the Lord. Psalm 145.1

Welcome to the Communication Center. No not when we walk over there in a few minutes. Welcome to here. This chapel is the communication center, the center of the most important communication on campus. Here is where God speaks to us in his Word on a regular basis. It's appropriate that we will soon walk from here to the newly remodeled building, the Communication Center, for that building, as all others on this campus, draws its purpose, its reason for being, from here.

As if this chapel is beautiful faceted gem, all the other campus buildings and programs reflect its light. Each facet lights each program in its own special way: Communication, Fine Arts, Athletics, Music, Business, the Library, the Administration wing – each individual office and class reflects a facet of this gem. None reflects it better than the others but each reflects in its own way the message we hear most often **here**.

In the Communication program and its building we dedicate today we are prompted to reflect on some of the deepest spiritual mysteries. We find there the close connection of communication with our Christian purpose. We become more deeply aware that our Lord Jesus is, as the Evangelist John was inspired to write, identified not as "the event" – though he was the central event of the world's history – nor as "the example" – though he certainly was that too – but as a communication concept: "In the beginning was the **Word**." John 1.1 The **Word** was the instrument of creation: "...and God **said** let there be..." Genesis 1.3 etc. The **Word** is an instrument of the Holy Spirit to change lives, in fact to bring the dead to life by bringing condemned sinners to faith through the central Means of Grace, the **Word**. Which of us, however astute in linguistics or rhetoric or any of the various disciplines of communication, can fully understand such things?

What power there is in the word! What spiritual wonders we work with and study every day!

Our study focuses too on the human aspects of communication. This enables us to observe with disappointment how humankind has corrupted this marvelous gift from God. How easy it is to sin with words: lying, cursing, boasting, smutty jokes, sharp words that cut and hurt, planning evil, not to mention our failures to speak up for the needy, for justice and for truth. We speak of sinning "in thought, word, and deed"; "word" is in the middle because it's almost always involved in sins of thought and of deed.

That's when we need God's Word most. God authorizes us to do the most important speaking of all: "*Comfort, comfort ye my people – **speak ye** comfortably to Jerusalem and **say** to her that her iniquity is pardoned....*" Isaiah 40.1f. "*Speak to one another,*" we are urged, "*with psalms and hymns and spiritual songs.*" Ephesians 5.19 Let the **Word** refresh us with the assurance that through Jesus the Word, all our sins are forgiven. Moved by the sacrifice of Jesus and depth of God's love we have reason to study excellence in communication, to strive for it in our own lives as a tribute to God's love, and to recognize and appreciate it, whether by a Christian or not, in theory or practice, in interpersonal settings, in organizations, in the media, in public life and in private life.

The current "Five Talents" capital campaign, which many of you support and which provided this building, reminds us that "*to whom much is given, much is expected.*" Luke 12.48 To us in the Communication Program much has been given: a remodeled building with its equipment and furnishings, strong administrative support for the program, an able and spirited faculty, willing and talented students, supportive parents and grandparents, and friends far and near. So it gives us pause to know that of us much will be required. Shortcomings there are and they are ours, but our strength is from God. The Communication Center we dedicate is nothing, no matter how impressive, if not a reflection of this communication center here. **This** is the gem, **that** is a reflection of one facet. What we do there is done in the power of God, as spoken in our motto from Psalm 145: "*My mouth will speak in praise of the Lord.*" That is why we dedicate it to God and God's glory.

†

November 1, 2000

Nahum Peace

INI

Some here have been in combat. Not I, not most of us. The most of that experience we can get is an inkling from the *Saving Private Ryan* movie. Ask even those who have been in war to go a step further: you at least had armor, weapons, a capability to defend yourself. Suppose you didn't!

Suppose to make your way to chapel this morning across the campus mall you had to duck between the pillars of the colonnade for fear of a sniper. Suppose to avoid the above ground crossfire, you wanted to take the tunnel but were warned not to for fear of a deadly terrorist gas grenade in that enclosed space. Suppose as we sit here, we suddenly heard the whistle of incoming ordnance and by reflex we duck under the seats – not that it would protect us from a direct hit but at least we might be shielded from glass splinters flying from the windows from a hit just outside. Suppose we were forced to view this beautiful chapel, which many of us have come truly to love, reduced to piles of rubble and this would be our last view of campus altogether as we gather what is most precious to us into a bundle to carry and set off afoot down some road in some direction we believe might be safe from the invading army on its way.

We are perhaps too used to peace, so much that we don't appreciate it as we should. You know, of course, there are right now many places in the world where reality is more as I've described. One of those places is the "holy land" – I don't call it that, because there have been more wars and bloodshed in those few square miles than any other place on earth.

In one of the most vivid memories I have of a visit there two summers ago, our tour bus was traveling on a paved road on the Golan Heights. We had just stopped at a bluff high above the Sea of Galilee where we could see how easily, just a few years earlier, Syrian soldiers had lobbed mortar shells onto Israeli kibbutzim at the lake's edge. The children there had to sleep in underground bunkers every night. Since then, Israel had occupied the Golan Heights so we tourists could pass safely through – we thought. As our bus rolled along, it suddenly slowed down and stopped. The road ahead was blocked by a military battalion moving in from our left, crossing the road. I looked left and saw, not 30 yards away, a Sabra tank which slowly swung its turret in our direction until its cannon was pointing right at our bus. At that moment someone asked in a whisper, "Is it ours?" "Ours" was "Israeli" and of course it was. This army unit was on maneuvers and a tank gunner decided to test his sights on us. No danger – but it was a stark reminder: this is a nation at war. We got just a tiny taste of what it would be like to live at war and maybe that helped us to appreciate peace just a little more.

Could it be the same in our spiritual lives? How sheltered we are from the great cosmic battles over our souls! We sing "a mighty fortress is our God" with little feeling of how precious it is to **have** a fortress, an armed, fortified refuge to which we can flee from the great danger pressing on us from all sides. Even that hymn tries to express that danger to our souls, perhaps comparable to dodging sniper bullets or fleeing terrorist gas attacks.

> *The old evil foe now means deadly woe*
> *with deep guile and great might – on earth is not his equal*
> *Devils all the world might fill all eager to devour us*

We're mostly shielded from all this – and why? Because Someone else has effectively fought this battle for us. He **won**! And leaves us in peace.

How remarkable it was in a country racked by war, occupied by a powerful enemy, pre-occupied with secret talk of rebellion and armed revolt, there appeared a Man who spoke gently of peace.

"Blessed are they," he said, in words we repeated in yesterday's chapel service. *"Blessed are meek, the merciful, the poor in spirit, the peacemakers."* Matthew 5 How startlingly different was this teaching than anything heard before. This man teaches of peace. It's not surprising he spoke of peace, for he was, he is peace. He fought for us the battle against sin, death and Satan; he won that battle for us and emerged the victor in his resurrection from the dead. He leaves us as we are now, with sins forgiven, assured of eternal life through faith in him. We are at peace.

The Old Testament prophet Nahum wrote to a people frightened and tired by war, under immanent threat of attack by Assyria, the superpower of that day. Listen to him as he speaks of how the Lord God takes on our enemies for us and leaves us with peace. Listen to the talk of war undertaken on our behalf by the Lord and by that more fully appreciate His peace.

> An oracle concerning Nineveh. The book of the vision of Nahum the Elkoshite. The Lord is a jealous and avenging God; the Lord takes vengeance and is filled with wrath. The Lord takes vengeance on his foes and maintains his wrath against his enemies. The Lord is slow to anger and great in power; the Lord will not leave the guilty unpunished. His way is in the whirlwind and the storm, and clouds are the dust of his feet. He rebukes the sea and dries it up; he makes all the rivers run dry. Bashan and Carmel wither and the blossoms of Lebanon fade. The mountains quake before him and the hills melt away. The earth trembles at his presence, the world and all who live in it.

Who can withstand his indignation? Who can endure his fierce anger? His wrath is poured out like fire; the rocks are shattered before him. The Lord is good, a refuge in times of trouble. He cares for those who trust in him.... Look, there on the mountains, the feet of one who brings good news, who proclaims peace! Celebrate your festivals, O Judah, and fulfill your vows. No more will the wicked invade you; they will be completely destroyed. Nahum 1.1-8, 15, 2.1-2a

†

November 2000

A Loving Not Cruel Deal

INI

I have here a handful of one-million-dollar bills. Well, you are right to be skeptical, so let me rather put it this way. Suppose I had ten million-dollar bills and offered to give you one. You'd have to earn it, of course. All you'd have to do is take a running jump and land on Mars. A funny joke? Not really – to get your hopes up and then put on an impossible condition, that would be a **cruel** joke.

Most people think that Christianity is a deal with God. On our part, we behave and by that we earn rewards from God. But this can't be God's plan and if you understand why not, you'll have the basis for a profound and joyous Thanksgiving this week. Listen to this reading, the words of Moses to the people of God just after he has laid out for them all the laws from God.

> When all these blessings and curses I have set before you come upon you and you take them to heart wherever the LORD your God disperses you among the nations, and when you and your children return to the LORD your God and obey him with all your heart and with all your soul according to everything I command you today, then the LORD your God will restore your fortunes and have compassion on you and gather you again from all the nations where he scattered you.

[here I'm skipping few verses, which we'll come back to]

> ...Then the LORD your God will make you most prosperous in all the work of your hands and in the fruit of your womb, the young of your livestock and the crops of your land. The LORD will again delight in you and make you prosperous, just as he delighted in your fathers, if you obey the LORD your God and keep his commands and decrees that are written in this Book of the Law and turn to the LORD your God with all your heart and with all your soul. Deuteronomy 30.1-3, 9-10

Without the verses I skipped, this sounds like a deal with God: the people obey and God rewards. But it doesn't take deep insight to realize that this by itself couldn't be the plan of a loving God. This could only be the plan of a cruel God ruling over an obnoxious, insufferable people. Consider: a loving God wants his people to be good and holy. A deal of strict reward for behaving can only create an awful people; everything we do would be selfish, to earn that reward. There could be no real **self-lessness.** Even acts of service for others would be to get points for ourselves. There could be no **humility** since that too would be reason for pride. There could be no **love**, for even that would be to serve ourselves. A behave-and-reward deal between God and us would produce a people full of pride, arrogance and selfishness, not what a loving God would want as his people.

What's more, a behave-and-reward deal would be the deal of a cruel god, especially since God knows (and we also know) that the behavior could never earn the reward. "Obey him with all your heart and with all your soul according to everything I command you today." Anybody here done that? Raise your hand – and if you do, you've piled lying atop your other sins. The demanded behavior is impossible for any of us. It's like the offer at our start today; just as jumping to Mars is physically impossible, keeping God's commands is morally impossible. It would only be a cruel joke for God to offer a reward for something he knows we can't do.

But our God is not cruel and unloving but kind and loving. To understand this matter of behave-and-reward properly we need those missing verses. Here is the key:

> The LORD your God will circumcise your hearts…, so that you may love him with all your heart and with all your soul, and live. Deuteronomy 30.6

Circumcision, you will recall, is the Old Testament ritual of dedication to the Lord. Look who's doing it here. Is it us, dedicating ourselves to earn reward? **No!** *"The LORD your God will circumcise your hearts."* God himself is the one who gives us the capability to measure up. He does that through his Son Jesus Christ. God's love recognized our inability and hopelessness. God's love prompted him to take the initiative. He sent his Son Jesus to live that life that was totally pleasing to God. He lived the life that indeed earned Heaven, then he took on himself the shame of our shortcomings, the burden of our sin, and paid for them with his life. Since our sins laid on Jesus have been paid for in full, Jesus' own perfection is credited to us so that God now looks on us and on our works as having the perfection of Jesus.

Now look again at the behavior-and-reward deal. Our efforts to do good, to please God, to love him and serve each other, all these efforts though weak and flawed God views through the work of Jesus. Because of Jesus God sees our work as worthy of reward, and he rewards them. We read,

> Then the LORD your God will make you most prosperous in all the work of your hands and in the fruit of your womb, the young of your livestock and the crops of your land. The LORD will again delight in you and make you prosperous. Deuteronomy 30.9

The LORD has made us prosperous. He has rewarded our faithfulness to him. Remember where that faithfulness came from: it's the perfect faithfulness of his Son Jesus credited to us by grace. That is the basis for our Thanksgiving.

†

December 18, 2000

Visit Bethlehem

INI

You can't visit Bethlehem now. It's too dangerous. It's in the "West Bank" and been the site of several clashes between Israelis and Palestinians leading to a number of fatalities. That's not only a tragedy for the poeple involved, but I'm sure that's a disappointment to visitors who might have to arrive in Israel and leave again without standing in that narrow cave beneath the Church of the Holy Nativity viewing the very place where it is said Jesus was born, with the manger carved out of the cave wall just a few feet away.

Still, it's not an utterly profound experience. It's diluted by change. It doesn't look at all like it must have then. It's been all fancied up in ways I'd consider tacky. The incense is thick enough to make one ill and the press of more tourists coming down the narrow stairway forces you out again after only a few moments, to encounter the annoying street vendors selling cheap plastic manger scenes for "one American dollar." Then you drive away past the tracts of land bought up by various Christian denominations, each claiming to be the authentic shepherd's field.

No, you won't be closer to Jesus' birthplace there than you are here, as you listen to these inspired, simple, profound words once again:

> While they were there, the time came for the baby to be born, and she gave birth to her firstborn, a son. She wrapped him in cloths and placed him in a manger, because there was no room for them in the inn. And there were shepherds living out in the fields nearby, keeping watch over their flocks at night. An angel of the Lord appeared to them, and the glory of the Lord shone around them, and they were terrified. But the angel said to them, "Do not be afraid. I bring you good news of great joy that will be for all the people. Today in the town of David a Savior has been born to you; he is Christ the Lord. This will be a sign to you: You will find a baby wrapped in cloths and lying in a manger." Suddenly a great company of the heavenly host appeared with the angel, praising God and saying, "Glory to God in the highest, and on earth peace to men on whom his favor rests." Luke 2.6-14

What an amazing story! Can you hear it again, as if for the first time? Can you sense, in these few words, the range of emotions? The annoyance of Joseph and Mary having to make that inconvenient journey; their anxiety that there was no room; all that was involved in a baby being born; the terrified shepherds startled in the middle of the night; their great joy with the realization that they would be seeing the long-promised Messiah; their excitement as they found the Baby.

But the most powerful excitement for them, as it should be for us, comes from just a few words: "to you." "A Savior has been born to you." The announcement is not just a "baby is born" but "a baby is born to you." When you hear those words, you're at Bethlehem. When you believe those words it draws you right up to the stable for you know what's happening there: this cute little baby, this sweet little child wrapped in swaddling cloths in the warm glow of the manger under angel-filled skies, this holy infant so tender and mild came to die. He came to die for your sins and mine. While we sing in welcoming him: "O come, O come Immanuel, and ransom captive Israel," remember what the ransom price is: his own life! "Come" we are inviting him, "Come so that you can die for me!"

And he comes.

As poet-composer Jan Nelson wrote, drawing us close-in to the Christmas manger:

> And in a bed of hay
> There the little Christ child lay
> and he smiles, yes, he smiles
> Though my debt he must pay
> still he smiles, he smiles for me.

No, you can't visit the town of Bethlehem these days. It's too dangerous. But if you ponder these words of God once again this Christmas – "unto you is born a Savior, which is Christ the Lord" – you've been to Bethlehem.

†

January 2001

This Special Person Knows You

INI

Did you ever wonder: would you have believed in Jesus if you had been his contemporary and lived in Palestine when he did? Of course God chose you before creation but still you might wonder what you would have thought of Jesus if he had grown up as the kid next door or a guy you met in school. A nice guy, sure, but – God?!

Today because of the distance in time and place it may be easier for us to think of Jesus as God than to think of him as man. Probably for the people who lived with him the opposite was the case; it was easy to view him as a man, but God? Those who visit Israel today find it easier to be impressed with the humanity of Jesus. He walked here, around this lake, beside this wall, through this olive grove. That's why the writer to the Hebrews, many of whom did live with Jesus and most of whom knew people who did, started his letter with a strong assurance of the divinity of Christ. He is more exalted than angels. He is very Son begotten of God. Hear the words:

> For to which of the angels did God ever say, You are my Son; today I have become your Father"? Or again, "I will be his Father, and he will be my Son"? And again, when God brings his firstborn into the world, he says, "Let all God's angels worship him." Hebrews 1.5-6

Jesus exalted: what does that mean for us?

We have a president here at Bethany Lutheran College. He's busy, but pretty accessible. We see him in chapel, around campus, in fact, his door is open. Still, each of us thinks it's special if the Bethany Lutheran College president spends time with us, asks us how we are, what we're doing, shows interest and concern. This is our president, the only one we have. His attention makes us feel special.

Tomorrow the United States inaugurates a new president.[1] It would surprise any of us to the point of disbelief, I'm sure, if we would receive a personal phone call – or a visit! – from the new president. What if the president of the United States, the leader of the free world, would show interest, concern, care just about you? I don't expect such a call, nor do you, but wouldn't it be a moment to celebrate and remember and talk about forever?

How many infinities must we ascend above the president of the United States to reach the planes of which this Bible writer speaks? Hear again: *"For*

---

[1] This was George W. Bush, succeeding Bill Clinton.

to which of the angels did God ever say, You are my Son; today I have become your Father? Or again, I will be his Father, and he will be my Son? And again, when God brings his firstborn into the world, he says, Let all God's angels worship him." This Jesus, the very only Son of God, is exalted above hierarchies that exceed the powers of our imaginations.

Yet he visits us – "God brings his firstborn into the world" – he becomes one of us in his incarnation, lives as we do so he knows how we live and not just in general but this Shepherd knows each of us his sheep by name, knows our lives, our thoughts, joys, fears, sorrows. And our sins. He knows each one of our sins, for he took each sin into own being. By paying the penalty of his own life to remove that sin from weighing against us in judgment, he accounted for it and all the others before God, not because we were at all worthy or deserving but purely because he loves us that much! You and I have been, each person individually, visited and touched by this Savior. Shouldn't this be something to celebrate, to remember, to talk about?

How can you worry about anything? How can you be afraid of anything? While emotions, happy and sad, may come and go, how can there be anything other than a foundational Christian joy bearing up your life when you know that this Lord, the Son of God exalted above all angels, has come to you, sought you out, become your Rescuer, your Savior, your Friend, your Brother?

Would we have been Christians living in his day in his land? Yes, the Holy Spirit would have called us then as he has now. We might have known Jesus differently had we lived then. Want to know him better? Continue in his Word.

†

February 1, 2001

Fullness

INI

If your studies here at Bethany Lutheran College have any value you've at least at times found them challenging. You've encountered big ideas that stop you and puzzle you for a long time. That's what a good education should do. And that's the challenge in the words of Scripture before us now. We're invited to consider a concept so big we'll never understand it. Listen to these words of Paul – especially the word "fullness."

> See to it that no one takes you captive through hollow and deceptive philosophy, which depends on human tradition and the basic principles of this world rather than on Christ. For in Christ all the fullness of the Deity lives in bodily form, and you have been given fullness in Christ, who is the head over every power and authority. Colossians 2.8-9

Consider "*all the fullness of the Deity*" – an older translation says "*fulness of the Godhead,*" all of God! There's a concept we'll never get our minds around. Oh, we grasp a notion of parts of it, we apply big words like omnipotence and omni-presence and omniscience and other Latin terms. But then we find we can't even understand these pieces; what can it mean to be all-powerful, to be present everywhere, to know all things?

Paul clearly isn't expecting us to understand "*fullness of Deity,*" but as clearly he wants us here to know three things about it:

First, it's in Jesus. "*For in Christ all the fullness of the Deity lives in bodily form.*"

Second, that's a reason! That's a reason why we should watch out for, and turn from "*hollow and deceptive philosophy, which depends on human tradition and the basic principles of this world.*" Paul is quite clear, as he writes on, about what those philosophies, traditions, and principles are: they are the common human belief that we save ourselves by what we do. Such ideas are opposite of Christ. We are to give them up because Christ is fully God, and being fully God, his death was not just the death of one innocent man but a death of God, of infinite value, enough to pay fully for the sins of everyone in the world including yours and mine. Any claim we help out in the least diminishes and insults Jesus and his work.

Paul said first, the fullness of God is in Christ, and second, that's the reason why we should cling to him. Then third, **it transfers to us!** Right after Paul wrote "*fullness of God in Christ,*" he said, "*And you have been given fullness in Christ!*"

Can I even start to describe – can any of us start to understand this fullness given to us? Jesus **is** the fullness of God and we are given fullness. That which Christ is, is passed on to us. We'll know fulness fully only after we pass through that portal at life's end. That's a doorway to fullness in full. What a future to look forward to!

But don't wait for it till then. Get started now. In fact, it has started already. After all, the Apostle uses past tense: "*And you have been given fullness in Christ.*" We're already beginning to know the fullness of God. We know the full and free forgiveness of all our guilt and wrongdoing. But let's speed things along. Let's pray that Christ's fullness becomes more and more ours. As he knew and submitted to His Father's will, pray and study to know God's will for you. As he exercised the power of God, pray for and depend on God's strength as you face the tasks of life. As he dealt patiently with followers weak in faith, pray for patience to deal with the weaknesses of friends and roommates. As he spent himself to help the sick and needy, look for ways to show your concern for those in need. As Jesus "sinners doth receive," pray for the strength to forgive those who trespass against us. Let Jesus' love fill us with the love that gives up self to serve others. Pray with the hymnwriter:

> Be with us, God the Father, be with us God the Son,
> And God the Holy Spirit, most blessed three in one.
> Make us your faithful servants, you rightly to adore
> and fill us with your fullness both now, and evermore.

†

February 27, 2001

Up to Jerusalem

INI

Wasn't it great, a week ago, to have a long weekend for Presidents' Day? Very refreshing! And I know, with the weather continuing as it is, and midterm exams coming this week, and the cabin fever that hits all Minnesota colleges in late winter, we are all looking forward to next weekend, the beginning of Spring Break.

In Minnesota, when people take a break from the routines and troubles of life, they often go "up to the lake." Nobody in Minnesota ever goes "over to the lake" or "down to the lake" or even just "to the lake." They always go "**up** to the lake." Today I'll ask you to let the phrase "up to the lake" represent any kind of refreshing break, and I'll point out, on the basis of these verses of Scripture that we can go up to the lake because Jesus went up to Jerusalem.

> Jesus took the Twelve aside and told them, "We are going up to Jerusalem, and everything that is written by the prophets about the Son of Man will be fulfilled. He will be handed over to the Gentiles. They will mock him, insult him, spit on him, flog him and kill him. On the third day he will rise again." The disciples did not understand any of this. Its meaning was hidden from them, and they did not know what he was talking about. Luke 18.31-34

The Minnesota phrase "up to the lake" probably comes from maps where north is up and most of Minnesota's 10 or 15 thousand lakes are north of everyone. In Bible lands, "up" means elevation, climbing hills and mountains. Most of the important happenings in the Bible took place on mountains. Moses went up Mount Sinai to get the Ten Commandments. Yesterday in church we heard again about the marvelous transfiguration of Jesus on top of a mountain. So it's appropriate that Jesus goes **up** to Jerusalem – and approaching Jerusalem from almost any direction is quite an uphill climb – because what would happen to him there was **the** most important event in all history.

And it wouldn't be a refreshing vacation. Jesus describes it: *"Everything that is written by the prophets about the Son of Man will be fulfilled."* That is, God's entire salvation plan for all humankind, laid out since before the world was created, actively underway since Adam and Eve first sinned, foretold by all the inspired writers of the Old Testament – all was now going to be fulfilled! Jesus went into detail: *"He will be handed over to the Gentiles. They will mock him, insult him, spit on him, flog him and kill him."* No, this was not a trip for refreshment. Not **his** refreshment. It will be good for us to review again this coming season of Lent the passion (the word means "suffering") of Jesus when he went **up** to Jerusalem. It was not for his refreshment at all.

But rather for **ours**.

Consider the **burden of sin** he lifted off of us when he took them all with him and paid for them on the cross. Consider the **peace** he established between God and us by removing any reason why God must be our enemy. Consider the **liberty** he provided us by freeing us from slavery to Satan. Consider the **load of dread** he cast off us by tearing out the sting of death. Consider the **riches** he transferred to us as he made us his sisters and brothers, heirs of God himself.

Truly it is a refreshing vacation in the fullest sense of word, an escape from our most profound needs, that Jesus provided us when he went **up** to Jerusalem.

Do you remember the last sentence of the Bible verses I read? *"The disciples did not understand any of this. Its meaning was hidden from them, and they did not know what he was talking about."* Those closest to him didn't understand what he was doing for them. Certainly they didn't adequately appreciate it.

And there we are too, aren't we? We enjoy our breaks, our vacations, our trips to Greece or Italy or home or whatever, with little thought to how dreadful all those things would be – in fact how dreadful all our lives would be – if we were still bearing all the burdens Jesus removed from us. We **can** really enjoy the good times God blesses us with. We can go **up to the lake only** because of what Jesus did when he went **up** to Jerusalem.

The same is true in bad times. Life isn't all fun, we know, and we're not always full of joy. Things happen to us – illness, accident, failure – that we can't understand. When Jesus told his disciples he was going up to Jerusalem, they didn't understand either. But he went anyway and did for them in love what they needed most. So in our bad times too – sickness, accident, failure, even persecution and even martyrdom – though we often don't understand what's happening to us, Jesus hasn't changed. He is still working in love for us to do what we need most. We can take great comfort in knowing that, in times of joy and times of sadness, we can be **up at the lake** because Jesus went **up to Jerusalem**.

†

April 2, 2001

Three Word Gospel

INI

How long since you asked the childhood questions about God? How big is God? How strong is God? How much does God know? These are questions with no answer big enough to be complete.

But here's a question with an answer we know: How much does God love us? The answer is a favorite Bible passage: So much that He gave his one and only Son, so that whoever believes in Him should not perish but have eternal life. John 3.16

That passage is a favorite because it gathers the entire Gospel message into one sentence. But there is an even more concise expression of the Gospel earlier in John's book (and we teachers of communication are great fans of conciseness). It's the Gospel in three words:

> The next day John saw Jesus coming toward him and said, "Look! the Lamb of God, who takes away the sin of the world." John 1.29

There it is in three words, the entire Gospel message: *"Look! God's Lamb!"*

It's all the more starkly plain and beautiful coming from this source: John, the crazy preacher out in the Judean desert, who specialized in preaching Law, not Gospel. Quite the Law preacher, this John was! Really strong on God's rules for our lives. **Repent** was his message. **Turn** from your sinful ways. And he had just the right zinger to hit the conscience of each of his listeners personally. To the tax collectors, you guys are thieves. To the soldiers (imagine saying this to Roman soldiers), you guys are bullies. To everybody, you're a bunch of snakes! Tough talk, but he did that to prepare the way for the Savior.

It's a message we need too, and for the same reason. Martin Luther talked about the need for daily repentance. Every day, repent of our sins.

That's not natural for us. Something in us always tries to play down our sin. It tells us we're not so bad. At least we try, sometimes. At least we go to chapel. At least we're not as bad as some other folks. Or at least we do some good things that can make up for what we do wrong.

None of it works. Our sins are still there, our sinfulness is still there. That was John's message about our sin. I can't look at your faces and see your special sins. But you know them, as I know mine, and God knows them all. None of these "at leasts" can possibly make up for any of it. Sin has to be removed, or else it will crush us in God's judgment.

Once John had his listeners realizing that, he had done his job of preparation. Then he could turn to them, point out Jesus as he approached, and say, "Look! God's Lamb!"

Those three words were enough among a people who knew their sin and knew about lambs. Lambs were killed, their blood spilled on the temple altar in the symbolic payment for sins. But those animals were the **peoples'** lambs. Here, Jesus, was **God's** lamb, the One who would make the **real** payment, spilling his blood on the altar of the cross. Those three words were enough.

But just to make sure (and to make **us** sure) John added, "*Look! The Lamb of God, that takes away the sin of the world.*"

Of all the world! Of course, that includes you and me. It's that fact which draws us to the cross in our worship. Because we know, though God's Lamb was slain many years ago and far away, we – you and I – were there. Our sins were loaded on him, and he took them away, paid their full price of punishment, guilt and shame, and left us, in God's view, **sinless**, **pure**, fit for Heaven, and prepared to live as his children here on earth.

How big is God? How strong? Those are questions for which no answer is big enough. But look to the cross on which Jesus died. Then we will again glimpse the answer to the question, how much does God love us?

†

April 4, 2001

We Know the Ending

(see Easter at Peace 2008)

INI

Don't you hate it when somebody gives away the ending? There's a movie you want to see, the ads say you'll never guess the twist at end. Then somebody tells you before you go. You're reading a book, really caught up in it. Then somebody says "Oh you're reading that book, watch out for..." and they tell you ending! It wouldn't be much fun watching a basketball or baseball game if you knew in advance who will win. Last Friday the Bethany debate team found itself in a round that would determine a national championship. They debated well against a tough and experienced California team, and then had to wait more than 30 hours, till the award ceremony the next night, to find out if they won or lost.[1] It was a time of great tension, but a delicious tension, one that would have been spoiled if someone had leaked the results to them before the ceremony. There are times we don't want to know the ending before the ending.

But not when it comes to the ending of life. When life it at stake, it becomes anguish not knowing the ending. I can remember twice in my life I've had to get into a car, after hearing of an emergency involving someone I love, and drive for hours – out of contact – to the scene, not knowing whether, when I got there, my loved one would be dead or alive. That's not fun. When it's not pretending, not a game, then not knowing the ending can be anguish

And what if it's not just life, but eternity at stake? What an underlying disquiet we would feel all through our lives if we didn't know where we would spend eternity. Worse still, what an anguish would gnaw at us, sometimes deep inside, but sometimes dominating our consciousness, when we are honest with ourselves and realize that when we face God in judgment, fallen far short of the holiness he demands, our eternity would be nothing but loss, and loss, and loss.

But there was Easter, the day God gave away the ending. On Easter God said, want to know how it ends – how your life ends? I'll show you, in advance, so you don't have to worry about it, so you don't have to travel your life in

---

[1] This was the debate team of Aaron Lambrecht and Jon Schmidt who won a gold medal at the Phi Rho Pi National Tournament in Jacksonville, FL. Since I worked in the tabulation room I knew in advance that they had won but succeeded in not letting them know until it was announced at the award ceremony. The same thing happened with the teams of Leah Olson and Britta Monson at the national tournament in Atlanta and Jon Loging and Dan Schneider in Milwaukee; each of these teams also won gold.

anguish wondering and fearing. Here's the ending: Jesus rose from the dead, and so will you. You will rise from the dead, just as Jesus did.

Remember that suspense, that anguish of wondering and fearing? It comes from the Law of God. The power of the Law lies in its ability to threaten us, to convict us. to show us the many ways we've fallen short.

But Jesus fulfilled the Law perfectly for us, never breaking it, always obeying it. Then he died on Good Friday, not for his own sin (he had none) but for ours.

When God the Father raised him up, that was his seal of approval on Jesus' work. **It is enough – sins are all paid for – all of them**. Our sins are now forgiven. The Law can't condemn us anymore. The Law is no longer a factor in determining our future. It has no power over us. And when the Law loses its power over us, death loses its sting. We know our future – not loss, but victory.

These days after Easter, feel the comfort of knowing this important ending – no more anguish that we are moving toward death, no more fear of what will happen to us then.

God told us the ending. Hear it in his Word:

> Where, O Death, is your victory? Where, O Death, is your sting? The sting of death is sin, and the power of sin is the law. But thanks be to God, who gives us the victory through our Lord Jesus Christ. 1 Corinthians 15.55-57

†

September 2001

Our Words are Us

INI

You and I may have had some tough weeks in our lives, but none as bad as this one had been for Jesus. His enemies, growing in number, were out to trap him into saying something that would cause him to lose whatever following he had. Failing that, some were starting to plot to kill him. Even his mother and family were trying to distract him and draw him off-task. In the middle of it Jesus, disappointed at the unbelief that surrounded him and tired of the constant attacks, aimed some sharp words at his enemies.

We're glad he did, because his words contain some important lessons for us.

> Make a tree good and its fruit will be good or make a tree bad and its fruit will be bad, for a tree is recognized by its fruit. You brood of vipers, how can you who are evil say anything good? For out of the overflow of the heart the mouth speaks. The good man brings good things out of the good stored up in him, and the evil man brings evil things out of the evil stored up in him. But I tell you that men will have to give account on the day of judgment for every careless word they have spoken. For by your words you will be acquitted, and by your words you will be condemned." Matthew 12. 33-37

On these Tuesdays, according to the chaplain's plan, we are going to hear some lessons from Jesus, advice on how to live. I want to show you two things this morning: first, what that lesson is this time, and then, what the purpose of these lessons really is.

What is the lesson this time? It's not difficult. We are to recognize what psychologists today call "congruity." Jesus spoke of it 200 years ago. Peoples' outside reflects their inside. The fruit reflects the quality of the tree. As Jesus says, "*The good man brings good things out of the good stored up in him, and the evil man brings evil things out of the evil stored up in him.*" That's especially clear regarding words. What you say is who you are. Again as Jesus puts it, "*For out of the overflow of the heart the mouth speaks.*"

OK, the lesson is plain, and it's not a new one to any of us. You heard it from your mom: watch your mouth! or some such warning. Do I need to repeat here what you already know? -- That you **can** judge people by the way they talk. That others will judge **you** by the way you talk – whether it be "foul language" or careless use of the Lord's name or boastful speech or words that hurt others or words that use others or words that mislead others – our words are us!

And not only do we judge each other by words, but **God** judges us by our words. Jesus says, *"But I tell you that men will have to give account on the day of judgment for every careless word they have spoken."*

And that brings us for sure to the second point – why these lessons?

It seems like these Tuesday lessons are to teach us how to live – what we can do to please God and show love to each other. Well that's right. But before that they have a far more important purpose: They are to show us how far short we fall of pleasing God and loving each other. In these lessons Jesus will lay out before us his requirements – perfect behavior! Perfect words! Perfect thoughts! And our first response is to be **wow** I don't do that! I'm way short of that! And when we realize how far short we fall of pleasing God it hits us: we need **help.**

Here's where Jesus becomes our Hero. He is the one whose words are himself. Just as our words are who we are, Jesus' words are who he is, someone whose words are never foul, never deceptive, never hypocritical – whose words, even when harsh as they are in this reading, are always spoken in love, and always always **true**. Test his words! They are always **true**. And especially test his words of promise:

> Come to me you weak and burdened, and I will give you rest. Matthew 11.28
> I have come to seek and save the lost. Luke 19.10
> The one who believes in me will never die. John 11.26
> This is my body, my blood, given and shed for you for forgiveness of your sins. Luke 22.15f

Hear his words, and then see how his words are him. In the terms of our reading, *"This truly good man brought wonderfully good things out of the good stored up in him,"* as he gave his life away to pay on the cross the penalty we owed God for our falling short of his requirements. This man of completely unselfish love and completely loving and true words has restored us to God's favor.

That's what we'll be doing here on Tuesdays – hearing how we should live, realizing how bad we are at it, finding comfort in the forgiveness we have in Jesus, and by that gaining the strength to try harder and do better.

Today's lesson: go out and make your words good ones – words of love, kindness, and help. Then come back each week for more lessons, and most important, for more reassurance of our forgiveness won by Jesus Christ.

✝

October 3, 2001

To Live Is Christ

INI

Invisible cells of enemies intent on our destruction – not far away in distant lands but right here where we live – sneaky and clever, studying to catch us with our guard down – putting us in potential danger every moment of our lives, whatever we are doing.

I don't think it belittles the disaster of Sept 11,[1] or the dangers we are newly aware of these days, to observe that words like these are not new to Christians who know their Bibles or even just their hymnbooks. These words exactly describe enemies not at all new, but (as Luther put it) the "old evil foe who now means us deadly woe, deep guile and great might are his dread arms in fight – on earth is not his equal." [*A Mighty Fortress...*] Satan and his cohorts, the world and our own sinful flesh have been seeking our destruction since the day we were born. Those are the terrorists who are in fact the most dire threat to us, for they are plotting our eternal death.

But the news in this war is good. The victory is already won. Jesus Christ defeated the forces of evil, entering their very own hiding place as he suffered the punishment of God and death for our sins in our place, then burst out alive and glorified on Easter morning.

It's good for us to contemplate the glorious future we all look forward to after this life because of Jesus' Easter victory. But it's also good to ponder why we remain here for a while – *"to live is Christ."* We are encouraged by our national leaders, as our country proceeds in its battle against terrorists, to go on living our daily lives without fear. So too in this battle with spiritual enemies, we should know the tactics of the enemy, stay on the alert, all those things, yes, but still go on living a full life in Christ, confident that in him the victory is already won.

Hear the words of the Apostle Paul, written in trouble, in danger of death, after he has been imprisoned for preaching the Gospel, and see how he plans to spend whatever days God permits him to remain on this earth, serving his Lord by serving others.

> For I know that through your prayers and the help given by the Spirit of Jesus Christ, what has happened to me will turn out for my deliverance. I eagerly expect and hope that I will in no way be ashamed but will have sufficient courage so that now as always Christ will be exalted in my body, whether by life or by death. For to me, to live is

---

[1] The tragedy happened less than a month before this.

Christ and to die is gain. If I am to go on living in the body, this will mean fruitful labor for me. Yet what shall I choose? I do not know! I am torn between the two: I desire to depart and be with Christ, which is better by far; but it is more necessary for you that I remain in the body. Convinced of this, I know that I will remain, and I will continue with all of you for your progress and joy in the faith, so that through my being with you again your joy in Christ Jesus will overflow on account of me. Philippians 1.19-26

†

October 15, 2001

Rebekah

INI

Expecting a new baby in the family, as some of you know and others will someday, is a memorable time of anticipation, tension, and excitement. Imagine how it would be, knowing the baby is at the center of God's plan. It was that way for Rebekah, and today we'll view baby-having through her eyes.

> This is the account of Abraham's son Isaac. Abraham became the father of Isaac, and Isaac was forty years old when he married Rebekah daughter of Bethuel the Aramean from Paddan Aram and sister of Laban the Aramean. Isaac prayed to the LORD on behalf of his wife, because she was barren. The LORD answered his prayer, and his wife Rebekah became pregnant. The babies jostled each other within her, and she said, "Why is this happening to me?" So she went to inquire of the LORD. The LORD said to her, "Two nations are in your womb, and two peoples from within you will be separated; one people will be stronger than the other, and the older will serve the younger." When the time came for her to give birth, there were twin boys in her womb. The first to come out was red, and his whole body was like a hairy garment; so they named him Esau. After this, his brother came out, with his hand grasping Esau's heel; so he was named Jacob. Isaac was sixty years old when Rebekah gave birth to them. The boys grew up, and Esau became a skillful hunter, a man of the open country, while Jacob was a quiet man, staying among the tents. Isaac, who had a taste for wild game, loved Esau, but Rebekah loved Jacob. Genesis 25.19-28

Here we have Rebekah, one of the most intriguing people in those Old Testament families led by the patriarchs, Abraham, Isaac, and Jacob. She was the wife of Isaac, mother of Jacob, right in the middle of what must impress us as three quite dysfunctional families. I wish I had time to retell her whole story, but I can only sketch it briefly, recall it to your mind if you've heard it before, and urge you to read it all in Genesis. She was quite a woman, who served God in a special way.

We first met Rebekah in the Bible when she was a young woman, perhaps just a girl between 15-20 years old. Remember how Abraham sent his servant back to his ancestral home to find a wife for his 40-year-old son Isaac. Remember how the servant met Rebekah and was impressed not only with her beauty but her kindness and industriousness as she gave him water and cared for his camels as well? Remember how he asked her brother for her hand, how her brother asked her if she would go off to a strange country and marry a man she had never met – the ultimate blind date – and she willingly agreed? How she traveled far and stepped off her camel into a marriage. And the Bible says, Isaac loved her. Surely they started marriage with an assurance that many young people today only hope for – the confidence that God had truly meant them for each other. I'm inclined to attribute to Rebekah as much as to Isaac that they were the only monogamous couple among the patriarchs. Despite 20 years of having no children, there was for Rebekah no "here's-my-handmaid-bear-a-child-for-me" foolishness. There was no alternate wife. She waited patiently, trusting in God's promise. And finally it became baby-having time.

You heard the story of it in the reading. She had no way of knowing she was bearing twins. Feeling odd movements like a struggle in her womb, and wondering what it meant, she consulted the ultra Ultra-sound – she asked the Lord. We don't know just how she did that, but it's significant that she went directly, not through her husband – this is the first time we know of that a woman ever consulted the Lord directly – and she got the answer you heard: twins, the older would serve the younger. Rebekah remembered that word from God. It made a difference in what she did.

The twins were born and now, sadly, these parents chose favorites. Esau was the macho outdoor type. Trouble is, he didn't take God seriously. Though he had the right of the first-born, and with it would have carried the promise of the Lord, he didn't care, and traded it away to his younger twin brother one day in return for a plate of stew because he was hungry. Add to that his messing around with the girls of the unbelieving neighborhood. He married two of them, much to the distress of his parents. Still he was his father Isaac's favorite.

There isn't any indication in the Bible that Isaac was very bright. In fact, born of a father Abraham and mother Sarah well past child-bearing age, he may even have been slow. We know that his half-brother Ishmael made fun of him. We know he was much attached to his mother and missed her terribly for a long time after she died. If Isaac and Rebekah's twin boys had any smarts, they probably got them from their mother. And now Isaac was indulging the wrong son. That may be why Rebekah felt she had to act.

Her favorite was Jacob, who wasn't outdoorsy at all but stayed home around the tents. Jacob as a youth wasn't that much of a Godly person either. Like many young people of all times, he wasn't very devout or religious and it took many years and lots of life experiences before Jacob could be renamed Israel, a real man of God. But he did know who the true God was, and his mother Rebekah saw the promise in him. More important, she had heard God's word. Recall again the story we don't have time here to relate. When it seemed the aged, blind and feeble father Isaac was about to bestow the blessing of the family and the Lord on Esau, Rebekah took charge, connived with Jacob to fool the old man into blessing Jacob instead, and then she sent her favorite son fleeing for his life back to her brother's house far away.

Who then was Rebekah? She was a generous, hard-working, faithful, resourceful woman who was dedicated to her husband, to her children, and to her God. Should we fault her for deceiving a blind old man to carry out what she knew was God's will? The Bible doesn't. She was a woman in a patriarchal age who got things done as best she could and that was well. She was willing to dare, and to take the consequences for her daring. And so she did, living out the rest of her life with an aged deceived husband and an angry son, never to see her beloved son Jacob again. She's the kind of woman I'd like for a wife – and have, I think – someone with the faith, sense, resourcefulness, and courage to take care of things when her husband gets silly.

What are we to make of these intimate stories of dysfunctional though God-fearing families? Well, we get pretty wound up in our own lives that we sometimes mess up terribly, with lives that resemble soap operas except far too dull. But we see in Rebekah's case that God works his will even through such messed up relationships and his will is love. The plan he was working through Rebekah's family was the blessing of the entire world, for from her children would come the promised Savior. Certainly this Bible family was special to God; they are in the Bible, after all, and central to God's plan. But so are you and I. God loves us no less than Isaac and Rebekah and Esau and Jacob. The blood of his Son was spilt on the cross to pay for their sins no less than yours and mine. And God is working in your life, no less than in theirs, to accomplish that portion of his will that will become real through your life.

Can we learn something from Rebekah? Yes. Stay faithful. Study the Word of God to know his will. Find it humbly, not arrogantly. Do it with daring. And then trust God to forgive our mistakes and work his will even through them.

That's the lesson of Rebekah.

†

November 6, 2001

Salt-Light

INI

It's a great shame when a Christian does something bad. It might be a greater shame when a Christian does nothing good.

Listen to Jesus' words right after he spoke the Beatitudes.

> You are the salt of the earth. But if the salt loses its saltiness, how can it be made salty again? It is no longer good for anything, except to be thrown out and trampled by men. You are the light of the world. A city on a hill cannot be hidden. Neither do people light a lamp and put it under a bowl. Instead they put it on its stand, and it gives light to everyone in the house. In the same way, let your light shine before men, that they may see your good deeds and praise your Father in heaven.
> Matthew 5.13-16

Jesus teaches us here that our greatest concern as redeemed Christians may not be that we fall into sin, but that we are useless.

This week here in chapel we are celebrating the saints. Popular view holds that these are especially good people, especially holy, serving God in ways beyond what any of us ordinary folk are capable of. So we might wonder, could I ever become one? – much like we might wonder if we might become president of the United States, or reach some other lofty lifetime achievement. Could I ever be a saint some day?

Well, if you know the Bible, you already know the answer to that trick question. It's not a matter of some day. You are one now. When you were baptized, when you became a believer in Jesus Christ, you became a member of the **Holy** Christian Church, one of the holy ones, one of the saints. That's because Jesus' work of salvation, by which he paid on the cross for the sins of all the world, became applied specifically to you. Your sins are removed, forgiven, gone. When God looks at you now through the work of Jesus, you are especially good – as good as Jesus whose goodness you wear. You are especially holy – as holy as Jesus whose sinlessness was transferred to you. That's your own special gift from God. Your sins and mine were carried by Jesus and he paid for them on the cross, while his perfection and holiness were credited to us. That means you and I are saints.

Now, Jesus is telling us, don't be useless! I told you at the beginning – for a redeemed Christian, that's the greatest shame, to be salt that's lost its saltiness, good for nothing, to be a light hidden under a bowl, lighting nobody and nothing. That's a huge shame.

How then to be "not useless"? Should we aspire to great deeds like saints are known for? Actually it's much easier than that. And at the same time much harder than that.

Look first at the easy part. Start with a simple prayer: "Lord, thank you for your gift of salvation. Now use me. Show me how to serve you." Pray that right now. See? That was easy! And it will work.

Next, look at Jesus' words which set up his observation about "salt and light." The Beatitudes describe saints perfectly. So then be poor in spirit – humble, knowing your sins and thankful for God's gift of forgiveness. Be ready to mourn with those who are sad. Be meek. Hunger and thirst after righteousness. Be merciful, and pure in heart. Be a peacemaker. There's a way to sum all this up: do everything you do in Jesus' name. Consider all that comes into your life, little or big, important or not, pleasant or unpleasant, as an opportunity for service of thanksgiving to Jesus.

And you know what will happen then? Doors start to open up, doors where your prayer ("Lord make use of me!") is answered. The Lord places you into opportunities where you can be for him what he wants you to be, where you can do for him what he wants you to do.

What that might be who knows? Important and spectacular in the eyes of the world? Could be, but probably not. Noticed by lots of people? Maybe, but not necessarily. Noticed by **anyone at all**? Maybe, but possibly not. Enjoyable? Could be, but maybe not at all. Jesus continued the Beatitudes describing Christians as those who are persecuted because of righteousness, "*when people insult you, persecute you and falsely say all kinds of evil against you because of me.*" That's typically what happens when Christians are useful to the Lord. Rejoice then, he says, because then you are not useless, but you are as his work made you: you are salt, seasoning and preserving the world, and you are light, shining God's love throughout the neighborhood.

Since you are redeemed and made holy by the work of Jesus, and when you respond with a life of usefulness to him by responding to the opportunities he places before you, then you are in every sense of the word a saint.

†

December 2001

God Serving Us?

INI

How do you picture Heaven?

We often picture Heaven as a place where we can serve God, singing and praising him perfectly without the distraction of our sinful world or our own corrupt flesh. In our reading this morning, we hear the words of Jesus who gives us another picture. Here Jesus describes Heaven not as a place where we serve God, but where God serves us. It's like a great banquet, he says, where we are the guests, where we relax, don't have to do the work, just sit back and enjoy.

God serving us, like a waiter at a banquet! Isn't that a startling thought? Especially considering what we, for our thoughtlessness, selfishness, thanklessness, neglect of God and his things, truly deserve from God? But that's the promise of Jesus himself! Still he sandwiches this marvelous promise between two slices of warning. Listen to Jesus' words:

> Be dressed ready for service and keep your lamps burning, *[note those words – we'll look at them later]* like men waiting for their master to return from a wedding banquet, so that when he comes and knocks they can immediately open the door for him. It will be good for those servants whose master finds them watching when he comes. I tell you the truth, he will dress himself to serve, will have them recline at the table and will come and wait on them. It will be good for those servants whose master finds them ready, even if he comes in the second or third watch of the night. But understand this: If the owner of the house had known at what hour the thief was coming, he would not have let his house be broken into. You also must be ready, because the Son of Man will come at an hour when you do not expect him. Luke 12.35-40

You heard that promise, didn't you? But you also heard that the promise is for those who are ready when He comes. Certainly we desire to be ready. But how, exactly, do we do that? How can we know for sure that we are ready? Well, the hard part of that has been done for us. Jesus has been here before, to do it. This coming, for which we need to be ready, is Jesus' third visit. The first two were to do the work of getting us ready for the third.

Jesus first came to live with us at the first Christmas – we're preparing now to celebrate its anniversary. That time he came to live, in our place, the sinless life of service that God demands of everyone. We could never do that, so Jesus came to do it for us. And then, to pay the world's debt of sin, to pay **our** debt to God's justice, he died in our place. What a great service he did for us at his first coming!

But since then he has come, a second time, for each of us in another very personal way. At your Baptism he came to you – in the Lord's Supper he comes to you – each time you attend to the Word of God he comes to you to make you God's child, to be our brother, to be with us daily in all we do. What a precious companion he is in his second coming!

So God has already done the work. He has made us ready for Jesus' final coming, when he comes visibly to end this age, and to start eternity. For us it's as simple as turning a page – turn to page 61 in the Hymnary. Respond now to those words in the middle of the page. I'll read the pastor's words:

"I ask each of you, in the presence of God who searches the heart: Do you confess that you have sinned, and do you repent of your sins?" **I do.** "Do you believe that Jesus Christ has redeemed you from all your sins, and do you desire forgiveness in His name?" **I do.**

When you sincerely say those "I do's", you demonstrate that God has gotten you ready. You are prepared for the final coming of our Lord Jesus. Your sins are forgiven, and you will enjoy being served by God himself in Heaven.

Want further evidence of it? Look to how you respond to the first words of Jesus that we read. *"Be dressed ready for service,"* he said, *"and keep your lamps burning."* The burning lamps remind us of our witness – how at all times we are presenting ourselves to those around us as the forgiven children of God that we are. And the encouragement to be dressed ready for service reminds us of where our attention is directed – service to others.

There is the service of Word, when we turn our attention to it regularly, read it and hear it. That's a sign that God has made us ready. There is the service of prayer, when we turn to our heavenly Father asking his help for those in need. That too is a sign that God has made us ready. There is the service of caring for those who need caring – be it our roommate, our friend, our enemy, the stranger at our door, the stranger far away. There is the service of preparing, as you are now heading into final exam week, working hard to become the best you can be, so you can serve even better in the future.

Any or all of these things are the signs that God has indeed made you ready, and that you will by God's grace always be ready to welcome the Lord when he comes for the final and most glorious time, so that he can welcome **us** to that place where we will be served by God.

God serving us. Why should that startle us? It's been happening all along.

†

January 21, 2002

God Bestows Dignity

On the observance of the Martin Luther King Holiday.
Theme: Human dignity, the basis for rights, was established by the sacrifice of Christ.

INI

The last time we held an assembly in this place, the South Gym at Bethany Lutheran College, it was our "Price of Freedom" Forum on Veteran's Day.[1] You heard that day from three inspiring speakers, Rev. and Mrs. McMurdie and Col. Heiliger, who had been thrust into the middle of important world-shaping events and responded with courage to do what they were called on to do. We honored them.

Today let me tell you of someone who was in the midst of important, world-shaping events, and didn't do anything. First, hear this portion of God's Word:

> For [the Lord] has clothed me with garments of salvation and arrayed me in a robe of righteousness, as a bridegroom adorns his head like a priest, and as a bride adorns herself with her jewels. Isaiah 61.10

I don't think it's hard to show how Martin Luther King Day and what it honors grows right out of solid Lutheran theology. Central in our beliefs is the doctrine of objective justification, that is, Christ's death paid for the sins of the entire world. All sins, everyone's, were paid for by that sacrifice on the cross. We believe what the Bible teaches, that every human being, though undeserving, has been redeemed by the blood of Christ. Every one of them, of us, could truly speak the words of Isaiah that I just read.

The adornment of bride and groom we take to be the pinnacle of human dignity. There is no occasion where dignity is more important than a wedding. When a person is redeemed by the blood of Christ, and thereby adorned as for a wedding, it follows that this person should not be reduced to sub-humanity by prejudice, oppression, poverty, or any other condition.

And if you don't trust the logic of that conclusion, then look at the direct words of Scripture to that effect. Hear the psalmist tell us how God's heart goes out to the lowly and oppressed e.g. Psalm 9.9, Psalm 10.17-18, hear Isaiah e.g. Isaiah 3.13-15; 10.1-2 and Amos e.g. Amos 8.4, and Micah e.g. Micah 2. 1-2; 3. 9-12, and Nehemiah e.g. Nehemiah 5.1-13 and other prophets condemn the powerful who oppress the poor, study the Ninth Commandment by which God protects opportunity, as

---

[1] Bethany had held an assembly in the gym, which had a larger capacity than the chapel, featuring two war veterans, Pastor McMurdie who had served in World War II, and Col. Heiliger, a good friend from Our Saviour's, our "home" church in Madison, Wisconsin, who had served and was a POW in Viet Nam.

much as by other commandments he protects marriage, property, reputation, and life itself, and look to the example of our Lord, who spent his time with the humble, the poor, the sick and disabled, the despised and oppressed.

As forgiven children of God, we can't leave people without faith in Christ so we preach the Gospel. But we also can't leave them in conditions that strip them of the dignity that Christ has won for them so we attack those oppressive conditions. The two go together. Concern with conditions without concern with faith is what's called "social gospel," and there the Gospel gets lost. But if we're concerned with faith without concern with conditions, we're condemned by the Apostle James who says faith without works is dead. The two go together. As the saying goes, "Do the one, but don't leave the other undone."

The person I referred to at the beginning, who found himself in middle of world-changing events and did nothing – that was me. In 1955, when Rosa Parks kept her seat in the front of the bus in Montgomery, I was a junior in high school. 1961, the year college students were risking and in some cases losing their lives joining in freedom rides to battle segregation in the South, I graduated from college. In 1963, the year King delivered his "dream" speech, I was in my second year of seminary. In 1968, the year King was assassinated, I was a doctoral student at Wisconsin. All those years I was not a supporter of the civil rights movement. In the church schools I was attending, our view of King was so pre-occupied with flaws in his theology that we missed his purpose. That's something I have since then always regretted. It took King's death to shock me into rethinking my views, and to realize how God was making Martin Luther King a gift to our nation.

Perhaps today's crisis atmosphere is one from which we can especially appreciate God's gift to us in Martin Luther King. Imagine if the oppressed minority in our country had chosen violent revolution as their strategy. Would the U. S. be like Northern Ireland today, with endless cycles of attack and retaliation? Suppose they had chosen terrorism as their strategy – and some advocated doing just that. Would the U. S. be like Israel and Palestine today, with nobody able to figure out how to stop the mutual hatred and killing? Martin Luther King, with his ability to understand and instill in others a commitment to nonviolence to accomplish desperately needed social change, was truly a blessing from God for all of us in our nation. I didn't appreciate that when he was alive. I do now.

What should you learn from my bad example? I don't feel guilty – God was leading me down the life path I'm sure I was to take. But I do regret being in the middle of a crucial time in our nation's history and missing it. So what I'd like to urge you this morning is this: stay alert to where the needy people are around you. Look for the people who are in need of the Gospel. Not only that. Look for the people who are being stripped of their dignity by oppressive conditions. Decide: somehow, that's where you should be – perhaps in person, perhaps only in spirit, but somehow be there.

Some of these places are nearby, easy to reach. How are the aged living in our community? Are children all getting the opportunities they need? People with disabilities? Are new immigrants encountering unfair discrimination? Are people near us being persecuted for their religion, their clothing customs, their life-style choices. It's easy to find opportunities to improve human dignity right near home.

But while we might work small, we needn't always think small. What would happen if we in the U.S. took the same effort that we are now putting into wiping out terrorism in the world – an effort most people support as fully justified – what if we would take the same effort, same billions of dollars we've been spending on bombs and military action, the same global diplomatic leadership (if not coercion), and dedicate it to wiping out world hunger within the next 15 years? It's possible, I'm convinced of that. Why don't we do it? Which of you here could find yourself involved, even instrumental, in launching and carrying out such a God-pleasing campaign for human dignity?

There are lots of opportunities. I pray that you don't need to look back late in life and regret that you missed them. Go with Jesus as he talked with a despised Samaritan woman, as he ate with despised tax collectors, as he welcomed the attention of a known prostitute, as he sought out the sick and the handicapped, as he went to the cross to pay for our sins, yours, mine, those of all the world -- and see how His presence transformed people. He didn't wait until they were somehow worthy or deserving first. Thank God He didn't wait until we were worthy or deserving before rescuing us. Rather, He went to the needy, and his presence transformed them, made them fit to stand in the presence of God, gave them dignity.

Now it's God's purpose for you. Where can you go? Whom can you help to realize the dignity that is theirs by knowing that *the Lord has clothed them with garments of salvation and arrayed them in a robe of righteousness, as a bridegroom adorns his head like a priest, and as a bride adorns herself with her jewels.*

†

February 11, 2002

Ruth

INI

Is your name Ruth? In a very real sense, everyone here can say yes, and so can I. It's a beautiful name, one that has endured in popularity since the first Ruth of whom we know lived some 33 centuries ago. Listen to the beginning of her story in the Bible book that bears her name.

> In the days when the judges ruled, there was a famine in the land, and a man from Bethlehem in Judah, together with his wife and two sons, went to live for a while in the country of Moab. The man's name was Elimelech, his wife's name Naomi, and the names of his two sons were Mahlon and Kilion. They were Ephrathites from Bethlehem, Judah. And they went to Moab and lived there. Now Elimelech, Naomi's husband, died, and she was left with her two sons. They married Moabite women, one named Orpah and the other Ruth. After they had lived there about ten years, both Mahlon and Kilion also died, and Naomi was left without her two sons and her husband. When she heard in Moab that the LORD had come to the aid of his people by providing food for them, Naomi and her daughters-in-law prepared to return home from there. With her two daughters-in-law she left the place where she had been living and set out on the road that would take them back to the land of Judah. Then Naomi said to her two daughters-in-law, "Go back, each of you, to your mother's home. May the LORD show kindness to you, as you have shown to your dead and to me. May the LORD grant that each of you will find rest in the home of another husband." Then she kissed them and they wept aloud and said to her, "We will go back with you to your people." But Naomi said, "Return home, my daughters. Why would you come with me? Am I going to have any more sons, who could become your husbands? Return home, my daughters; I am too old to have another husband. Even if I thought there was still hope for me – even if I had a husband tonight and then gave birth to sons – would you wait until they grew up? Would you remain unmarried for them? No, my daughters. It is more bitter for me than for you, because the LORD's hand has gone out against me!" At this they wept again. Then Orpah kissed her mother-in-law good-by, but Ruth clung to her. "Look," said Naomi, "your sister-in-law is going back to her people and her gods. Go back with her." But Ruth replied, "Don't urge me to leave you or to turn back from you. Where you go I will go, and where you stay I will stay. Your people will be my people and your God my God. Where you die

I will die, and there I will be buried. May the LORD deal with me, be it ever so severely, if anything but death separates you and me." When Naomi realized that Ruth was determined to go with her, she stopped urging her. Ruth 1.1-18

Here my assignment for this morning tells me I should stop reading, but I'd urge you sometime today or tonight to pick up your Bible and read the rest of the story. It's just four chapters long and you can finish it in 20 minutes. What follows is a delightful romance which was admired as such by no less a critic than Goethe, the story of how this foreign girl, this alien Ruth returns with Naomi to Bethlehem, finds her new husband Boaz, and becomes the great grandmother of King David and an ancestor of our Lord Jesus Christ. But the story's highlight, its most famous passage, is that pledge of devotion hailed by some commentators as unsurpassed in all literature. It was spoken not by husband or wife to each other – it often is used in wedding ceremonies that way – but by a devoted daughter-in-law to her mother-in law, and the words soar even more beautifully in the more famous King James translation:

> Intreat me not to leave thee, or to return from following after thee: for whither thou goest, I will go; and where thou lodgest, I will lodge: thy people shall be my people, and thy God my God: Where thou diest, will I die, and there will I be buried.

Why did she do it? Why did this foreign young woman decide to leave behind her own family, her own ways, her own hope of a future, and go instead to a strange land? It wasn't for comfort – two women traveling alone through some hundred miles of wild barren country to who knows what. It wasn't for material gain – two widows in those days had virtually no hope of a livelihood except for begging.

There was only one reason Ruth made this decision. God had sent her Naomi. There, perhaps, is the real hero of this story. Naomi had left her home ten years before with her husband and two sons, driven by circumstance to leave their homeland in order to survive. Now the men were dead. We aren't told the details, but it's clear that through those terrifyingly difficult years, Naomi did not lose her faith in God. She freely acknowledged that she had been dealt some devastating trials. But she wanted to go home because she knew God's promises, that his love was constant, that a Savior would come, and she knew that those promises would be fulfilled in Judah with God's people. She didn't want to lose sight of them in a foreign land, so she went home. We can't doubt, as we read this story, that it was Naomi's manner of coping with her troubles with sincere continuing faith in God that so attracted her daughters-in-law to her. And Ruth decided, "Naomi's God and her people will be mine too."

I asked if your name is Ruth. Mine is – quite likely, yours too. For consider how we were drawn to God's grace. We too were spiritual aliens, strangers to God and to his people because in our natural state we didn't know God and couldn't please Him. In some rare cases, people like us experience a sudden, dramatic conversion – we heard here in chapel some weeks ago about the case of Saul, persecutor of the church, who encountered Christ on the Damascus road and became Paul the Apostle. But most of us didn't experience any such dramatic change. Instead, for many of us, God sent us a Naomi, someone who somehow led us to Christ, a simple, sincere believer in God whose faith we observed and who drew us to God's grace, who turned our attention to God's promises because they were living in God's promises. That's the primary way God's family grows – by his Gospel, the good news that our sins are forgiven through Jesus' work, reaching new people across the relationships believers build with others.

So then, we can be named Ruth, each of us – someone drawn to the grace of God by seeing the Gospel at work in the life of a Naomi that God in his love has placed into our lives.

And once we have recognized our name is Ruth, perhaps next we can in turn become Naomi.

†

April 2002

A Christian's Song of Joy

INI

Hear Psalm 126:

> When the LORD restored the fortunes of (brought captives back to) Zion, we were like men restored to health. Our mouths were filled with laughter, our tongues with songs of joy. Then it was said among the nations, "The LORD has done great things for them." The LORD has done great things for us, and we are filled with joy. Restore our fortunes, O LORD, like streams in the Negev. Those who sow in tears will reap with songs of joy. He who goes out weeping, carrying seed to sow, will return with songs of joy, carrying sheaves with him.

"How are you feeling?"

This is one of those questions, often used in a greeting, to which we don't expect an honest answer. We expect the answer to be "fine" whether it's true or not. But though we're not used to talking openly in public about them, our feelings and emotions are important to us.

Fortunately, they're not important to our faith.

Well, wait a moment, let me modify that. It's one of those paradoxes of faith that we can truly say, our feelings and emotions are unimportant to our faith, and yet feelings and emotions are very important in our faith life. They are unimportant in the sense that we don't look to our feelings for assurance of our salvation. We don't depend on emotional highs to tell us that we have the love of God. Our faith looks outward, at God's promises, and at God's work on our behalf. Our faith focuses on Jesus Christ and his payment for our sins, and not inward on our fleeting, inconstant feelings. We thank God for that objective assurance of our salvation.

And yet our faith is associated with deep emotions. Chief among them is joy, as captured so beautifully in this psalm.

There are other emotions too in the course of Christian living. For example, the word "**fear**" occurs nearly 100 times in the New Testament. Usually it's telling us not to fear. But God transforms "fear" and it takes on a different meaning when applied to God, as when we are urged to "fear and love God."

The word "**love**" appears many times, as you would expect – over 350 times in the New Testament. It's a word that means lots of things to us, often an emotion. But again, "love" is transformed when we learn of God's love. Then it's more than an emotion – it's a commitment to see to the welfare of someone, whether we like them or not, even to the point of giving oneself fully for the benefit of the other.

We find the word "**anger**" only a little over a dozen times in the New Testament. When it's in people, anger is a sin to be shunned and avoided. But when attributed to God it is righteous and just.

"**Pity**" and "**compassion**" achieve new depths of meaning when attributed to Jesus, the usual New Testament use of these words.

Unlike "**anger,**" "**sorrow**" is not sinful, though it is surely negative. But like anger, God transforms sorrow, and His goal is to turn it to joy.

You see, God transforms all emotions.

But the basic Christian emotion is joy, an underlying constant joy which is there in our lives no matter what else is going on, and which bubbles up to affect and change whatever else is going on.

This psalm captures joy well and recognizes its source. Notice the images of the Gospel. Returning captives – we think of our former captivity to the Devil, a captivity broken by Jesus Christ. Restoration to health – we think of Christ the Healer of diseases, and the conqueror of that basic disease, sin. Water in the desert, bringing what was dead to life, is a reminder of the resurrection of Christ, and through his resurrection, our own eternal life. It's the work of the Lord that brings us joy, that gives us the good deep-down joyful feeling.

I know you've experienced it. It's like walking out of the doctor's office after an annual physical that found nothing wrong. It's like leaving the dentist's office knowing you don't have to come back for a long time. It's like knowing your team is in first place, at least for a few days. It's like the entire off-season after your team won the super-bowl. It's like knowing there is a vacation place waiting for you. It's like knowing that someone loves you even though they're not with you.

It's like…no, it actually **IS** hearing of the cancellation of your death. It's learning of your and my rescue from hell. It's pondering our newly cemented friendship with God. Those are good, deep, constant feelings of joy.

It's true that Christian joy is punctuated by many other emotions. There are emotional highs and lows of life with the births and the deaths. There is sorrow over our sins and their effects on our lives. There is compassion for those we are sent to serve and the sad realizations when we confront the work that is to be done.

On September 11, as you know, nearly 3000 people died in the New York City attacks. On same day (by conservative estimate), some 20,000 people throughout world died of hunger, most of them children. On September 12, there were no more attacks in New York City, but another 20,000 people died of hunger. And still another 20,000 on September 13, 14, and every day since then. And most, we can be sure, died without Baptism, without knowing of their Savior. Realizations like that must punctuate our joy – in fact, they can make us cry.

But finally the deep Christian joy resurfaces with the realization that the Lord has us in place to do his work, and that the Lord promises success in that work in which we serve him. That's why this psalm ends with these words:

"Those who sow in tears will reap with songs of joy. He who goes out weeping, carrying seed to sow, will return with songs of joy, carrying sheaves with him."

That's another one of the promises of God that should bring us joy.

†

June 19, 2002

In the Ron Younge Gymnasium/Assembly Hall,
a devotion to open a session of the Evangelical Lutheran Synod Convention

Don't Worry

INI

When we bow our spirits before the Lord each night to lay our sins before him in daily contrition and repentance as Luther urges, the list of sins we should bring is always longer than we realize. If you're like me, one of the sins we should confess more often, one easy to overlook but one so widespread it might even be called the prevailing sin of our time, is worry.

Like lust, covetousness, and hatred, worry is an internal, mental sin. Worry always anticipates the worst; it pre-occupies us, fills our consciousness with expected misfortune. God knows what we worry about. How we worry about our loved ones, about their health, their safety, their spiritual lives! How we worry about money, the stock and commodities markets, what the weather will do for the crops, what taxes will do to us! How we worry even about fun, whether we'll be able to continue to enjoy the pleasures and lifestyles we have gotten used to. And of course, there's plenty temptation to worry every time we open a newspaper or watch a TV news report!

This morning let Jesus teach us what to do about worry.

> Therefore I tell you, do not worry about your life, what you will eat or drink; or about your body, what you will wear. Is not life more important than food, and the body more important than clothes? Look at the birds of the air; they do not sow or reap or store away in barns, and yet your heavenly Father feeds them. Are you not much more valuable than they? Who of you by worrying can add a single hour to his life? And why do you worry about clothes? See how the lilies of the field grow. They do not labor or spin. Yet I tell you that not even Solomon in all his splendor was dressed like one of these. If that is how God clothes the grass of the field, which is here today and tomorrow is thrown into the fire, will he not much more clothe you, O you of little faith? So do not worry, saying, "What shall we eat?" or "What shall we drink?" or "What shall we wear?" For the pagans run after all these things, and your heavenly Father knows that you need them. But seek first his kingdom and his righteousness, and all these things will be given to you as well. Therefore do not worry about tomorrow, for tomorrow will worry about itself. Each day has enough trouble of its own. Matthew 6.25-34

Let's summarize from this what Jesus wants us to know about worry. First, he wants us to know its root cause. He says, "*O you of little faith!*" Worry is a problem of faith. Not "No faith." Jesus is speaking to believers like us. We know Jesus is our Savior and trust him fully to bring us to Heaven.

But worry exploits a weakness in our faith. That weakness is our reluctance to carry over our **saving** faith into rest of our lives. It's the difficulty we have spreading our confidence in our salvation into daily living. It's how we're willing to trust that God has assured our place at the heavenly feast but not trust that we will eat lunch today, or next week or next year. Isn't that strange? When we worry, how right Jesus is when he says, "*O you of little faith!*"

Well if the cause of worry is our weak faith, what's the solution? Jesus teaches us that too – it's the Gospel. Of course, only the good news of what God has done for us can strengthen faith. In this reading, Jesus' Gospel presentation starts with the birds. Want a great example of God's loving care and providence? Look at the birds!

There's a scholarly journal called *Birds of North America* which over the past 15 years has published careful detailed profiles of 610 species of birds, from the black footed albatross to the sedge wren. You can read all those articles and discover that not one of these bird species has been observed checking the stock market each morning or the weather report or commodities prices. And God takes care of them just fine.

Then Jesus points to the lilies. Do you know lilies? Of course there are the white ones we see and smell at Easter but have you looked carefully at the other kinds? Yellow, apricot, orange, pink, red, multicolored ones (red center blending into yellow petals or yellow centers blending into pink petals or red centers blending into white petals) – more than 100 different species, with new hybrids appearing almost daily with even more exquisite colors and patterns. Jesus was not exaggerating when he said that Solomon in all his glory was not dressed like one of these.

Look, Jesus says, at the grace, care, and providence of God all around you. See that this is God's way, providing in love for these lesser creatures. Then realize that God didn't send his Son to become a flower or bird but a human being, to become our brother, so he could lead for us the God-pleasing life we couldn't lead, so he could in his death wash away our sin with his own blood, so he could in his resurrection establish us before God's judgment to be sinless and righteous. That's the Kingdom of God. Jesus says, that's what should be on your mind. That's what should pre-occupy your consciousness. Seek first that Kingdom of God and that righteousness.

What happens, then, to all those things we worried about? Jesus says, all good things will be provided you. Oh, we don't ignore those things. Problems don't just magically disappear. But we don't worry about them. Instead, we **work** on them, **deal** with them, **confront** them with faith and trust that God will provide. We'll **plant and tend our crops** with trust in God and not worry. We'll **work at our jobs and build our businesses** with trust in God and not worry. We'll **carefully manage our financial blessings** with trust in God and not worry. We'll **step on the airliner** heading for convention to do God's work with trust in God and not worry. We'll **send our children off to military service** with trust in God and not worry. We'll **witness about Jesus to our spiritually struggling loved ones** with trust in God and not worry. We'll **discuss apparent divisions among us** and our differing perspectives and terminology about doctrine with trust in God and not worry.

Above all, just as we daily bring our sins before God confident in his forgiveness through Christ, we will daily heed the apostle who urges us, *"Be anxious for nothing, but in everything by prayer and supplication with thanksgiving let your requests be made known to God."* Philippians 4.6 Then, without worry, we await the Lord's answer as in the hymn:

> Fear not, I am with you. O, be not dismayed
> For I am your God and will still give you aid.
> I'll strengthen you, help you, and cause you to stand
> Upheld by my righteous, omnipotent hand.

†

September 3, 2002

A Strong Relationship

INI

Are you giving any thought these days to finding a lifelong companion – husband or wife? If it's going to happen right, the sequence of events might be something like this.

First you mature enough to get past all those games people play with each other – the ego stuff, the macho stuff, the flaunting of sexuality, and all those superficial behaviors that some people unfortunately never outgrow. We're talking "lifelong companion" here, and that usually starts when you find someone that you can respect and admire with all your heart – someone you want a relationship with just because of the kind of person he or she is. As you learn to know each other, at some point you recognize that love has arrived. That's more than just an emotion, certainly more than just physical attraction. It's a deep and profound dedication to all that's good for the other person. At some time you discover a trust for each other, the conviction that neither of you will ever be betrayed, ever let down, by the other. You can trust one another with all your heart. And at some point you together encounter the **big C** – commitment, the agreement and promise that from that point onward you will be taking the same path together for your entire life. Blessed are you if you have found someone in this way, as I know many of you have, as have I.

Whether or not you have yet found such a person in your life, or are even looking, there is another who loves you and who invites your relationship in ways just like these, though even more profound. Hear his invitation:

> Trust in the LORD with all your heart and do not lean on your own understanding. In all your ways acknowledge Him, And He will make your paths straight. Proverbs 3.5-6

I asked at the start if you've given any thought lately to finding a lifelong relationship with a husband or wife. Now I ask, have you been giving any thought to your relationship with God? What would you like that relationship to be? The Lord here and elsewhere tells us what **he** would like that relationship to be, and it contains the same elements we discussed before. There should be, God says, admiration and respect, love, trust, and commitment.

There's one big difference between any human relationship and our relationship with God: humans work themselves mutually into a relationship. They work on it and create it together. But our relationship with God is already there. He made it. God has set up our relationship with him and then put us into it.

How did he do that? By taking action to remove the barrier that separated us from God, that is, our sins. When God's Son Jesus Christ lived a flawless and sinless life, as we certainly do not, and then died a death of punishment suffering our punishment in our place, he removed the barrier of our sins that separated all people from God. Our sin was transferred onto him, and his holiness was credited to us. That work, entirely by God, re-established a good relationship between God and us.

The relationship is there. All the elements of a relationship we've spoken of earlier are there. Certainly God is worthy of admiration and respect. Certainly God has shown us he is loving. Certainly he is always trustworthy. And his commitment to us is shown in the sacrifice of his Son for our sake. God has gone to a lot of trouble to re-establish a good relationship with us. And he is certainly fulfilling his side of it. What is it, then, that he expects of us?

Simply, to enjoy it. Enjoy it with all our hearts. Enjoy being with God! Enjoy taking everything out of this relationship that he has put into it.

Consider admiration and respect. He wants us to embrace with all our heart our new role of "admirable." We have, after all, put on the holiness of Christ, and are in God's eyes as respectable as his Son. He wants us to live as – to actually **be** someone who deserves respect, for that's what he made us.

Consider love. He wants us to love God back, and to show it by loving each other with all our heart.

Consider trust. He wants us to trust him, fully and completely, with all our hearts. Not just as a someday future friend – as if years from now when I'm on my deathbed I'll call on him. Not just as a safety net – as if when I'm in trouble, or sick, or in need I'll look to him. Certainly God promises to be our powerful Help in just those situations. But he wants to be so much more. He wants us to enjoy this relationship in all our ways, with all our heart.

And he wants us to return his commitment to us with our commitment to him. He wants us to visit with him in his Word and in prayer, to dine with him at his special Holy Supper, to go down the same path with him daily, hourly, minute by minute and all our lives. That's when he will make our paths straight, and we will fully enjoy all his love can give us.

"Trust in the LORD with all your heart and do not lean on your own understanding. In all your ways acknowledge him and he will make your paths straight."

†

September 22, 2002

Your God

INI

"You've got mail!" That's an announcement that lifts the spirits of many people every day. *"There is a message for you."* Doesn't that make us curious, eager to find out what it says? *"It's a love note."* Who would ignore that? The letter is signed, *"I'm yours, truly."*

If you went to a Lutheran confirmation class once upon a time, you learned the "attributes of God." As soon as you learned what that big word "attributes" meant you got hit by more, bigger words. Omnipotent, omniscient, omnipresent – you learned what they meant: all powerful, all knowing, present everywhere, conceptions of God that would fill you with awe. Then came one more one more attribute and it became truly frightening: **holy**.

Let's see now, you would think – and you would be right: God is present everywhere so we can't hide from him; God knows everything, not only what we do and say, but what we think; God has power to do with us or to us whatever he will; then add holy, perfectly pure, morally without flaw – and we know the kind of trouble we are in, a truly frightening situation in which we know we and this awe-some God are enemies.

Until we add one more attribute, of which we are told in this reading. Let's see: omnipotent, omniscient, omnipresent, holy, and **yours!** Your God, dedicated to your welfare, devoted to your good, the ultimate in love – it's that kind of devotion that love is – so much yours that he willingly gave up his most precious his only Son so your sins could be forgiven and he could bring you into his eternal company. What a difference that attribute makes: God is *"yours, truly."* And if that is so, then this is also true: we are his truly.

Hear God's words to his people through Moses, words which can as well be heard by his people today, the members of the Holy Christian Church, believers in Jesus Christ:

> And now, O Israel, what does the LORD **your God** ask of you but to fear the LORD **your God**, to walk in all his ways, to love him, to serve the LORD **your God** with all your heart and with all your soul, and to observe the LORD's commands and decrees that I am giving you today for your own good? To the LORD **your God** belong the heavens, even the highest heavens, the earth and everything in it. Yet the LORD set his affection on your forefathers and loved them, and he chose you, their descendants, above all the nations, as it is today. Circumcise your hearts, therefore, and do not be stiff-necked any longer. For the LORD

your God is God of gods and Lord of lords, the great God, mighty and awesome, who shows no partiality and accepts no bribes. He defends the cause of the fatherless and the widow, and loves the alien, giving him food and clothing. And you are to love those who are aliens, for you yourselves were aliens in Egypt. Fear the LORD **your God** and serve him. Hold fast to him and take your oaths in his name. **He is your praise; he is your God,** who performed for you those great and awesome wonders you saw with your own eyes. Deuteronomy 10.12-21

†

October 9, 2002

Our Greatest Problem

INI

Jesus stepped into a boat, crossed over and came to his own town. Some men brought to him a paralytic, lying on a mat. When Jesus saw their faith, he said to the paralytic, "Take heart, son; your sins are forgiven." At this, some of the teachers of the law said to themselves, "This fellow is blaspheming!" Knowing their thoughts, Jesus said, "Why do you entertain evil thoughts in your hearts? Which is easier: to say, 'Your sins are forgiven,' or to say, 'Get up and walk'? But so that you may know that the Son of Man has authority on earth to forgive sins –" Then he said to the paralytic, "Get up, take your mat and go home." And the man got up and went home. When the crowd saw this, they were filled with awe; and they praised God, who had given such authority to men. Matthew 9.1-8

Do you share the values of Jesus? Is your worldview the same as his? In this reading we see how difficult it is for us to share the mind of our Lord. We tend to look at things so much differently. It's natural for us to downplay sin – especially our own which, we like to tell ourselves, isn't as bad as others, and doesn't matter that much anyway, because other problems are much worse. Jesus viewed sin as the world's worst problem – its root problem, and God made sin's removal the highest priority.

Put yourself in the place of the various parties in this incident. I'm not going to dwell on the church officials who were there, who were sharp enough to recognize that, when Jesus dared to forgive this man his sins, he was claiming to be God – for only God can forgive sins. Their offendedness, which Jesus read in their hearts and called "evil," gave the Lord the opportunity to present a lesson in who he really is.

That's exactly what he did when he asked them, what's easier to say – your sins are forgiven (unobservable when it happens; this utterance doesn't need to be backed up with visible action) – or is it easier to say, get up and walk (after that, something visible had better happen)? And then, to prove he had power to do the former, he did the latter.

But now put yourself in the place of this paralyzed man who was brought to Jesus to be healed. Which would you rather hear – your sins are forgiven, or get up and walk? I'm afraid I would have been tempted to think, when Jesus first said, "Your sins are forgiven," is that all I'm going to get? I would rather walk! I'm afraid I don't share the mind of Christ, who considered sin the more important, the root problem in the world, in my life, and in yours.

Just three days ago[1] I walked on ground that almost literally cried out to Heaven because of the magnitude of the sins that were committed there. I visited Oswiencim, Poland, a town whose name is internationally notorious in its Germanized version. I walked through Auschwitz last Sunday, and then, as if to an anticlimax that became even more compelling than the climax, I also walked through Birkenau, the neighboring camp even more awful because of its mammoth size – it held 100,000 victims at a time – and its even more focused dedication to mass killing. I asked myself as I walked and heard the stories and saw the instruments and accoutrements of unbridled cruelty – I asked, can Jesus' sacrifice have paid even for this? It was the wrong question, really. I should have asked, Can Jesus' sacrifice have been so great that it paid even for my sins, which in the eyes of a completely holy God are no less offensive?

Of course, the answer to both questions, thank God, is yes, because Jesus viewed sin as the world's root problem, and God made its removal the highest priority.

Jesus asked, which is easier to **say**. I ask today, which was easier for Jesus to **do,** heal this paralyzed man, or forgive his sins? Certainly the healing was easier, the forgiving much more difficult, because it meant Jesus would have to take upon himself the guilt and punishment which that man had earned – and not only his, but the horrible offenses of an extermination concentration camp, and then yours and mine, and all the sins of the world, and pay their penalty before God by dying on the cross. That he did, and because he died and rose again, the root problem of the world is indeed dealt with; God's highest priority is achieved. Our sins, in God's eyes, are gone.

We're not told by the Gospel writer the inner thoughts of the paralyzed man as Jesus dealt with him. But we are told this was a man of faith and so I want to imagine that he was not fearful or disappointed when Jesus said to him first, your sins are forgiven. I imagine that with those words a great flood of relief swept over him. He had heard the Gospel from the lips of Jesus himself – what a blessing! And the Gospel doesn't weaken faith, it strengthens it. What great faith this man had, then, when Jesus told him to get up and walk home. And he did just that.

Whatever afflictions, whatever illnesses, whatever disappointments trouble you, learn to adopt the outlook of Jesus. Hear with faith the words of the pastor, as valid as if coming from Jesus' own lips – the words that deal with your root problem: for the sake of Jesus' life, death, and resurrection, your sins are forgiven. Be of good cheer! Take heart! Our biggest problem has been taken care of as a matter of God's highest priority. We are restored to him.

---

[1] I had just returned from delivering a paper at a debate conference in Krakow, Poland.

October 22, 2002

Our Stuff

INI

Let's talk about your stuff. You have lots of it, don't you? So do I – we all do, we all have lots of stuff. You realize how much you have each fall when you carry all that stuff upstairs when you move in, box after box after box. And you'll realize it even more when you have even more stuff to carry out in the spring. When you're like me, you'll have not just a room full of stuff, but a whole house full, plus the garage, plus some storage sheds and lockers.

There's nothing wrong with having stuff, in itself. In our reading this morning, God establishes our right to own things. But we get in trouble when we set our hearts on those things. Listen to God's warning in this Old Testament verse:

> Do not move your neighbor's boundary stone set up by your predecessors in the inheritance you receive in the land the LORD your God is giving you to possess. Deuteronomy 19.14

Which of God's commandments is the most abused in our society today? It would be easy to argue for the 6th, the one about forbidding sexual sin. You heard about that here last week. It's so easy to see, all around us, God's wonderful gift of sexuality horribly twisted, exploited, and distorted. But there's another part of God's wonderful will that we get twisted up daily, continually. It's the part about property. God says, don't steal. Stealing happens when we set our hearts on stuff.

In the reading, God puts it in terms of moving a boundary marker, just nudging the stone over a little bit so I get more and my neighbor gets less. Most of us don't work with boundary stones anymore, but there are plenty of ways we have of trying to get more stuff for ourselves at the expense of our neighbor. When we are kids, we might take candy or a toy. Teens face the temptation of shoplifting, of borrowing and not returning, or of borrowing and returning damaged. As we move into an adult world, there is everything from pilfering from the office, through cheating on taxes, to mismanaging investments – we're talking about just plain basic integrity here, the lack of which is a problem as widespread and current as today's newspaper, and as close to us as the tempting voice in our heads that says "get more," "just take it" – to which we have listened too often.

All these sins have this in common: our heart is set on stuff. In our material age, it's one of our biggest problems, one of our most plaguing sins.

It's all so fleeting, really. As I backed out of our garage this morning with this chapel service in mind, my eye caught my old computer, an old Mac II, sitting there on a shelf. How I was in love with that machine when I first got it! Now there it was, awaiting disposal. My heart since then has passed on to my new computer. What is it with you? On what stuff do you easily set your heart? Your electronics? Your CD or MP3 collection? Your books? Your car? Your wardrobe? What's your favorite **thing** these days? Whatever it is, one day it will be in the trash.

How different it was with our Savior. Jesus had nothing. Birds have nests, foxes have holes, but – we are told in the Bible – the Son of Man had no place to lay his head. _{Matthew 8.20} When he died for us on the cross, his only possession of any value at all was his seamless cloak, for which the soldiers gambled. Jesus had given up all stuff, he had even left behind the riches of Heaven, so he could serve us, and save us, paying also for our sins of materialism. How different Jesus was.

Jesus taught us to pray for only enough to eat for today. *"Give us this day our daily bread."* Luther explains, this means all we need – clothing, shoes, meat, drink, house, home, spouse, children, fields, cattle, all our goods. Yes, that's what it means, but notice that Jesus' expression is minimal. Enough to eat for today. That's all we should desire.

The Divers sing – and rightly – *We Are Not What We Own*. They could as rightly add: We are whom Jesus owns. We belong to him, not because he stole us, but because he bought us at a great price, the price of his own holy precious blood and his innocent suffering and death, by which he purchased and won us from sin, from death, and from the power of the Devil. Our sins are forgiven.

So be what Jesus made you – God's purchased child – and don't set your heart on stuff. Certainly don't let any of it become so important that you start nudging the boundary stone, to get more of it at your neighbor's expense. Practice contentment. The Bible says, do you have something to eat? Do you have something to wear? That's enough! Be content. And if you have been blessed with lots of stuff, as we all have, do enjoy it – it's a gift of grace to you from God. Better, thank God for it, and praise him for his generosity to you. Best of all, plan how you can use your stuff for God's purposes. Think of your favorite things, the ones you are tempted to set your heart on, and figure out ways to use them to serve God by helping and serving others, especially those who are in need.

That's the only reason why God has given us all that stuff.

†

November 11, 2002

Assuring Our Future

INI

> So when you see standing in the holy place "the abomination that causes desolation," spoken of through the prophet Daniel – let the reader understand – then let those who are in Judea flee to the mountains. Let no one on the roof of his house go down to take anything out of the house. Let no one in the field go back to get his cloak. How dreadful it will be in those days for pregnant women and nursing mothers! Pray that your flight will not take place in winter or on the Sabbath. For then there will be great distress, unequaled from the beginning of the world until now and never to be equaled again. If those days had not been cut short, no one would survive, but for the sake of the elect those days will be shortened. At that time if anyone says to you, "Look, here is the Christ!" or, "There he is!" do not believe it. For false Christs and false prophets will appear and perform great signs and miracles to deceive even the elect if that were possible. See, I have told you ahead of time. So if anyone tells you, "There he is, out in the desert," do not go out; or, "Here he is, in the inner rooms," do not believe it. For as lightning that comes from the east is visible even in the west, so will be the coming of the Son of Man. Wherever there is a carcass, there the vultures will gather. Matthew 24.15-28

I like to think that as a redeemed Christian I am mostly in tune with my Lord. I have to confess – I'm not, with this passage. I like to be upbeat, optimistic, trusting in the Lord's blessing, trusting that he will keep my family safe from danger, that he will keep them faithful and true to him to the end, that my kids and grandchildren will have an even better life than Judy and I have had, that he will bless my work and my school – really his school, that it will continue to prosper and grow and succeed in the world of higher education, as it has and is doing now. Those are the thought patterns I easily fall into – maybe like yours, looking forward to good things lying ahead.

And now along comes my Lord, whom I love and trust above all else, to tell me I have a warning for you. You heard the words, dire, stark words. What am I... what are **we** to make of it?

First, I'm going to resist literalizing it, that is, trying to match each aspect of his warning with somebody I know or something I see now. Many try to do that and many have over the centuries been shown to be embarrassingly wrong in doing so. And yet in not literalizing Jesus' words of warning to me I don't want to water them down, reduce their seriousness. This was not a time of his life for Jesus to lack seriousness. It was just two days before the

Passover, at which he would become the Lamb sacrificed for the sins of the world. These warnings were very close to his last words to us, and that's all the more reason to take them to heart. What then should I take from them, to put into my heart and yours?

First, that if I am enjoying a period of blessing from God right now, I should be all the more thankful for it and certainly not take it for granted.

Second, I have a glimpse of an insight into the cosmic spiritual battles that our Lord waged and is waging for us, hidden from us most of the time but more real than the chair on which you sit. A deeply serious battle is being waged over our very souls. That's the reason why in our liturgies we so often pray *Kyrie Eleison*, Lord have mercy upon us.

Third, I should not be surprised when trouble comes, trouble that is dire, severe, trouble that is centrally spiritual and widely recognized to be so as people far and near grope desperately to find some kind of savior and fail to find the true Savior.

Fourth, this trouble will be personal, touching each of us, wherever we are in the midst of our ordinary daily activities and it will prompt us to flee for safety.

And finally (at least for this list) I am to take that trouble, dire as it is, as a sign of God's love for me. It is our loving Lord, after all, who is warning us. It is our loving Lord who assures us, even in the middle of the warning that it's all under the control of our loving God, that he can and will shorten the time so we can bear it, that we remain his elect, his chosen ones whom he will not permit to be lost, that God will still and always be **our** God, the one who provided this sacrificial Lamb to face all the worst powers and strongest efforts of sin, Satan, and death and to subdue – indeed to crush them, and by that to remove their power over us. Our sins are forgiven; they have no power to condemn us.

The warning then, though frightening, is for our comfort. It is a great comfort. It echoes the words of the psalmist: *"The Lord of hosts is with us, the God of Jacob is our Fortress,"* Psalm 46.7 and of the Apostle who asks, *"Who shall separate us from the love of God?"* – and then answers, *"For I am convinced that neither death nor life, neither angels nor demons, neither the present nor the future, nor any powers, neither height nor depth, nor anything else in all creation, will be able to separate us from the love of God that is in Christ Jesus our Lord."* Romans 8.38f.

That is the message our Lord wants to remain with us as he moves toward the cross where he assures our future, no matter what we face.

†

December 2, 2002

Christmas Want and Need

INI

You can tell it by the crowded parking lots at the malls, the music on radio stations, the lights appearing on homes: the Christmas season has started. It's a good thing too. We need a season for Christmas. It can't be just one day. It takes a while to get out of Christmas what we want and need.

What we want and need. That might sum up Christmas presents in general. Remember when you were a kid? There were some presents you got of things that you **needed** – new socks and underwear, never very exciting. You opened them and tried to look happy about it. Then there were the presents you **wanted**. No forced joy needed when opening those! The Nintendo, pound puppy, strawberry shortcake, cabbage patch or whatever the doll of the year was. I don't know if most of you go back that far, but you know what I mean. There are presents you need, and presents you want.

Do you know what we really want and need at Christmas? To find some moments in which the peace of God can rest in our hearts – that's what we want **and** what we need.

Now that's not something that just happens suddenly. It can take preparation, it can take a season. It can take a plan. Along with all the other Christmas plans we make – how we'll get home, where we'll go and whom we'll see, what we'll buy for whoever – let's make this plan. In the church, we call this season Advent. It's the period of weeks before Christmas when we prepare to get out of Christmas what we truly need and what deep down we really want. If you haven't started such planning yet, we can do it now. We can use this Word of God from the prophet Jeremiah as an invitation to enjoy during this season God's gift of the baby Jesus as a gift that we need, and a gift that we want.

> "The days are coming," declares the LORD, "when I will fulfill the gracious promise I made to the house of Israel and to the house of Judah. In those days and at that time I will make a righteous Branch sprout from David's line; he will do what is just and right in the land. In those days Judah will be saved and Jerusalem will live in safety. This is the name by which he will be called: The LORD Our Righteousness." Jeremiah 33.14-18

Jeremiah was one of the most dour and dismal of all those who ever spoke for God. His was the sad duty to warn God's people that their kingdom would soon fall and they would be carried into captivity. The cause of their troubles? The root cause of **our** troubles and those of the whole world then and since: a broken relationship with God, broken by unrighteousness, sins in mind and speech and actions against the will of God. Jeremiah's people facing captivity became acutely aware of their need. We should too. Advent is a penitential season, that is, one in which we become especially aware of our own sinfulness and our own need for rescue.

This is where the dour gloomy Jeremiah becomes Jeremiah the angel of joy. Here, sparkling like a gem in the middle of his prophecies of doom, we have this beautiful Gospel message, a prophecy of Christmas. You heard the words. Look how the whole plan of our salvation is built into them. He saw it, looking ahead, as clearly as we see it looking back.

God, he says, will solve this sin problem by intervening in history: *"The days are coming when I will fulfill the promise – in those days and at that time."* This intervention would be through the birth of a human being: *"I will make a branch sprout from David's line."* This man would live sinlessly, without any of the unrighteousness that separates us from God: *"He will do what is just and right in the land."* His purpose in coming is salvation: *"In those days Judah will be saved and Jerusalem will live in safety."* This man would at the same time be God: *"This is the name by which he will be called: the LORD our Righteousness."* Not "a righteous person' but the LORD, the same one who is declaring the promise. And finally he is *"the LORD our Righteousness,"* acknowledging the great substitution by which we are made righteous through the transfer of Jesus' sinlessness to us and the transfer of our sins to Jesus, sins for which he paid our full penalty before God by dying on the cross.

What a grasp of God's salvation plan for us Jeremiah had! Go back and read again those marvelous words.

There's lots of fun at Christmas. There's lots of pressure at Christmas, especially getting to Christmas. What we want and need most at Christmas is some moments of time in which the Christ Child simply rests in our hearts. Make a plan this Advent season to prepare for that satisfying Christmas. Many people around you are making available tools, materials, and opportunities. Take full advantage of them. Go to choir concerts and hear the Gospel of Christmas proclaimed in song. Join people from nearby congregations here in our chapel on Wednesdays for Advent services. Renew your focus in religion classes on the Gospel taught there. Refresh your own private Bible reading plans. Make full use of all the opportunities available to you to realize that this Child whose birthday we celebrate is the **LORD our Righteousness,** a present from God that we not only **need** but **want** and in fact, already **have.**

†

December 12, 2002

Reading the News

INI

[Read some news items from today's paper.]

This from Lebanon:

> Then Herod went from Judea to Caesarea and stayed there a while. He had been quarreling with the people of Tyre and Sidon; they now joined together and sought an audience with him. Having secured the support of Blastus, a trusted personal servant of the king, they asked for peace, because they depended on the king's country for their food supply. On the appointed day Herod, wearing his royal robes, sat on his throne and delivered a public address to the people. They shouted, "This is the voice of a god, not of a man." Immediately, because Herod did not give praise to God, an angel of the Lord struck him down, and he was eaten by worms and died. But the word of God continued to increase and spread. Acts 12.20-24

You could tell right away that this last item is not from today's paper. Actually it's the portion of the Bible assigned for today from the book of Acts. But it doesn't sound that much different, does it?

From time to time in Scripture we get a reference to goings on in the political world, the "news of the day" as it were. The most famous, perhaps, is in the Christmas story where we are told that a world-wide tax registration was going on while Cyrenius was governor of Syria. That's why Joseph and the pregnant Mary had to travel from Nazareth to Bethlehem.

Here, some 30 or more years later, we have a news-like reference to the gruesome death of Herod Agrippa, the grandson of the Herod who killed all those boy babies around Bethlehem after the Wise Men had worshipped baby Jesus and gone home another way. This Herod had started a persecution against this new sect called Christians, and was responsible for the martyrdom of James, the brother of John.

But why is this news story worth our attention during Advent, our preparation for Christmas? I'm going to present it to you this morning as a reminder that Christianity is an historical religion – that is, its essence comes from events that happened in real human history, just like the news.

We tend to "mythologize" Christmas. What I mean by that is, we take it out of reality. Our images of the birth of Jesus become fuzzy and sentimentalized.

As beautiful and precious as all the carols and legends are, they tend to make it all too sweet, too cute, too sugarcoated, too **unreal**.

We might, in fact, do that not just with Christmas, but with our Christian faith in general. Is Jesus an everyday reality to us or just an occasional thought? A safety net for trouble maybe someday, a sweet and cute story that has little to do with our daily lives? No, the fact is, Christianity is an historical religion based on things that really happened, as real as today's news. And what happened in history is that **God broke in.**

In the reading, a grandiose but wicked **man** got carried away when he was hailed as a god, and paid for it. That happened in history, reported to us not only by Luke but by Josephus. What also happened in history at Christmas time is that a gracious and loving **God** became **man.** It actually happened. The frustration, the annoyance, the anxiety of Joseph and Mary were real. The pains of childbirth without anesthetic was real. God has become a human being – that's real. God is in our world. It happened, just like today's news happened.

Does this news affect us? We wonder that sometimes, when we read the paper. But this news does. As the prophet foresaw: **"Unto us** a child is born, **unto us** a Son is given." Isaiah 9.6 As the angels proclaimed, **"Unto you** is born this day a Savior." Luke 2.11 God broke into history to assure us: Does God know what it's like to be human? Yes, Jesus was and is human. Does God know what it's like to be stressed? Jesus was stressed. Does God know what it's like to be tempted? Jesus was tempted. Does God know what it's like to be sad, burdened? Jesus was sad and burdened. Does God know what it's like to carry a load of sin? Jesus carried a huge load of sin, not his own, but ours. He carried it to the cross and paid for it there. God broke into history to assure us – to save us.

Now his presence with us is real and most powerful in his Gospel of forgiveness which we hear in his Word and receive in our Baptism and at the sacramental table. Never doubt the reality and the life-changing power of that Gospel, the proclamation that your sins are forgiven.

At the end of our Bible reading, this news report, we read, Herod died. *"But the word of God continued to increase and spread."* That's history. Make it also your history, real, a piece of daily news in your life. At the birth of Jesus, God broke into history, your history, and mine.

†

December 17, 2002

Who Can Understand?

INI

One of our most important goals here at Bethany Lutheran College is **under-standing. We**'ve been testing it all week. But Christmas is a time to celebrate a **lack** of understanding.

> This is how the birth of Jesus Christ came about: His mother Mary was pledged to be married to Joseph, but before they came together, she was found to be with child through the Holy Spirit. Because Joseph her husband was a righteous man and did not want to expose her to public disgrace, he had in mind to divorce her quietly. But after he had considered this, an angel of the Lord appeared to him in a dream and said, "Joseph son of David, do not be afraid to take Mary home as your wife, because what is conceived in her is from the Holy Spirit. She will give birth to a son, and you are to give him the name Jesus, because he will save his people from their sins." All this took place to fulfill what the Lord had said through the prophet: "The virgin will be with child and will give birth to a son, and they will call him Imman-uel" – which means, "God with us." When Joseph woke up, he did what the angel of the Lord had commanded him and took Mary home as his wife. But he had no union with her until she gave birth to a son. And he gave him the name Jesus. Matthew 1.18-24

Who can understand how God works? These words of Scripture take us back before Christmas to the real beginning of God's movement into history, the conception of the God-man Jesus Christ by the Holy Spirit. This mysterious hidden activity was perhaps the greatest, most important activity in the his-tory of the universe, a happening made necessary by the fallen condition of humankind and nature, a happening prophesied since nearly the beginning of time, a happening looked forward to by countless people. Now, after all those years, after all that waiting God at last was on the move. The fulfillment was beginning with the conjoining of God and humanity. But who can under-stand it?

Who can understand **the messenger?** An angel of the Lord appeared. Who can understand **the announcement?** The angel said – what kind of momen-tous announcement? – don't be afraid to take a wife! Who can understand the **biology** of it? A young woman, a virgin, was to bear a child. Who can understand the **secular politics** of it? This momentous act of God which would affect all nations was happening not in the great capitols where great issues were decided; God was bypassing all that earthly power. Who can understand the **church politics** of it? This momentous act of God central to religious belief was happening not in the great churches where important scholars and leaders were endlessly debating their fine points of doctrine; God was bypassing all that churchly power. Who can fully understand **the spirituality** of it? The eternal God now tied to time, the omnipresent God now confined to space, the Creator God now become a creature.

How can Joseph understand what is happening in his life, to his beloved, to their plans? There is no understanding it. Joseph didn't need to understand it. He only believed, and by believing, he served God and all of us.

It's not hard to make application to us, not hard to find encouragement by acknowledging at times we don't understand. Just trust God's ways. There are plenty of times we should remember that.

But today let's not focus on application. Let's not focus today on self because we know the applications. We live with them daily as our most precious comfort; the substitution, Jesus becoming human so he could live under God's Law and fulfill it in our place; the satisfaction, Jesus remaining God so his payment for all sin would be universal and complete; the exchange of our sin with his righteousness; being drawn close to God again; the confidence we have in the care and love of God and of Jesus our best friend. All those things are the **why** and are very important to us.

But today, and in coming days as the blessed day of Christmas approaches, let's focus on the **what**, cover ourselves with the awe of what God did and float in the mystery behind the angel's message to Joseph. *"Joseph son of David, do not be afraid to take Mary home as your wife, because what is conceived in her is from the Holy Spirit. She will give birth to a son, and you are to give him the name Jesus, because he will save his people from their sins."*

How could he understand? But he simply believed and thereby served God and us.

†

January 29, 2003

God of Healing

INI

Ever since we can remember, we are taught to count on healing. As a toddler, when we fell and bumped an elbow and cried, Mommy kissed it and sure enough, it felt better. We got sick, tucked in bed and given medicine, and soon we were better. We scraped ourselves – on goes the bandage and in a few days sure enough, the scrape was healed.

It's one of our deepest fears that one day, something will happen to us that can't be cured. And to some of us here, it will happen. We'll sit in front of a doctor, who will tell us the test results are back and they don't look good. This time there won't be any cure. If that's me, or you, we won't be any worse off than anyone else. Because we are all subject to a sickness unto death, the sickness of sin, which is carrying all of us toward the grave.

Now, those are mighty glum thoughts to bring to you on a Monday morning, but I don't apologize for them, because they are a prelude to hope, and I hope that hope predominates by the time we are done. These thoughts must be quite similar to how the people must have felt to whom the Prophet Jeremiah was speaking in today's reading. They were facing death – their city was under siege, and it would fall. What's more, they knew they deserved it. That's when the Lord, through the prophet, brought them (and us) these words – dire words that describe a situation, and then words of hope.

> For this is what the LORD , the God of Israel, says about the houses in this city and the royal palaces of Judah that have been torn down to be used against the siege ramps and the sword in the fight with the Babylonians: They will be filled with the dead bodies of the men I will slay in my anger and wrath. I will hide my face from this city because of all its wickedness. Nevertheless, I will bring health and healing to it; I will heal my people and will let them enjoy abundant peace and security. I will bring Judah and Israel back from captivity and will rebuild them as they were before. I will cleanse them from all the sin they have committed against me and will forgive all their sins of rebellion against me. Then this city will bring me renown, joy, praise and honor before all nations on earth that hear of all the good things I do for it; and they will be in awe and will tremble at the abundant prosperity and peace I provide for it. Jeremiah 33.4-9

Two simple facts. The first our situation: by our sins we bring destruction on ourselves. The second is our hope: our God is a God of healing.

One of our favorite images of Jesus is found in the Gospel of Luke. He was in Capernaum one peaceful evening on the banks of the Galilee Lake, and we read,

> Now when the sun was setting, all they that had any sick with divers diseases brought them unto him; and he laid his hands on every one of them, and healed them. Luke 4.40

It's an amazing yet comforting scene. We can picture it as Jesus moved from cot to cot, group to group, family to family – at each He paused, from each a shout of joy went up – a pleasant and comforting scene.

But look more deeply and see what is really going on. We are given that view by another prophet, Isaiah, when he wrote of the Savior.

> Surely he hath borne our griefs, and carried our sorrows: yet we did esteem him stricken, smitten of God, and afflicted. But he was wounded for our transgressions, he was bruised for our iniquities: the chastisement of our peace was upon him; and with his stripes we are healed. All we like sheep have gone astray; we have turned every one to his own way; and the LORD hath laid on him the iniquity of us all. Isaiah 53.4-6

In today's reading, Jeremiah tells us **that** God is a God of healing. Here Isaiah tells us **how** God is a God of healing. It's like a doctor who heals by drawing the disease onto himself. Jesus healed the sick that evening in Capernaum by taking on himself the cause of sickness – their sins. Jesus deals with the putrid puss of our sin by drawing it onto himself. He stops our tumble toward death by getting there before we do and dying in our place. That took the sting out of death and removed the grave's victory, giving it instead to us, and making them instead the doorway to Heaven.

One of our great fears is fear of the incurable. The angels on Christmas morning proclaimed, "Fear Not!" Luke 2.10 The fear of the incurable is another one of those fears we can put aside because of the arrival of the Christ child, who as our God of healing took upon himself what made us all sick unto death, and for us cured the incurable.

†

February 2, 2003

Happy Marriage: Just One Example

Suppose I offered you this deal – would you take it? I have a construction job for you. I'd like you to build a house – for yourself. When you're done, you keep the house. And for the work I will pay you a million dollars.

If you say, I know nothing about construction, I'll reply that I'll show you how to do it, furnish all the tools, material, know-how that you need. I'll give you complete instructions, make sure you can do the job. What's more, I'll pay you the million up front. Keep the money whether the job gets done or not. What I'll do is, I'll give you the million, then give you extra incentives for actually doing the job. Do the basement and I'll give you a bonus. Do the framing and I'll give you some jewelry. And so on until the job is well started. And since probably you can't really do it all, I'll finish it for you. Is a deal like that one you'd be interested in?

Every comparison is imperfect. But this deal is in some ways like how God treats us. God says first, I have a job for you. Keep my laws – which is finally for your own good – and in return your reward is Heaven.

But wait, God says. Since I know you aren't able keep my laws perfectly, I'll give you the payment up front. Heaven is yours already, since my Son Jesus did the work for you, and on the cross paid for your failures. Your sins are forgiven. Salvation is yours (like the million dollars) without your earning it. But meanwhile, while you are enjoying that free gift, stay busy. Do the work anyway, as best you can. I'll empower you. I'll give you all the tools you need, and if you do any of the work, I'll reward you, give you additional benefits as if you earned them – even though you didn't really, because it was all my work in and through you.

That's God's way of dealing with us. We find instances of it in promises throughout Scripture. The psalm before us today is one example, where God makes some promises about one of the greatest gift-blessings God can give, a gift-blessing many of us here have enjoyed and many others of you are looking forward to, with good reason, the reward, gift, blessing of a long and happy marriage.

> Blessed are all who fear the LORD, who walk in his ways. You will eat the fruit of your labor; blessings and prosperity will be yours. Your wife will be like a fruitful vine within your house; your sons will be like olive shoots around your table. Thus is the man blessed who fears the LORD. May the LORD bless you from Zion all the days of your life; may you see the prosperity of Jerusalem, and may you live to see your children's children. Peace be upon Israel. Psalm 128   †

February 17, 2003

A Glimpse for Encouragement

INI

After six days Jesus took with him Peter, James and John the brother of James, and led them up a high mountain by themselves. There he was transfigured before them. His face shone like the sun, and his clothes became as white as the light. Just then there appeared before them Moses and Elijah, talking with Jesus. Peter said to Jesus, "Lord, it is good for us to be here. If you wish, I will put up three shelters – one for you, one for Moses and one for Elijah." While he was still speaking, a bright cloud enveloped them, and a voice from the cloud said, "This is my Son, whom I love; with him I am well pleased. Listen to him!" When the disciples heard this, they fell facedown to the ground, terrified. But Jesus came and touched them. "Get up," he said. "Don't be afraid." When they looked up, they saw no one except Jesus. As they were coming down the mountain, Jesus instructed them, "Don't tell anyone what you have seen, until the Son of Man has been raised from the dead." Matthew 17.1-9

There are many things for which I must ask God's forgiveness. I hope God (and you) will forgive me also for speaking tonight on this passage of Scripture without emphasizing doctrine. I know, it's the Lutheran thing to do – stress the doctrine! And there is so much doctrine in this piece of Scripture – the Trinity – resurrection – two natures of Christ – other equally rich and important doctrines. But today I would rather bring to mind, mine and yours, more precisely what I believe is the purpose for which Jesus brought these three disciples (and through their report, us) to this mountaintop. It wasn't as much for an impression on the head than for an impression on the heart.

It was for encouragement.

Jesus knew what was coming in the next few days. From the glories of the mountaintop they were to descend to the hill called Calvary. Jesus knew that then his followers would need all the encouragement they could get. And for their encouragement, he gave them a glimpse of Heaven. It works. Has it worked for you? Have you felt the comfort and encouragement of knowing that, after all the difficulties, uncertainties, and fears of this life there is a wonderful place waiting for you?

Judy and I are fortunate to own a week worth of timeshare in Florida. Sometimes when days get stressful, it relaxes me simply to think, I can go there! That feels good. But even when I'm there for a week and having a good time, at the end of each day I have to think, one day gone, six to go – half the week is gone now, only a few days left – last night here, we leave tomorrow.

It's almost silly to compare a week in a vacation timeshare with Heaven, to compare a week of "counting down" with an endless eternity of joy. That place waiting for us, one of those "many mansions" in his Father's house that Jesus said he was going to prepare for us John 14.2 – the anticipation of that should be for us the ultimate encouragement. Have you had that glimpse? Probably not a timeshare, but at some other event you thought you'd never want to leave? A wonderful choir concert? A moving worship service? I remember some I wished would never end.

But don't get caught in the mistake of Peter, who got so excited he started to focus on the place. "Let's build here," he said. It's the kind of focus on sacred places that lies at root of conflict in Jerusalem even today. But God interrupts in the middle of Peter's place-based plans, and booms with a great voice, "**No!** Look at Jesus! This is my Son – listen to him."

There is the true glimpse of Heaven, where we see the love of God shown to us in Jesus Christ. As we look forward to this gift from God, this refuge, this rest, don't forget what it cost – not what it cost us, for to us it's a free gift, but what it cost God. Jesus came down from the mountain where he had given his followers a glimpse of Heaven and headed for Jerusalem where he would endure what we in the church call "his passion." That is, he began the course of his suffering that led to his death on the cross to pay for our sins.

In about three weeks we will be invited once again into the season of Lent during which we turn our special attention to those parts of God's Word that describe the cost to God of our free gift, the forgiveness of our sins. Meanwhile, feel the comfort and encouragement that comes from Jesus showing us a glimpse of our future, a glimpse of Heaven.

†

February 27, 2003

The Word Grows

INI

How would your life be different if you weren't an American? Assuming you aren't one of our valued overseas students, one of the things overseas travel does for a us Americans is to make us newly appreciative of the blessings and prosperity we have. It's good once in a while to consider how our lives would be different if we weren't Americans.

How would your life be different if you weren't a Christian? That too is a question we do well to ask ourselves from time to time and for the same reason. Most of us here have grown up Christians from our Baptism as infants and it becomes very easy to take all its blessings for granted.

This morning I'd like for us to consider how the Word of God has made a difference in our lives. Our theme for the week is "the Word of the Lord Grows" and by "grows" we mean, it makes a difference. Listen, please, to this portion of Scripture describing some strange goings on.

> God did extraordinary miracles through Paul, so that even handkerchiefs and aprons that had touched him were taken to the sick, and their illnesses were cured and the evil spirits left them. Some Jews who went around driving out evil spirits tried to invoke the name of the Lord Jesus over those who were demon-possessed. They would say, "In the name of Jesus, whom Paul preaches, I command you to come out." Seven sons of Sceva, a Jewish chief priest, were doing this. One day the evil spirit answered them, "Jesus I know, and I know about Paul, but who are you?" Then the man who had the evil spirit jumped on them and overpowered them all. He gave them such a beating that they ran out of the house naked and bleeding. When this became known to the Jews and Greeks living in Ephesus, they were all seized with fear, and the name of the Lord Jesus was held in high honor. Many of those who believed now came and openly confessed their evil deeds. A number who had practiced sorcery brought their scrolls together and burned them publicly. When they calculated the value of the scrolls, the total came to fifty thousand drachmas. In this way the word of the Lord spread widely and grew in power. Acts 19. 11-20

Imagine the excitement in Ephesus when the Word of the Lord first came among them. Excitement is too small a word. From this reading we get the impression that the city was turned upside down. Lives were being impacted and changed. Can we who are lifelong Christians begin to appreciate what a provocative, powerful, life-changing message this Word was for the

Ephesians, and is for us? It might be true that a person never can fully feel the pleasure and relief of freedom unless he has just been released from prison. In just such a way, try to imagine the excitement of a person understanding God's Word for the first time.

First, it makes an impression; then, it works big changes.

Look at the attention the name of Jesus got in the Ephesus of our reading. Supported by miracles of healing Jesus' name spread among all the people. Many of them, misunderstanding its purpose, misused it, tried to exploit it, leading to one of the most darkly comic scenes in the Bible where a man possessed by a demon turned on the phony exorcists, beat them up and chased them out.

Today, even without spectacular miracles, the Word gets attention. Yes, it's still often misunderstood and people attempt to exploit it. Those who truly understand its message are startled by its uniqueness. Among all the religions of the world, this Word brings a message totally unique: that the relationship between us and God, broken by our wrongdoing, is restored not by our efforts but alone by God's love. Christianity is the only religion which teaches that we are restored to God through God's work, not our own. That unique Christian message, which frees us from the unbearable burden of having to keep God's law perfectly for our salvation, is so utterly liberating that it shocks those who come to understand it fully.

Do we too much simply take it for granted?

Not only does the Word get attention but it works powerful changes. It does this first by **reporting cosmic changes** – that by the work of Jesus Christ our sins are forgiven and the gulf between us and God who was our enemy has been removed. We have been brought close to God, adopted by God our loving Father. The Word announces this cosmic reversal in our relationship with God that in turn leads to an **internal change** in each of us believers. Our old sinful nature is removed from control and a new person is born in each of us. This internal change shows itself **externally** as well, as the new believers in Ephesus publicly confessed their sins, changed their occupations, reformed their lifestyles literally burning their bridges to their sinful past. That's how the Word grew. It made a powerful difference in the lives of more and more people.

Are we aware of changes of similar magnitude in us?

If not, perhaps that too is good news for it reminds us that all this work in us is not ours but the work of God the Holy Spirit in us. God has begun the process of change in you and me. But now God invites us to join in the work as individuals and as a community. Are there changes we can still make in our campus community that will say ever more clearly, God's Word is active here? Are there personal changes still to be made in our lives – a sinful habit or a way of thinking or dealing with others that needs to go up in figurative smoke? Can we be granting that new person born in us by the Gospel more and more control over our lives, guided by the Word?

If so, then it truly will be said of us individually and as a Christian campus, as it was said in Ephesus: *"In this way the word of the Lord spread widely and grew in power."*

†

April 10, 2003

Wearing Jesus on Your Sleeve

INI

Shipwrecked, flogged, imprisoned, stoned, mugged, nearly drowned in flash floods – these are just some of the items on Paul's list of suffering he has undergone for the Gospel. To all those add this (many here would gladly undergo the former to avoid this one): he had to give public speeches. Here is an important one, given at his own trial. Quickly the setting: at the Jerusalem temple Paul had been roughed up in a riot stirred up against him by church leaders. He had to be rescued by being arrested, and through a series of hearings and narrow escapes had been brought before Felix, current Roman governor of Judea. A lawyer representing the church leaders spoke first, leveling some false charges against Paul. Then we read...

> When the governor motioned for him to speak, Paul replied: "I know that for a number of years you have been a judge over this nation; so I gladly make my defense. You can easily verify that no more than twelve days ago I went up to Jerusalem to worship. My accusers did not find me arguing with anyone at the temple or stirring up a crowd in the synagogues or anywhere else in the city. And they cannot prove to you the charges they are now making against me. However, I admit that I worship the God of our fathers as a follower of the Way, which they call a sect. I believe everything that agrees with the Law and that is written in the Prophets, and I have the same hope in God as these men, that there will be a resurrection of both the righteous and the wicked. So I strive always to keep my conscience clear before God and man. After an absence of several years, I came to Jerusalem to bring my people gifts for the poor and to present offerings. I was ceremonially clean when they found me in the temple courts doing this. There was no crowd with me, nor was I involved in any disturbance. But there are some Jews from the province of Asia, who ought to be here before you and bring charges if they have anything against me. Or these who are here should state what crime they found in me when I stood before the Sanhedrin – unless it was this one thing I shouted as I stood in their presence: 'It is concerning the resurrection of the dead that I am on trial before you today.'" Then Felix, who was well acquainted with the Way, adjourned the proceedings. Acts 24. 10-21

That was a long reading, so the rest of this must be short. I'm going to entitle it "wearing Jesus on your sleeve." You know the expression, wearing your heart on your sleeve. It means, your emotions are apparent to everyone, nothing you feel is hidden from those around you. When you wear Jesus on your sleeve, it means your faith in Jesus is apparent to everyone, your life in Jesus is never hidden from those around you.

That's what the apostle shows us in this reading. When the governor abruptly adjourned this trial, Paul would be two years in custody in Caesarea. Then he'd be sent on to Rome. So far as we know, Paul would never again on this earth be a free man. This then was a huge turning point in Paul's life – from freedom to prisoner, from leading to being led, from almost frantically active to patiently passive, from making plans about things to making the best of things.

This speech reflects Paul's awareness of that change in his life. It's not a spectacular speech, it's straightforward, no attempts to be clever. It's what theorist Quintilian would call an *"an sit"*[1] defense – he's saying, I didn't do anything, and they can't prove that I did.

But in this speech Paul's listeners can discern something else even more important: They can tell that this guy is a Christian – Jesus is there on his sleeve. In a humble and unobtrusive way, Paul is revealing the character of a believer in Jesus.

Look at the character revealed – the courage to be in Jerusalem in the first place despite warnings of danger, the desire personally to deliver gifts from collection for the poor, the care he took not to violate laws, civil or religious, and to stay out of trouble.

We can also detect his realism – he's not really expecting a fair trial. We sense his realization that you don't depend on government even as you take part in it, and his awareness not to expect much good when religion gets mixed up with politics.

Still we can also witness his fearlessness, his refusal to be intimidated in this important forum, on this pivotal occasion in his life. And then most important is his bold testimony – yes I am a believer – yes I look for a resurrection from the dead. Much about this sequence reminds us of Christ, on trial, as he too changed from active preacher to passive servant.

Surely it was Paul's faith in this Gospel, his faith that God who had supplied Paul's salvation through the **active service** and **passive suffering** of Jesus Christ his Son – this God would surely care for him in any situation, capacity, position, circumstance, or predicament. It's the Gospel that gave Paul

---

[1] Latin *an sit?* translates "whether it even is," that is, did an act even occur? Paul is saying, "Nothing they are accusing me of happened." Other possible defenses, according to Quintilian, include *"quid sit?"* "what might it be," that is, "I may have committed the act but by definition it is not against the law," and *"quale sit?"* that is, "What I did may have been against the law, but the moral nature of the act is good." Paul chose the appropriate defense.

courage to **action** when it was called for in his ministry, and it's the Gospel that gave Paul courage to **passion** – to resting in the Lord – when he reached this big change in his life.

We don't know what lies ahead in our lives. We can make plans, but we've experienced how uncertain they can be. It's the Gospel – God's care for **us** in Christ, his forgiveness of our sins for Jesus' sake – that gives us courage to **action** when it's called for in our lives. And it's the Gospel that gives courage to **passion** – to just resting our cares in the Lord – when that's what is called for in our lives.

This is how Christians – ones with Jesus on their sleeves – act. It means, your faith in Jesus is apparent to everyone, always, and your life in Jesus is never hidden from those around you. That's worth thinking about and planning about.

†

May 5, 2003

Ezekiel's Shepherd

It won't be long now. These last days of the school year are rushing by – days packed with busy-ness, writing those last papers, studying for finals, celebrating accomplishments, joining year-end parties, spending precious moments with friends. Soon we'll be leaving what has become a familiar routine, leaving those good friends at least for a while, leaving maybe a very special friend for a while, and we easily wonder, what will happen? What will happen before we see each other again?

It's a good time to enjoy one of the greatest blessings God has given us in his Word, the message about the Lord as Good Shepherd who seeks, gathers, and cares for us, the sheep that he loves. We are most familiar with this picture from Jesus' own words, where he said "*I am the Good Shepherd,*" John 10.11 and told the story of how the Good Shepherd leaves the 99 sheep who are safe in the flock and risks everything to seek out the one lamb who has strayed into danger, finds it, and brings it back to the flock amid rejoicing. Matthew 18.12 Those who heard these words for the first time from Jesus' own lips were surely aware that Jesus was referring to the earlier expression of this idea from many years before and indicating that He is the fulfillment of that prophecy. Those words are our assigned reading for today.

> For this is what the Sovereign LORD says: I myself will search for my sheep and look after them. As a shepherd looks after his scattered flock when he is with them, so will I look after my sheep. I will rescue them from all the places where they were scattered on a day of clouds and darkness. I will bring them out from the nations and gather them from the countries, and I will bring them into their own land. I will pasture them on the mountains of Israel, in the ravines and in all the settlements in the land. I will tend them in a good pasture, and the mountain heights of Israel will be their grazing land. There they will lie down in good grazing land, and there they will feed in a rich pasture on the mountains of Israel. I myself will tend my sheep and have them lie down, declares the Sovereign LORD. I will search for the lost and bring back the strays. I will bind up the injured and strengthen the weak, but the sleek and the strong I will destroy. I will shepherd the flock with justice. Ezekiel 34.11-16

At last Friday's formal banquet, your student president spoke eloquently of how we came here last fall as individuals from different places, but our experiences this year have drawn us together and made us one. While she didn't refer to Scripture, it's surely a scriptural notion: that we are important to God both as individuals and as a group. Nowhere is this idea so clear as in the Bible picture of the Shepherd and his sheep. In it the Lord reassures us of his care for us as a group and as individuals. Both are important, both hugely comforting.

No serious shepherd, after all, has only one sheep. Shepherds gather their sheep into flocks, into groups. Our Lord cares for us as a group by gathering all believers into his Church, where they can care for and support one another, where faithful under-shepherds can feed the flock with God's Word, can increase its number through Baptism, can nourish its members with the special meal of the Lord's own body and blood given on the cross so we can be forgiven and restored to God. Being a group, flock, church, coming together as one in faith – that's important to our God, and to us.

The Shepherd picture also teaches us that our Lord cares for us as individuals. He knows when his sheep are in trouble or danger. He gives special attention to those who stray. He creates his flock by **seeking** us one by one. All of us have strayed by our selfishness, stubbornness, and rebellion – in fact, we were born strays. He calls to us, seeks us out, won't let us go, finds us, and brings us back to the group, flock, church, where we can be cared for by faithful under-shepherds.

How do we know this is true? How do we know God is committed to this care? Because of Easter, which we celebrated again a few weeks ago. That's the day God the Father, by raising his Son from the grave, put his seal of approval on that Son's sacrificial work, certifying him as The Good Shepherd, who by giving his life for his sheep took onto his own back all of the foolishness, the straying, the sinning we have done and paid the penalty for it before God's justice, so that we could be spared, could be freed from what we deserved, could instead simply lie down with our sins forgiven and experience the joy of the green pastures and cool still waters our Shepherd has prepared for us.

Last night, while I was thinking about these things, I looked up and saw our piano. In our house, the piano is loaded with photographs of children and grandchildren, the most dearly loved ones to us like your own family and friends are to you. It's at such times that one can truly appreciate the beauty and comfort of the Bible's shepherd picture of our Lord's promise. Hear again the words:

> For this is what the Sovereign LORD says: I myself will search for my sheep and look after them. I will rescue them from all the places where they were scattered on a day of clouds and darkness. I myself will tend my sheep and have them lie down, declares the Sovereign LORD. I will search for the lost and bring back the strays. I will bind up the injured and strengthen the weak. I will shepherd the flock with justice.   †

September 10, 2003

Slides from Our Life Trip

INI

It's an old joke – there's nothing more boring than having to watch home video of someone else's vacation. But today I'm going to take a chance and present to you a slide show of a trip. What will make this show not boring, I hope, is your realization that it's not someone else's trip but yours, a trip you are in the middle of even now.

This trip of yours, remarkably enough, was already foreseen before you started it. Talk about getting your photos back quickly![1] This Bible writer already had the pictures of your trip a couple thousand years ago. Since this slide show is from Bible times don't expect a lot of technology. In fact, the pictures are in words. Where are you going? It's a very important destination: back to God. The thing that makes this trip so important, so needed is the distance, the great distance, between you (us) and God in the first place.

That's the single biggest trouble in this troubled world. The trouble from which all other troubles emerge is the separation of humankind from God. But let's not talk about humankind. Let's talk about you and me and how without help **we** are separated from God by our sin.

How do we get back? The Bible writer gives us a map, with pictures, of two contrasting routes. Each of them goes by way of a mountain. The first is Mt. Sinai. Yes, you remember correctly – it's the mountain where God gave Moses God's Law, the Ten Commandments. And yes, that is a way that can lead us back to God. All we have to do is keep God's Law perfectly and we will be acceptable to him, back with him. But look at the pictures we are shown of this route – burning mountain, untouchable, dark, gloomy storm swirling, trumpet blast right in our ears, intolerable voice both in tone and content, **death!** for the seemingly trivial act of an animal touching, the leader Moses trembling with fear.

And for good reason! That's a truly frightening trip because it's a journey that leads us to hell. Oh yes, it **could** lead us back to God if we could keep the law perfectly but we can't. Let's get past some detours that would mislead us. Let's get past our focus on how bad other people are and focus on ourselves. Let's get past the idea that maybe if we try hard that will be good enough. Let's get past the idea that we **can** even try hard. We have failed

---

[1] We were still in the days when you took your pictures on film and had to take it to a drug store for developing, then wait a week or so for the finished pictures to come back.

miserably and continue to fail, day after day, to keep God's Law. If that's our only route back to God, we are lost.

But thanks be to God! that's not the route we are on. We are going by way of another mountain, Mt. Zion, that lovely, desired, longed-for mountain goal, with its shining beautiful city, the heavenly Jerusalem with streets of gold. Look at these pictures! There the crowds of angels are having fun – imagine joining rejoicing angels! There is the Church, the gathering of the privileged, the firstborn. We are there! There is God – the Judge, yes, but not the frightening Judge, for there God is judging people in mercy in view of Jesus the Christ. And Jesus is there, making sure it goes as planned because central to the scene is the blood that reverses sin – not Abel's blood of the first heinous sin of murder but Jesus' blood shed for us to satisfy on our behalf the aweful judgment of God.

God, we know, must be a stern and fair Judge, for his Law is perfect. But here he is also the merciful judge looking at us through the sacrifice of Jesus, and for his sake he pronounces us clean, made perfect, worthy to be restored once again to him. By this route, we have arrived. By setting us on this path, God through the work of Jesus has returned us to himself. Listen once more to this astounding travelogue in word pictures:

> You have not come to a mountain that can be touched and that is burning with fire; to darkness, gloom and storm; to a trumpet blast or to such a voice speaking words that those who heard it begged that no further word be spoken to them, because they could not bear what was commanded: "If even an animal touches the mountain, it must be stoned." The sight was so terrifying that Moses said, "I am trembling with fear." But you have come to Mount Zion, to the heavenly Jerusalem, the city of the living God. You have come to thousands upon thousands of angels in joyful assembly, to the church of the firstborn, whose names are written in heaven. You have come to God, the judge of all men, to the spirits of righteous men made perfect, to Jesus the mediator of a new covenant, and to the sprinkled blood that speaks a better word than the blood of Abel. Hebrews 12.18-24

These are the pictures of our trip. That's the journey you and I have been placed on and have already begun, a trip that is truly a *bon voyage* – a beautiful journey. Live now as you are enjoying the trip.

†

October 2008

The Compassion Mirror

INI

Sometime before you go to bed tonight, you will probably look in a mirror. May I teach you now to look into your mirror in a new way? Our reading invites us to learn something about compassion and we'll see it's all about mirrors – not mirrors in the negative sense as in the deception of "smoke and mirrors," but in the positive sense: this is a mirror that we look into and see the truth about ourselves.

In this Old Testament passage we find a few simple rules and the reason for them:

> Do not deprive the alien or the fatherless of justice or take the cloak of the widow as a pledge. Remember that you were slaves in Egypt and the LORD your God redeemed you from there. That is why I command you to do this. When you are harvesting in your field and you overlook a sheaf, do not go back to get it. Leave it for the alien, the fatherless and the widow, so that the LORD your God may bless you in all the work of your hands. When you beat the olives from your trees, do not go over the branches a second time. Leave what remains for the alien, the fatherless and the widow. When you harvest the grapes in your vineyard, do not go over the vines again. Leave what remains for the alien, the fatherless and the widow. Remember that you were slaves in Egypt. That is why I command you to do this. Deuteronomy 24. 17-22

There are other rules like this in this section but these are enough to teach us something about compassion, a deep **awareness** of the suffering of another coupled with the **wish** to help. It's feeling another's pain and wanting to relieve it because it is like our own.

Don't confuse compassion with pity, feeling sorry for someone. There is a place for pity but not in godly compassion. Most people don't like being pitied. It implies that someone is looking down on them, seeing them as somehow different, inferior in their need.

Compassion doesn't come from recognizing difference but from recognizing same-ness. How do we know that? Look at the reading, especially at the reason for the commands. We are to provide for the needy not because we feel sorry for them but because we "*Remember that you were slaves in Egypt and the LORD your God redeemed you from there. That is why I command you to do this.*" People in need are a mirror for us. Look at them and you see yourself because you are them! You and I are among the needy. We're not talking about "There but for the grace of God go I," but rather, "there go I!" We are one, alike together exactly! Compassion means identifying with the needy, feeling solidarity with them, recognizing we are one with them.

We see it in the reading; we see it in our Savior. How many times in the Gospels do we read of Jesus' compassion? Typical is this passage: "*And Jesus, when he came out, saw much people, and was moved with compassion toward them, because they were as sheep not having a shepherd: and he began to teach them many things.*" Mark 6.34 It's exactly that compassion that moved the Son of God to leave his heavenly throne, to set aside his true superiority over us and in fact to become one with us, to take on human flesh and blood so that he could rescue us from our profound need by means of a lifetime of pleasing God in our place and a death to pay for everything about us that did not please God.

Compassion means becoming one with the needy to help them. When we look at the needy, we are to see ourselves. They are a mirror to us.

But not only that: we are to be a mirror to them. They are a mirror and you are a mirror. God is compassionate, says today's theme. God is compassionate – it starts there. But it doesn't end there. Compassion received becomes compassion given.

God is compassionate; we know that from what he has done for us in Jesus Christ. How will other people know that about God? How will needy people find comfort in God's compassion? Only when we show compassion. In today's reading, the effect of compassion is not a feeling, but a plan. "*Leave behind some food for the needy.*" A common sense plan. It may not be common sense to one who doesn't feel compassion, but for one who does, it's obvious. **Of course** you leave them some food! When you know you are one with the needy you do those things that provide relief.

Several times a day you look into your mirror. Once in a while (not always) let it remind you of God's compassion – how needy people around us are a mirror in which we see ourselves and how God wants **us** to be the mirror that reflects to others the compassion God has shown us.

†

September 9, 2003

What to Do?

INI

What to do?! How often the question torments us. What should I do? Which choice should I make? Facing a tough decision? About friends? health? marriage? About your future? Bring it here.

By here, I mean wherever God can speak in his Word. It might be in another church or in your room with the Bible. But Trinity Chapel is a good "here," any time of day. Bring your major decision-making here.

I don't mean that you'll find a specific answer, like opening a fortune cookie. But here God can fill you with an awareness of him and of his love. Be assured that he has bought you with the blood of his Son, that you are now a member of God's own family and your Brother Jesus is sitting next to you. Then in that awareness face your decision.

Do that especially if your decision has a moral dimension, if it involves right and wrong. Come here to make it. Even more especially if you feel pressured to make the wrong decision by so-called friends or by your own sinful nature – that is, by enemies. Come here to make that decision for sure and find the strength you have from knowing your sins are forgiven.

There's another time when you should come here besides when facing a tough decision. It's when you're **not** facing a tough decision. Because you know what, maybe you should be. And God's Word when we encounter it here sometimes has a way of surprising us. This is never a boring place. At any minute, God's Word can jump us, shake us up, bring us face to face with a decision we **should** be making like, what to do with our lives.

Join me please in an old prayer, 3000 years old or so, a prayer of a person longing for guidance from the Lord, a prayer of all of us.

Give ear to my words, O LORD, consider my sighing. Listen to my cry for help, my King and my God, for to you I pray. In the morning, O LORD, you hear my voice; in the morning I lay my requests before you and wait in expectation. You are not a God who takes pleasure in evil; with you the wicked cannot dwell. The arrogant cannot stand in your presence; you hate all who do wrong. You destroy those who tell lies; bloodthirsty and deceitful men the LORD abhors. But I, by your great mercy, will come into your house; in reverence will I bow down toward your holy temple. Lead me, O LORD, in your righteousness because of my enemies – make straight your way before me. Psalm 5.1-8 Amen.

†

October 24, 2003

Loving God

INI

Did you ever get lied to? If you did, you know how it makes you feel, how angry it makes you. Imagine how angry God gets when he is lied to. And he knows it every time. Did we just lie to God? What did I sing in the hymn that opened our worship service just now? "Lord, thee will I love with all my heart"! ELH 409 Did we just lie to God?

If "Love God" is a command that we must keep perfectly to get to Heaven, we should tremble. Luther says it is a command. He starts the explanation to every commandment with the phrase, "We should fear and love God" so that we do this, or so that we don't do that. It's exactly because we do **not** fear and love God that we disobey those commandments often, every day.

By every measure of **human** love, we fall far short of loving God. We love each other so poorly – even those we claim to love most, brothers, sisters, parents, children, spouses. So often our love for them fails due to our own selfishness. How much more poorly we love God.

Consider any notion of love we have. What's an important aspect of love? Commitment? What is really first in our lives? Always God? Or usually self? Love means longing to be together with the one we love. How many times have we pretended and wished that God wasn't there so we could do what we know is wrong? Love means communication. How much time do you spend in prayer? And then is it little more than a quick automatic "Come Lord Jesus" at some meals, if that? Love means going all out to please, and not disappoint the one we love. I'm not even going to comment on our failure there. If "love God" is a command, we are lost.

Fortunately, while "love God" is a command, it is even more so a response. Listen to the psalm verses assigned to us this morning. David wrote this psalm, we are told, while a fugitive on the run from King Saul. We read the opening verses:

> I love you, O LORD, my strength. The LORD is my rock, my fortress and my deliverer; my God is my rock, in whom I take refuge. He is my shield and the horn of my salvation, my stronghold. I call to the LORD, who is worthy of praise, and I am saved from my enemies. Psalm 18.1-3

Through David, the Holy Spirit here is reminding us that for whatever life situation we are in, God is there for us. Only that can enable us to love God.

David not surprisingly uses military imagery – fortress, shield. Luther too, often lived in mortal danger and used the thought of this psalm and others to inspire the Reformation hymn, *A mighty fortress is our God* – we'll sing it again next week. As for us, we are unlikely (thank God) to be in danger of our lives because of our faith, though it could happen. But certainly in whatever other dangers we face God is there for us.

His fundamental assurance is of our salvation. As part of fulfilling our obligation for us Jesus loved God perfectly. Is **commitment** central to love? Jesus' commitment to his Father was unquestioned all his life long. Even at an early age he told his earthly parents he had to be about his Father's business. **Communication**? Again and again we read that Jesus was in prayer. **Doing all He could to please God?** Of course, and never so clearly as in Gethsemane Park, where facing the agony of death he prayed to his Father, not my will but yours be done. And then he went to the cross to pay there for all of our failures to love.

When David perceived what God had done for him, he responded, "I love you, O Lord, my strength." And so do we. There's an old song some of us remember that goes, "You made me love you; I didn't want to do it." That's how it is with us and God. To use language that is more Scriptural, we love God because he first loved us. 1 John 4.19 When we learn the Good News of how God cares for us, body and soul, we **do** love God, even though feebly compared to as we should.

Now knowing our salvation, we can work on improving our love for God. **Communication?** If someone says, there is a love note waiting for you in the mail room, who of us could resist going to see what it said, who it's from? There **is** a love note waiting for you, daily in chapel, each week at church, whenever you turn to your Bible, or remember your Baptism, or kneel at the Lord's table. That's communication in love.

Commitment? That means doing all we can to please him, and we show that by **loving other people**. Certainly it means loving our families, friends, teammates better than before. But it also means loving strangers and even our enemies. We all have much to learn about love.

I don't know if "unlove" is a word, but you remember the prayer of the sick child's father to Jesus when he said, *"Lord I believe, help thou my unbelief."* Mark 9.24 Let our prayer today be "Lord I love thee, help thou my unlove!" Make the prayer we are about to sing heartfelt. Make a change in your life today.

> O teach me, Lord, to love thee truly with soul and body, mind and heart,
> And grant me grace that I may duly practice fore'er love's sacred art.
> Grant that my every thought may be directed e'er to Thee.

†

November 13, 2003

Keep the Faith

INI

Please pardon my voice this morning. Like many of you, I'm suffering from a cold, but I'm not suffering from being a Christian. Are you? Most of us, I expect, are enjoying being Christians, and don't feel we have suffered for it. But others have. St. Paul who had just lost his freedom because of his faith wrote this encouragement to young pastor Timothy:

> So do not be ashamed to testify about our Lord, or ashamed of me his prisoner. But join with me in suffering for the gospel, by the power of God, who has saved us and called us to a holy life – not because of anything we have done but because of his own purpose and grace. This grace was given us in Christ Jesus before the beginning of time, but it has now been revealed through the appearing of our Savior, Christ Jesus, who has destroyed death and has brought life and immortality to light through the gospel. And of this gospel I was appointed a herald and an apostle and a teacher. That is why I am suffering as I am. Yet I am not ashamed, because I know whom I have believed, and am convinced that he is able to guard what I have entrusted to him for that day. 2 Timothy 1.8-12

Paul wrote this at a time when the Christian church was growing perhaps faster than at any other time. And he is suffering for it. Notice well: a growing church and suffering appear together. There is something that causes both of these things to happen.

And what is it that prompts the suffering? What tempts us to try to avoid suffering, to "be ashamed"? Paul says, "Don't be ashamed to **testify about our Lord.**" It's good preaching and faithful witnessing! It's living like a Christian and not hiding it. Where Christians keep the faith without shame, that is where we should expect suffering. That in turn is where the Kingdom of God flourishes.

Did you hear Paul's invitation? He asks Timothy and us to *"join with him in suffering for the Gospel"* and urges us not to be *"ashamed"* of it or of him.

Have you ever been ashamed of the Gospel? Oh, I doubt that you or I have ever hung our heads and said, "I'm ashamed of the Gospel." But it's a sign of being ashamed when we try to avoid the suffering, when we hesitate to speak God's word, and when we fail to live it. We are ashamed of the Gospel whenever we give in to peer pressure to scale back what God says. We can so easily do that with both of the great teachings of Scripture, the Law and the Gospel.

We water down the Law when we think or say or show by our behavior that we think disobeying God "isn't so bad." Ideas like these are popular all around us, and to avoid being scorned by others, we might buy into them. "OK, maybe God **did** say thou shalt and thou shalt not but he doesn't really mean it. We are all pretty much OK, nobody's perfect of course so God can't expect us to be, we are good enough if we try sort of hard, we deserve credit, God will have to accept us just as we are." You recognize that all these are widely popular views these days, but they are watered-down Law, not God's Law, and if we go along with such views it's because we are ashamed of God's Word.

We can water down the Gospel too – pretending among the people we hang around with that we're not really **that** Christian, I'll use some of the words they use so that I fit in, just don't identify me too closely with Jesus, I'll just "tone down" my religion with these people so I won't suffer, so that I can keep them as friends, they'll like me, think I'm cool, or whatever. That's being ashamed of Jesus.

On the other hand, when someone testifies to the real Law of God and points out that God condemns sins, all of them, big and small, and thereby condemns us sinners to eternal punishment and separation from God and all that is good in hell – that brings the potential that we'll suffer for it, because nobody likes to hear that truth.

And when someone testifies to the real Gospel, that (as Paul says in this reading) God "*has saved us and called us to a holy life, not because of anything we have done but because of his own purpose and grace. This grace was given us in Christ Jesus before the beginning of time, but it has now been revealed through the appearing of our Savior, Christ Jesus, who has destroyed death and has brought life and immortality to light through the Gospel*" – when people hear that truth, their natural self doesn't like to hear that either because everybody wants to take some of the credit for themselves. Again, if we are the messenger we may suffer.

When you testify with your words and your way of living to the truths of God's word, then expect trouble and suffering and pressure to feel ashamed and back off and water down your faith or even hide it.

But Paul says join with me in suffering for the Gospel, by the power of God. This temptation to feel ashamed of the Gospel you can overcome, by the power of God. By the power of God you can testify to God's stern Law and to the sweet precious Gospel. By the power of God you can keep the faith. And then you can expect trouble, yes, but also something else. You can expect the kingdom of God to grow and flourish around you, by the power of God.

If you haven't felt you have experienced suffering yet, expect that sometime you will. If you have felt pressure to feel ashamed, pressure to water down the message or hide your faith in the face of disagreement, accept this encouragement to keep the faith by the power of God.

Here's what to do. First understand what God's Word teaches us about ourselves. Apply God's Law to your life, fully and without holding back, so you are sure that without help you are a lost and condemned sinner. Then apply God's Gospel to your life, fully and without holding back, so you are certain that Jesus' blood washed away **your** sins too, every one of them. Then live accordingly, not just getting better and better at keeping God's Law, but getting better and better at living the Gospel, seeking forgiveness for your own failures, and freely granting forgiveness for those of others.

Finally practice speaking and explaining God's Law and Gospel whenever there is an opening. In other words, **keep the Faith**, confident with the Apostle that our Lord is keeping the faith with us even to this day.

†

December 2003

Being Ready

INI

I have one announcement before we begin: to make the most efficient use of time, the administration has decided that Final Exams will be moved ahead two weeks. Your first final exam will be given next hour right after chapel.

Now hear our appointed reading for today, these words of Jesus:

> Be dressed ready for service and keep your lamps burning, like men waiting for their master to return from a wedding banquet, so that when he comes and knocks they can immediately open the door for him. It will be good for those servants whose master finds them watching when he comes. I tell you the truth, he will dress himself to serve, will have them recline at the table and will come and wait on them. It will be good for those servants whose master finds them ready, even if he comes in the second or third watch of the night. But understand this: If the owner of the house had known at what hour the thief was coming, he would not have let his house be broken into. You also must be ready, because the Son of Man will come at an hour when you do not expect him." Luke 12.35-40

While the reading you just heard was serious and genuine, the announcement I opened with, as most of you realized immediately, was bogus. You can relax. Final exams have **not** been rescheduled for today. I said those things to try to conjure up for just a moment that feeling of anxiety you get when you suddenly discover you are **not ready** for something important. That's what Jesus is doing in this reading – prompting us to consider whether we are ready for him to come again.

There are few things sadder than missing a great opportunity because we're not ready. I saw a professional football coach on TV after a playoff loss. He said, "We had a good week of practice and I thought we were ready – but we weren't." Sometimes we can think we are ready, but we're not.

That's why Jesus encourages us here as he does. Jesus says, think of being a burglary victim. If you've ever been victimized by a thief, you know the feeling the next day when you discover it – you feel angry, violated, fearful, vulnerable – and knowing you could have prevented it if you had taken some precautions. If those are our feelings the day after a theft, imagine how you would feel the day after Jesus comes, and you had not been ready.

We should be especially concerned with one bad readiness habit it's easy for students and teachers to develop. It's the "I still have the last minute" thought habit. We learn to think, I get a lot done at the last minute, so I can put off worrying about meeting God face to face till later. That means you're satisfied with not being ready now. But **this** final exam really could be moved up to the next hour right after chapel.

What then does it mean to be "ready"? It's the difference between **oh yes** and **oh no**. When we're surprised – and Jesus says we will be surprised when he comes – we have a reflex reaction. If it's an unwelcome surprise, our reflex is **oh no**! If it's an anticipated and welcome surprise, our reaction is **oh yes**!

What could happen at Jesus' sudden coming for our reflex response to be **oh no**? If he comes when we are caught in a sin? If he comes when we are so much attached to this world that we don't want to leave? Certainly we don't want ever to be in a position where, when Jesus comes, our reflex is **oh no**.

What will assure that we have a reflex **oh yes** when Jesus comes? He tells us in this reading: "Be dressed ready for service and keep your lamps burning." Dressed for service – we know that picture from elsewhere in the Bible. We read about "robes of righteousness" – those are robes of Jesus' righteousness which he earned for us. By his life and death, he covered over our sin, and dressed us in his holiness so that we are worthy of meeting a holy and righteous God. Jesus dressed us; knowing and believing that, is being ready.

But he didn't dress us for nothing, and certainly not so we could ignore him and continue in our sinful lives. It cost him dearly to dress us; it cost him his life. So we are dressed for a purpose. He says, be dressed **for service** and with our lamps burning. Keeping lamps burning means we are giving his possible coming regular attention, watching for him any and every minute.

Remember then these two things about being ready. Jesus dressed us with his righteousness – that makes us ready. He dressed us for service – that keeps us ready.

When the aged Simeon saw the baby Jesus, whom his parents had brought to the temple to fulfill the law, his heart burst forth with a joyful prayer. We know it as the "*Nunc dimittis*" – we sing or say it frequently as part of our worship liturgy. "*Lord, now let your servant depart in peace, for my eyes have seen your salvation.*" Luke 2.29 He was saying, now I'm ready. I've seen the Savior, and now I'm looking forward to the completion – to what Jesus describes in our reading when he says, "*It will be good for those servants whose master finds them watching when he comes. I tell you the truth, he will dress himself to serve, will have them recline at the table and will come and wait on them. It will be good for those servants whose master finds them ready.*"

Let Simeon's prayer be ours, every moment until Jesus comes.

†

April 2004

By Grace

INI

It was in a January 31 basketball game between Giltner and Hampton, two Nebraska high schools. The news report said, "Giltner's Brandon Kohmetscher brought the whole package of weapons to the York City Auditorium Thursday night, as the Hornets upended No. 2 seed Hampton 61-57 to earn a berth in the Crossroads Conference finals. While most of those in attendance sat with their mouths hanging open on some of Kohmetscher's drives and athletic moves to the basket, Giltner head coach Laurel Roth has come to expect the unexpected from his senior guard. Nothing surprises me anymore, commented Roth on the play of his senior. I've seen him do it so many times, that nothing he does surprises me."

It's an expression heard a lot: nothing surprises me anymore. It's spoken when something otherwise surprising becomes commonplace, so we take it for granted. It's a shame when that happens. What is surprising should stay surprising.

Do you enjoy pleasant surprises? Let me encourage you to experience a new pleasant surprise every day. You can do that if you pay close attention to God's Word every day. Listen carefully to what it tells you and me about our sin, what you and I do every day that earns us God's anger and punishment. Take that seriously, or you won't be surprised at what else the Bible tells us.

If you fully understand that your behavior has earned you nothing but eternal punishment, then you will be on your knees in sorrow and repentance. And I'm not talking about the kind of sleazy apology that was modeled for all America on TV last night,[1] where I start out with "I've had a rough week," a kind of invitation to feel sorry for me because I've suffered some for what I did wrong, and follow that with a lie, saying "What I did was unplanned and unintentional" and finally put the blame for the trouble on God by wording the apology carefully like "I'm sorry **you** were offended." That might satisfy a TV network, but God sees right through that kind of smirky, arrogant nonsense. No, if we take God's standards for our behavior seriously, we are on our knees, staring into hell.

And when that happens, you will truly be surprised when you hear how God rescued you. And it wasn't because of anything you or I did, or even because our repentance was sincere. It was purely out of **grace** – God's love for us

---

[1] I wish I could remember to what this referred, but it doesn't matter because we still hear "apologies" like this often today.

which is totally undeserved. That's what grace is, and that's why it is so surprising. It's entirely God's love in the work of Jesus Christ on our behalf that makes it possible for the Apostle Paul to write as he did in our assigned reading this morning.

So don't say it doesn't surprise me anymore. Read a passage like this daily. Take it to heart and be surprised every day. Keep grace **amazing**.

> But we ought always to thank God for you, brothers loved by the Lord, because from the beginning God chose you to be saved through the sanctifying work of the Spirit and through belief in the truth. He called you to this through our gospel, that you might share in the glory of our Lord Jesus Christ. So then, brothers, stand firm and hold to the teachings we passed on to you, whether by word of mouth or by letter. May our Lord Jesus Christ himself and God our Father, who loved us and by his grace gave us eternal encouragement and good hope, encourage your hearts and strengthen you in every good deed and word. 2 Thessalonians 2. 13-17

†

April 2004

He Went Willingly

INI

Are you looking forward to the end of the school year? to graduation? to the celebrations, and to the release from the pressures of college expectations and assignments due? That will be fun, won't it? It's easy to look forward to that.

Some of us, perhaps, face some less pleasant events. Have a dentist appointment coming up? A root canal, wisdom tooth removal? Anybody here scheduled for surgery? Those things are not much fun, and every time we are reminded that this is coming, we cringe, tighten up – the thought ruins our moment. To events like these we go because we must, out of self-interest perhaps, but we go reluctantly, not willingly.

Jesus knew what awaited him in the last hours of his life. Today we are filled with wonder as we realize, he went forward to it willingly.

Our assigned reading takes us to Gethsemane Park just across the Kidron valley from the walls of Jerusalem. It begins after we have read about Jesus agonizing in prayer because of his coming ordeal.

> So Judas came to the grove, guiding a detachment of soldiers and some officials from the chief priests and Pharisees. They were carrying torches, lanterns and weapons. Jesus, knowing all that was going to happen to him, went out and asked them, "Who is it you want?" "Jesus of Nazareth," they replied. "I am he," Jesus said. (And Judas the traitor was standing there with them.) When Jesus said, "I am he," they drew back and fell to the ground. Again he asked them, "Who is it you want?" And they said, "Jesus of Nazareth." "I told you that I am he," Jesus answered. "If you are looking for me, then let these men go." This happened so that the words he had spoken would be fulfilled: "I have not lost one of those you gave me." John 18.3

Here was Jesus facing a hostile mob. Many times before he had walked safely through a crowd bent on destroying him because "his time had not yet come." e.g. John 7.30 Now his time had come. The gang of thugs that came to Gethsemane encountered no resistance from Jesus. He introduced himself to them freely. Even when his evident power caused them all to fall over backward, he made no attempt to flee, no attempt to hide who he was, though he had more than a chance to do both. Clearly Jesus was not being forced onto the path he was about to take. He went willingly.

While his willingness amazes us, it shouldn't surprise us. It started long before this, when he the Son of God came from heaven to be born into this world – why would he want to do that? Why would anyone want to leave Heaven and come here? His willingness became fully apparent once again when he headed to Jerusalem for the last time and his disciples said, are you crazy? The last time you were there they wanted to kill you? And he replied, this is my time. This is why I came.

If we are amazed at his willingness to enter into his passion, it's because we recognize how unnatural that is. People just don't willingly embrace unpleasantness, and what Jesus knew he faced was the ultimate in physical and spiritual suffering. He himself showed us how unnatural, how difficult this was by his struggles in prayer in the park, imploring his Father if there was any other way to save us. But there was none.

And so he undertook our salvation, quite willingly. He said to his captors, here I am, let's go.

By his life, his suffering, his death, and his resurrection, Jesus brought us comfort. But he also brought us discomfort.

The comfort is clear. I hope it's why you love to come to chapel every day, where you can hear afresh that great news, why you remember your Baptism frequently, and enjoy the Lord's special meal as often as you can. In those places we are assured that we are once again God's friends, that God has discarded all our sins for Jesus' sake, that everything that could possibly separate us from him has been put aside, that he is caring for us now, and is preparing a place of caring for us forever. That's a deep and abiding comfort. This is not our choice. It doesn't depend on any willingness on our part – it is entirely God's gift, so that we can be truly comforted.

But there is discomfort too, to which we are sometimes called. God has some tasks for us to do – that's why we're here. They aren't always pleasant. God's plans aren't always our plans. And what then? Where is **our** willingness?

My brother has been an overseas missionary for many years and in many countries. I remember friends asking me, how does your brother like it in Peru or Ghana or Kazakhstan or wherever he was at the time. I appreciated the question – it showed caring and concern – but upon reflection I found it rather odd. Does anyone uproot his family and go to a distant and possibly dangerous part of the world because he likes it? Because it is pleasant for him? I can't imagine that to be so. Missionaries go not because it is fun, but because they are willing.

And where does that willingness come from? The same place that Jesus' willingness came from – after all, they learned their willingness from him. I hope missionaries "like it" where they go. But that isn't why they go. It isn't pleasure. It certainly isn't self-interest. It isn't even duty. It is love.

Young people – older ones sometimes too – wonder what love really is. Look here. Jesus is showing you by being willing – willing to perform unselfish service to others even when it is most unpleasant. Am I saying that willingness to serve is a measure of love? Perhaps it is. But I would rather put it this way – and listen closely – Love is what transforms reluctance into willingness.

Did you ever watch water drops running down a glass window? They zigzag down always finding the easiest path. Is that your life plan? Are you looking always for what's most pleasant, what's easiest, what's most comfortable?

If you are living the life of a water drop, what will happen when God calls on you to take on an uncomfortable challenge? To move outside your comfort zone, to make the harder choice, to leave the pleasant and easy path, in order to do something God wants done? What will prompt us to reverse the gravity of our natural desire for the pleasant?

Lord, as you went willingly to serve us, teach us your love – the love that makes us willing.

†

April 22, 2004

Now Raised

INI

I hate feeling stupid, don't you? It's happened to me when traveling overseas in a country where I don't know the language or even the alphabet, can't read street signs, don't know how to do the simplest things like parking, using a telephone, or even the bathroom. It's easy to feel stupid. Have you ever been in a situation where you feel stupid?

Here's the good news from today's reading. You don't ever need to feel stupid about being a Christian. The traditional Easter greeting contains both a proclamation and an assurance. He is risen (proclamation, and the reply is assurance) He is risen indeed.

In today's reading from the Bible's famous resurrection chapter we find both, but in reverse order. It starts with assurance from the back side. Assurance from front side occurred a few verses before, where the Apostle listed eyewitnesses to resurrection, challenging readers of his day to go and interview them if they wanted to double check. That's powerful assurance that "He is risen indeed."

Here in these verses is the other side of the assurance coin. Paul shows he is fully aware of what's at stake in his preaching the resurrection. What if it's **not** true? Well then, feeling stupid would be just one of the consequences. After exploring them, the Apostle concludes by repeating the proclamation.

Be confident in your faith! Be certain of your own some-day resurrection. Hear the proclamation: he is risen – believe the assurance: he is risen indeed. Let's hear the Apostle tell it, as he deals with some who seem to think they are Christian but who don't believe that the dead can come back to life.

> But if it is preached that Christ has been raised from the dead, how can some of you say that there is no resurrection of the dead? If there is no resurrection of the dead, then not even Christ has been raised. And if Christ has not been raised, our preaching is useless and so is your faith. More than that, we are then found to be false witnesses about God, for we have testified about God that he raised Christ from the dead. But he did not raise him if in fact the dead are not raised. For if the dead are not raised, then Christ has not been raised either. And if Christ has not been raised, your faith is futile; you are still in your sins. Then those also who have fallen asleep in Christ are lost. If only for this life we have hope in Christ, we are to be pitied more than all men. But Christ has indeed been raised from the dead, the firstfruits of those who have fallen asleep. 1 Corinthians 15.12

†

May 2004

Joining the Flowing Crowd

INI

I've never before been in a flowing crowd of people like I was in yesterday. A week ago a team of walkers from Bethany Lutheran College took part in the walk against MS here in Mankato. There was a good turnout, people thought, and we had a good time following this flow of walkers around a five-mile course.

But that was a mere trickle compared to yesterday's "Run for the Cure" to fight breast cancer in the Twin Cities. Some of the crowd ran for a cure, most walked. I walked. An estimated 50,000 people took part. That's about the entire population of the Mankato area. It was startling to see all of France Avenue by the Southdale Mall, a boulevard eight lanes wide at that point, closed to vehicles and flooded instead with people walking. The walk was pleasant, easy to follow, hard to get lost. We just moved into the flow and followed the crowd.

There have been other flowing crowds of people in history. Some more diffuse, like the Oregon trail, lasted for years. That was a lot harder to follow, much more dangerous, easier to get lost.

One flowing crowd we can all look forward to being a part of is the one on the day of judgment that leads to Heaven. As the hymn writer foresaw,

> From earth's wide bounds, from ocean's farthest coast
> Through gates of pearl, streams in the countless host
> Singing to Father, Son and Holy Ghost, alleluia!

That will be quite a flowing crowd.

But sadly not the biggest. Most, Jesus tells us, will be going in the other direction. Is this one where it's easy to get lost?

We men have this reputation where we'd rather get lost than ask directions. On our way to Heaven we don't want to let our pride get in the way, and insist on going our own way so that we get lost, for then we are really lost.

Where are the directions? Join the psalmist this morning. Our reading is a prayer asking God to show us the path. In these few verses we at the same time recognize where the directions are, and in the closing phrase "*make your face shine*" we acknowledge the essence of those directions, the love of a kind and forgiving God in Jesus Christ.

Your statutes are wonderful; therefore I obey them.

The unfolding of your words gives light; it gives understanding to the simple.

I open my mouth and pant, longing for your commands.

Turn to me and have mercy on me, as you always do to those who love your name.

Direct my footsteps according to your Word; let no sin rule over me.

Redeem me from the oppression of men, that I may obey your precepts.

Make your face shine upon your servant and teach me your decrees.

Psalm 119.129-35

Amen.

†

19 August 2004
At the opening of the Faculty Workshop

Ambassadors

INI

We're not close enough to the start of classes for me to conduct a classroom exercise. But if we were, I might hand out a blank half-sheet of paper and ask you to write, in 40 words or less, your answer to this question: What makes Bethany Lutheran College a Christian college? What is its uniqueness? One good answer is in this reading:

> God was reconciling the world to himself in Christ, not counting men's sins against them. And he has committed to us the message of reconciliation. We are therefore Christ's ambassadors, as though God were making his appeal through us. We implore you on Christ's behalf: Be reconciled to God. 2 Corinthians 5.19-20

You know by now the theme of this workshop; I was asked to speak on that theme this morning – it's at the top of the worship sheet. You heard yesterday about what an ambassador is and does.

I want to focus for a moment on the "therefore."

What is it that makes us ambassadors? What prompts us to have any interest in being ambassadors? This reading says: Whatever "ambassadoring" happens in a Christian setting, it centers in this term: reconciliation.

Paul tells us here plainly first of all what God did: in Christ he reconciled the world to himself.

One wordsmith observes that "reconcile" is a complex concept. It includes no less than four aspects: (1) disruption of friendly relations because of (2) presumed or real provocation, (3) overt behavior designed to remove hostility, and (4) restoration of original friendly relations. It's not hard for experienced Christians to acknowledge how each of these four applies to us.

We have disrupted the friendly relations with our kind and generous Creator by the real provocation of our sins, which we continue to commit every day. But God has acted to remove the hostility, by sending his Son Jesus to bear the guilt and punishment of those sins for us, so that God doesn't have to count our sins against us anymore. In that way, the whole world is reconciled to God once more. The original friendly relations have been restored. It happened. God did it. It's objective fact.

Now here's the "therefore," what makes Paul an ambassador: he says he and his colleagues are ambassadors of Christ because they have been given a message to bring to the world. What the representative and ambassador does is bring us this message and urge us to know it, believe it, and live as befits it: be reconciled to God. When we know this reality – that we are friends again with God – there are ways we respond.

Students are coming in a few days; Audrey will tell us how many. Some, perhaps many simply don't know that God has reconciled them to himself in Christ. Others may know that, but don't know fully what that means for them in their lives. In fact, none of us knows fully what that means for us in our lives. That's why the ambassador's urging is still relevant to us: be reconciled to God.

Here's where we take our place in the ambassadorial chain. We too, echoing Paul, can urge our students to recognize and cling to the fact of God reconciling the world to himself through Christ. We can model and teach our students to study and explore what it means fully to be reconciled to God. We can be ready to speak about Christ and his work for us. We can be an example of devotion to his Word in chapel. We can be reconciled to each other! And in many other ways we can help our students explore, each in their own lives, what it means fully to be reconciled to God.

What makes Bethany a Christian college? What makes us unique?

- We know and proclaim the "one thing needful" Luke 10.42;[1]
- We acknowledge what makes ours an education that lasts beyond a lifetime;
- We are a community of sinners whom God has reconciled to himself through the blood of Jesus Christ,
- And who have gathered to explore together that Gospel in all areas –
- Probing it deeply in every academic discipline,
- searching it out in administration, campus life, and all the other groupings we'll gather in today.

We've gathered on this campus to explore together fully what it means to be reconciled to God. If we are dedicated ambassadors for that, everything else will fall into place.

†

---

[1] "One Thing is Needful" has been the motto of Bethany since its beginning. It refers, of course, to the Gospel of Jesus Christ.

October 2004

Celebrating with (Strange) Fellow Christians

INI

Let me ask you to do something **if** you are comfortable doing it. I'd like you to shake hands with the person next to you.

Now in that touch I want you to feel the presence of a fellow Christian. This is someone who like you and me knows about the infection of sin, knows that the only chance of escape lies in God's love, depends on the work of Jesus Christ the Son of God for forgiveness, for help in this life, and with confident hope in the next. This is a fellow Christian. It feels good to be together, to touch.

Now close your eyes. Remember that touch and pretend that the person you were touching is a different fellow Christian, just as real, but not one you know personally. This fellow Christian lives in Kenya or Singapore or Shanghai or it is any of the many many fellow Christians all around the world this very minute. Feel the same connection with them!

And now finally, pretend this touch is of a fellow Christian from another time, from long ago, from perhaps over 2500 years ago. I'd like you this morning to feel a connection with some fellow Christians of long ago who were having a celebration. They were enjoying a celebration of God's grace, a celebration of their own spiritual renewal, a celebration of **their** connection with you and me. It's pictured on the front of your worship folder and in many ways it would seem to us quite strange. As I read about it from the Old Testament book of Chronicles, you'll hear some of the obvious strangeness, just as you can see them in the picture. But I especially want you to feel your kinship with these people and enjoy their celebration with them. They are fellow Christians.

The two books of Chronicles, today's assigned theme, are a quick summary of the history of God's people from Creation to King Saul, and then a more detailed telling of the history of Judah until its conquest by Babylon. This celebration before us this morning began after the death of King Ahaz, one of the most wicked of Judah's kings. The new king was young man, not much older than many of you.

> Hezekiah was twenty-five years old when he became king, and he reigned in Jerusalem twenty-nine years. His mother's name was Abijah daughter of Zechariah.

[I'll comment here that Abijah is a heroine's name. Hezekiah certainly didn't learn about the true God from his father. He must have had a faithful mother.]

He did what was right in the eyes of the LORD, just as his father David had done. In the first month of the first year of his reign, he opened the doors of the temple of the LORD and repaired them. He brought in the priests and the Levites, assembled them in the square on the east side and said: "Listen to me, Levites! Consecrate yourselves now and consecrate the temple of the LORD, the God of your fathers. Remove all defilement from the sanctuary. Our fathers were unfaithful; they did evil in the eyes of the LORD our God and forsook him. They turned their faces away from the LORD's dwelling place and turned their backs on him. They also shut the doors of the portico and put out the lamps. They did not burn incense or present any burnt offerings at the sanctuary to the God of Israel. Therefore, the anger of the LORD has fallen on Judah and Jerusalem; he has made them an object of dread and horror and scorn, as you can see with your own eyes. This is why our fathers have fallen by the sword and why our sons and daughters and our wives are in captivity. Now I intend to make a covenant with the LORD, the God of Israel, so that his fierce anger will turn away from us. 2 Chronicles 29.1-10

Let me comment: It might appear on the surface that the king was following the religion of the world, trying to earn God's favor by good works. But we can be confident that this celebration was one of thanks for God's grace. That is, we can be confident this celebration was Christian.

We know this because

- They were guided by God's Word,
- They sang psalms of David who wrote the "*Lord is my Shepherd*," Psalm 23.1 and "*Wash me, and I will be whiter than snow*," Psalm 51.7
- The king's spiritual counselor was Isaiah who wrote "*All we like sheep have gone astray, but the Lord has laid upon him [Jesus] the iniquity of us all*," Isaiah 53.6
- The sin offerings reminded everyone that sins would be paid for by the shedding of blood, and
- They knew that their sacrifice of thousands of animals was not a payment but a reminder that the real valued sacrifice would be the shedding of the blood of God himself.

Following the word of the LORD, the priests went into the sanctuary of the LORD to purify it. They brought out to the courtyard of the LORD's temple everything unclean that they found in the temple of the LORD. The Levites took it and carried it out to the Kidron Valley. They began the consecration on the first day of the first month, and by the eighth day of the month they reached the portico of the LORD. For eight more days they consecrated the temple of the LORD itself, finishing on the sixteenth day of the first month. 2 Chronicles 29.15-17

Early the next morning King Hezekiah gathered the city officials together and went up to the temple of the LORD. They brought seven bulls, seven rams, seven male lambs and seven male goats as a sin offering for the kingdom, for the sanctuary and for Judah. The king commanded the priests, the descendants of Aaron, to offer these on the altar of the LORD. 2 Chronicles 29.2-21

The priests then slaughtered the goats and presented their blood on the altar for a sin offering to atone for all Israel, because the king had ordered the burnt offering and the sin offering for all Israel. He stationed the Levites in the temple of the LORD with cymbals, harps and lyres in the way prescribed by David and Gad the king's seer and Nathan the prophet; this was commanded by the LORD through his prophets. So the Levites stood ready with David's instruments, and the priests with their trumpets. 2 Chronicles 29.24-26

The whole assembly bowed in worship, while the singers sang and the trumpeters played. All this continued until the sacrifice of the burnt offering was completed. When the offerings were finished, the king and everyone present with him knelt down and worshiped. King Hezekiah and his officials ordered the Levites to praise the LORD with the words of David and of Asaph the seer. So they sang praises with gladness and bowed their heads and worshiped. Then Hezekiah said, "You have now dedicated yourselves to the LORD. Come and bring sacrifices and thank offerings to the temple of the LORD." So the assembly brought sacrifices and thank offerings, and all whose hearts were willing brought burnt offerings. The animals consecrated as sacrifices amounted to six hundred bulls and three thousand sheep and goats. The priests, however, were too few to skin all the burnt offerings; so their kinsmen the Levites helped them until the task was finished. There were burnt offerings in abundance, together with the fat of the fellowship offerings and the drink offerings that accompanied the burnt offerings. So the service of the temple of the LORD was reestablished. Hezekiah and all the people rejoiced at what God had brought about for his people, because it was done so quickly. 2 Chronicles 29.28-36

Do you feel the kinship we have with these fellow Christians? Like they, we enjoy a ritual of renewal right here in chapel every time we hear that our sins have been forgiven through the blood of the Lamb of God. Here is the power of spiritual renewal

- Its author: the Holy Spirit,
- Its motive: recognition that something has gone wrong in our lives,
- Its means: the Word of the Gospel, and
- Its effect: rededication, sacrifice, lives in harmony with God's will.

I hope you felt close to these strange but admirable fellow Christians and I hope you felt a little part of their celebration. A massive ritual like theirs we might never experience until Heaven. But our small rituals can connect us with them – our worship forms here in chapel, the Lord's prayer alone in your room, our confession: "I believe in the Holy Christian Church." This **is** the Holy Christian Church. We **are**, with them and many others, fellow Christians.

†

October 2004

The Blessing of Work
On the Tenth Commandment

INI

Jesus was busy all his life fulfilling God's Law for us. His parents started it on his behalf, taking him to the temple when he was eight days old for the circumcision ceremony. Luke 2.22-24 The first conscious effort of his own that is reported to us happened when he was 12 years old. Luke 2.42-49 On that occasion, he was fulfilling for us the 10th Commandment.

What we've seen so far, I hope, in the chapel series on the Ten Commandments is the multi-layered blessing these commandments are to us. Their first purpose is to show us our sin and bring us to an acute awareness of how desperately we need a savior. But we also see how God by these commandments is setting up protections for us around the essential areas of our lives. They define for us what a life of happiness can be. What would we do without any of them?

A quick review: the 1st Commandment, that we have no other gods, protects the preeminence of God in our lives. 2nd about taking God's name in vain: truth. 3rd: worship. 4th urging us to honor parents: authority. 5th: life. 6th: marriage. 7th which says don't steal: property. 8th: reputation. 9th as we heard last week, about our place to live: opportunity, and I'd even say liberty.

Now we're at 10 which says: Thou shalt not covet thy neighbor's wife, nor his manservant, nor maidservent, nor cattle, nor anything that is thy neighbors. Listen to the reading assigned for today and see how it elaborates this commandment perfectly.

> But godliness with contentment is great gain. For we brought nothing into the world, and we can take nothing out of it. But if we have food and clothing, we will be content with that. People who want to get rich fall into temptation and a trap and into many foolish and harmful desires that plunge men into ruin and destruction. For the love of money is a root of all kinds of evil. Some people, eager for money, have wandered from the faith and pierced themselves with many griefs. But you, man of God, flee from all this, and pursue righteousness, godliness, faith, love, endurance and gentleness. 1 Timothy 6.6-11

What important aspect of life does 10 protect? It's about work and its rewards. It says, notice those people and other creatures that serve your neighbor? Don't selfishly and unfairly interfere with that important mutual service relationship. The 10th Commandment (along with many other directives in Scripture) tells us that workers should work hard and faithfully, and that in turn employers should reward workers fairly and treat them well.

How precious to us is the gift of work! Yes, we often complain about having too much of it, but consider the alternative: how stressed those are who are unemployed, how bored those are who have nothing to do, how having work means satisfaction, happiness, and being worthwhile. In the beginning, when the world was perfect and without sin, God set Adam and Eve to work tending the beautiful park Eden.

But sin ruined everything, including this blessing, and that's why we need a commandment about work. Look around: There's a big 10th Commandment problem in the world today. It's spelled **greed**, and it has a little brother named **getting something for nothing** – in our reading it's called the "love of money." There are many "problems of society" that concern us, and they should. But I'd suggest that far more people are trapped in sin against the 10th Commandment than will engage in a gay marriage or even an abortion. Greed and selfishness, dreams of riches at any cost, win a lottery and I'll have it made, lusting after the lifestyles of the rich and famous – all these plague our culture, and infect our minds.

And they can center right at that employer-worker relationship, where sin happens on both sides. Workers shirk and call in sick and start late and leave early, employers exploit workers, CEOs pad profits by mergers and out-sourcing jobs with no regard for the workers they are displacing, pensions are squandered, and many other shady dealings we read about almost daily in the news, all for the sake of the love of money.

But (as usual) we don't have to look that far for Commandment problems. Ever take shortcuts in your work? Ever steal the work of others – cheating, plagiarism? Are you satisfied with sloppy work, with careless work? If you do it now, you'll do it later.

Do you dream of riches? Set money-making as a life goal? The 10th Commandment says, watch your values! Our reading warns: "Some people, eager for money, have wandered from the faith and pierced themselves with many griefs." Like any sin, this one too earns hell.

I've got some good news too. Jesus worked. He knew the job he had to do. Already at age 12 he astounded his parents when they found him in the temple by saying, "*I must be about my father's work.*" Luke 2.49 If you are reading John's Gospel these days as part of the 21-day writing challenge, you'll find Jesus very aware of his work. Two days ago you read about the disciples offering him food at Jacob's well and he replied, "*My food is to do the will of him who sent me and to finish his work."* John 4.34 Yesterday you read of him saying to the Pharisees who challenged him, *"My Father is always at his work to this very day, and I, too, am working."* John 5.17 Today you'll read Jesus define the goal of his work by saying, *"The work of God is this: to (get you to) believe in the one he has sent."* John 6.29 In his long prayer in Gethsemane Park, Jesus said to his father, *"I have brought you glory on earth by completing the work you gave me to do."* John 17.4 And on the cross where he paid penalty for our sins also against the 10th Commandment he said at last, *"It is finished."* John 19.30

By keeping this commandment for us Jesus changed it for us, from obligation to privilege. By paying to God what we owe for breaking this commandment, Jesus has empowered us to learn how to obey it.

If some day you are an employer, maybe even a leader of industry, can you be one who *"flees love of money and pursues righteousness, godliness, faith, love, endurance and gentleness"*? Can you right now be a teacher, administrator, or student – whatever your current work – who *"flees love of money and pursues righteousness, godliness, faith, love, endurance and gentleness"*?

Can you in setting your life's goals, model them after Jesus who *"though he was rich, yet for your sakes he became poor, so that you through his poverty might become rich"*? 2 Corinthians 8.9

Can our values be like those of the widows about whom Paul wrote to Timothy, who were admired for good deeds, such as bringing up children, showing hospitality, washing the feet of the saints, helping those in trouble and devoting herself to all kinds of good deeds 1 Timothy 5.10 – then and now, among the lowest-paid jobs of society, but among the most valuable.

In the end, our work is of value only because of Jesus and the future in Heaven he has provided us. As for money (our reading says) *"we brought nothing into the world, and we can take nothing out of it."* And so the apostle urges us, *"Whatever you do, work at it with all your heart, as working for the Lord, not for men, since you know that you will receive an inheritance from the Lord as a reward. It is the Lord Christ you are serving."* Colossians 3.23

For that opportunity, thanks be to God.

†

November 2004

Worthy for the Supper

INI

Today let's explore another of the great paradoxes of the Christian faith.

> For I received from the Lord what I also passed on to you: The Lord Jesus, on the night he was betrayed, took bread, and when he had given thanks, he broke it and said, "This is my body, which is for you; do this in remembrance of me." In the same way, after supper he took the cup, saying, "This cup is the new covenant in my blood; do this, whenever you drink it, in remembrance of me." For whenever you eat this bread and drink this cup, you proclaim the Lord's death until he comes. Therefore, whoever eats the bread or drinks the cup of the Lord in an unworthy manner will be guilty of sinning against the body and blood of the Lord. A man ought to examine himself before he eats of the bread and drinks of the cup. For anyone who eats and drinks without recognizing the body of the Lord eats and drinks judgment on himself. 1 Corinthians 11.23-32

It might seem odd to you that we are considering a Lord's Supper passage in a service where we are not celebrating the Lord's supper. I hope to show you that it is not odd at all.

Notice first of all that this meal is central to a Christian's life. It's significant that our Lord chose to establish, as the "means of grace" by which the Holy Spirit creates new life in us, activities that resemble our most common, everyday actions. **Baptism** is a **washing** – something we do multiple times each day. The **Word of the Gospel** is conveyed through **speaking** and we are told "faith comes by **hearing**," common human activities. And of course, we eat and drink every few hours in order to live. Eating and drinking are **central to life** and eating and drinking **this** meal – the supper of our Lord – is central to the **Christian's life**. And so it isn't so out of place to speak of the Lord's Supper on an occasion when the Sacrament is not present, for what we will say about the Supper applies to our entire Christian life.

The point Paul is making about the meal in this portion of Scripture is this: Self-examination is central to this meal, which is central to the Christian life.

Paul says, before partaking of this meal, look inside yourself. Look for what? Are we to look for worthiness? He says, *"Whoever eats the bread or drinks the cup of the Lord in an unworthy manner will be guilty of sinning."* Worthiness means, of course, having worth. To most, it means "deserving" – somehow deserving. Are the poor "worthy of help?" we might wonder. Perhaps so if they are working hard, perhaps not if they are lazy. If we consider people worthy, we might associate ourselves with them, even in a helping relationship. But if we find them unworthy, we avoid them and don't even think about them.

But Paul is not telling us to examine ourselves for worthiness. We are not to look for that. Hear again what he says: *"A man ought to examine himself before he eats of the bread and drinks of the cup. For anyone who eats and drinks without recognizing the body of the Lord eats and drinks judgment on himself."*

What are we to look for? The body of the Lord! But that's not something we would find inside ourselves. Paul here is engaging in a logical leap. He has skipped a couple of links because he knows that for a Christian believer they are obvious. What he means is this. When we look inside ourselves and examine ourselves carefully, what we find turns our attention to the body of the Lord, which comes to us in the sacramental meal. We look inside ourselves, and what we find forces us to look outside ourselves.

This is the Christian paradox we forecast earlier: we are worthy when we find ourselves unworthy. We become worthy to receive the Sacrament only when we have examined ourselves, held ourselves up to the requirements of God's Law, and found ourselves so wanting, so far short, so much moral failures, that we realize the only escape is to turn to Jesus Christ, to plead "Lord have mercy, I am totally unworthy, please help me." And that makes us worthy to receive the Supper, because we recognize what we need so much, the real body and blood of our Lord Jesus, given and shed for us on the cross of Calvary.

Then we are, as Paul puts it, recognizing the Lord's body. Luther's words too are familiar to many of us from confirmation class: a person is truly worthy and well prepared for the Sacrament who has faith in these words: given and shed for you for the remission of sins.

Sometimes we decide to dress up for a meal – doing that makes it more special. The message from the Bible tonight is about the Lord's meal. Dress for this dinner, we are told, by putting on Christ. Wrap yourself for this dinner with the sinlessness that he has won for you by paying your debt and mine on the cross where he gave the same body and shed the same blood that you are taking into yourself at this miraculous meal.

And finally realize, this food and drink are central to your life. Our entire life is to be one of self-examination, and recognition that all our worthiness comes from God, on whom we depend in faith.

If you are worthy for this supper, you are worthy all the time, even now.

†

December 10, 2004

A Child of Hope

INI

Ever wish you could see yourself when you were a baby? See your folks as they looked then – young, excited at your arrival. And you were so cute!

There always seems to be excitement around the birth of a baby. The whole relationship anticipates it, gets ready for it. And when it finally happens – to the Mom it seemed like forever – the word goes out, the pictures are in the mail or on the internet. There's a lot of excitement around the birth of a baby.

And that's just as it should be. Consider the wonder of birth, how the tiny cells multiply, each of them knowing whether to become an eye, or an ear, or a button nose, or whatever – there's lots of whatever. And how finally it all becomes a human person, full of all the potential in the world.

The second thing everyone asks, after "Is everyone OK," is what did you name the baby? Should you use one of the popular names? Last year Jacob topped the list, followed by Michael, Joshua, Matthew, and Andrew. For girls it was Emily in first place, followed by Emma, Madison, Hannah, and Olivia. Maybe you should use a name that's been in the family? Or a name you've always liked? Or just a name that has a funky sound?

The only downer comes when we remember that beneath all the excitement, the baby is stained, as we all were, with sin that was inherited all the way from our first parents. All of us are stained like that, and even as we are born, we are set off into a world of trouble, sickness, struggle with our own sins, and finally death.

Still, we enjoy the excitement of a birth, and this is only what we might call an **ordinary** birth of someone like you and me. Consider how much more excitement, how much more widespread the excitement over an extra-ordinary birth, a very special birth, a promised birth. Consider the greater excitement over a birth that has been anticipated not for a few months but for centuries, the birth of a "Child of Hope."

Consider the greater wonder of what is developing in that virgin womb – a tiny creature, yes, but at the same time the creator – a human by design, but at the same time the divine Designer, one whose being is so complex and mysterious that wise theologians over the ages have applied long lists of obscure Latin terms trying to describe it, and still they admit they do not understand it.

We **do** understand that this baby had to be human so he would live fully under God's Law and fulfill it for us; so he could suffer temptation and resist it for us; so he could die.

We understand too that he had to be God so that his death would be of such infinite value that it could pay for **all** sins, including yours and mine. And naming this baby? Names meant a lot more to people back then. They didn't choose names just because they liked them, or because they sounded good. Names often provided a profound description of the essence of who this person was. Elijah – the Lord is my God. Isaiah – the Lord is salvation. Jesus – Savior. The names captured the person, forecast the mission, identified the purpose of this life.

And what about the stain? In this special baby there was none, and that indeed was his purpose and mission – to remove all of our stains by taking them on his innocent stainless self, to overcome all the evils that result from sin, to wash our stain away as we are baptized in his name, to open our graves and raise us to eternal life.

This is a time for us once again to become excited about the birth of this Baby – not only excited, but repentant, and thankful, and humble, and re-dedicated. Relive the anticipation recorded centuries before the event by the prophet Isaiah.

> The people walking in darkness have seen a great light; on those living in the land of the shadow of death a light has dawned. You have enlarged the nation and increased their joy; they rejoice before you as people rejoice at the harvest, as men rejoice when dividing the plunder. For as in the day of Midian's defeat, you have shattered the yoke that burdens them, the bar across their shoulders, the rod of their oppressor. Every warrior's boot used in battle and every garment rolled in blood will be destined for burning, will be fuel for the fire. For unto us a child is born, unto us a son is given, and the government will be on his shoulders. And he will be called Wonderful Counselor, Mighty God, Everlasting Father, Prince of Peace. Isaiah 9.2-6

†

December 21, 2004

Micah in Bethlehem

INI

I wouldn't advise you to visit Bethlehem now – it's too dangerous. While this year authorities have been working hard to assure tourists that for the first time in five or six years a visit would be safe, still Americans aren't much liked in most of world, maybe especially there. I'm not sure if there will ever again be a time when it's safe for us to go there to stand in the narrow cave beneath the Church of the Holy Nativity viewing the very place where, it is said, Jesus was born, with the manger carved out of the cave wall just a few feet away.

Still, it's not an utterly profound experience. It's diluted by change. It doesn't look at all like it must have then. It's been all fancied up in ways I consider tacky. The incense is thick enough to make one ill and the press of more tourists coming down the narrow stairway forces you out again, after only a few moments, to encounter the annoying street vendors selling cheap plastic manger scenes, oddly enough, depicting the manger in a wooden shed, not the cave where you just were.

The truth is, the "little town of Bethlehem how still we see thee lie" was frequently far from quiet and peaceful. Just a couple of years ago, militants took possession of the Church of the Nativity and had to be flushed out by a military operation. You can still see the bullet holes in the stone church walls, both external and internal.

Violence in Bethlehem is not new. It wasn't two years after Jesus was born when King Herod sent his soldiers to murder all the babies and toddlers in the area in an attempt to rid himself of a prophesied Jewish King born there. Today's reading goes back still farther to the days of the prophet Micah. It was a time when in that part of the world whole regions were ruled by the latest biggest bully, where the people lived in constant fear of the thugs who ruled the tribe or country next door. It's still like that over there today – only the weapons have changed.

That's the atmosphere in which Micah preached, with the land facing immanent invasion by the chief thugs of the day, Assyria, and he drew attention to this little town with these words.

> But you, Bethlehem Ephrathah, though you are small among the clans of Judah, out of you will come for me one who will be ruler over Israel, whose origins are from of old, from ancient times. Therefore Israel will be abandoned until the time when she who is in labor gives

birth and the rest of his brothers return to join the Israelites. He will stand and shepherd his flock in the strength of the LORD, in the majesty of the name of the LORD his God. And they will live securely, for then his greatness will reach to the ends of the earth. And he will be their peace. Micah 5.2-5a

We are too used to peace. Suppose to make your way across the mall to chapel this morning you had to duck between the pillars of the colonnade for fear of being picked off by a sniper. Suppose to avoid the crossfire above ground, you decided to take the tunnel, but were warned not to for fear of a deadly terrorist gas grenade in the enclosed space. Suppose as we sit here, we suddenly heard the whistle of incoming ordnance and by reflex duck under the seats – not that it would protect us from a direct hit but at least we might be shielded from glass splinters flying from the windows from a hit just outside. Suppose we were forced to view this beautiful chapel, which many of us have come truly to love, reduced to a pile of rubble. And this would be our last view of campus altogether as we rush to our rooms to gather what is most precious to us into a bundle or single suitcase to carry, and we set off afoot down some road in some direction we believe might be safe from the invading army we know is on its way.

We are perhaps too used to peace. So much that we don't appreciate it as we should. You know, of course, there are right now many places in the world where reality is as I've described. One of those places is the so-called "holy land," the land of Bethlehem. I never call it "holy," because there have been more wars, more blood shed in those few square miles than any other place on earth. We don't appreciate peace as we should.

Could it be the same in our spiritual lives? How sheltered we are from the great cosmic battles over our souls. We sing "a mighty fortress is our God" with little feeling of how precious it is to **have** a fortress, an armed, fortified refuge to which we can flee from the great danger pressing on us from all sides. Luther in that hymn tries to express the danger to our souls, perhaps compared to dodging sniper bullets or fleeing terrorist gas attacks.

> The old evil foe now means deadly woe with deep guile and great might ... on earth is not his equal... Devils all the world might fill all eager to devour us.

We're mostly shielded from all this -- and why? Because as Micah foretold, Someone else has effectively fought this battle for us, won it, and leaves us in peace.

How remarkable it was, in a country racked by war, occupied by a powerful enemy, pre-occupied with secret talk of rebellion and armed revolt – how remarkable that out of the little town of Bethlehem, just as Micah had prophesied, there appeared a man who spoke gently of peace. *Blessed are they...* he said, in words we repeat frequently in chapel. *Blessed are the meek, blessed are the merciful, the poor in spirit, the peacemakers.* Matthew 5 How startlingly different was this teaching than anything heard before. This man teaches of peace!

But it's not surprising he spoke of peace, for he was, he is peace. He fought for us the battle against sin, death, and Satan. He won that battle for us, emerged the victor in his resurrection from the dead, and leaves us as we are now – with sins forgiven, assured of eternal life through faith in him, and enjoying the peace of God which passes all human understanding.

The Old Testament prophet Micah wrote to a people frightened and wearied by war, under immanent threat of attack by Assyria, the superpower thugs of the day. He spoke of how the Lord God takes on our enemies for us and leaves us with peace.

No, it's not wise to visit the town of Bethlehem these days. It's too dangerous. But if you ponder once again this Christmas those words of the angels' song, *"Peace on earth ... for unto you is born this day in the city of David a Savior, which is Christ the Lord"* Luke 2.10 – if you ponder those words, you've been to Bethlehem.

†

January 10, 2005

God Tips the Balance

INI

The basketball teetered on the edge of the rim for what seemed an endless moment. Which way would it fall, in or out? What was at stake was a trip to the state tournament and it was crisis time, a tied score with a few seconds left in the third overtime of that regional tournament game between Minnesota Valley Lutheran and Morristown in 1987. If it fell in our team would have a marvelous state tournament experience; if it fell out we would all just go home in great disappointment.

Today I'm called upon to introduce you briefly to the Old Testament book of the prophet Nahum. We don't know much about him apart from what is in his short book. The subject of his prophecy, delivered a couple hundred years after the reign of King David, is the approaching complete and final destruction of Nineveh, the capital of the great and flourishing Assyrian empire which was threatening Judah, God's people. The prophet Jonah some years earlier had gone to Nineveh by way of the belly of a big fish to deliver a similar message. That time Nineveh repented and was spared. This time Nineveh indeed fell, giving way to the Persian Empire. Today the troublesome city of Mosul is located in Nineveh province in Iraq.

Here are the verses from the prophet I've been assigned to read. Some of these words are addressed to Judah, God's people, and some to Nineveh, the enemies of God's people.

> This is what the LORD says: "Although they have allies and are numerous, they will be cut off and pass away. Although I have afflicted you, [O Judah,] I will afflict you no more. Now I will break their yoke from your neck and tear your shackles away." The LORD has given a command concerning you, [Nineveh]: "You will have no descendants to bear your name. I will destroy the carved images and cast idols that are in the temple of your gods. I will prepare your grave, for you are vile." Look, there on the mountains, the feet of one who brings good news, who proclaims peace! Celebrate your festivals, O Judah, and fulfill your vows. No more will the wicked invade you; they will be completely destroyed. An attacker advances against you [Nineveh]. Guard the fortress, watch the road, brace yourselves, marshal all your strength! The LORD will restore the splendor of Jacob like the splendor of Israel. Nahum 1.12-2.2

I can still see that basketball teetering on the rim and think of it often as a symbol of crisis time, a time when a little difference can make a big difference. Here is the message I am bringing to you from today's reading: **God nudges the ball our way.**

I'm not claiming that God is all that interested in a ball game but I **am** talking about crisis moments, big and small, bringing you the message of Nahum, that God is in those crisis moments with his strength and with his love for us.

Nahum wrote at a time of war and described it vividly. In our time we've had vivid depictions of war: for the Vietnam war the *Deer Hunter* did it strongly; for World War II it was *Saving Private Ryan*; maybe you saw *Blackhawk Down*. For the Assyrian invasion in the 8th Century B.C. long before movies it was Nahum. Listen to this description of battle:

> The shields of his soldiers are red; the warriors are clad in scarlet. The metal on the chariots flashes on the day they are made ready; the spears of pine are brandished. The chariots storm through the streets, rushing back and forth through the squares. They look like flaming torches; they dart about like lightning. He summons his picked troops, yet they stumble on their way. They dash to the city wall; the protective shield is put in place. The river gates are thrown open and the palace collapses. Nahum 2.3-6

Perhaps only those of us who have been there can fully visualize the crisis of battle. We spoke of that here before Christmas while examining the prophet Micah who lived in similar times anticipating invasion. I'm not going to compare crisis sizes today and argue that one is greater than another. In a class discussion yesterday, one student said she sometimes longed for simpler days when her biggest problem was which friends to invite to her birthday party. Well, from here that seems like a trivial crisis, but back then, to her it was a big one. If the crises we face today in faith might be relatively small perhaps they are preparation for facing big ones later on and facing them in the power of God.

Wherever your crisis falls on the importance scale, whether it's winning the game or facing a challenging semester or encountering illness in your family or yourself or going to war or being engulfed by a giant wave,[1] the Lord urges us this morning through the pen and experience of Nahum, *"Look, there on the mountains, the feet of one who brings good news, who proclaims peace!"* That is, have faith in our Rescuer, the One who tips things our way. Find peace in the assurance of his love, the love that prompted him to sacrifice his

---

[1] During the previous month, December of 2004, a tsunami had devastated a dozen countries in south Asia.

own Son for us. In God's love, everything that happens will, as the apostle puts it, "*work together for good.*" Romans 8.28

It may not be as we imagine, or even as we wish. The ball might drop off the rim in the direction that disappoints us. The test grade might not please us. The medical report might not be what we had hoped for. And I'm certain that watching all I own and love washed away in a flood of water would be a mammoth test of my faith. But I suspect that if Jesus' own disciples had been asked their wishes at the time of Jesus' unfair trial, I'm almost certain they would have wished that Jesus not be condemned to death, that Pilate would be a fair judge and let Jesus go. If they had it their way, they and you and I would all still be lost in our sins. But it happened God's way, not their way. And so our sins are now forgiven.

It may not be the way that we would wish but in faith we know that, whichever way the ball falls, **the God who loves us and gave his Son for us tipped it our way.** Carry that faith into this semester's tasks and carry that faith into your life's tasks.

†

January 27, 2005

They Testify of Me

It's nice to hear in the hymn ("Bright and Glorious is the Sky" ELH120) an echo of Christmas which should never fade away. I'm picturing a Christmas tree still decorated; most prominently hanging from a central bough is a golden key, which we'll talk about this morning.

Have you ever lost your key? Depending on what the key unlocked, it was at least a minor annoyance, at most a near catastrophe. A jewelry box can usually be smashed and opened. A lost room key at Bethany can be replaced, but it will cost you 10 or 20 dollars. If a master key at a place like BLC is lost, it could cost several tens of thousands of dollars to replace all the locks.

Jesus here is talking to some people who have lost a very important key – it's a key you and I have. Hear his words, and especially the last verse.

> *[Jesus here is speaking to his enemies, those who didn't believe in him]* If I testify about myself, my testimony is not valid. There is another who testifies in my favor, and I know that his testimony about me is valid. You have sent to John and he has testified to the truth. Not that I accept human testimony; but I mention it that you may be saved. John was a lamp that burned and gave light, and you chose for a time to enjoy his light. I have testimony weightier than that of John. For the very work that the Father has given me to finish, and which I am doing, testifies that the Father has sent me. And the Father who sent me has himself testified concerning me. You have never heard his voice nor seen his form, nor does his word dwell in you, for you do not believe the one he sent. You diligently study the Scriptures because you think that by them you possess eternal life. These are the Scriptures that testify about me. John 5.31-39

Jesus is talking about the inseparable connection between himself and Scripture. The key to understanding Jesus is Scripture, of course. We would know very little about Jesus without Scripture. But here Jesus reverses that saying. He says, the key to understanding Scripture is Jesus. It goes both ways. Jesus presented himself as the key to the Scriptures, just as the Scriptures are the key to himself. Any interpretation of one without the other is wrong.

As proof, Jesus directs us to his life. Look at what he said about how his life and work emerged from the Scripture. Here is a short list.

- He said he was the Son of David, the Son of Man named in the Old Testament as the Son of God. Matthew 9.6 and other places
- He named himself the Good Shepherd foretold by the prophets Isaiah and Ezekiel. John 10.11f.

- He identified himself as the Servant spoken of by Isaiah, who would take on himself the suffering of his people. Matthew 12.17f.
- He told the congregation in Nazareth that he preached in fulfillment of Scripture about him. Luke 4.16f.
- He told Matthew he healed in fulfillment of Scripture. Matthew 8.17
- He went to his death knowing it was fulfilling Scripture. Heading to Jerusalem for the last time, he told his disciples, *"Behold we go up to Jerusalem, and all things that are written by the prophets concerning the Son of Man must be accomplished."* Luke 18.31
- At the last supper: *"The Son of Man goes as it is written of him."* Luke 22.22
- When Peter started to fight with a sword to prevent his arrest, Jesus stopped him, saying, *"Do you think I can't ask my Father, and he will immediately send me more than twelve legions of angels? But how then would the Scripture be fulfilled, that this must be so?"* Matthew 26.53-54
- He went to his death trusting his father to raise him again, and after he did, he came back and explained to his disciples what it all meant. *"These are my words which I spoke to you when I was still with you, that everything written about me in the law of Moses, and the prophets, and the psalms must be fulfilled... Thus it is written, that the Christ must suffer, and on the third day rise from the dead, and that repentance and forgiveness of sins should be preached in his name to all nations."* Luke 24.44f.

Jesus presented himself as the key to Scriptures, just as Scriptures are the key to himself. Any interpretation of one without the other is wrong.

More than that. He presented himself as the key to life itself. In our reading Jesus tells those who don't believe in him. *"You diligently study the Scriptures because you think that by them you possess eternal life.* (He is saying, in effect, you're right about that part – Scripture does provide eternal life – but not without the key. He goes on.) *These are the Scriptures that testify about me. – I'm telling you this so that you might be saved."*

You have this key not in your pocket or purse but in your heart. Treasure it! Take advantage of every opportunity you have to study Scripture. I don't know **all** that it will open for you in your life. I do know that it starts with the forgiveness of all your sins that Jesus won for you, that it removes from us the fear of death, that it removes all fear of the future since we know our future is in the hands of a loving God, who sent his Son to restore us to himself. It's the assurance of Heaven, and a life full of purpose.

Jesus is the key to Scripture. It opens us up to life. Don't lose that key.

†

February 22, 2005

Under the Word

INI

What do you plan to do with your brain? Let me save you the trouble of puzzling over that odd question by pointing out that you have already answered it. Your presence here on this campus is an answer to the question: you plan to use your brain as fully as you can. Your presence here in chapel is another answer to the question: you plan to use your brain in a certain way.

Our survey of Bible books has brought us this morning to Corinth and to two wonderful letters that the apostle Paul wrote containing some scolding (which we still need), lots of encouragement (which we still appreciate), and many directions on how to live as Christians (which we still try hard to follow). Today's assigned reading speaks to the question of what we should do with the brains, the intelligence God gave us.

> For the message of the cross is foolishness to those who are perishing, but to us who are being saved it is the power of God. For it is written: "I will destroy the wisdom of the wise; the intelligence of the intelligent I will frustrate." Where is the wise man? Where is the scholar? Where is the philosopher of this age? Has not God made foolish the wisdom of the world? For since in the wisdom of God the world through its wisdom did not know him, God was pleased through the foolishness of what was preached to save those who believe. Jews demand miraculous signs and Greeks look for wisdom, but we preach Christ crucified: a stumbling block to Jews and foolishness to Gentiles, but to those whom God has called, both Jews and Greeks, Christ the power of God and the wisdom of God. For the foolishness of God is wiser than man's wisdom, and the weakness of God is stronger than man's strength. 1 Corinthians 1.18-25

Intelligence? Wisdom? Scholarship? Does God want us to engage it or not? Paul's answer: It has to do with attitude.

The fact that you are here on this campus indicates that you intend to use your brain to the fullest, to grow in your knowledge and your skills. You work hard at that here and so do your teachers. The administration works hard to bring to this campus qualified scholars and teachers to guide and encourage you. The faculty works hard to maintain and upgrade their academic qualifications. We have a great respect for scholarship and academic integrity here. There is no questioning the many benefits that have been brought to us by science, medicine, technology, and the advance of knowledge in all areas of study. On this campus, we search it all out. By being on this campus, you join us in respecting and engaging in scholarship of the highest quality.

But why then does St. Paul seem so negative about it in this reading? It has to do with attitude, with who is in charge of our scholarship? Is it the world, or is it the Word? Paul's warning, you see, was about **how** intelligence is used. He was observing that if our brains come under the control of the world, they become our idols. Paul nails the cause exactly. In the verses right after our reading, he observes the motive of the world: it likes to boast. The world wants to expel God from its thinking so it can vaunt its own accomplishments. Paul says,

> But God chose the foolish things of the world to shame the wise; God chose the weak things of the world to shame the strong. He chose the lowly things of this world and the despised things – and the things that are not – to nullify the things that are, so that no one may boast before him. ... Therefore, as it is written: "Let him who boasts boast in the Lord." 1 Corinthians 1.26-31

Paul says, don't be fooled or intimidated by the so-called wisdom of the world. Don't worry about who the world considers smart, or powerful, or wise. Bring your intellect under control of the Word and learn there of Christ to find real wisdom and power, the wisdom of God, and the power of God.

Don't worry, there is plenty of intellectual power there. We don't have shelves in the lobby where we expect you to check your brain before you enter this chapel. I know you are using plenty of brain power just to follow what I'm saying. Look at Paul himself. There is no questioning his intellect. He studied under Gamaliel, the top Rabbi of his day and probably took some credits studying Greek philosophy and literature at Tarsus University, a top Hellenistic school in his hometown. Consider his power as writer. Consider chapter 13 in this same letter to the Corinthians where he wrote, *"If I speak in the tongues of men and of angels, but have not love, I am only a resounding gong or a clanging cymbal...* 1 Corinthians 13.1 *And now these three remain: faith, hope and love. But the greatest of these is love."* 1 Corinthians 13.13 Or in chapter 15: *"Where, O death, is your victory? Where, O death, is your sting? The sting of death is sin, and the power of sin is the law. But thanks be to God! He gives us the victory through our Lord Jesus Christ."* 1 Corinthians 15.55-57 What profound thoughts, under God's Word!

Look at Luther; there is no questioning his towering intellect. He submitted it to the control of God's Word. There have been marvelous intellects in our own church, not least Dr. S.C. Ylvisaker, former president of Bethany after whom the YFAC was named. His widely renowned and respected scholarship was under God's Word.

Look at Jesus himself as a model. No questioning his intellect, or his knowledge. Though it was divine, he submitted to the Word. The phrases echo throughout his speaking: *"Behold, we go up to Jerusalem, and all things that are written by the prophets concerning the Son of Man shall be accomplished."* Luke 18.31 At the Last Supper he said, *"The Son of Man goeth as it was written of him,"* Matthew 26.24 and a little later, *"This Scripture must be fulfilled in me, he was reckoned with transgressors."* Luke 22.37 In Gethsemane park, he stopped Peter's fighting impulse by saying, *"Do you think that I cannot appeal to my Father, and he will at once send me more than twelve legions of angels? But how then shall the Scriptures be fulfilled, that it must be so?"* Matthew 26.53-54 He ended a life obedient to Scripture by dying for us, in obedience to Scripture, trusting his father to raise him from death according to Scripture.

And so he rose, returning to explain it all to his disciples, and to us, using Scripture, saying, *"Thus is it written, that the Christ should suffer and on the third day rise from the dead, and that repentance and forgiveness of sins should be preached in his name to all nations."* Luke 24.46-47 Living, dying, and living again, Jesus was under the Word. In that forgiveness of sins he won for us, we find the power of God to restore us to him and to change our lives.

That's why, on this campus and in this chapel, as Paul says, *"We preach Christ crucified: a stumbling block to Jews and foolishness to Gentiles, but to those whom God has called, both Jews and Greeks, Christ the power of God and the wisdom of God. For the foolishness of God is wiser than man's wisdom, and the weakness of God is stronger than man's strength."* 1 Corinthians 1.23f.

When you use your brain subject to God's Word it is no idol, but God's gift. You are in the marvelous company of many great, intelligent men and women of faith, and following the model of our Lord himself. As we said at the start, your presence on this campus shows you intend to use your brain to the fullest. Your presence in this chapel shows you intend to use your brain in a certain way, not under the world, but under the Word.

In that spirit, you can sing in your heart the words of another great intellect of our church, Norman A. Madson as he translated the Kingo hymn:

> I pray thee, dear Lord Jesus, my heart to keep and train
> That I thy holy temple from youth to age remain.
> Turn thou my thoughts forever from worldly wisdom's lore.
> If I but learn to know thee, I shall not want for more.

†

March 31, 2005

God's Mystery's Ending

See "We Know the Ending" in 2001 and "Easter at Peace" 2008

INI

It's a great season for basketball fans. You know that, if you are one. You've had some exciting moments because of some very close endings. The endings make the game great.

My sister and brother-in-law are fervent Wisconsin Badger fans. A Badger tournament game was scheduled to start at the same time as a holy week church service. They set their VCR, went to church, and on the way home were careful not to listen to the radio or in any other way find out how the game had ended. They wanted to watch it on tape as if it were live. They didn't want to know the ending in advance.

I'm a bit different. My wife Judy and I were on the road some 38 hours last weekend[1] and one of the ways we made time pass quickly was to slip in an audio tape of the radio broadcast of some of our favorite basketball games from the past when our son's high school team was playing in postseason tournaments. In those cases we knew as we listened how the game ended. That didn't detract at all from our enjoyment of the game; in fact it was more fun to listen, knowing our team won in the end. Of course, we listened only to the games we won. The ending makes all the difference.

If you have ever participated in serious sports you know that's true. It might have been a rough and bruising game but if you won, you can look back on it all with pleasure. Even the bumps and bruises can feel good if they were a part of what led to victory.

Life of course is much more than a game. It too can certainly be rough and bruising at times and there is a clock that runs out.

The joy of Easter in which we are still basking afresh comes precisely from this: Easter tells us the ending in advance. It tells us how your life and mine is going to turn out. It's not going to be ultimate defeat, and death, and grave. Because of Jesus Christ and his good life which substitutes for ours, his sin payment which substitutes for ours and his resurrection which is a model for ours, the ending is going to be victory. And the ending makes all the difference.

Yes, it's a great season for basketball fans. It's a greater season for Christians. It's a great season for all humankind. The Easter message calls for all the

---

[1] Must have been a spring break trip; I don't remember where.

eloquence we can muster. There isn't any way I am going to be able to match the eloquence we heard here on Tuesday, or the unmatchable beauty of the musical celebration we heard here yesterday.[1] So permit me just to let God's Word say it plainly and clearly in a passage that, when I conducted funerals, was my favorite part. It might sound odd to hear about a favorite part of a funeral but a Christian can have one. For me it was the moment when I could stand at the graveside and read these words of God penned by the Apostle Paul.

> Listen, I tell you a mystery: We will not all sleep, but we will all be changed – in a flash, in the twinkling of an eye, at the last trumpet. For the trumpet will sound, the dead will be raised imperishable, and we will be changed. For the perishable must clothe itself with the imperishable, and the mortal with immortality. When the perishable has been clothed with the imperishable, and the mortal with immortality, then the saying that is written will come true: "Death has been swallowed up in victory." "Where, O death, is your victory? Where, O death, is your sting?" The sting of death is sin, and the power of sin is the law. But thanks be to God! He gives us the victory through our Lord Jesus Christ. Therefore, my dear brothers, stand firm. Let nothing move you. Always give yourselves fully to the work of the Lord, because you know that your labor in the Lord is not in vain. 1 Corinthians 15.51-58

If you are one of those who doesn't want to know the ending in advance, I apologize. I just gave it away – your ending and mine. And remember: the ending makes all the difference

†

---

[1] I don't remember who the "eloquent" speaker was. The music was probably an Easter concert.

April 19, 2005
God Reverses the Sequence
INI

The school year is almost at an end. Are you ready? Ready for what comes next? For many, it will be a new routine, going home – but it's not the same being home after you've been away. For some, it will be graduation, and the real world. Are you prepared?

Let me assure you this morning that you are, by drawing a lesson from a peanut butter sandwich. I learned a long time ago, when preparing a peanut butter sandwich for a three-year-old (did you ever do that?) that successful preparation is a matter of sequence – what comes first and what comes next. You see, I made the mistake of putting the jelly on first. That makes sense – it soaks into the bread better that way. But no! a 3-year old will have nothing to do with a peanut butter sandwich made that way. The peanut butter goes on first!

Today we come in our Bible book survey to the letters of St. Peter. There are two of them, and they provide us an important lesson in sequence, and how sequence relates to being ready, being prepared.

The letters of Peter are crammed with passages familiar to any Christian who has been around a while: encouragement to holy living, holding up under suffering, resisting the enemies of our faith. Listen to just a few of many such passages

> For it is written: "Be holy, because I am holy." 1 Peter 1.16

> Therefore, rid yourselves of all malice and all deceit, hypocrisy, envy, and slander of every kind. 1 Peter 2.1

> Dear friends, I urge you, as aliens and strangers in the world, to abstain from sinful desires, which war against your soul. Live such good lives among the pagans that, though they accuse you of doing wrong, they may see your good deeds and glorify God on the day he visits us. 1 Peter 2.11-12

> For it is commendable if a man bears up under the pain of unjust suffering because he is conscious of God. But how is it to your credit if you receive a beating for doing wrong and endure it? But if you suffer for doing good and you endure it, this is commendable before God. 1 Peter 2.19-20

> Humble yourselves, therefore, under God's mighty hand, that he may lift you up in due time. 1 Peter 5.6

> Be self-controlled and alert. Your enemy the devil prowls around like a roaring lion looking for someone to devour. Resist him, standing firm in the faith. 1 Peter 5.8-9

There are many more like that and when we read them, we may think, that's the life of a Christian, wow! I'd like to live the life of a Christian, but can I do that? As we sing in the school song, "When I leave Bethany's sheltered side," and move out into the world, am I ready? Am I prepared for this?

That's where the importance of sequence comes in. Here sequence is vital and St. Peter is going to show us a sequence that is counter-intuitive; it runs the opposite direction of what we might expect. "Be prepared" suggests to us this sequence: work hard, then you'll be ready, you'll be prepared. That's what school is all about: work hard, learn a lot, develop the skills, and you'll **be prepared.**

God gives us a difference sequence involving being prepared. He reverses it. In God's plan, we are prepared first, then we work hard. If you don't mind, I'm going to compare a Christian to a turkey, a Thanksgiving turkey. When we say, on Thanksgiving eve, "I hope the turkey will be prepared," we are not talking about the turkey doing anything to get ready. The preparing is **done to the turkey,** and after that, after it is prepared (and all the work is done by someone other than the turkey) **then** it fulfills its delicious appointed task.

That's the sequence, the important sequence in God's plan for us. First we are prepared – by God, entirely his work, there is nothing that we do to get prepared – and then, once we are prepared, we are ready to do the work we are meant to do. Our work is not preparation; our work comes **after** the preparation

How does St. Peter teach us this? That brings us finally to today's reading. It's the opening words of his first letter. Those other things I read before, about how we are to lead a Christian life? All that comes later, it's second in the sequence. In these opening words, Peter tells us what comes first. Listen for this list – it's all God's work to prepare us. He says we are elect, chosen by God to be followers of Christ, cleansed by his blood, our sins forgiven. He says we are newly born. He says we already have been guaranteed an inheritance. He says we are already protected by God from anything that would take salvation from us. All this comes first. This makes us prepared:

> Peter, an apostle of Jesus Christ, to God's **elect**, strangers in the world, scattered throughout Pontus, Galatia, Cappadocia, Asia and Bithynia, who **have been chosen** according to the foreknowledge of God the Father, through the sanctifying work of the Spirit, for obedience to

Jesus Christ and sprinkling by his blood: Grace and peace be yours in abundance. Praise be to the God and Father of our Lord Jesus Christ! In his great mercy **he has given us new birth** into a living hope through the resurrection of Jesus Christ from the dead, and into an **inheritance** that can never perish, spoil or fade – kept in heaven for you, who through faith are **shielded by God's power** until the coming of the salvation that is ready to be revealed in the last time. In this you greatly rejoice, though now for a little while you may have had to suffer grief in all kinds of trials. These have come so that your faith – of greater worth than gold, which perishes even though refined by fire – may be proved genuine and may result in praise, glory and honor when Jesus Christ is revealed. Though you have not seen him, you love him; and even though you do not see him now, you believe in him and are filled with an inexpressible and glorious joy, for you are receiving the goal of your faith, the salvation of your souls. 1 Peter 1.1-9

You are ready. You are prepared, entirely by the loving work of God through our Lord Jesus Christ. That's why we love God. Now go forward, here on campus for a few more weeks and on into the summer and the rest of your life, loving each other, and doing the work of a Christian.

†

May 11, 2005
In the Good Shepherd Chapel for the Vicar Workshop

Two Attitudes

INI

Esteemed faculty, Christian friends, families and visitors, especially students dear to our hearts, grace and peace be yours on this special day.

There are pivotal moments in life. Some of them occur when we stop from our routine, step back to consider what we have been doing and what we are about to do next. Days like today can be considered pivotal. You've immersed yourselves in lots of advanced, graduate-level learning. You've engaged in lots of sophisticated and complex parish experiences. This might be a time to go back once more to the basics.

I have no interesting stories for you, not even any stimulating metaphors. I just ask for the chance to point your attention to two verses of this wonderful psalm that are special for pastors just entering their calling, just as they are special for pastors nearing the end of their journeys. These are two verses you will speak often in your ministry. The first occurs regularly in the first part of our liturgies, the second you might pray softly each time you enter the pulpit.

> Create in me a clean heart, O God, and renew a right spirit within me.
> Psalm 51.10

> O Lord, open thou my lips, and my mouth shall show forth thy praise.
> Psalm 51.15

I focus on these two verses because they engender two basic and proper attitudes of the pastor: **humility** and **confidence.**

"Create in me a clean heart, O God, and renew a right spirit within me." This prayer uttered sincerely engenders **humility.** It reminds us of our heart problem. All of us have a heart problem. Our hearts are by nature unclean and impure. We all know how we have been often led astray by sins of all kinds. Before long pastors know about temptations to which they are especially prone. Not the least of these is pride and self-righteousness. Yes, even among those who preach salvation by the merits of Christ alone how easy it is to believe we are doing God a favor in our calling, to comfort ourselves by dwelling on the sacrifices we think we are making, to believe ourselves indispensable to the Lord as if he couldn't get along without us, to exalt our own importance to the Lord's kingdom. Because of these and all of our other sins we need continually to cry the *kyrie eleison*. We need daily to pray, *"Create in me a clean heart, O God, and renew a right spirit within me."*

The Lord knows our need, of course. He knows our heart problem even before we pray. In **Baptism,** he has replaced our dead stony heart with a clean pure heart of flesh. Through his **Word** he instructs it and makes it strong. Our hearts are renewed every time we are fed with **Christ's body and blood.** When God's Law crushes our own heart daily and we beg for a new one we remain humble even as the Lord creates in us a pure heart and renews a right spirit within us.

"O Lord, open thou my lips, and my mouth shall show forth thy praise." This prayer uttered sincerely engenders **confidence.** We have not only a heart problem, but also what we might call a lips problem. Our lips are naturally closed.

Who here is naturally eloquent? Who here doesn't find it too easy to hesitate, to be embarrassed, to be reluctant to speak up for the Lord? To resent the grind of sermon preparation, to bypass opportunities to express what we know is God's will? We need the Lord to open our lips. He alone must do that, and he does. He brings the dead to life. The spiritually dead can't speak, but he has created in us a clean heart and restored a right spirit within us.

Then he gives us the **message** we are to speak, he gives us the **motive** to speak it, he gives us the **courage**, he gives us the **office**, the authority, the command and the promise of blessing on our words. He enables us with his gifts, different gifts for each of us. Each of us has been given some strengths; each of us has some limits. But each of us can be confident that we are gifted with strengths and weaknesses exactly as God intended.

The Lord indeed opens our lips and the result is to show forth his praise. I'm not talking here of some inane praise song where you repeat "praise the lord" fifty times – well, some of those might be fun sometimes too – but much more than that you are empowered to preach the Gospel. That's showing forth God's praise, telling the story of what God has done, preaching the incarnation at Christmas time, telling how God broke through the barrier separating human from divine and God the Son became human flesh, Jesus Christ; preaching the active obedience of Christ, telling how Christ, fully human, fulfilled every jot and tittle of God's Law on our behalf; preaching the passive obedience of Christ, telling how he subjected himself to the anger of God at our sins and suffered our punishment in our place – our sins are forgiven; preaching the resurrection of Christ, telling how God the Father put his seal of approval on the vicarious work of Christ, and assured us of eternal life; preaching sanctification, how God the Holy Spirit brought us to faith in Christ by which faith alone we are restored to God, made heirs of Heaven and empowered to live lives of value to God and to the people around us.

That's the Gospel. When God opens our lips to make that Gospel ring in the ears and hearts of our listeners we are most profoundly showing forth God's praise. Humility: create in me a clean heart O God and renew a right spirit within me! Confidence: O Lord, open thou my lips, and my mouth shall show forth thy praise.

Two verses, two attitudes. May they carry you far into many years of God pleasing ministry.

†

May 17, 2005

You're Doing OK

INI

You're doing OK. That's the message I want you to hear this morning. It's a message from God.

We Christians are well aware of our sin, shortcomings, failures. It's important for us to do that. God's Law is a vital teaching of Scripture, and it is entirely appropriate for us to hear from this place all that God expects us to do, and to not do. It is entirely appropriate that we are brought to realize again and again that we don't measure up to God's expectations and demands of us. That's entirely appropriate because when we realize our moral shortcomings fully, only then are we prepared for Christ. Only then are we ready with longing hearts to hear the sweet Gospel, and to find peace for our troubled consciences in the assurance that Jesus by his life and death did all that was needed to be done. His work has rescued us from God's anger and punishment. To prepare us for the Gospel, there is a time for us to ponder our sins.

But there is also a time for us to hear: You are doing OK. To resist that message is to deny the power of the Holy Spirit. When we are brought to faith in Jesus and taught by the Spirit to trust in him, our lives are changed; the things we can do and the things we can do together can be considered OK.

Are we too Lutheran to accept a compliment like that? Listen to this morning's assigned reading. In our survey of Bible books we've reached the two letters of St. Paul to the Thessalonians. That was a very young church. Paul spent barely three weeks there founding that church before he was forced to flee. He worried about them like a father worries about a child he has had to leave behind. But when Timothy brought news about how they were doing, Paul knew with joy that the Holy Spirit had been working among them. He wrote to tell them, Nice going – you are doing OK.

There are parallels perhaps, as well as differences between us gathered here and the Christian group at Thessalonika. When we read a passage like this, written to a group of Christians other than ourselves, we may feel an urge to compare ourselves to them, to see if we match their achievements. But this morning, as I conclude with the reading, I invite you not to compare, not to turn this very nice compliment into more law, as if the apostle is describing more standards to which we can't measure up. Rather listen as Paul, writing by God's direction, tells this group of believers, you are doing OK. Recognize that the Holy Spirit has planted the same faith in us and among us, a faith that has not lost its power to change us, as it changed them, into people to whom God can say, you may not be perfect yet, and you may have a lot of work to do – and remember: it's not anything you do but what Jesus did that saves you. Your sins are already forgiven. But, here is the message for today: For Jesus' sake, by power of the Spirit, **you are doing OK.**

Hear and be encouraged by the opening of Paul's first letter to the Thessalonians.

> Paul, Silas and Timothy, To the church of the Thessalonians in God the Father and the Lord Jesus Christ: Grace and peace to you.
>
> We always thank God for all of you, mentioning you in our prayers. We continually remember before our God and Father your work produced by faith, your labor prompted by love, and your endurance inspired by hope in our Lord Jesus Christ.
>
> For we know, brothers loved by God, that he has chosen you, because our gospel came to you not simply with words, but also with power, with the Holy Spirit and with deep conviction. You know how we lived among you for your sake. You became imitators of us and of the Lord; in spite of severe suffering, you welcomed the message with the joy given by the Holy Spirit. And so you became a model to all the believers in Macedonia and Achaia. The Lord's message rang out from you not only in Macedonia and Achaia – your faith in God has become known everywhere. Therefore we do not need to say anything about it, for they themselves report what kind of reception you gave us. They tell how you turned to God from idols to serve the living and true God, and to wait for his Son from heaven, whom he raised from the dead – Jesus, who rescues us from the coming wrath. 1 Thessalonians 1.1-10

†

June 18, 2005
For the ELS Historical Society

History Influence Purpose

INI

Scripture contains many eloquent blessings. One which seemed to me especially appropriate for opening our studies today is this one:

> May the God of peace, who through the blood of the eternal covenant brought back from the dead our Lord Jesus, that great Shepherd of the sheep, equip you with everything good for doing his will, and may he work in us what is pleasing to him, through Jesus Christ, to whom be glory for ever and ever. Amen. Hebrews 13.20-21

We will hear today of **history** – it's why this society exists. We will hear today of **influence** – it's in the program. Combine them, and the study of influence through history is fascinating. We see both in this blessing, along with a 3rd dimension: **purpose.** Let's look at each.

History: things that happened. Things that actually happened. The older you get, the more interested you are in history. Maybe it's due to the length of memory. Almost anybody can remember what happened last year, or two or three years ago. But when you remember something, and you realize it was 40 or 50 years ago, that's startling! Young people are preoccupied with **making history;** older people realize that the greater challenge is to **know history.** Somehow it seems that should be the other way around.

In any case, the writer of the blessing in these verses from Hebrews before us knew the centrality of history, for he bases his blessing on history's central event. He says, *"May the God of peace, who through the blood of the eternal covenant brought back from the dead our Lord Jesus...."* He reminds us that Christianity is a thoroughly historical religion, based on events that actually happened, chief among them the incarnation. When at Christmas the eternal God broke into time, the Ultimate Spirit took on flesh and became a human being. He did that because of another momentous historical event, the fall into sin by our first parents. Since then all history – yes, even your and my personal history – has been dotted and blotched and infected by sin.

But Jesus Christ, the great Shepherd of the sheep, **entered history at the first Christmas, satisfied God's will** by his spotless life in our place, **satisfied God's just anger** at our sins by his substitutionary death in our place. And in the historical event that turned history around he **rose from the dead on Easter.** Paul puts it most plainly: if Christ did not rise from the dead, we are still in our sins, and we are of all people most foolish. But, he quickly adds, now is Christ risen from the dead, and become the firstfruits of those that slept. 1 Corinthians 15.19

That **history**, then, brings us to **influence**. Firstfruits – Christ rose first, so that others, we, can follow so that we can become like him. The writer of the blessing before us puts it this way: *"May the God of peace, who through the blood of the eternal covenant brought back from the dead our Lord Jesus, that great Shepherd of the sheep, **equip you with everything good....**"*

Influence: it's not a word we quickly associate with the works of God. We are used to associating God with startling, awe-filled sudden changes like the conversion of the Apostle Paul, or the crossing of the Red Sea, or indeed like the Resurrection of Christ. The word "influence" seems too slow and too ordinary to be a work of God. And yet that seems to be how the Holy Spirit chooses to make the most profound changes in the lives of most of us. It's a matter of equipping us – equipping us with everything good.

We imagine an equipment manager coming in with one piece at a time. First **faith**, established by Baptism. Then a little **knowledge** here, and little **understanding** there, some heavy study and research which yields a little **wisdom**, and finally a **lifetime of growth and sanctification** all nurtured over years and years by continuous and repeated contact with Word and Sacrament.

Influence is indeed a word that captures that work of God in and for all of us.

And that brings us to **purpose**: why should we want to know and to grow, why learn history? How then should we live? The blessing puts it plainly: *"May the God of peace, who through the blood of the eternal covenant brought back from the dead our Lord Jesus, that great Shepherd of the sheep, equip you with everything good **for doing his will**, and may he work in us what is **pleasing to him**, through Jesus Christ, to **whom be glory for ever and ever.**"*

Our study today, and our enjoyment today, joins these three: history, and influence, and purpose. These three are also central to our faith:

History: Christ actually came, and died, and rose again.

Influence: the Holy Spirit over a lifetime equips us with every good thing.

Purpose: so that we can then do God's will and carry out what is pleasing to him.

Long before there were Germans or Norwegians, Christians rejoiced in how God influenced them through events in history. Let's close with these words of joy from the Psalms:

When the LORD brought captives back to Zion, we were like men restored to health.

Our mouths were filled with laughter, our tongues with songs of joy. Then it was said among the nations, "The LORD has done great things for them."

The LORD **has** done great things for us, and we are filled with joy.

Restore our fortunes, O LORD, like streams in the Negev.

Those who sow in tears will reap with songs of joy.
He who goes out weeping, carrying seed to sow, will return with songs of joy, carrying sheaves with him. Psalm 126

†

September 14, 2005

Citizens of Heaven

INI

He cursed his country. I know the words he used but won't speak them from this place. And then he said, "I wish that I may never hear of the United States again!"

By that utterance before a court of law, according to the story by Edward Elliot Hale, a young army lieutenant from Fort Adams, Philip Nolan, condemned himself to more than 50 years in exile, till his life ended. He was kept continuously aboard a ship at sea, never touching land. Those around him were under strict orders never again to let him hear the name of the United States, or even news of it. He became known as – and his story was entitled – "the man without a country."

It was a terrible sentence, to be made a citizen of nowhere. Sir Walter Scott wrote,

> Breathes there the man with soul so dead,
> Who never to himself hath said
> "This is my own, my native land!"

Philip Nolan himself, the story goes, when he died, was found clutching a Bible and a slip of paper on which were written these words: "Bury me in the sea; it has been my home, and I love it. But will not someone set up a stone for my memory at Fort Adams or at Orleans, that my disgrace may not be more than I ought to bear? Say on it: IN MEMORY OF PHILIP NOLAN LIEUTENANT IN THE ARMY OF THE UNITED STATES. He loved his country as no other man has loved her; but no man deserved less at her hands."

Citizenship – belonging to a country – is an extremely precious thing. It is coveted. Especially, we are told, U. S. citizenship is coveted by many. I myself have witnessed three naturalization ceremonies involving family and close friends. It's a time of great joy and rejoicing.

Most of us are born into our U. S. citizenship, and so we can easily take it for granted. But even so, especially on days of observance like Constitution Day which we observe here tomorrow, or the other patriotic festivals around the year, we can feel the emotion of the Lee Greenfield song,

> I'm **proud to be an American**. where at least I know I'm free,
> And I won't forget the men who died who gave that right to me.

In the Bible portion before us this morning, St. Paul says we are citizens of Heaven. That's not in opposition to our citizenship in the United States, but rather it's in opposition to belonging to the world. He says

> Many live as enemies of the cross of Christ. Their destiny is destruction, their god is their stomach, and their glory is in their shame. Their mind is on earthly things. But our citizenship is in heaven. And we eagerly await a Savior from there, the Lord Jesus Christ, who, by the power that enables him to bring everything under his control, will transform our lowly bodies so that they will be like his glorious body.
> Philippians 3.18

How did this citizenship come about? Not by natural birth. By natural birth we were aliens to God, citizens of a different country. Not just aliens, we were enemies. We were Al-Qaeda. We were Osama bin Laden. And if you are thinking, oh no, I'm not as evil as somebody who would fly airplanes into a building and kill innocent people, you are looking at yourself through your own eyes, not the eyes of God, whose standard is perfection and anything less is unholy and evil. Because of our sin and our sinfulness, which tugs on us even now, God should in his justice hunt us down in the caves from which we would try to hide from him, and destroy us. That would be just. But God is not only just, he is merciful.

Over the past four years many sons and daughters have died trying to destroy Osama bin Laden. Would you give your life, or your son's life, to **save** Osama bin Laden? That's what God did for us. He comes to us now in his Word and shows us there how in love he gave up his only begotten Son to die for us. Because Christ satisfied the justice of God on the cross in our place, God can come to us who were enemies, and say, you are now a citizen in my country. This is my gift to you, which cost me the life of my precious Son. Not by birth, but by re-birth in Baptism, you are now a citizen of heaven. Your sins are forgiven. You belong here, God says, in my beautiful country, with me.

That's a country we will belong to when we leave this one. But more than that, it's a country we belong to now. Paul did not say, we will be citizens of heaven, but we **are**. We've heard a lot about death here in chapel this week – the theme is "Keys to Hell and Death." But Paul is talking here about living – about living now, and living later, beyond a lifetime – and about living up to our citizenship. We don't want, as citizens of the United States, to do anything to disgrace our country. Certainly we don't want, as citizens of Heaven, to bring shame upon the Christian faith by anything we do. Doing that is renouncing your citizenship, as surely as Philip Nolan who cursed his country, and to his deep regret was exiled from it forever.

Think for a moment of things you will be doing in Heaven. Practice doing them here. And if there is anything you know you shouldn't be doing in Heaven, stop doing it here. Let your living here at Bethany Lutheran College be a study, a learning, a practice of your citizenship, of living in Heaven.

Last week our good friend and colleague Prof. Christopher Johnson lost his brother. That was a hard hard time. The night before the funeral, I got an email from Chris. After an information update, he added this paragraph.

> As teachers at Bethany remind your students that the one thing BLC prepares them for the most is this (and too often we all take it for granted). We all will face difficult times like this in our lives and it is during these times that we will cherish a Bethany education most, appreciate daily chapel and most of all a place where we are taught to enjoy God's wonderful creation here on earth while focusing on the ultimate goal – being with him in Heaven.

That's living as a citizen of Heaven – here for a while, but knowing where we are going, focused on living up to our citizenship, and looking forward to those unimaginable changes when God will transform this weak and corrupt body to become like Christ's heavenly body, according to the tremendous power which makes everything – sickness, natural disasters, terrorism, everything we fear including death itself – it's all subject to Christ, the very one who in utmost love gave himself so we could belong in the presence of God. Rejoice in that citizenship, and live up to it, so we can proclaim our allegiance, paraphrasing the song:

> I'm proud to be a Christian, 'cause for sure I know I'm free,
> And I won't forget the One who died to give that gift to me.

†

November 15, 2005

Sorting Left and Right

INI

What's on your mind this morning? What is the most important thing in your life right now? Making the team? Success of the play, the concert? Doing well in a class? Making a relationship work? What is it?

I'm here to tell you this morning, that whatever it is, it's of no importance. And then I'm going to tell you that whatever it is, it's of the greatest importance. Perhaps you'll understand that apparent contradiction as soon as I read the Bible verses assigned us today. Jesus is speaking.

> When the Son of Man comes in his glory, and all the angels with him, he will sit on his throne in heavenly glory. All the nations will be gathered before him, and he will separate the people one from another as a shepherd separates the sheep from the goats. He will put the sheep on his right and the goats on his left. Then the King will say to those on his right, "Come, you who are blessed by my Father; take your inheritance, the kingdom prepared for you since the creation of the world. For I was hungry and you gave me something to eat, I was thirsty and you gave me something to drink, I was a stranger and you invited me in, I needed clothes and you clothed me, I was sick and you looked after me, I was in prison and you came to visit me." Matthew 25.31-36

We read here about one of God's greatest gifts to the world. It's the gift of morality. Jesus is telling us, right and wrong matter, because there is a final accounting, a sorting day. Jesus is telling us that we live in a moral universe and that is a great gift.

Not only do right and wrong matter, they matter profoundly and overwhelmingly. Right and wrong establishes how each of us will be placed on that sorting day, and that makes right and wrong so much more important than any of our other concerns – making the team, or how well the concert goes, or doing well in class, or whether or not he or she really likes me, or whatever you had in mind a moment ago – all these are, in comparison, of no importance at all.

That becomes especially clear when we consider what it means to be sorted to the left. How we hate being dismissed by anyone, held in contempt by anyone. Here we would be dismissed and held in contempt by God, forever – forsaken by God forever, no more turning to God for help, no more holding out hope, no more trusting God, because we have from that moment on established ourselves as God's enemies forever. When we look at ourselves honestly, we recognize that this is where we belong – on the left, dismissed by God – because with each sin we have committed, with each moment of stolen wrongdoing when we think God isn't watching, with every time we go ahead and sin not caring if God **is** watching, with each thought of lust, or envy, or scorn, or selfishness – with every such moment we **are** establishing ourselves as enemies of God. If we dismiss <u>God</u> so often, shouldn't he dismiss <u>us</u>? If we show by our continuing sin that we prefer evil now, God will justly sort us with evil forever. It's what he must do, it's what he will do.

Except for his love for us. That love prompted God to prepare our rescue. It wasn't easy, nor was it cheap. It cost God what is dearest to him, the life of his own Son Jesus Christ. There on the cross, God sorted Jesus himself to the left, punished him with the tortures of hell so that he had to cry out, *"My God, why have you forsaken me."* Matthew 27.46 Instead of us the sinners who should have been dismissed, Jesus was dismissed by God in our place, so that we could be placed on the right.

Those big concerns of yours – remember them? Compared to this moment of sorting, none of these things is important at all.

But because of this moment of sorting, all of these things are of utmost importance. Look what Jesus does as he conducts this sorting. Jesus connects his judgment **then** back to what you and I do **now**. This sorting day isn't just some far off future event. It's clear from what Jesus says that what happens on **that** day relates directly to what is happening **this** day, today – to what you did this morning, and what you will do when you leave this chapel, and what you are doing right now. That makes those concerns of yours today of utmost importance. On sorting day, Jesus will look back and say to you, I remember what you did with those.

Now let's be clear. Being sorted to the right side is a gift. It's not something that we earned by these good deeds of ours that Jesus lists. We know that, not only because of what we learn elsewhere in Scripture but also because of his words here. Look closely: *"Come, you who are blessed by my Father."* That's the only cause of our being sorted to the right – God's love, grace, and blessing. *"Take your inheritance,"* he says, *"the kingdom prepared for you since the creation of the world."* – that is, long before we did any deeds, good or bad, God knew where we would be placed.

This list of deeds isn't the cause of the blessing, it's the effect of the blessing. Christian believers are the people who in joy and gratitude spend their lives in service to others, who look for, find, create opportunities to help those in need.

Should we look for opportunities to feed hungry people? Of course. To provide clothing for the needy? Certainly. To visit prisoners, look after the sick, of course. But Jesus isn't providing a list of six things to do. He is speaking in specific terms of a general spirit, a spirit that characterizes Christian believers in everything they do, a spirit of repentance, a spirit of turning away from sin toward doing good, a spirit of service, of focusing not on self but on others, especially others in need. And so you see, all those activities that seemed important to us, activities which pale in importance compared to that great sorting day, all these activities assume the greatest importance **because of** that sorting day. It's our Christian spirit in everything we do that will be recalled on that sorting day, when Jesus observes: we did it for him.

We hear often here in chapel about death. There's something in our nature that makes us cringe, reluctant to think about death – unless we have listened to God's Word. For one thing, it teaches us that we should expect not to die. We should expect to be still living when Jesus comes, when that real orange glow arises that Chaplain Moldstad spoke of a few days ago. I know, it's a conflict between statistics and God's promise. Statistically, it is probable that we will die. But Jesus said, behold I come soon, and that's why I expect not to die but to be alive when Jesus comes. Either way, that's when we will experience the first great gift of Heaven – the sorting day.

We don't usually look forward to facing judges, especially when there is a lot at stake. But this one we **can** look forward to, because we know what the judgment will be. We arrive at the sorting day wearing the sinlessness Jesus won for us. And he is the Judge. That's why we can enjoy the Scripture-based words of the Paul Manz anthem:

> Peace be to you and grace from him who freed us from our sins,
> Who loved us all and shed his blood that we might saved be.
> Rejoice in Heaven all ye that dwell therein,
> Rejoice on Earth ye saints below,
> For Christ is coming, is coming soon,
> For Christ is coming soon.
> E'en so Lord Jesus, quickly come, and night shall be no more.
> We need no light nor lamp nor sun, for Christ will be our all.

†

December 8, 2005

The Best Christmas Ever

INI

This could be the best Christmas ever!

I wanted to talk about Christmas today. Imagine how pleased I was when I saw the Scripture portion assigned for today, a beautiful Christmas text.

> But the day of the Lord will come like a thief. The heavens will disappear with a roar; the elements will be destroyed by fire, and the earth and everything in it will be laid bare. Since everything will be destroyed in this way, what kind of people ought you to be? You ought to live holy and godly lives as you look forward to the day of God and speed its coming. That day will bring about the destruction of the heavens by fire, and the elements will melt in the heat. 2 Peter 3. 10-12

Wait a minute, I hope you are thinking. This is a Christmas text? Where are the singing angels, the shepherds and wise men? the cute baby and the manger? Answer: while none of those appear in these verses, these verses put us right in the middle of all of those. Without knowing what these verses say, we don't know what Christmas is all about.

It's easy to view this as a scary text. You think Katrina or the tsunami or the Asian earthquake caused huge destruction? Certainly they did. But here we are talking about the destruction of everything, including every form of human help, protection, or rescue. There is no government agency, no group from outside the disaster area that can send help when this happens. It's the destruction of all that we know, indeed, all that is.

And it will come by complete surprise, like a thief. Certainly it won't happen while I'm here speaking to you. We wouldn't expect that at all would we? But wait – unexpected!

Yes, this could easily be viewed as a scary text. Surely one part of us will consider this scary, the part that has listened to God's rules for our lives. Whether those rules speak to us out of our own consciences or out of God's Word, they bring us face to face again and again with how we don't please God. God's rules condemn us to be part of the destruction by fire.

But the Apostle Peter tells us, even as he describes this awesome scene, that we should look forward to it – see those words there? *"As you look forward to the day."* How can we look forward to that terrible day of destruction?

Because of Christmas. Peter tells us to look forward to this day, because he is sure we know about Christmas, about how the angels sang of God's good will toward humankind, about how the shepherds and wise men recognized and responded to the most momentous event of all history between the creation of the world and the destruction of the world, that is Christmas. It's the event by which God himself, the Creator and Destroyer, entered into this world, became a human creature, lived and died and came back to life again to restore us to God's favor. Christmas assures us that for Jesus' sake our sins are forgiven, and since our sins are forgiven we will be brought through the great destruction into the new Heaven and new earth that God will make for us. Christmas assures us that we have a loving heavenly Father to whom we can pray, as Jesus our brother taught us, *"deliver us from evil."* Christmas assures us that he will indeed deliver us while all else is destroyed.

Never get tired of this talk about the end of all things that we hear frequently in church before Christmas, in this season known as Advent. It's a design to make Christmas more meaningful, more sweet, more refreshing.

Want to make Christmas especially joyful and meaningful this year? The best Christmas yet? Then spend time now getting deep inside Bible messages like this one. Let the coming destruction remind us of our sins and let the knowledge of our sins drive us to repentance – that is, to examine ourselves, **confess** our sins and **trust** in God's forgiveness won for us by Christ. Then, assured of our salvation and moved by God's gracious promise of protection through the coming destruction, we can work to become worthy of it.

As Peter says, *"Since everything will be destroyed in this way, what kind of people ought you to be? You ought to live holy and godly lives as you look forward to the day of God and speed its coming."*

Peter is saying, this looking forward to it is meant to be active. It's not just a passive longing, not a lazy waiting, but continually working on what Peter calls our *"holy and godly lives."* What are you working on today? If your feeling is "I'm OK, I'm pretty good just the way I am," you are not getting it. Look into your life. Identify some part of it where you should live a more holy, godly life, and get to work on it, asking God's help to do so.

When something happens they don't like, the kids say, Oh No! When something happens they do like, the kids say, Yessss! What will be your reflex response when Jesus comes? You don't want to be in a place where your reaction is, Oh no! You want it to be "Good, at last, thank God!"

Peter says, look forward to it, be ready for it, let God's promises so fill your life that when that day comes by total surprise your automatic reflex response will be, yesss! Because you'll know that, if it happens today, that will make this the best Christmas ever.

†

January 12, 2006

Bless the Children

INI

Enter "heroes of the Bible" into Amazon.com and you will find dozens of books out there with that phrase in the title. I didn't find any called "Jerks of the Bible," but that would make a good book.[1] In this reading assigned for this morning we have both appearing within a few sentences.

> People were bringing little children to Jesus to have him touch them, but the disciples rebuked them. When Jesus saw this, he was indignant. He said to them, "Let the little children come to me, and do not hinder them, for the kingdom of God belongs to such as these. I tell you the truth, anyone who will not receive the kingdom of God like a little child will never enter it." And he took the children in his arms, put his hands on them and blessed them. Mark 10.13-16

It's easy to spot the jerks here. Those poor disciples of Jesus, they got battered pretty much here in chapel yesterday for their awful behavior [fighting over who was greatest Luke 22.24f.] and they will again today. They just didn't get it. We have to add that, by God's grace, by the time some of them wrote down these incidents for us to read, they had caught on. And they wrote about them so that **we** would catch on.

Look what they were doing! They were keeping people away from Jesus! Moms bringing their little kids to Jesus to connect them to the Lord, and the disciples were scolding them and shooing them away! And you know what? They thought they were helping Jesus, that they were doing the Lord's work. "We've got to help the Lord," they must have thought. "He is much too busy – and by the way we are much too important – to be bothered by these women with their children. We're doing religion here, and that's man's work. Get out of here you moms and kids and stop bothering us."

But now I'm wondering if there ever was a time when I've kept someone from Jesus. Can you think of any time when you have kept someone from Jesus? We can do that in many ways – for example, by our behavior when we're with a crowd that should know Jesus but doesn't, and instead of behaving like Christians we choose to behave like they do – they look at us and they should see Jesus in us but they don't. We turn them away from Jesus.

---

[1] After I presented this, someone looked and found a book with that title – Google it.

Sometimes, like the disciples, we can do that in the belief that we are helping Jesus. When we talk about religion we can get condemning and argumentative instead of inviting and loving. That can turn people away from Jesus.

We keep people from Jesus when we are not concerned about his work. And we also turn people from Jesus when we are concerned about his work selfishly and with a what-would-God-do-without-me self-importance.

What is our Lord's response to this? We read his response to the disciples. He was "indignant." I doubt that this English word fully captures the strength of the word it translates. This is the only place in the Bible that this word is used of Jesus. We might say Jesus was very, very upset. His response reflects the enormity of wrong done by those who would prevent children from coming to Jesus. They are trying to keep children away from that which God has prepared for them at the cost of the life of his own Son.

Jesus said, "*Let those little children come to me, absolutely do not get in their way, for the kingdom of God belongs to such as these. I tell you the truth, anyone who will not receive the kingdom of God like a little child will never enter it.*"

Please don't misunderstand this. Jesus is not saying, "OK everybody, get your faith in shape now – if you want to get into God's kingdom you have to make the effort to try to have faith like a little child." That would make this passage Law, something God demands of us. But Jesus here is speaking not Law but Gospel, what God does for us. **He is describing the nature of the Kingdom of God** especially regarding **how one enters it**. Jesus is not making a demand, but simply describing what happens. This, he says, is how anybody enters the Kingdom of God – it's by believing like a little child does. No matter the circumstances. For many they enter the Kingdom of God at Baptism when a baby, when to human eyes it might seem impossible for a baby to have faith in Jesus but the Word assures us that the baby indeed does believe. Or it might be that someone enters the Kingdom of God as an adult, the most hardened skeptic after a pounding of apologetics has cleared away the intellectual garbage and debris that have prevented him from giving Jesus serious attention, and he comes face to face with the Word of God which convicts him of his lost condition, and assures him of his rescue in the blood of Jesus Christ. In every case God brings a person to a moment of simple, childlike trust and dependence on the Lord Jesus Christ. That is how you entered the Kingdom of God. That is how I entered the Kingdom of God. That is how God brings anyone into His Kingdom – through faith like that of a child.

And so we read, "*And he took the children in his arms, put his hands on them and blessed them.*"

There are two words in this reading that are written in an especially emphatic form in the original language. We've spoken of the first – Jesus was indignant. Here is the second – he blessed them. He really specially blessed them. This was not a material blessing. Here it's not even the blessing of a cure, as Jesus provided on other occasions, or anything physical, but a pure and simple, powerful spiritual blessing, a blessing of the inner life of the spirit: these children will grow as children of God. That is, they will believe. Welcome into my Kingdom, Jesus is telling them, a place of purpose in this life, blessedness for now and happiness for all eternity.

We expend a lot of effort on this campus trying hard to help you students become more sophisticated in your faith, to strive for higher levels of critical thinking and intellectual attainment. I might even claim that nobody tries harder to do that than I. The many good reasons for doing that are a subject for another time. And yet there is no doubt in my mind that the most important thing I have ever done – that God has given me the privilege of doing – is to follow his command and pour water on the head of a little baby, apply the Word of God by saying "I baptize you in the name of the Father and Son and Holy Spirit," and by doing that, bring that child into friendship with God through the work of Jesus Christ. That's the most important thing I have ever done.

Let's not forget the heroes – remember, both heroes and jerks here in a few sentences? I've never seen these heroes mentioned in any of the *Heroes of the Bible* books, but they should be there. The heroes are these moms, who persisted in bringing their children to Jesus, despite the disciples. They believed in the power and holiness that were in his touch and in his prayer. They trusted his tenderness and gentleness. Jesus' response forever consecrated, in this scene of utmost gentleness and tenderness, the act of a parent with love and faith bringing a beloved child for blessing. And the blessing is entry into the Kingdom of God.

Remember your own parents this morning, or whoever it was that brought you to Baptism, heroes of faith, and remember your own Baptism. In fact remember your Baptism every morning. It's the time when Jesus laid his hands on you, and specially blessed you. It's the time God gave you faith like that of a child and welcomed you into his Kingdom. Remembering that time, you can even now once again dismiss all your doubts and imagine yourself taken up into Jesus arms, feel on your shoulders the arms that were outstretched for you on the cross, feel on your head the hands that were pierced to pay for your sins and mine, and you can once again know his blessing: welcome into my Kingdom.

†

February 9, 2006

Working on Our Christian Life

INI

First comes anger, then embarrassment and shame, followed by realization, appreciation, and effort.

I don't know if you recognize that sequence of emotions, but I'm almost certain that you have experienced it, maybe more than several times, in your life. And it's a good sequence, not always pleasant, but biblical and God-pleasing. It's triggered when someone you know and respect whispers in your ear, notifying you of something you have done wrong. It might be as simple and innocent as a piece of spinach stuck on your front teeth, or a clothing tag sticking out behind your neck, or some other clothing malfunction. Your best friend comes to you and whispers in your ear, "Did you know you've got a bzzz." There goes the sequence.

1. **Anger**: well, why did you have to tell me that!
2. **Embarrassment and shame**: boy, I wonder how long I've looked stupid?
3. **Realization and appreciation:** yes, I should have known better and my friend is helping me.
4. **Finally effort:** I'll fix it, and never let it happen again.

I guess that's a sequence I went through when I re-read the Scripture assigned for today, and I invite you to as well. Because this is more serious than an outward appearance problem – like most of Scripture this strips away externals and gets at the center of who we are. Listen as someone we respect, the Apostle Paul (no, it's really God the Holy Spirit through the apostle), comes and whispers in our ear:

> Now you are the body of Christ, and each one of you is a part of it... But in fact God has arranged the parts in the body, every one of them, just as he wanted them to be. If they were all one part, where would the body be? As it is, there are many parts, but one body. The eye cannot say to the hand, "I don't need you!" And the head cannot say to the feet, "I don't need you!" ...*there should be no division in the body, but that its parts should have equal concern for each other.* If one part suffers, every part suffers with it; if one part is honored, every part rejoices with it. Now you are the body of Christ, and each one of you is a part of it. 1 Corinthians 12.18-21, 26-27

From the last line we know that God is teaching us here about how we deal with each other, with fellow believers. Our life here at Bethany Lutheran College, where we are a gathering of believers in Christ, is exactly what he is talking about. Now I said that when I read these words again, it started me down the sequence of emotions. Did it for you? Let's see how.

Step one: Anger: God is telling me here something he wants done, that I'm not doing so well. And when somebody tells me I'm not doing something well, that I should be doing well, I get annoyed. That's our natural reaction to hearing what God expects of us, that is, to God's Law: just get off my case! And we're angry with God. In this instance, he is talking about how we should regard one another. And I know – and don't you also? – how I fail here, how easily I get negative thoughts about others, when I should have positive thoughts. How when someone else does well I get envious, how I covet the honor someone else receives, how I put down others in order to build myself up, how I might consider others dorky or unworthy of my attention, or even hold them in contempt. And when God comes to me in His Word and says in my ear, here is the way you **should** be - *there should be no division in the body, but that its parts should have equal concern for each other* – my first natural reaction is annoyance and anger.

But next comes **step two: embarrassment and shame.** Or maybe I should better call it contrition and repentance. Because then I think, y'know he's right. I should have known better. I should have done better. But I didn't, and I have to confess it's my own fault. And it's serious. In a matter of our inner selves like this, in this matter of **who we are**, we know that flaws like these are not trivial or unimportant, but that they are offenses against God's people, they divide the body of Christ, they separate us from God, and steer us straight to hell.

Fortunately we also know more about this one who is whispering to us, and that brings us to **step three** in this four-step process: **realization and appreciation** – we know he is a friend who loves us, and who means only our good. He has proved that to us by what he has done to turn us away from our destruction, and to rescue us from these sinful inclinations and thoughts and acts – not only these but everything in our nature that would separate us from God.

Our Lord Jesus Christ lived his entire life in perfect unity and harmony with God – something we could not do. He gave his attention equally to all people, along with his concern and his very life, and God in his love transferred that merit to us. Then our Lord Jesus Christ accepted into his person all those evil inclinations of ours, together with our hurtful and offensive actions, and willingly bore the punishment for them which we deserved, in our place. Our sins are forgiven. That's how we know that when this God the Holy Spirit whispers in our ear about things that we should be and things that we should do, we know that he is a friend, who means it for our good and our happiness.

That realization leads us finally to **step four: effort.** In gratitude for all that God has done for us in love, we are moved to respond to his whisper, to work on our Christian lives. You've heard the expression "working on a marriage." If you are married, you probably know what it means – a successful marriage isn't something that just happens automatically to two lazy people. No, if it is to develop and grow the relationship takes dedication and effort – it's a joyful dedication and effort, but it's also work. The same can be said of our Christian lives. This area, which the Holy Spirit has whispered to us about in these verses, gives us a good area of our Christian lives that we can work on.

"There should be no division in the body, but its parts should have equal concern for each other." If one part suffers, every part suffers with it; if one part is honored, every part rejoices with it.

Respecting, honoring, rejoicing in others. This is a project we can work on for a while. Yes, that's something I can work on starting today, right here on the Bethany Lutheran College campus.

It's a God-pleasing sequence, these four emotional steps, one we can go through again and again, daily, as we work on our Christian lives. It starts with turning to Scripture, regularly, because it is through his Word that God the Holy Spirit whispers into our ears about how we should be. Then we should get quickly past the anger that naturally wells up in us, acknowledge in repentance that yes, we should have known to do that but we haven't, realize that the work comes from God who loves us and has sacrificed what is most precious to him in order to save us, and finally let that move us to work with dedication and effort to be better and better Christians every day.

To God Alone be the Glory.

†

April 14, 2006
At St. Paul's in North Mankato for the *Tre Ore* Service on Good Friday

Truly Finished

INI

"I am the Way, the Truth, and the Life." Jesus once said. Jesus is the Truth – that's important, for he was without sin in our place. But never was it more important that Jesus is the Truth than at the moment he said these words:

> When he had received the drink, Jesus said, "It is finished." With that, he bowed his head and gave up his spirit. John 19.30

It is finished, he said. The work for which the Son of God was prepared before the creation of the world was finished. The events that were foreseen and forecast and looked forward to by believers for centuries, for millennia, was finished. The perfect, holy life lived in the place of our stained and sin-filled lives was finished. The suffering in full payment for the sins of the world was finished.

Jesus is the Truth. It is unthinkable that Jesus lied when he said it is finished with nearly his last breath. But the importance of his words for us can be brought home to us if we consider…

What if it wasn't finished?

If it's not finished, then we have something left to do.

If it's not finished, then our salvation might not yet be won.

If it's not finished, we live our lives, and face our death, in uncertainty and fear, wondering what yet has to be done.

It would be horrible, and your life and mine would be much different if these words of Jesus were not true. But of course, they are true. Jesus doesn't lie. But oddly, many people act as if he did.

There are traditions even within Christianity that openly teach that it isn't finished. They make Jesus a liar: he said it is finished, but they teach that it really isn't. Some teach things like that it wasn't really finished on the cross, but Jesus has to be sacrificed over again, again and again, in what they call the mass. Others teach things like that it wasn't really finished on the cross, but we have to do something to complete the job Jesus left undone, like we have to live a good life, or we have to decide to invite Jesus into our hearts, or we have to do something.

It's a serious matter, teaching things that make Jesus a liar. But of course, we can do the same thing. When troubles come into our lives and worry grips us and we forget the all-enfolding love of God Jesus won for us, then we are saying, "No, Jesus, you didn't finish it, things still aren't right between God and us."

When our many sins oppress us and drive us into depression, and we doubt that God can possibly love and forgive us, then we are saying, "No, Jesus, you didn't finish it, my sins are too great for you."

When we think that we are pretty good people for going to church and being nice and preserving true doctrine, and that things **we** do earn us credit with God, then we're saying, "No, Jesus, you didn't finish it, I still have to do some things to help you out."

Our failure to trust, our lack of faith, our sinful pride, all these would make Jesus a liar when he said, "*It is finished.*" But Jesus is the Truth. he does not lie. He said it is finished, and it **is** finished. Even our sins of weakness and pride have been borne by him and wiped away. They are gone.

We can have full confidence in those words: it is finished.

A little over 120 years ago, on September 4, 1885, one of the great teachers of Lutheranism, Dr. C. F. W. Walther spoke to his students some remarkable words that fit so well here that I want to bring them to you. He spoke in German, of course, but here in an updated translation is what he said. Notice how boldly he says we can approach the Almighty God Himself, and that is because Jesus was speaking truth when he said, "It is finished." Walther said,

> Cling to that word by faith. If I do that, I can confidently meet God on the Last Day; and if he were preparing to condemn me, I could say to him: "You can not condemn me without making yourself a liar. You have invited me to place my entire confidence in your Word. I have done that, and therefore I cannot be condemned, and I know you will not do it....it is impossible that we should be sent to perdition. Here is Christ. You will have to acknowledge, O God, the ransom which your Son has given as **payment in full** for our sin and guilt." (Walther: p 347)

He said, it is finished.

That's the confidence we can have, as we live, and as we die, and as we rise again with Christ in the great resurrection. For we can face life, and face death with these words of Jesus ringing in our minds. Christ's work is done. It is finished. Our sins are gone. It is finished. Jesus' holiness is given to us. It is finished. Heaven is ours. It is finished.

Thanks be to God.

†

May 11, 2006

Help with Our Praying

INI

The comfort of the familiar is about to end. We're at a time of transition, a time of relief, of celebration, of satisfaction to be sure, but also a time of uncertainty. We are leaving a routine, leaving what we are used to, what we know we can manage, and going to situations and challenges we might not manage.

It's a good time for prayer.

We need help with our prayer. We undervalue prayer. And when we undervalue prayer, we are undervaluing God. Despite God's invitation, despite God's urging, despite God's promise to answer our prayers, we pray far too seldom. Our regular prayers such as at mealtime (though nice) are superficial, often thoughtless and tossed off, sometimes even skipped. We get really serious about prayer only when we are in trouble. We need help with prayer.

We get help with prayer. We get overwhelming help with prayer. Listen to the Apostle Paul.

> The Spirit helps us in our weakness. We do not know what we ought to pray for, but the Spirit himself intercedes for us with groans that words cannot express. And he who searches our hearts knows the mind of the Spirit, because the Spirit intercedes for the saints in accordance with God's will. And we know that in all things God works for the good of those who love him, who have been called according to his purpose. Romans 8.26-28

We sometimes ask people to help with our prayers. When in trouble, when sickness strikes, the word goes out: pray for me. We have prayers for individuals in times of trouble here in chapel. It feels good to know that someone else is joining you in praying for the same thing. Look who this portion of the Bible says is joining us in prayer: God himself, the Holy Spirit.

Just as we often undervalue prayer, we undervalue the Holy Spirit.

We hear often in church and chapel (and appropriately so) of the love of God the **Father.** His love prompted him to send his Son Jesus Christ to die as payment for our sins. We hear and think often (and appropriately so) of God the **Son**, whose love for us prompted him to leave his heavenly home, to enter this sinful world, to live and die and rise again to rescue us from sin and from death and from lives in the grip of the Devil. Jesus loves me this I know, we sang when we were children.

We undervalue the Holy Spirit. The primary work we ascribe to God the Father, creation, is done. The primary work we ascribe to God the Son, redemption, was completed when Jesus said "it is finished" on the cross. The work of the Holy Spirit goes on and on with great intensity.

God the Holy Spirit knows us, knows what we need, knows what we will face even in days of transition and uncertainty like these. And the Holy Spirit prays for us intensely. While there's no children's song that goes "The Holy Spirit Loves Me This I Know," the Holy Spirit does love us, and works earnestly and constantly for our good.

It feels good to know someone else is praying for you – grandma, parents, your sponsors, your pastor, your congregation, they all do. But also the Holy Spirit, God himself.

This is who is praying for us – the ultimate Pray-er, praying for what we really need (even though we might not know what that is), praying with supreme earnestness in expressions beyond human language that God's purpose will be fulfilled in us.

This is the confidence with which you can move into your future, whatever it is. God has promised to answer **our** prayers. Would he not answer his own? That is why the apostle can assure us, that all things work together for good to those who love God.

We are here in the final regular chapel service of school year. I want to wish you a "God be with you" as you leave Bethany, perhaps for a little while, perhaps for a long time. I want to wish you a "God the Holy Spirit be with you."

We don't spend much time here each morning. Today you might want to linger a bit before you leave. If you are a regular chapel go-er you know that the essence of Bethany Lutheran College is here in this room. And if you are like many before you, this is the part you will miss most – the chance to gather with fellow believers every day, to engage in praise and prayer, to listen to God's word, and through that word receive the blessing of God the Holy Spirit.

†

September 6, 2006

This Moral Universe

INI

How delicious is the feeling when your team wins! That's the point of the current top box office movie, *Invincible*, about a guy who raises the spirits of all of Philadelphia by helping the Eagles football team become a winner.

Even those who believe that pro sports are over-hyped can see that the highs and lows felt by many when the Vikings beat the Packers or the Packers beat the Vikings – those feelings are substantial, they mean a lot to the people who have them.

God comes to us in the first psalm and tells us **this is real**: "You are on the side of the winner." We are there because God put us there, and he urges us in this psalm to stay there, and not be lured away.

> Blessed is the man who does not walk in the counsel of the wicked or stand in the way of sinners or sit in the seat of mockers. But his delight is in the law of the LORD, and on his law he meditates day and night. He is like a tree planted by streams of water, which yields its fruit in season and whose leaf does not wither. Whatever he does prospers. Not so the wicked! They are like chaff that the wind blows away. Therefore the wicked will not stand in the judgment, nor sinners in the assembly of the righteous. For the LORD watches over the way of the righteous, but the way of the wicked will perish. Psalm 1

We would expect this very first psalm to be somehow basic and in this sense it is: it is laying out a fundamental, first principle. This psalm proclaims that we live in a moral universe, a world in which good and evil matter. The Greeks knew this over 2000 years ago, and in a few weeks we will all have a chance to enjoy a demonstration of that, as in our theatre we watch *Oedipus the King* run headlong into the moral force of the universe. We live in a world in which good and evil are real. They are not just social constructions, or products of cultural development. There is **good** and there is **evil**.

The world was made to be good, not evil. When he first created all things, God pronounced them all "very good," and that not just because things worked well (as they certainly did) but it was especially true in a moral sense. Even though corrupted by the entry of sin, nature still proclaims God's glory. Nature follows the laws God laid down in a way that glorifies God and serves his creatures. And even when nature becomes destructive, it illustrates what Paul described as nature "groaning and suffering," awaiting (just as we are) the liberation from sin that will come at the last day, when nature too will be made anew.

People of all cultures discover from experience that the world was not made to sin in, that it is easier, safer, more advantageous not to sin in a world like ours, and that sinning brings disease, hardship, and suffering to the sinner and all those around. As Dr. Dau said in his introduction to C. F. W. Walther's epic *Law and Gospel*, "Fully to suit sinners, the world would have to be made over again."[1] We live in a moral world, a world in which sin is the alien, the intruder, and (this psalm tells us) inevitably the loser.

It doesn't always look that way to us. Sin wouldn't survive very well without its companion temptation, and we may look around us and be lured. It looks sometimes like the sinners are having all the fun, getting all the money, wielding all the power, and winning all the attention and celebrity status.

The psalmist says, don't be fooled. They are chaff. The side of good is going to win and God has put us on that winning side. Notice I said God put us there. We were not there by birth. In our natural state we were on the alien, sinful side, on the path with the losers, the chaff, those on the way to perishing.

Don't try to understand what I'm about to say, because you can't. But for reasons we can attribute only to the mystery of God's love, he chose you and me, before we were born, to transfer over to the winning side. He accomplished that at great cost to himself, the cost of the life of his only and much beloved Son. Jesus was the ultimate righteous one described in this psalm. Through his moral life as the substitute for all people, through his innocent death paying for sin as the substitute for all people, through his resurrection by which he conquered sin and death once and for all, Jesus Christ shifted us from the side of evil to the side of good, from losers to winners.[2]

He put us here. And now in this psalm he encourages us, don't be lured away, don't leave. The temptations will come. You know the ones that come to you. It will look delicious to you sometimes to walk in the counsel of the wicked, or stand in the pathway of sinners, or sit in the seat of mockers. You know those temptations. Stay where you are! – for the sake of Jesus who did so much to put you where you are, delighting in the Word, continuing to enjoy the refreshing streams of spiritual water by which the Lord nourishes our inner lives, relishing the feeling – the reality of being on the winning side through the work of Jesus Christ.

†

---

[1] *The Proper Distinction between Law and Gospel*, translated by W.H.T. Dau. St. Louis: Concordia Publishing House, 1928, p. vi.

[2] Recognize that "the Man" spoken of in the first verse of this psalm is Jesus whose righteous ways were for us. We would expect this "basic" psalm to refer to Jesus, since all of the Psalms are about him. See the references to him in Psalm 2, the companion to this one.

November 6, 2006

Mercy Seat

INI

When was the last time you especially wanted God to be near you? Probably at a time of sickness or trouble. And when was the last time you pushed God away? We do both.

Some people want God to go away from them permanently. They've talked themselves into believing there is "no god." The Bible calls such people fools, and to them God will say, let it be as you wish. You are apart from me, the source of all that is good, forever.

We join these people when we push God away. When you're about to commit that sin, when you're with that crowd you hang with that makes fun of faith and you say nothing, at times like these we are telling God to go away, and we risk, at that moment, God saying, let it be as you wish; you are apart from me forever. We all do it, don't we?

But God in love will not let us go. God takes the initiative to bring us back to him. God wants us to know: God is with us. He shows us his presence. Our reading this morning describes how God did that for his Old Testament believers. It's the story of a box with a lid. The box was made of acacia wood, not very big, about 4 feet long, 2 or 3 feet high. It was covered inside and out with gold. God told the Israelites to place into the box the two tablets of stone on which were inscribed the Ten Commandments Moses brought down from the mountain of God, Sinai. This box has come to be called "**the ark of the covenant.**" Then God provided directions about how to make its lid. Imagine, from these words, how it would look.

> Make an atonement cover [Luther: "mercy seat"] of pure gold – two and a half cubits long and a cubit and a half wide. And make two cherubim [angel figures] out of hammered gold at the ends of the cover. Make one cherub on one end and the second cherub on the other; make the cherubim of one piece with the cover, at the two ends. The cherubim are to have their wings spread upward, overshadowing the cover with them. The cherubim are to face each other, looking toward the cover. Place the cover on top of the ark and put in the ark the Testimony, which I will give you. There, above the cover between the two cherubim that are over the ark of the Testimony, I will meet with you and give you all my commands for the Israelites." Exodus 25.17-22

This precious box containing God's Law with its specially designed, ornate cover was the central object in the tabernacle, the tent church used by the Israelites as they moved through the desert on their forty-year journey to the promised land. What was it for? It was a continuing reminder of God's presence. It worked in four ways:

First, it was a **sign of the covenant**, the legal agreement, what we sometimes call the "testament" between God and his people. They were to keep the laws inside that box, and God would save them. It was the "ark of the covenant."

Second, it was a **source of revelation.** Note the last words of the reading: "There, above the cover between the two cherubim that are over the ark of the Testimony, I will meet with you and give you all my commands for the Israelites." That's where Moses heard from God the words of the first five books of the Bible. God appeared in the space above the lid, between the angel wings. It was a source of revelation.

Third, it was a **guide**. When the Israelites moved their camp, the ark, covered with a skin cover and a blue cloth, was carried before them, seeking out where they should go next. It was a guide.

Fourth (and most important) it **represented redemption**, what we today call the Gospel, a cleansing from sins. In an important ceremony once a year on the festival called the Day of Atonement (Yom Kippur), the high priest would enter the room where the ark was kept, bringing the blood of a sacrificed lamb, and he would sprinkle the blood on the mercy seat, on the lid of the ark. Note well what that portrayed. Between the commandments in the box (commandments none of us have kept) and the presence of God between the angel wings – in between those two was the blood of the sacrificial lamb. The ark taught those Old Testament people the Gospel.

The box is long lost and it no longer can assure us of God's presence with us. But we have a new covenant, a new testament, a new and even better assurance of God's loving presence. We call that assurance the Means of Grace, that is, the means by which God brings his loving presence to us. And we identify them as his Word, and his Sacraments, Baptism and the Holy Supper. These do for us what the ark did for Old Testament believers. Remember its four functions? God's Word and Sacraments do for us the same thing. They are the sign of the **NEW covenant**, the new testament. They are the **Revelation** of God's plan to save us, fulfilled in the life, death, and resurrection of his Son Jesus Christ. They are a **Guide** to what we are to believe and do as we accept with gratitude the gift of salvation.

But before all that they are a **cleansing from sins**. When we were baptized, when we hear the Gospel, when we eat and drink the body and blood of our

Lord given and shed for the forgiveness of our sins, we have what they all proclaim. Our sins are forgiven, even our sin of so often pushing God away.

Is God with you? Present with us? Old Testament Christians had a beautiful sign of God's presence, the precious ark with its mercy seat cover. We of the New Testament are more blessed. We have the Means of Grace. No one is closer to God than you were in your Baptism. When you symbolically went under the water, you were joined with Jesus in his death and burial. And when you symbolically came up out of the water, you were joined with Jesus in his resurrection. Our death is over. Our life is assured. No one is closer to God than you are at the Lord's Supper, when you take into yourself by eating and drinking the very body and blood Jesus gave to pay for your sins. No one is closer to God than when you turn to his Word; it is God speaking to you, inviting you to call upon him as your dear and loving Father and teaching you that Jesus is your Good Shepherd, who knows your name.

Look forward to Christmas again this year, when we rejoice in the coming of that Baby named "Immanuel," which means, "God is with us."

†

August 15, 2007
For the Faculty Workshop opening the school year

Godlike

INI

A few years ago my exercise tape was an audiobook reading of Homer's ancient Greek epic poem, the *Odyssey*. I noticed how often the poet describes a character as "like a god." Usually it described physical appearance, "looking like a god," and it was one of highest compliments, reserved for the best. Homer wasn't hesitant to call someone godlike. Is there anyone you know you would describe as "like God"? As much respect as I have for all of you here, there is nobody I'd apply that to, would you? Yet we are called on in Scripture to be like God, especially to be like Jesus Christ. Listen to Jesus' words:

> Jesus called them together and said, "You know that the rulers of the Gentiles lord it over them, and their high officials exercise authority over them. Not so with you. Instead, whoever wants to become great among you must be your servant, and whoever wants to be first must be your slave – just as the Son of Man did not come to be served, but to serve, and to give his life as a ransom for many." Matthew 20.25f.

Today we start to focus formally on the shape of our service for this coming school year. We just heard Jesus' words: our service should be like his. You are committed to service. I'm confident that everyone who works at Bethany is committed to serve our Lord Jesus by serving students. I hope this Word of God can strengthen and deepen that commitment as the school year opens.

Begin by taking stock of our service here. I said a moment ago: it's pretty good, right? But Christians know that even our attempts at serving others are deeply flawed. God's prophet says his own attempts to do good are filthy rags. Isaiah 64.6 Consider. Too easily impatient with students? Too frequently annoyed with fellow workers? Lapses in worship, laziness in Bible study, forgetfulness in prayer, few prayers of thanksgiving, few prayers asking for help for students, for fellow workers, for ourselves?

Now it's true, we may not be as bad as others. Our faculty politics, jealousies, and resentments are not as bad as they might be at other schools. Bethany is a good place to be. But our reading does not say we should be better than St. Olaf or MSU. The standard we are to measure up to is to **be like Jesus,** and when we measure all we do against that requirement we realize how unworthy we are to be blessed with the opportunity to do the Lord's work here at Bethany.

Yet purely out of his grace, God chose you and me to serve him by serving students at BLC. More than that, he **enables** us to serve him. It starts with Jesus serving us. Hear our reading: "*He did not come to be served, but to serve, to give his life a ransom for many (that is. for us).*" With that ransom paid on the cross, Jesus covered our sin with his righteousness like a nice long clean shirt. Now God, for Jesus' sake, looks as us standing in that shirt and sees not our weakness and flaws in service but he counts it as precious and valuable service.

Still more: our service is **guided** by Jesus' service. Again our reading: "*Whoever wants to become great among you must be your servant, and whoever wants to be first must be your slave– just as the Son of Man did not come to be served, but to serve.*" Jesus' model becomes our path of life and Jesus' spirit empowers our feet down that path like lively shoes to take us where he wants us to go.

Well, if the robe of righteousness is like a long shirt covering our sin and weaknesses and if Jesus' Spirit is like lively shoes carrying us down his path, then we can truly state the theological version of that often-seen sign: "no shirt, no shoes, no service." We'll reverse that. We **are** covered with the shirt of Jesus' righteousness and we **are** propelled with the shoes of his Spirit, so we can and do serve. We **can** muster extra patience for a needy student, we can support and uplift a stressed fellow worker, we can be faithfully in chapel, and regular in personal Bible study, we can pray often for staff, for students, for Bethany, we can forgive quickly those who sin against us and we can study to make Jesus our model in all we do. All this we can do because Jesus is at the center of our service, in our minds, in all our activities, especially in our study of his Word. We can know him better and find in that Word the shirt and the shoes so our service becomes more and more like his service and we become, with his power and at his urging, more like God.

†

September 12, 2007

Adventures in Evangelism

INI

Take a deep breath – now quietly in your head say "Thank you God for that breath." Have you ever thanked God before for a breath? Look at your hands – wonderful tools. Have you ever thanked God for your hands? Do it now. And then thank God for the gift of language that enables you to say thank you. These are all simple everyday things, that we take for granted. But these and many other things that contribute to our happiness are of course gifts to us from the living and loving God.

St. Paul made that point in our reading for today. I have to give you some background to this reading, which we can call "adventures in evangelism" or "you never know what will happen when you are out there teaching about Jesus." Paul and Barnabas had gone out on their first missionary trip and they came to a little village in Asia Minor, present day Turkey, named Lystra. There Paul healed a man who had never walked because of a birth defect. When the villagers saw that, they went wild. They thought their Greek gods had come to them in human form. Since Paul spoke the most, they started calling him Hermes, the messenger, and Barnabas they called Zeus. The priest of Zeus in a nearby temple ran out some bulls and started to offer them as sacrifices to Paul and Barnabas. That brings us to this reading:

> But when the apostles Barnabas and Paul heard of this, they tore their clothes and rushed out into the crowd, shouting: "Men, why are you doing this? We too are only men, human like you. We are bringing you good news, telling you to turn from these worthless things to the living God, who made heaven and earth and sea and everything in them. In the past, he let all nations go their own way. Yet he has not left himself without testimony: He has shown kindness by giving you rain from heaven and crops in their seasons; he provides you with plenty of food and fills your hearts with joy." Even with these words, they had difficulty keeping the crowd from sacrificing to them. Acts 14:14-18

What an odd situation! And what a strong reaction by the apostles! No modern-day talk here about "My how quaint these religious customs are but we have to accept them, after all we are all going to the same place so it's OK, we're all worshiping the same god only in different ways." There is none of that from the Apostles. They tore their clothes, rushed into crowd shouting, "Stop this! Turn from worthless things to the living God!" Notice the basic contrast: worthless things/ living God. Anything that does not honor the true and living God – that is the triune God that Paul represented, Father, Son

Jesus Christ, and Holy Spirit - any worship, indeed any activity that does not honor the living God is a **worthless thing**.

Why should the whole focus of our lives be on this living God? Because, Paul says, the true and living God created everything and continues to bless you and me with his kindness, giving us rain, and crops, and food – and we might add language and hands and breath, all the ordinary things we take for granted that can fill our hearts with joy and happiness.

The kindness of God upon everyone – these are signs of God's love. They are love letters to us from God. Paul didn't have a chance on this occasion even to get to the part about Jesus. Sadly, the crowd at Lystra didn't let him. But happily you and I know about Jesus who is the ultimate gift and sign of God's love, who cements our happiness with the forgiveness of our sins, restoration of friendship with God and the assurance of God's love and help for us in every situation. That means we can turn from all those worthless things around us that are empty of God and make everything we do **a tribute of thanks to the living God.**

> Make your **next breath** a tribute of thanks to God.
>
> Make the next **work of your hands**...
>
> Make the **next assignment** you hand in...
>
> Make your **sports** or **music** or **speech** or **theatre performance**...
>
> Make your **Saturday night plans**...
>
> Yes, even make your **difficulties**, **troubles**, and **challenges** a tribute of thanks to God who has assured us that he is with us in all of them.

That's how we can turn from worthless things to the living God. For all he has done, let us thank God through everything we do. We pray:

Almighty God, merciful Father, you open your hand and satisfy the desire of every living thing. We give you most humble and hearty thanks that you have crowned the fields with your blessing and are permitting us once more to gather in the fruits of the earth and have heaped this harvest atop many other precious gifts that we enjoy every day. We ask you to bless and protect the living seed of your Word sown in our hearts, that in the abundant fruits of righteousness we may always present to you an acceptable thank-offering in all we do; through Jesus Christ, your Son, our Lord, who **lives**![1] – and reigns with you and the Holy Spirit, one true God, now and forever. Amen

†

---

[1] I emphasized to seminary students the importance of using vocal emphasis to proclaim the resurrection in this often-used portion of our worship. Some still do. Most do not.

September 2007

Remember: We Are Creatures

INI

Going to sleep well tonight? Been sleeping well lately? Thankfully, I have, but around the anniversary of 9/11 I sometimes still wake up with those images in my head that we saw over and over on television – you know which ones I mean. When that happens, my first morning thought is hope that it was only a nightmare, followed by the sinking realization that it wasn't.

Maybe with the psalmist, we need to be reminded that we are creatures.

Why can that help? Well, when we look outward at God's creation – the beauties of nature and the wonders of the heavens at night – we are easily filled with awe at God's power. But when we look inward at God's creation of ourselves, we not only sense God's power, but also his care. Let's see that again in words of the psalmist David:

> For you created my inmost being; you knit me together in my mother's womb. I praise you because I am fearfully and wonderfully made; your works are wonderful, I know that full well. My frame was not hidden from you when I was made in the secret place. When I was woven together in the depths of the earth, your eyes saw my unformed body. All the days ordained for me were written in your book before one of them came to be. How precious to me are your thoughts, O God! How vast is the sum of them! Were I to count them, they would outnumber the grains of sand. When I awake, I am still with you. Psalm 139. 13-18

This is David's celebration – let's make it ours! This is David's celebration of being a creature – a creature of God. What does it mean to be a creature? It means wonder, and it means comfort.

Hear the wonder in David's perceptions – wonder at God's skill, wonder at God's knowledge, wonder at God's wisdom. God knows how to make a self – think of all that's involved in that, in **your** self. God made it! God knows how to make a body. Here I wish I were my son,[1] with his intimate knowledge of the wonders of the human body. I certainly don't know human biology or physiology or anatomy like he does, and probably you don't either. But neither did David, and still he was filled with wonder as he considered his body and his self as creatures of God, and we share that wonder.

---

[1] Dr. Matthew Kuster, Professor of Biology and Exercise Science, teaches Human Physiology and Gross Anatomy at Bethany Lutheran College.

But knowing we are God's creatures doesn't just fill us with wonder. It also fills us with comfort, comfort in God's care. David looks at God's deeds and his thoughts and finds them very personal to him. These deeds of God are not impersonal, like the creation of some distant star (marvelous as that is). But God knew intimately what was going on in that hidden place, as you and I first came into being inside our mother. And even at that time, before I was born, David observes, God knew what would happen every day of my life. That's not just knowledge – it's care.

David acclaims the many thoughts of God, too vast in number for any of us to comprehend them all. Certainly among those celebrated thoughts of God was the Gospel that David knew, the promise of the Savior that would come from his own descendants. We, looking back, know the Savior even more perfectly, and are able to see him, Jesus Christ, as the surest pledge of God's love and care. Through Jesus' work, we have the certain assurance that our sins are forgiven.

The God who in wisdom and power made us so wonderfully has even more wonderfully arranged for our eternal care by sending the Savior, a divine Friend and Brother, a Substitute before God in our deserved punishment, a Champion who overcame death and the grave by bursting out on Easter morning, and One who then comes to us with the gentle invitation: cling to me and I will bring you through both life and death.

It helps from time to time to look inward, to see ourselves as God's own creatures, to feel the wonder, and enjoy the comfort.

Then, no matter how troubled our sleep by horrible events, we can say with the psalmist to God our Creator and our Savior, whether it be on another morning in our life, or on the morning after death, *"When I awake, I am still with you."*

†

October 9, 2007

Dinner with Sinners

INI

Nobody likes to be scolded. And once we're past a certain age, as you and I are, we don't expect to be rebuked like a child.

I'm embarrassed to tell you the latest time it happened to me. It was just a couple of weeks ago in a town about 30 miles to the west of here which will remain unnamed. I was hauling some yard waste – grass clippings – to the compost site. As I drove in through the gate the site watchman yelled at me. I stopped and he came to my window and started to scold. It seems I hadn't stopped for the stop sign behind the gate. As he yipped at me I thought, who are you to talk to me like that, you 40-cents-an-hour dumpsite janitor? I'm a semi-dignified college professor with advanced degrees. And besides the sign wasn't there the last time I came, and it's over there half-hidden behind the shed so how can you expect...?!

See, I'm still not quite over it!

But I was soon ashamed of my anger. I was wrong, the stop sign was there and I missed it. But the bad feeling from being scolded stayed a while.

Jesus scolded – he issued a sharp rebuke in our reading.

> As Jesus went on from there, he saw a man named Matthew sitting at the tax collector's booth. "Follow me," he told him, and Matthew got up and followed him. While Jesus was having dinner at Matthew's house, many tax collectors and "sinners" came and ate with him and his disciples. When the Pharisees saw this, they asked his disciples, "Why does your teacher eat with tax collectors and 'sinners'?" On hearing this, Jesus said, "It is not the healthy who need a doctor, but the sick. But go and learn what this means: 'I desire mercy, not sacrifice.' For I have not come to call the righteous, but sinners to repentance." Matthew 9.12-13

You know the characters here. The Pharisees were the self-righteous church people who knew their Old Testament Bibles down to the letter, and thought they were observing every one of them. The tax collectors were the despised collaborators with the occupying Roman army, their cheating and exploitation well known. Jesus sat down and ate dinner with these so-called sinners. And the Pharisees thought, look at that, he's condoning their sin.

Jesus' reply is a sharp rebuke. "Go learn what this means," he said, and he quoted a Bible passage. Wow! That was like someone telling Albert Einstein, you are so wrong, don't talk to me till you go and review your arithmetic! "Go learn what this means," he said, and he quoted a passage from the Old Testament prophet Hosea, *"For I desire mercy, not sacrifice."* Hosea 6.6 And then he added, *"For I have not come to call the righteous, but sinners to repentance."*

In this episode, which side do we more identify with? Would you rather be standing with the Pharisees, or sitting with the sinners? If we don't identify more with the tax collectors than the church leaders, we haven't been paying attention to our Bibles which teach us clearly that we are sinners. We don't measure up to what God expects and demands of us.

Jesus reaches out to sinners. He has a love for sinners, and a passion to reach out to them. Don't imagine it was only to those **we** might consider "deserving" sinners. He loves and reaches out to dirty rotten undeserving sinners like us. He tells the Pharisees (and us), that's what he came to do. It's based on a timeless principle about God: He prefers mercy to sacrifice.

You see, sacrifice involves rituals, it's what **we** do. Mercy (undeserved love) is what God shows to sinners, to us, and it's what God wants us to reflect to sinners around us. We do value our rituals, our liturgies, our worship. They are precious and beautiful. But if we do them self-righteously, without love – St. Paul says if we speak with the tongues of angels, without love it's nothing. 1 Corinthians 13.1 If our faith is not translated into how we deal with others, into how we reach out to sinners, it's nothing.

Reaching out to sinners: we don't have to look hard for them. There might be some in this very room. Each of us should know of one really bad sinner in this room. No don't point down the row, that's not the idea here. This room is full of undeserving sinners. There are more elsewhere on this campus, and still more stand at the edge of our campus from time to time.[1] With whom do we most identify? Do we still identify with the undeserving sinners?

It's easier not to. It is easier to gather behind our fobbed doors and talk with each other about how right we are on that issue. Don't misunderstand: we are with God's Word on that issue. But as Paul teaches and Jesus shows us here, without love being right means nothing.

I have to ask myself: do I love undeserving sinners? Do I love them as Jesus loves them? Do I love them as Jesus loves me? Do I have the inclination to reach out to sinners? Do I have the burning desire that Jesus had to reach out to them? Do I have a plan to reach out to them? If we have no plan or

---

[1] This was shortly after the time when "Soul Force," the crusading gay rights group, had picketed our campus. That's the time all of our campus buildings were equipped with new door locks accessible with "fobs."

inclination to reach out to sinners, Jesus might say to us, *"Go learn what this means...."*

I'll accept Jesus' rebuke, as I hope you will too. We should accept a rebuke every day as we examine ourselves against God's law. Jesus' rebuke is, as with all he does, a loving one, one we should accept not with anger or shame, but with repentance, and a determination to do better, moved by the assurance that Jesus eats with sinners. More than that. he lifts our sins from us, puts them on his own back, and carries them to the cross where, through his intense suffering and death, he makes them disappear forever. By doing that, he qualifies us to join that heavenly banquet, where we will sit with Jesus.

Out of gratitude, let's try to help assure that every sinner we know, and that we know of, will also be there.

†

March 30, 2008
At Peace Lutheran Church, North Mankato

Giving Away the Ending

See April 4, 2001 We Know the Ending

INI

Last week Pastor Kerkow did something that usually annoys me very much. But when he did it, far from being annoyed, I was very grateful. We'll talk about that in a moment; first, let's turn to the portion of Scripture we will consider together this morning:

> Where, O death, is your victory? Where, O death, is your sting? The sting of death is sin, and the power of sin is the law. But thanks be to God! He gives us the victory through our Lord Jesus Christ. Therefore, my dear brothers, stand firm. Let nothing move you. Always give yourselves fully to the work of the Lord, because you know that your labor in the Lord is not in vain. 1 Corinthians 15.55-58

The thought I want to impress on you this morning, is that **the ending makes all the difference.** It makes all the difference in how we face death. It makes all the difference in how we face life.

This is a great season for basketball fans. You know that, if you are one. You've had some exciting moments because of some very close endings. The endings make the game great. My sister and brother-in-law are fervent Wisconsin Badger fans. A Badger tournament game was scheduled to start at the same time as a holy week church service. They set their VCR, went to church, and on the way home were careful not to listen to the radio or in any other way find out how the game had ended. They wanted to watch it on tape as if it were live. They didn't want to know the ending in advance.

Don't you hate it when somebody gives away the ending? There's a movie you want to see, the ads say you'll never guess the twist at end. Then before you go somebody tells you. You're reading a book, really caught up in it. Then somebody says "Oh, you're reading that book, did you get to the part where..." and they tell you ending! The Lord warns us against temptation to murder, but it might almost be justified at times like that. We don't want to know the ending.

But that's not the case when it comes to the ending of life. When life is at stake, it becomes anguish not knowing the ending. I can remember twice in my life I've had to get into a car after hearing of an emergency involving someone I love, and drive for hours – out of contact – to the scene, not knowing whether, when I got there, my loved one would be dead or alive. That's not fun. When it's not pretending, not a game, then not knowing the ending can be anguish.

And what if it's not just life, but eternity at stake? What an underlying disquiet we would feel all through our lives if we didn't know where we would spend eternity. Do you know where that suspense comes from, that anguish of wondering and fearing what the ending will be? That **fear of death**? It comes from the Law of God, God's rules for our lives, what God expects of us. The power of the Law lies in its ability to threaten us, to convict us, to show us the many ways we've fallen short of what God requires of us. That anguish can gnaw at us, sometimes deep inside but sometimes dominating our consciousness when we are honest with ourselves and realize that when we die, when we face God in judgment, fallen far short of the holiness he demands, our eternity would be nothing but loss, and loss, and loss.

Our reading says it plainly: "The sting of death is sin, and the power of sin is the law." But then it goes on immediately to say, "But thanks be to God! He gives us the victory through our Lord Jesus Christ." You see, there was Easter, the day God gave away the ending. That's what Pastor Kerkow did last week on Easter Sunday, something that usually annoys me. He gave away the ending – of our lives, and what a pleasure it was to hear it! He was (as always) bringing us a message from God. On Easter God said, want to know how it ends, how your life ends? I'll show you, in advance, so you don't have to worry about it, so you don't have to travel your life in anguish wondering and fearing. Here's the ending: Jesus rose from the dead, just as you will. You will rise from the dead, just as Jesus did.

How does that work? How does Jesus' resurrection from the dead become ours? Well, *The sting of death is sin, and the power of sin is the law.* That's the Law Jesus fulfilled perfectly for us, never breaking it, always obeying it. Then he died on Good Friday, not for his own sin (he had none) but for ours, paying to God the punishment we owed. When God the Father raised him up on Easter, that was his seal of approval on Jesus' work. **It is enough – sins are paid for – all of them!** The Law can't condemn us anymore. God's rules are no longer a factor in determining our eternal future. The Law has no power over us. And when the Law loses its power over us, death loses its sting.

We know our future – not loss, but victory. **The ending makes all the difference.**

We've seen how it makes all the difference in **how we face death** because what we know as death is just the doorway to eternal life. But the ending also makes all the difference in **how we face life.**

If you have ever participated in serious sports you know that the ending of the game makes all the difference. It might have been a rough and bruising game but if you won, you can look back on it all with pleasure. Even the bumps and bruises can feel good if they were a part of what led to victory.

Life of course is much more than a game but it too can certainly be rough and bruising at times. There are good times, to be sure, times of happiness and contentment for which we are thankful. But then there is sickness, fear of sickness, accidents, fear of accidents, relationship problems, failures, struggle with sin, bumps and bruises, and like in a game, there is a clock that runs out.

But we know the ending. It's victory. It's rising with Christ. And when we look back on all the bumps and bruises we can say, well that wasn't fun. I wish this or that hadn't happened. But they were the pathway to the ending. They kept us close to Jesus in faith and when some day we look back we will know that even the bumps and bruises can feel good when they were part of what led to victory. That's why the apostle urges us, in our reading,

> Therefore, my dear ones, stand firm. Let nothing move you. Always give yourselves fully to the work of the Lord, because you know that your labor in the Lord is not in vain.

That's how Easter makes all the difference in how we face life. The joy of Easter in which we are still basking afresh comes precisely from this: Easter tells us the ending in advance. It tells us how your life and mine is going to turn out. It's not going to be ultimate defeat and death and grave. Because of Jesus Christ and his good life which substitutes for ours, his sin payment which substitutes for ours, and his resurrection which is a model for ours the ending is going to be victory. And the ending makes all the difference. So I was grateful for the pastor's message last week even though he gave away the ending. In fact, it was **because** he gave away the ending.

Let me join him. Permit me once more to let God's Word say it plainly and clearly in a passage that, when I conducted funerals, was my favorite part. It might sound odd to hear about a favorite part of a funeral but a Christian can have one. For me it was the moment when I could stand at the graveside – you've all been at one of those, haven't you? – and read aloud these words of God penned by the apostle Paul which contain today's reading:

> Listen, I tell you a mystery: We will not all sleep, but we will all be changed – in a flash, in the twinkling of an eye, at the last trumpet. For the trumpet will sound, the dead will be raised imperishable, and we will be changed. For the perishable must clothe itself with the imperishable, and the mortal with immortality. When the perishable has

been clothed with the imperishable, and the mortal with immortality, then the saying that is written will come true: "Death has been swallowed up in victory." Where, O death, is your sting? Where, O grave, is your victory? The sting of death is sin, and the power of sin is the law. But thanks be to God! He gives us the victory through our Lord Jesus Christ. Therefore, my dear ones, stand firm. Let nothing move you. Always give yourselves fully to the work of the Lord, because you know that your labor in the Lord is not in vain. 1 Corinthians 15.51-58

If you are one of those who doesn't want to know the ending in advance, I apologize. I just gave it away again, your ending and mine. And remember: the ending makes all the difference.

†

April 2008

Like Mike

INI

Ever want to "be like Mike"?

You'll remember the ad campaign of a few years ago in which kids said they wanted to be like Mike, that is, of course, Michael Jordan, the greatest basketball player of all time. Usually being "like Mike" involved buying some merchandise, so you could have the same brand of shoes, or breakfast cereal, or whatever Mike was endorsing.

But what if I were to order you this morning to **be like Mike?** Go out and get on a professional basketball team, become the NBA league Most Valuable Player five times, go ahead and lead your team to an NBA championship 6 times, be the MVP of the playoffs all 6 of those times, and set all those other records too. Go ahead, be like Mike! There aren't very many people in this room who can say, OK I'll do that. We might say I'm pretty hot at intramurals or noon ball,[1] but like Mike? We'd have to say, impossible, I can't do that.

In our Bible reading for today, we are told to **be like Jesus.** Who can do that?

> Let this mind be in you which was also in Christ Jesus, who, being in the form of God, did not consider it robbery to be equal with God, but made himself of no reputation, taking the form of a bondservant, and coming in the likeness of men. And being found in appearance as a man, he humbled himself and became obedient to the point to death, even the death of the cross. Philippians 2. 5-8

You frequently hear sins listed in this chapel, sins we are warned against, sins we are rebuked for. That's good, we need those reminders from God. But these verses remind us that sins go deeper than just a list of things we shouldn't do, like don't steal, lie, or kill. Sin isn't just what we do, it's how we naturally are. The Apostle is reminding us here about a general attitude problem that comes from who we are. The first verse of the reading, in the NIV translation, says, "Your attitude should be the same as that of Christ Jesus." What's he talking about?

Look back two verses before our reading, where it says, "*Do nothing out of selfish ambition or vain conceit, but in humility consider others better than yourselves.*" That's the attitude problem St. Paul is addressing, and it gives us a chance to check ourselves. How's our attitude on these things? Selfish

---

[1] Many faculty and staff members got exercise by meeting in the gym over lunch to play basketball. It was rumored to get pretty rough at times.

ambition? Vain conceit? Isn't that the way we naturally are? Isn't it just natural for us to look out for ourselves first? Isn't it just natural for us to think we're pretty good? Isn't it just natural for us to think other people – at least some of them – aren't as good or as valuable as we are? That's the way we are, right? It's natural.

And it's sin. Jesus wasn't that way.

Is Paul saying it's a sin to not be like Jesus Christ? After all, he was perfect, even in his attitude. How can we be perfect? Even though it's impossible, does God demand that we be like Christ?

Yes. And if we're not as perfect as Christ, does that mean we are doomed to hell for all eternity? **That's exactly right.**

So let's get perfect, like Christ. OK? Well, that's even harder than being like Mike. There's only one way that we can be that perfect, and that is to accept the Gift. And the Gift is... all the perfection of Christ's holy life, given to us, credited to us as a free present from God's grace.

Look at the Bible verses before us. Jesus Christ is God, it says. The claim of being equal with God was not something beyond his right. But he chose to become a creature – not just a holy creature, but a lowly one, like a slave, a creature that would die. And not just an ordinary death, but the most **humiliating** and **excruciating** – the word excruciating comes from the experience on the cross – the most excruciating form of death men have ever devised.

Why?

Because he believed that you are more important than he. Think of it – Jesus Christ, God's only Son, believed that your life was more valuable than his. So he laid his down, so that you could have the life he wanted for you.

That's the attitude that Jesus had. That's the attitude that God now sees when he looks at you. All of Christ's holiness has been transferred to you when you simply believe that it's true. You don't face hell anymore. His death paid for all your sins, and his holiness is transferred to you. You inherit Heaven.

Now, after that, how can you not? How can we not respond to the Apostle's urging and try to live up to what Jesus has sacrificed so much to make us. Can you catch yourself? Next time your nature tells you to look down on someone, next time you feel the impulse to make fun of someone, next time **self** importance reasserts itself, next time old grudges come up and we despise someone, next time those natural attitudes re-emerge, **there is Jesus who left heaven and went to the cross for us.**

Be like Jesus.   †

April 2008

Toughest Exam

INI

What's the toughest exam you ever took? Was it recent? Do you remember awful exams for a long time? They are probably not a pleasant memory. Tough can mean two things. It can mean there is a lot at stake – maybe a final and your course grade depends on it, or maybe it's an entrance exam and an important part of your future depends on it. There's a lot at stake.

Tough can also mean it was so challenging, so much of it was beyond you that there's a good chance you failed it. Maybe it wasn't a mind exam, but a physical one, an exam by a doctor, looking for something wrong. In that case tough means the same two things: there is a lot at stake, maybe your life, and there's a good chance you'll not pass. They wouldn't be looking if they didn't think something is wrong. But add to that: it'll probably hurt because doctors come at you with needles and things.

Let's move one step more: what if it's not needles but a sword, and not a mental or physical exam, but a spiritual one? Now there's really a lot at stake! What's at stake is your relationship with God, your life not only now but for all eternity. This exam will be really really painful because this examining sword will invade you, penetrate to the core of who you really are – not your body (that's external), but your spirit, your soul, and poke and carve and pry to uncover every sin, every wrong deed, every shameful act, and every flicker of a sinful thought. It will open everything up and bring it all out into light for everyone to see. And worst of all you know that this spiritual exam you **will** fail!

Tonight I'll read to you four verses from the Bible. Here are the first two:

> For the word of God is living and active. Sharper than any double-edged sword, it penetrates even to dividing soul and spirit, joints and marrow; it judges the thoughts and attitudes of the heart. Nothing in all creation is hidden from God's sight. Everything is uncovered and laid bare before the eyes of him to whom we must give account. Hebrews 4.12-13

Are you ready for that exam? What's at stake is everything that really matters to you for all eternity. Can you imagine how it will hurt when all your sins are laid out in open? And can you think otherwise than that you will fail it? The examination instrument is the Word of God, and the standards against which we are measured are God's own standards. To pass this exam requires not just trying hard, not just being as good as we can. Passing this spiritual exam requires us to be as sinless and righteous as God!

But I haven't finished reading the Scripture verses before us this evening.

There are four verses, I've read only two. It goes on, and it goes on remarkably. In the very next verses, the Bible writer says (and it might surprise us to read it) that since this tough spiritual exam is coming we should approach God with what? with confidence and joy! Listen!

> Therefore, since we have a great high priest who has gone through the heavens, Jesus the Son of God, let us hold firmly to the faith we profess. For we do not have a high priest who is unable to sympathize with our weaknesses, but we have one who has been tempted in every way, just as we are - yet was without sin. Let us then approach the throne of grace with confidence, so that we may receive mercy and find grace to help us in our time of need. Hebrews 4.14-15

Did you get that!! It's as if God is proceeding with this spiritual exam, thinking no-one is going to be able to pass it but Jesus steps up to God and says: Look! Somebody did it. I did it, Jesus says. I passed the test!

And so he did. He lived just like everyone else, tempted by all the same temptations but overcame them all and remained without sin. He fulfilled all the obligations God laid on us including the most profound, to love. He fulfilled that obligation with the most profound act of love, giving his life for us on the cross of Calvary. Jesus can say to God, "I passed this test, I did it and what's more, **they** did it too." Jesus is saying, "We've gone to them with the Word, we've gone to them with Baptism, and it has brought them to faith, to believe and trust in me. By that faith, they have put on what I did and now" (it's as if Jesus says to the Father) "you look at them (who believe in me) as if you were looking at me. What I did, they did; what I am, they are too."

How can we approach God's throne with confidence? Can we submit to the spiritual exam without fear, but with joy? Imagine approaching this exam with what Jesus has: Jesus the Son of God has God's love and total devotion and commitment, and so do we. Jesus the Son of God has his own sinlessness, the righteousness of God! And so do we. What does it take to pass this spiritual exam? Does it take sinlessness and the righteousness of God? **We have that!** It was given to us by Jesus. **We will pass** the test – we can't fail. That's why we can (as the writer says) *approach the throne of grace with confidence, so that we may receive mercy and find grace to help us in our time of need.*

†

June 2008

An Invitation to Rest

INI

We got another wedding invitation the other day – have you? An invitation to a wedding always promises a good time – for those yet unmarried, perhaps a dream of their own to come. For those long married, a precious reminder of their own special day. You might get other invitations from time to time: to dinner, perhaps or an invitation to apply for a job, for young people maybe an invitation to attend a college, especially valued when accompanied by a scholarship offer. All invitations have this in common: they show that someone values your presence and wants your company.

It's usually best not to tell people about invitations we have received; they may not have gotten one and they'd feel left out. But this morning we have an invitation we can mention anywhere, everywhere. Listen:

> At that time Jesus said, "I praise you, Father, Lord of heaven and earth, because you have hidden these things from the wise and learned and revealed them to little children. Yes, Father, for this was your good pleasure. All things have been committed to me by my Father. No one knows the Son except the Father, and no one knows the Father except the Son and those to whom the Son chooses to reveal him. Come to me, all you who are weary and burdened, and I will give you rest. Take my yoke upon you and learn from me, for I am gentle and humble in heart, and you will find rest for your souls. For my yoke is easy and my burden is light." Matthew 11.25-30

May I bring you today, in his name, our Lord's invitation to rest.

It's important to note first of all who is issuing this invitation and for whom he intends it; it's an invitation from a powerful Savior to children.

And then it's important to note secondly, what the invitation asks us to do; it's an invitation to exercise our faith, that is, to rest.

To whom is this invitation extended? Is it for us? For you? for me? Jesus says, *"I praise you, Father, Lord of heaven and earth, because you have hidden these things from the wise and learned and revealed them to little children. Yes, Father, for this was your good pleasure."*

When you heard these words did you find it remarkable – Luther did – that Jesus expressed praise for two things: that the Father had **hidden** these things from some, and that the Father had **revealed** these things to others.

Are there some for whom the invitation is **not** intended? It's not, Jesus says, for the *"wise and learned."* Luther says it's referring to "those wise in their own conceit." Conceit means having a high opinion of your own qualities or abilities, especially one that is not justified; it involves self-importance, pride, and arrogance. These words describe plenty of people in religious circles. I think of British biologist Richard Dawkins who wrote the book named *The God Delusion,* an argument for atheism that has been on the best-seller lists for months and has sold 1.5 million copies in 31 different languages. I think too about the anti-God factions in the scientific community who go absolutely crazy in their attacks on any suggestion that God exists and has created the universe. It's easy to understand why God would be angry and withhold his gracious message from arrogant people like this.

And then I think of myself. I'm worse. If you or I ever think we're better than those guys, that we deserve something from God because we're not that bad, then we are not yet one of the children. Conceit – having a high opinion of one's own qualities – is that me, before God? Is it you? Do we have **any** reason to regard our own qualities as worthy before God?

Not if we have heard and heeded God's Law. God has brought us face to face with the mirror of his law and shown us our true natural condition, prompting us sincerely to say with the psalmist, *"There is no soundness in me for thine anger, nor any rest because of my sin. For mine iniquities have gone over my head, they have become too grievous to bear."* Psalm 38.3-4 Like the publican in the temple, we smite our own breast and cry, "God be merciful to me, a sinner!" Luke 18.13

You remember, I am sure, the Bible incident when Jesus took a child, placed it in front of his disciples and said, if you don't enter the Kingdom of Heaven like a little child, you won't get in. Mark 10.15 These are the children to whom Jesus' gracious invitation comes – those who are meek, humble, seeing no value in themselves, those who are weak and heavy laden, weary and burdened, poor sinners, who feel the weight of sin, the burden of a Law they have not kept, and the threat of losing everything good in eternal hell.

Now here comes this invitation to us who have been stripped of all conceit by God's Law and made humble children; **it's an invitation to rest. It comes from a Savior.** Only a Savior could issue an invitation like this, and Jesus is the one and only Savior. Hear Jesus' majestic assertion: *"All things have been committed to me by my Father. No one knows the Son except the Father, and no one knows the Father except the Son and those to whom the Son chooses to reveal him."*

Last week the *Pew Forum on Religion and Public Life* reported a survey of Americans affiliated with a religion or denomination – that is, church people – which found that most (70 percent) believed that "many religions can lead to eternal life." The report praises this result, says it's a rejection of "intolerance." I rather interpret it as an embrace of misinformation. People who believe that "many religions can lead to eternal life" don't know Jesus or what he said. He said, *"No one knows the Son except the Father, and no one knows the Father except the Son and those to whom the Son chooses to reveal him."* People who do not acknowledge Jesus as God, the second person of the Holy Trinity, do not know God, and they have no Savior. We are not intolerant when we accept and believe what Jesus said. We don't say it with pride. We don't despise or wish to persecute those of other religious traditions. We even defend their right to worship as they choose. But rather we adopt the spirit of our Lord, who sat on the hill above Jerusalem and wept over those who would reject him. How greatly he desired, he said, to gather them as a hen gathers chicks beneath her wings, but they refused. Luke 13.34

The invitation before us comes from Jesus, the only one who knows God the Father. He is the only Savior, the only path to God. Only a strong powerful Savior could relieve us of our burden of **fulfilling God's Law perfectly**. He did that in our place and the Father counts his perfect righteousness as ours. Only a strong powerful Savior could relieve us of our burden of **paying the death penalty for our sins.** He did that by suffering God's punishment for our sin in his own innocent death and the Father counts **our** sin-debt as fully paid by Jesus' death. Our sins are forgiven.

The invitation before us today is first of all from a Savior to children who humbly know they need him. It's important to note secondly, what the invitation asks us to do: it's an invitation to **exercise our faith**, that is, **to rest.**

Jesus says, *"Take my yoke upon you and learn from me, for I am gentle and humble in heart, and you will find rest for your souls. For my yoke is easy and my burden is light."* The invitation is to exercise faith, that is, believe it – that is, insofar as our salvation is concerned, do nothing. Even our faith is not our doing; it's God's gift to us. Rest entirely and completely on the work of Jesus for us, rest from the burden of earning anything from God, rest from the fear of punishment. It's the rest spoken of by the prophet Isaiah when he said, *"Comfort, comfort my people, says your God. Speak tenderly to Jerusalem and proclaim to her that her hard service has been completed, that her sin has been paid for, that she has received from the LORD's hand double for all her sins."* Isaiah 40.1-2

Faith and trust in Jesus provide soul-rest. It assures us of Heaven but more than that, it serves us on earth.

Jesus says, *"My yoke is easy, my burden light."* There is a burden that comes with being a Christian. We're asked to do things as Christians, and to endure things as Christians. We give up some activities that this world considers pleasures. We take jobs with the church that won't make us rich. We give some of our earnings to the church. Sometimes we might be ridiculed or persecuted for our faith. Things like these are the yoke and burden Jesus invites us to take on. But our faith transforms them. When we exercise the faith God has given us, it changes our attitudes toward these burdens, and makes them light, because with every burden he asks us to bear there is a promise to which we cling by faith in his Word.

Is it a burden to give money to church? Read the promise of God through Malachi: *"Bring the whole tithe into the storehouse, that there may be food in my house. Test me in this, says the LORD Almighty, and see if I will not throw open the floodgates of heaven and pour out so much blessing that you will not have room enough for it."* Malachi 3.10 It's like the Christian farmer said: "When I shovel from my bin into the Lord's, the Lord shovels from his bin into mine – and the Lord has a bigger shovel." Exercise your faith with the burden of giving to church, and it will become light.

Is it a burden as a **teenager** to endure ridicule and peer pressure? Exercise your faith in the promise expressed by Paul, who said *"I am not ashamed of the Gospel of Christ, for it is the power of God unto salvation..."* Romans 1.16 The ridicule may not stop, but you'll have the power of God unto salvation, and that burden will become light.

Is it a burden to keep **taking care of the kids**, or to keep working hard at the **job**, or to keep working on your **marriage**, or to keep studying hard in **school**, when it's not appreciated and you face burnout? Remember God's promise, *"And let us not be **weary in well doing**: for in due season we shall reap, if we faint not."* Galatians 6.9 You'll still work hard, but your faith will make the burden light.

Is it a burden to **suffer persecution** for the Gospel, as has happened frequently to Christians, and is happening even now to some in Iraq and China and Peru and other places? God preserve us from serious persecution, but if it should occur, remember the promise: *"The sufferings of this present time are not worthy to be compared with the glory that will be revealed in us."* Romans 8.18 Exercise your faith in the face of persecution, and we have Jesus' own word that it will become light.

And so with sickness, or unfaithfulness, or any of the other reverses life is full of. They can't interrupt the soul-rest provided by Savior. We have the promise that the Lord will not burden us beyond our ability to bear it, and if the load becomes too heavy, he places himself with us beneath the burden. Whenever that happens, the burden binds us closer to Jesus. We need only exercise our faith.

And so it is especially when we face death, that ultimate burden. It's our faith in God's promise, expressed many places in Scripture, that will make that burden light. Hear it this time by the apostle writing to the Corinthians:

> We know that the one who raised the Lord Jesus from the dead will also raise us with Jesus and present us with you in his presence.... Therefore we do not lose heart. Though outwardly we are wasting away, yet inwardly we are being renewed day by day. For our light and momentary troubles are achieving for us an eternal glory that far outweighs them all. 2 Corinthians 4. 14-18

That's the apostle, exercising his God-given faith in God-given promises. When we do the same, the yokes become easy and the burdens light.

Today again our powerful Savior has invited us, his children, to cast our burden of sin upon him who has given himself to remove that burden. He has invited us because in love he wants us with him, because he wants you in every moment in life to exercise your faith in his work and in his promises.

Then, whatever happens, our Savior will keep your soul at rest.

✝

September 11, 2008

Getting Involved in Hope

INI

If you told some friends back home that all this week in chapel at Bethany we've been talking about death, they might say, what a downer! And I hope you'd reply, no, not if you were there. Renew that impression again this morning with this word from God.

> Therefore, since we have been justified through faith, we have peace with God through our Lord Jesus Christ, through whom we have gained access by faith into this grace in which we now stand. And we rejoice in the hope of the glory of God. Not only so, but we also rejoice in our sufferings, because we know that suffering produces perseverance; perseverance, character; and character, hope. And hope does not disappoint us, because God has poured out his love into our hearts by the Holy Spirit, whom he has given us. Romans 5. 1-5

When you arrive at Bethany for your first year, you are invited to participate. The faculty hopes for your participation in class. Believe me, nothing delights your teachers more than to see you take the risk of participation. You are also urged (how is it always put?) to "get involved" in activities – get involved in extracurricular, co-curricular, and social activities. It's part of Bethany; since you are here, participate fully!

In this reading, God urges us to participate in our Christianity by getting fully **involved in hope.**

Look at the reading again, at the first phrase. It describes our new condition, what has happened to us. Though we were sinners – though we *are* sinners – we have been, we are justified. That is, God's has assigned the just and sinless life of Jesus to us, even as Jesus paid the penalty for our sins on the cross. This forgiveness of sins has become ours in the only way possible. We can't earn it. Jesus earned it. Our sins are forgiven when we simply believe it.

So then, since we are justified by faith we should get fully involved in the Christian life in which God has put us. Since we're at Bethany, get involved in Bethany. Since we are Christians, get fully involved in your Christianity. The rest of this Scripture reading describes this Christian life. We have peace with God, where before, our sins made us God's enemy. We have access, where before, our sins separated us from God. And then this seems to be a key on which we will dwell a bit this morning: **we have hope,** the essence of involvement and participation.

Hope is one of the great three in Paul's letter to the Corinthians. *"Now abide these three: faith, hope, and love."* 1 Corinthians 13.13 He goes on in that letter to extol love in words that have become familiar. And in other places we hear much about faith. That's as it should be, since faith is the empty hand with which we accept the gift of salvation won for us by Jesus. But in the passage before us the hero is hope. It's the center of that Christian life in which we should fully participate.

The word meant something a bit different in the New Testament than it does to us. For us, hope expresses a preference. I hope it won't rain for our picnic. It might, or might not, but I prefer not. That, for us, is hope. For St. Paul, hope meant not only a preference, but an expectation. Hope referred to something he was certain would happen, and that's at the center of the Christian life.

Paul says, we **rejoice** in the hope of glory. The word rejoice suggests more than just being happy. It means that we talk about it, that we even boast of our hope – that we live in it fully, always, and continuously, because what we hope for will surely happen. Hope makes us future oriented. We have grace now. Paul says we stand in grace, in God's declaration that our sins are forgiven and we are righteous for Jesus sake. We have grace now, but glory is coming. That is our hope, and we live it, we speak it, we boast of it, we participate in it fully.

More than that, we rejoice (same word), we boast of our suffering. When things go wrong (and they do) we actually remain cheerful, as we remember this chain: this suffering I am enduring has a purpose. It brings perseverance (I'm going to stick this through), and perseverance builds character, and character brings what? It brings hope. The hardships we endure sharpen our focus on the glory that is to come. So we rejoice in it, talk of it, boast about it, participate in it fully.

All three of Paul's great three, faith hope love, are here in this Scripture passage. Hope is the link between the other two. Hope links us to our glorious future. The proof is at the end of this reading. *"Hope does not disappoint us, because God has poured out his love into our hearts by the Holy Spirit, whom he has given us."*

God's love is sometimes depicted as shining on us from outside, from somewhere above. Here we read instead that it enters us, is in us now, in our inmost being, in our hearts. What beats in Christian hearts is God's love. When the Christian heart stops beating, God's love remains. That is our sure hope. Hope is the link between the *now* of this life and the *then* of the next life. Hope carries us across the threshold which is death into the life of glory beyond.

There will come a time for each of us – probably not in as spectacular a disaster as occurred seven years ago on this day, September 11, 2001. Haven't we all wondered what it felt like for those on the top floors with the world trade center smoking and burning below them, when they realized there was no hope. Maybe a time came for a loved one of yours when a doctor came in and said there's no hope. Surely a time like that will come for each of us, when we face the end of life, and someone will say, there's no hope.

That's when the Christian will reply, no. No doctor, you are mistaken. Now is the time at last for the greatest hope of all. In a few days, or hours, or minutes, I'll wake up with Jesus in glory.

That's participating fully in the *Christian life.*

†

September 2008

Forgiveness 101

INI

> Jesus said, "Peace be with you! As the Father has sent me, I am send-
> ing you." And with that he breathed on them and said, "Receive the
> Holy Spirit. If you forgive anyone his sins, they are forgiven; if you do
> not forgive them, they are not forgiven." John 20.21-23

Ooo I wish I hadn't said that! No not reading these beautiful words of Jesus;
I could do that over and over. I'm thinking of something else I said earlier.
Ever want to take back something you said? Ever want to redo something
you messed up? Wouldn't it be nice if life were like a video tape, which you
could rewind sometimes and try it over? Or maybe something even simpler
– an eraser, so when you make a mistake, you can just remove it.

Mistakes hurt because they cost us. I watch Andy Overn[1] sketching. He never
makes a mistake, no wrong lines. If I tried to draw, I'd be erasing all the time,
and the picture would be ruined. Do you remember learning how Bill Bukowski painted the fresco?[2] They put a few square feet of wet plaster on the
wall, and then before it dries, he paints on it. **No mistakes allowed!**

You know about mistakes on a test. Some are more serious than others, just
as some tests are more important than others and then correcting mistakes
starts to cost more – maybe you are required to re-take the test. The mistakes aren't just erased, they are paid for.

But test mistakes only hurt ourselves. More serious still are the mistakes we
make that hurt others, mistakes that are personal, interpersonal. Those mistakes destroy relationships. They drive wedges, sometimes permanent ones
that can never be repaired. And then we say, Oooo, I wish I could take that
mistake back! It becomes very costly, hard work, to try to repair those mistakes.

Finally we are getting to the subject of sin. All these examples of mistakes,
even the ones that hurt people badly, pale when compared with sin. Sin is
not just a "mistake," an oops, but an offense against God, a violation of God's
will, that hurts us because it separates us from God. Sin can't just be overlooked by God, it can't be set aside as if it didn't happen. It has to have its due
consequences. Separation from God is hell, a place of punishment and suffering. A mistake in a football game could mean loss of game, perhaps of a

---

[1] Professor of Media Arts at Bethany Lutheran College (and my son-in-law).
[2] Campus artist Prof. William Bukowski painted the famed "Creation Fresco" in the Meyer
Hall of Mathematics and Science at Bethany Lutheran College.

championship. A sin **for certain** means loss of life; the wages of sin is death, eternal death. Romans 6.23 How do we erase sin? We really need a sin eraser.

We have one. Jesus said, "*Peace be with you! Receive the Holy Spirit. If you forgive anyone his sins, they are forgiven; if you do not forgive them, they are not forgiven.*" When we hear words of forgiveness from the pastor, it is as if we are hearing them from God himself. If it's not the music, the atmosphere, the opportunities for prayer and fellowship, that alone – hearing the pastor pronounce forgiveness – should bring us regularly to chapel and to church. What a wonderful thing, the Gospel! What a wonderful thing, forgiveness!

But it cost. Sometimes it costs money to avoid mistakes. I lived in a time before computers or even copy machines (how old must I be!). Yes, we had fire and the wheel, but not computers or copy machines. Now we have white-out, and even better, delete keys. When people used typewriters and carbon paper, a graduate thesis and dissertation had to be typed, with five carbon copies, with no errors, no erasures. Make a mistake on a page, and you start it over. I could never type a full page without a mistake; there would always be a blot on it somewhere. That's why people would usually pay someone, a professional, to type the final draft. Lots of women paid their husband's way through graduate school by typing theses and dissertations – another industry gone by the wayside. I was depending on Mrs. Kamin not to make any mistakes, to type a mistake-free dissertation in my place.

In a trivial way, is that a picture of Christ? I can't live a day, an hour, a minute without a blot of sin on my life. I need someone who can live that perfection for me. Jesus did it. And what about the blots that were there? My sin, which had to be punished, was! It had to cost, a price had to be paid. Sin was punished but not in me, or in you; rather, it was punished in God's own Son, Jesus Christ. Sin wasn't just overlooked. It was substantively dealt with, removed, erased and now is permanently gone! The perfect pages of life he wrote for us are now our pages and the blots were whited out by the payment he made on the cross. The white out of our sins was red, the blood of God's Son. **That's forgiveness.**

Watch out for one thing. Erasers make mistakes easier. If we know we have an eraser, sometimes we are not so careful. If we have a delete key, we don't feel the pressure to be mistake-free that we felt with five layers of carbon paper. Don't let the knowledge of forgiveness we have in Christ lead us to sin more easily. That would be an unrepented sin. That's why there is the second part of Jesus' saying: "*If you forgive anyone his sins, they are forgiven; if you do not forgive them, they are not forgiven.*" Unrepented sins stick to us, with the same authority of God as forgiveness does. What a tragedy, to be condemned to hell for a sin that has been paid for by Jesus' blood, just because we wouldn't give it up. That's why, in our services, as often as we hear the pastor pronounce in God's name that **we are forgiven**, just as often we sing or pray, "**Lord have mercy upon us.**"

Remember your forgiveness always. Let it be the foundation blessing for all others – all the many others. Let it provide that deep inner peace that characterizes a Christian, no matter what your personality, no matter what the turmoil in your life. Jesus said, "*Peace be with you!*" Luke 24.36 etc. And let the knowledge of our forgiveness and what it cost prompt us (in relieved gratitude) to avoid sin, stay in Word, keep searching out God's will for our lives.

Then we can fulfill God's loving purpose in forgiving us, that is, if we have made a mistake get it right the next time. That's the key to our happiness, which in his love, is God's intention for us.

†

October 14, 2008

Why No Fear

INI

They told us last week that on Wall Street there are only two emotions: greed and fear. What we have witnessed there these past weeks is that, strong as greed is, fear is stronger. The economy is in deep trouble.[1] How afraid should we be?

We are engaged, we are told, in a great struggle against terrorism. Terrorism gets its very name and whatever power it has over us from its capability to instill fear. How afraid should we be?

In today's reading the inspired apostle reminds us that there are worse things to fear than a falling market, or even terrorism. Hear the apostle writing to the Ephesians.

> Finally, be strong in the Lord and in his mighty power. Put on the full armor of God so that you can take your stand against the devil's schemes. For our struggle is not against flesh and blood, but against the rulers, against the authorities, against the powers of this dark world and against the spiritual forces of evil in the heavenly realms. Ephesians 6.10-12

The Holy Spirit here reveals that there are powers of evil out to destroy us. You heard here yesterday how Jesus told Peter, Satan has asked for you. Luke 22.31 What a thought that is, Satan asking for someone by name. Has Satan asked for **you** by name? or me? Be sure that Satan knows where you live.

Remember that image from St. Peter's letter that scared us when we were kids? The Devil, he said, is like a roaring lion stalking around looking for someone to devour. 1 Peter 5.8 We sing it in Luther's most famous hymn: "The old evil foe means deadly woe, deep guile and great might are his dread arms in fight." And at a time when his society faced their own earthly threat from militant Islam, Luther added about Satan, "On earth is not his equal."

What's at stake? Satan wants us in hell, which Luther described as a place of **endless fear and terror.** To me the most scary part of hell isn't even the fear and terror. It's the endless part. In this life, we can get past bad experiences, like a root canal, by thinking, OK it'll be over with soon. With time, this will pass. But not in hell. The fear and terror will never be over with. And when

---

[1] In 2008 at the end of the George W. Bush presidency, the economy had fallen into the deepest recession since the Great Depression of the 1930's.

we examine ourselves and hold our lives up against God's Law, his rules and requirements of us, we know hell is where we deserve to go.

So how afraid should we be? Don't be afraid.

The first proclamation of the Gospel in New Testament times began just that way. The angels on Bethlehem's plain, on the night of Jesus' birth, came to the shepherds and said, "Fear not!" Certainly, the shepherds were startled. But the angels meant more than that – look at their words. They didn't say, don't be afraid because we won't hurt you. They said, don't be afraid because a Savior has been born to you. Luke 2.10 That is the reason to not fear.

God's plan to free us from fear is in two parts. One involves what he does; the other what he gives us to do.

What he does is send a Savior, his Son Jesus Christ. As Jesus took our sins onto himself, to pay for them with his death in our place, he **challenged** all the powers of evil in direct battle, **subjected** himself to every temptation, but remained without sin. He defeated the Devil, **faced** the most fearful of all human experiences, death, and even entered it in order to burst out of it again in glorious resurrection. Before the Son of God, death and all the powers of evil tremble and run. They have been conquered for us. One little word can fell them.[1] That's what God has done – rescued us from hell and set us on the path to eternal life. He told us, don't be afraid of anything.

Now he gives us another gift. He asks us to do something – to keep us mindful that we are not uninvolved, that this is not some distant fight unrelated to us. He gives us something to do. He asks us to respond to his goodness by taking up the fight ourselves. Using the equipment he provides us we are to clean out every influence of evil from our lives. In our reading, Paul says, "*Put on the full armor of God so that you can take your stand against the devil's schemes.*"

In the verses following, the apostle surveys the weapons God has given us for this fight. A lot can be said about those weapons, too much to go into now. So I invite you, sometime this evening, to pick up your Bible, turn to Ephesians 6. Read that list of weapons God has for you to use and think about how you can use them: the belt of truth, the breastplate of righteousness, your feet fitted with the readiness that comes from the Gospel of peace, the shield of faith, with which you can extinguish all the flaming arrows of the evil one, the helmet of salvation and the sword of the Spirit, which is the Word of God. Ephesians 6.14-17 What powerful weapons to fight the forces of evil! God doesn't

---

[1] From Luther's hymn, *A Mighty Fortress Is Our God.*

want us to wield them out of fear. He wants it to be with thankfulness, and a reflection of the love he has shown us.

Let our prayer this morning be this hymn which captures God's message with two stanzas of encouragement and one of prayer.

> O little flock, fear not the foe
> who madly seeks your overthrow;
> Dread not his rage and pow'r.
> What though your courage sometimes faints,
> his seeming triumph o'er God's saints
> Lasts but a little hour.

> As true as God's own Word is true,
> not earth nor hell with all their crew
> Against us shall prevail.
> A jest and byword are they grown;
> God is with us, we are His own;
> Our vict'ry cannot fail.

> Amen, Lord Jesus, grant our prayer;
> great Captain, now thine arm make bare.
> Fight for us once again!
> So shall thy saints and martyrs raise
> a mighty chorus to thy praise
> World without end. Amen.

†

Tuesday, November 4, 2008

The Fundamental Issue

INI

We have before us, I believe, a perfect passage from Scripture for our national election day.[1] We read in the Old Testament prophecy of Isaiah, these words:

> He will swallow up death forever, And the Lord GOD will wipe away tears from all faces. The rebuke of His people He will take away from all the earth, for the LORD has spoken. And it will be said in that day: "Behold, this is our God; we have waited for Him, and He will save us. This is the LORD; we have waited for Him; we will be glad and rejoice in His salvation." Isaiah 25.8-9

If you're a serious U. S. citizen – and we at Bethany hope that if you are a U. S. citizen you're a serious one, not only a voter but an informed voter – then you have been researching and mulling over some big issues this election. You've considered the status of race relations in our land. You may have wondered how qualities of leadership may be affected by gender. You've pondered questions of how matters of morality, ranging from abortion and marriage to waging war and protecting the environment, translate into wise public policy. You've puzzled about how government policy should affect our economy. And many of these issues, this year, have become close and personal – for most of us here, questions like "Will there be a job for me when I graduate?" and for some of us here, questions like "What will my retirement account look like next week?"

It's easy for us to become anxious about this election. And it can be deep anxiety, when it looks like our preferred candidate may not make it. To that add more anxiety from other areas of life: how am I going to get all those projects done as the semester dwindles quickly? Will this new relationship I'm working on turn out well? How safe is my brother/sister, dad/mom, son/daughter/ friend, or whoever it is we know in Iraq or Afghanistan?

It doesn't belittle those big issues to bring this to your attention: none of these is the biggest problem we face. The biggest problem we face is our standing before God. And it's not even "How does our nation stand before God." The biggest problem we face is "How do *I* stand before God."

That's why this word of God from the pen of Isaiah is a good text for today. Isaiah lived in troubled times too. People then faced some big issues, matters

---

[1] At this point we did not yet know that Barak Obama would defeat John McCain for the presidency. The country was in a deep economic recession.

not only of faith and morals, but of economics and national security. In the midst of all these troubles and anxiety, in a section of his book dealing with how God's people are surrounded by faithlessness, attacks on the true religion, and threats of every kind, Isaiah in these verses brought God's people down to this our basic, biggest problem. He brings us face to face with the question, how do I stand before God?

And he gives us this reassuring answer: *"He will swallow up death forever, And the Lord GOD will wipe away tears from all faces."*

Isaiah's words are fundamental. Central to God's care for us is the destruction of death itself. Isaiah, looking forward from his time, saw what we know looking back from our time: how God in his love attacked the central problem of humanity, our sin which prevents us from standing before a holy and just God. Jesus Christ, God's Son, took his sinless life to the cross where he suffered death, the punishment for our sins, in our place. Then, with all sins paid for, he burst out of the grave, conquering death forever. Our sins are forgiven. Because of that gift of forgiveness, we **can** stand before God, who views us as sinless because of the work of Jesus. When we contemplate that sacrifice, and that gift, and that measure of love from God, it isn't hard to know that he will surely also wipe away every tear from our eyes.

In this world, troubles pass. In the next world, where we are bound for, troubles pass away. Some of us have been around a while and remember a time when the biggest problem our country faced was the Vietnam war. Some here even remember when our biggest problem was the Korean war. Contrary to opinion, none of us remembers the Civil War. But still that war passed, as did the Korean and Vietnamese, and this current war will pass, as will the next one unless Jesus comes again very soon. And so too will pass the economic downturn, and the relationship problems you may be struggling with, and the other challenges you face. All these troubles pass by in this world and will pass away in the next. But what remains is God's love and forgiveness and care in Christ Jesus.

Don't misunderstand. I'm not claiming that the problems we face today are not serious or worrisome. Many of them are big huge problems that will need a lot of effort, attention, and sacrifice to resolve. They are big problems, but they are not fundamental. Our fundamental problem is, how do we stand before God. And Isaiah urges us to rest in the assurance that God has taken care of that problem. Through Jesus Christ, death itself has been swallowed up. The tears from our struggles will be wiped away.

What then of these troubled times, and the problems they bring us? We should be concerned about important issues. They matter. We should devote time and energy to solving, if we can, the problems with government, with our studies, with our relationships, with war, with illness, with all the troubles that surround us.

But as we struggle and work, we can and should regularly come back to the basics. Daily we should confess our sins that would separate us from God and we should rejoice in the forgiveness won for us by Jesus that brings us back close to him. Isaiah reminds us that, in the midst of any anxiety, we can rest in the Lord, that whatever happens in elections, or relationships, or illnesses, or bank accounts, or any other challenges we face, God is still in charge, he loves us, and has dealt with our most fundamental problem. God has swallowed up death forever, and he will wipe away our tears, as we look forward to the time when we join the throng of all the saints of whom we sing in the hymn, and we will say in that day, "*Behold, this is our God; we have waited for Him, and He will save us. This is the LORD; we have waited for Him; we will be glad and rejoice in His salvation.*"

Thanks be to God, through Jesus Christ our Savior.

†

April 2009

Separate

INI

These weeks can be a time of mixed feelings. Consider the pressure of final exams, and the huge relief that will come from having them over with. Consider the exultation of a task well completed with the end of the semester, a milestone achieved with graduation, and then the sadness of separation, leaving roommates, friends, and colleagues, at least for time, but in some cases probably forever.

Separation is most often sad. It's even used as punishment for wrongdoing. The worst punishment in prison is isolation – solitary confinement, separation from everything of human value.

I recall a workshop I once attended, where they described an exercise so cruel that the leaders refrained from asking us actually to do it, but rather they simply described it. May I do that for you now?

The workshop explored addictions, such as to drugs, alcohol, or gambling. To help us understand the effects of addiction, the exercise asked us to list the 20 things most important in our lives, the things most valuable and precious to us. Well, listing 20 precious things isn't hard. Along with family and religion, the list would probably include our homes, our education, and maybe a computer or car or CD collection, among other things.

After making the list, the leader would ask us to narrow it down. Pretend you had to give up 10 of the items, which would they be? Cross out 10 of the 20 items, leaving only the most precious ones. Well, it would be only a little hard to strike out some of the material things – the computer and the car could go, if it could mean leaving such things as health and home and education.

Next the leader said, take your list of 10 things and cut it in half. If you had to give up 5 of the items what would they be? Now it's getting really hard. Should you give up your home or your health? Your health or your education?

After you pare down the list to the 5 most precious things in your life, the leader says, cut out three of them. Of the top five, you can keep only two. How painful, now, to cross off what? your parents? your children? your job? in order to keep the top two, perhaps your faith, and your spouse. But at last you have given up everything except the two most precious things in your life.

Now, says the leader, cross off those two also.

I told you it was a cruel exercise. It's meant to illustrate the effects of addiction. The addict will, in fact, finally give up all those things for the sake of the addiction.

But it's also a good illustration of the pain of separation. It's an illustration of the pain of punishment, of being separated from everything that is good, of the pain of being without God. It's an illustration of hell.

Now hear this promise of the Gospel from God the Holy Spirit through the Apostle Paul. **No separation**! Reverse the whole picture: restore that list of good and valuable things and add to it. **God loves us**! Jesus Christ, God's Son, came to remove all that would separate us from God – our sins, by which we deserve the punishment of separation. But those all are gone, and now, asks the apostle,

> Who shall separate us from the love of Christ? Shall trouble or hardship or persecution or famine or nakedness or danger or sword?... For I am convinced that neither death nor life, neither angels nor demons, neither the present nor the future, nor any powers, neither height nor depth, nor anything else in all creation, will be able to separate us from the love of God that is in Christ Jesus our Lord. Romans 8.35-39

Along with the joy of accomplishment at school year's end, you'll feel some pain of separation. Remember throughout the summer, throughout your life, what was taught us by the psalmist at the end of the most famous psalm, the 23rd:

> Surely goodness and mercy will follow me all the days of my life, and I will dwell in the house of the Lord forever. Psalm 23.6

✝

May 2009
In the Good Shepherd Chapel for the Vicar Workshop,
Bethany Lutheran Theological Seminary

Why Me?

INI

What a sinful and rebellious people! Rather than following God's Word and seeking out his will, they are deciding they know by themselves what is best. They insist that God fit into **their** plans, rather than conforming themselves to God's plans.

These words could apply to any humans of any age. They apply today. In our reading today, they applied to the children of Israel who had decided they wanted a king to rule over them.

God's prophet Samuel, even as he prepared to anoint a new king for them, made clear the wickedness of their motives. When the people expressed remorse, the prophet spoke to them as reported here.

> And all the people said to Samuel, "Pray for your servants to the LORD your God, that we may not die; for we have added to all our sins the evil of asking a king for ourselves." Then Samuel said to the people, "Do not fear. You have done all this wickedness; yet do not turn aside from following the LORD but serve the LORD with all your heart. And do not turn aside; for then you would go after empty things which cannot profit or deliver, for they are nothing. For the LORD will not forsake His people, for His great name's sake, because it has pleased the LORD to make you His people. Moreover, as for me, far be it from me that I should sin against the LORD in ceasing to pray for you; but I will teach you the good and the right way. Only fear the LORD and serve Him in truth with all your heart; for consider what great things He has done for you. 1 Samuel 12.19-24

"Why me?"

It's a phrase often heard from someone suffering some kind of misfortune. It expresses the belief that the speaker feels he doesn't deserve whatever it is that happened to him. Let's turn the situation around and make it the expression of someone to whom something good, something wonderful has happened. Let's make it our expression. Lord, by the sacrifice of your holy blood, you have made us your own. Each of us can look into our hearts and know how thoroughly we don't deserve it. Each of us can cry, "Why me?"

This is no new experience for you. Just as the great prophet Samuel in this reading, you know Law and Gospel. As he did on the occasion reported here, you have preached Law and Gospel. You've done it first to yourself, as I have to me. God's Law showed us how we ignore God's will and try to redefine what **we** want as what God wants. We have repented of that sin and many others and turned to the comfort of the Gospel. We've learned that Jesus, by his unceasing conformity to his Father's will, has fulfilled in our place this obedience to God where we have failed. He sought out his Father's will ***for us*** and obeyed ***for us***. And for our disobedience, those times we went our own way, or even wished to, he went to the cross to pay in full the punishment we deserved. That he did, as Samuel said in this reading, because "*it has pleased the LORD to make you His people.*"

Why me? The only answer is in the depth of God's incomprehensible love: "*It pleased the Lord.*" Beyond that, I don't know why me. "*It pleased the Lord.*" That is enough reason for me to know, gratefully, why me.

Besides this wonderful thing, that God has made each of us his own for Christ's sake, for which we can cry why me, there is this other wonderful thing: God has called us to bring these same messages to his people, to wield his Word which enables his kingdom to grow. For that wonderful privilege, we might well be moved again to cry, why me? And again, the answer can be found only in his grace: it has pleased the Lord.

Let our response of gratitude be to model our ministry after that of Samuel in the words of our reading once more, applying Law and Gospel faithfully and prayerfully to ourselves and to our flocks. Can these words of Samuel be our words to the flocks to which God sends us?

> "Do not fear. You have done all this wickedness; yet do not turn aside from following the LORD but serve the LORD with all your heart. And do not turn aside; for then you would go after empty things which cannot profit or deliver, for they are nothing. For the LORD will not forsake His people, for His great name's sake, because it has pleased the LORD to make you His people. Moreover, as for me, far be it from me that I should sin against the LORD in ceasing to pray for you; but I will teach you the good and the right way. Only fear the LORD and serve Him in truth with all your heart; for consider what great things He has done for you."

†

August 9, 2009
At Peace Lutheran Church, North Mankato

New Life in Christ is Like...

INI

Let's talk today about "our new life in Christ."

Most people think that **how we live** is the essence of the Christian life. Popular opinion says, **good behavior**, what we should do – that's what the Christian life is all about. Today I hope to remind you, on the basis of this one verse from Scripture, that this popular opinion is mistaken. We will see there, that

- our new Christian life starts by God's choice, not our works,
- it expects tough times, not prosperity, and
- it is filled with serving others, not ourselves.

And finally we'll see what a comfort all this is.

Listen again to St. Paul.

> As a prisoner for the Lord, then, I urge you to live a life worthy of the calling you have received. Ephesians 4.1

This verse first addresses this question: How does our Christian life begin? It's the question all humankind must face: how can we who are sinners stand before a just and holy God? Or in other words, how do we get to Heaven?

The answer: this verse speaks of "the calling you have received," or more exactly translated, "the calling by which you were called." We begin our Christian life by being called, by God's choice and not by anything we do.

Now, the popular opinion out there has a different view. Let's have a conversation this morning with Popular Opinion. Here is Popular Opinion speaking:

> How do we get to heaven? It's automatic. Everyone who dies goes to heaven. I'll proclaim it in the news when a celebrity or sports star dies, or when anyone's relative dies, I'll just say they are now in heaven with loved ones, or perhaps looking down on us now, or something like that.

That's what popular opinion says, isn't it?

But sadly it's not true. The Bible teaches it plainly. In Romans we read, "*As it is written: There is no one righteous, not even one; there is no one who understands, no one who seeks God. All have turned away, they have together become worthless; there is no one who does good, not even one.*" Romans 3.10f. The Psalmist says, "*Lord, no man living is righteous before thee.*" Psalm 143.2 In Revelation it speaks of Heaven and says, "*Nothing impure will ever enter it, nor will any-one who does what is shameful or deceitful.*" Revelation 21.27 So it's clear that not everyone who dies goes to heaven. In fact, sinners are shut out of heaven, and everyone is a sinner. Broad is the path, says Jesus, to destruction.

Ah, but here comes Popular Opinion again. It says,

> Wait a minute, we're not **that** bad. OK, we do some bad things, but we do some good things too, maybe many good things. Don't those earn points with God? At least we try. Certainly God can't expect more than that.

The Bible answers that clearly too. In Galatians we read, "*All who rely on the works of the Law* – [the things **they do** to earn points with God] – *are under the curse.*" Galatians 3.10 Martin Luther, commenting on this passage, says, those who think they earn points with God by trying are sinning **doubly**; they are not only overlooking their own deadly sins, but are adding pride and arrogance on top of them.

It's easy to respond to mistaken popular opinion out there by citing the Bible. But you know, it's in us too. The reason these false views are so popular is that they are part of all of us. They are built into our old sinful natures, which always want to try to claim some credit for ourselves.

So these false opinions try to sneak back into **our** thinking. Can't we easily catch ourselves thinking, well I'm not **that** bad, I'm a Christian after all, I go to church and all that, and haven't done any **major** sins like murder. And where I fall short, well, I thank Jesus for making up for my failures by his death on the cross.

Doesn't that sound a lot like popular opinion? Do you see how that kind of thinking insults our Lord, and cheapens Christ's sacrifice on the cross? Did his death only *make up for our failures*? That's as if we did most of the work for our salvation, and Jesus had only a little left to do. Did we do **anything** to earn our salvation? If we think that, we are setting the value of Christ's sacrifice at nothing. We are sinning doubly, adding pride and arrogance to our other sins.

No, the Bible teaches that we were **dead** in our trespasses and sins. Ephesians 2.1 Dead people can do nothing. We didn't need somebody to make up for our lack. We needed rescue. We needed reviving. We needed to be brought back from the dead.

How then **do** we sinners stand before a righteous and holy God? Look again at this verse before us. It says, we are chosen. It speaks of "*the calling by which you were called.*" We are selected by God's grace, called out, elected by

God, without any merit on our part. It's all God's work. By the death of His Son Jesus Christ on the cross God wiped out all the sin and punishment that was due us. Then God the Holy Spirit came to us in Baptism, and again repeatedly through his Word, and he comes to us again today in his special meal, bringing us the Gospel message that our sins are forgiven in Jesus Christ.

And we believe in him. That faith God counts as righteousness and holiness. St. Paul says, "*But now the righteousness of God has been manifested apart from the law.*" Romans 3.21 –that is, separate from anything we do. Again Paul says, "*The one who through faith is righteous shall live.*" Romans 1.17 And Jesus himself said, "*I am the door. No one comes to the Father, but by me.*" John 10.9 And in Revelation, speaking of Heaven, here's the rest of the verse we read before: "*Nothing impure will ever enter Heaven, nor will anyone who does what is shameful or deceitful, but only those whose names are written in the Lamb's book of life.*" Revelation 21.27

Listen to the Bible, not popular opinion or your old sinful self. Your name is written in the Book of Life. Mine is too. It's not because of anything we do. We are chosen for heaven, we are "called" by God's grace.

What then should we expect in this new Christian life to which we are called? Look at these words: "*a prisoner.*" The apostle wrote this letter while in prison in Rome, possibly awaiting execution. He is enduring some tough times. He reminds us here that we are called to a life of struggle, even suffering, and not to ease and prosperity.

But here's popular opinion again:

> Believing in God should mean good times, relief from everything that burdens us, no more troubles, God will even make you rich! God wants you to be wealthy and prosperous and **if you** turn your life over to him, **if you** decide to invite God into your life, then God will be pleased with you, and bless you, and make you happy.

That's popular opinion, isn't it? Have you heard the TV preachers saying that? Did you notice how they make it depend on **us**, the thing **we** are supposed to do to earn God's favor?

That mistaken view is in us too. That's why it's popular opinion, because it's built into our old sinful nature. Isn't it easy for us to think of God as the big ATM machine? That's where we go when we need something, right? We can forget about God most of the time, but when we need something, then we pray. And how easy it is when we do pray, to fill those prayers with selfish requests – God do this for me and that for me, give me this and give me that.

And if we then don't get this or that, we think God has failed us. It's as if God is **our** servant, rather than that we are God's servants.

Well, God is very patient with us in our sin, and he does prosper and bless us. We thank God for those blessings, and for his patience. And yes, God urges us to call on him in the day of trouble, so we should pray when we need help.

But listen to the Bible, not popular opinion, about trouble and suffering. Saint Paul is in prison! The Christian life can be tough. Living as we should can be hard. Even the simple everyday course of our Christian lives is a challenge. Raising your kids, for example, isn't always easy. Of course we know they are a blessing from God, and of course we love them. But that doesn't always make it easy. In your worship folder every Sunday is this note: it says, "Parents – for your convenience there is a cry room available which has been equipped for listening to the service." Notice, it doesn't say anything about children. When I first read that, I thought, wonderful! My church understands! They have a place where parents can go to cry!

Yes, it's wonderful to have the assurance that we are called, that our names are written in the book of Heaven, and so are our children's when they are baptized. But in this world things still happen. There is sickness, there are accidents, there are problems with people, there is war and violence and suffering. And there is death. Popular opinion says, "Doesn't God care? Doesn't God want us to be happy? Prosperous? Even wealthy?" I only know what the Bible says. The Bible says, God wants us to be **saved**. And all he does, all that happens to us, is to that end.

Ask any Christian who has gone through hardships, and you'll find someone who has been drawn closer to God, someone who has learned more and more to depend not on their own strength, but on God's.

God knows suffering. God himself suffered death and hell on the cross in the person of his Son Jesus Christ, for us, in our place, so we would be clothed in His righteousness and fit for Heaven. When we look at Jesus on the cross, we see the enormity of our sins that put him there. But more than that, we see on the cross the enormity of God's love for us. God reveals the **essence of his being, love**, through the suffering of his Son Jesus. God's love is manifest in his suffering. We can find God's love in our struggles, and hardships, and illnesses. His strength is made perfect in our weaknesses. That's why St. Paul, writing to the Corinthians, can describe himself and all believers *"as sorrowful, yet always rejoicing; as dying, and behold we live."* 2 Corinthians 6.9f.

Listen to the Bible, not popular opinion, about how God can make trouble and suffering, too, into a blessing for our eternal good.

Finally, we notice that our new Christian life is filled with service to others, not ourselves. In this verse before us, Paul urges us to live a life worthy of the calling we have received.

You know how Popular Opinion talks about "number one." No that's not God, although it should be. We all know that "Take care of number one" means "Take care of yourself." Here's Popular Opinion again: "Have it your way, live life to the fullest, go to the **me** university, you deserve a break today, and on and on."

Our old selves find that appealing too. That's why the apostle here urges us to overcome that old self and live worthy of our new calling. Then he goes on to talk about humility and serving each other.

How does this happen, this serving others? We're talking here again about what we do, and remember from before, we don't do these things to earn anything from God. We can't. There is nothing to earn. Jesus has earned it all for us and given us eternal life as a gift.

Now, can our old sinful self sneak back in here and tempt us to see value before God in our Christian service to others? Can we start to be proud and satisfied when we do good things for others, and think we are pleasing God by what we do? Don't give that old self the slightest crack to get back in. Listen to the Bible. It tells us just to keep on confessing our sins, as we say with the Psalmist in our Sunday liturgy, "*I said: I will confess my transgressions to the Lord.*" Psalm 32.5 Let's keep saying, "Lord have mercy upon us!" Let's heed St. Peter who says, "*God gives grace to the humble,*" 1 Peter 5.5 and our Lord himself who said, "*Whoever humbles himself will be exalted.*" Matthew 23.12 Let's not look with even a smidgen of pride at anything we do.

Yes, of course we do good things as Christians. Here's a better way to look at any good things that we do: they happen because by God's grace Jesus lives in us, and so the good things we do are not our works, but they are the Lord's works in us. And since they are the works of Jesus, that's why God is pleased with them. As St. Paul says a few verses beyond our reading for today, "*Therefore be imitators of God, as beloved children.*" Ephesians 5.1 That's how our works can be totally selfless – not to get or earn anything for ourselves, not from other people, not from God, but humbly, without any inkling of pride, or even of awareness that we are doing good works.

All of this is a lot to learn from one little verse of Scripture. But I don't want to stop before I'm sure you know the blessing that comes from what we've reviewed today.

We've seen first that our new Christian life starts by God's choice, not our works, so our calling is sure – the pressure of earning our way to Heaven is gone, everything is already done for us by Jesus. What a blessing and comfort that is!

We've seen, second, that God's love can be found especially in tough times. Our Lord, who knows suffering, who saved us and brought us to new life through his own suffering, and whom we know better through our troubles – that Lord is with us, always, and makes our burdens light. What a blessing and comfort that is!

Finally, we've seen that since Jesus lives in us by faith, he fills our life with serving others. We don't have to worry about good works, or even notice them. We just do them, because living the Christian life, living worthy of our calling, is doing the work of Jesus who dwells in us. What a blessing and privilege that is!

For all that, may thanks forever be to God!

†

August 2009

How to Love Jesus

INI

Is there anyone here who is in love? I'd ask for a show of hands, but if you raised your hand you might startle the people around you, including perhaps the person you believe you are in love with. Love among humans is complex and often confusing, something you may have puzzled about or agonized over. You might be doing such things right now.

Let me turn the question a bit: do you love God? We know we ought to, but do we? Do you love Jesus? How can you tell?

We said love among humans is complex and confusing. Love involving God is complex too, but in our reading this morning, Jesus makes it very simple and I hope less confusing. Look at this brief sentence from John's Gospel:

If you love me you will obey what I command. John 14.15 NIV

We all have a great deal to learn about love, all our lives long, and of course the best place to learn about it is from God in his Word. Jesus spoke the words before us at a very important time. It was at the last supper, the night before he was arrested, tried, and crucified. He spoke at length that night with his disciples. His words are recorded for us by the Holy Spirit in the Gospel of John. In that conversation the word "love" occurs some two dozen times. If you are puzzled about love, you would do well to go to John's Gospel and read the 14th 15th and 16th chapters. You'll learn a lot about love there.

I'll repeat the questions of a moment ago: Do you love Jesus? How can you tell? Do you look inward for some kind of feeling? Feelings come and go. Jesus here makes clear what people who have a mature love learn over a lifetime. Love may involve emotions but emotions are not the essence of love. He says, if you love me you will obey my commands. Love is not essentially an emotion. Love is a determination. Love is a matter of will and of action. Love is doing.

It's important to note the order of events here. First we love Jesus. Then we obey his commandments. It's **because** we love Jesus that we obey his commandments. If obeying the commandments came first, we could never love Jesus because we can't keep the commandments. Check the list of which we are singing in this morning's hymn, built on the Ten Commandments. We can't keep even one of them! So how can we possibly love someone who lays upon us commandments we can't keep and when we fail we deserve to be punished eternally? Nobody could love Jesus if we **first** had to keep his commandments.

But here is the greatest demonstration that love is not an emotion but a determination and an action. We read in Romans, God demonstrates his own love for us this way: while we were still sinners, Christ died for us. Romans 5.8

There is love! Though we were totally unlovely, dead putrid corpses in our sins, God determined to love us and took action to save us by sending Jesus to cleanse us from our sins by his sinless life in our place, and by his death on the cross, taking on himself the punishment we deserved. God showed his love for us in his will, determination, and action to save us. Only those who know what God has done for us can love God. Only we who gratefully cling to the gift of eternal life Jesus won for us on the cross – only those with faith in Jesus can love Jesus.

How do we know that we love Jesus? He says it here: if you love me you will keep my commandments.

You've probably heard the expression, "working on a marriage." Married couples with mature love for each other know that their love is much more than an emotion; it's a matter of doing things, often self-sacrificing things for each other. Loving relationships don't just automatically take care of themselves. They need attention, and work. And work done in love is pleasurable work.

Jesus is urging us in these words before us to work on our relationship with him. Of course we love him. We know what he has done for us and we love him. What naturally follows? We keep his commandments.

At least we try to. And we try **hard** to. But of course we fail. We certainly don't always keep Jesus' commandments. We love him imperfectly. When we realize that, we can only turn once more to his most important commandment, the one he spoke at the very beginning of the discussion from which the words before us are taken, spoken that night before he went to the cross for us. He said, "*Do not let your hearts be troubled. **Trust in God; trust also in me.***" John 14.1

There is the commandment that saves. There is the commandment that best shows our love for Jesus. He says, **trust** me. **Believe** in me. Have **faith** in me. **Rest** all your hopes in me. And by the strength of **his Spirit**, we do that and know that that we are his, and we are saved.

We love Jesus. Remember: love means action.

†

September 1, 2009

Keep Your Mouth for Jesus

INI

I know you've been hurt at some time in your life by something someone said. I know that's happened to you because it's an experience common to all people everywhere. And that's because it's so easy, when we want to hurt someone, to do it with our words, with our mouths, with our tongues.

So it's useful this morning to give our attention to these words of God.

> Do not let any unwholesome talk come out of your mouths, but only what is helpful for building others up according to their needs, that it may benefit those who listen. And do not grieve the Holy Spirit of God, with whom you were sealed for the day of redemption. Ephesians 4.29-30

Language and speech are surely wonderful gifts from God. In my communication classes these very days we are spending significant time looking closely at this uniquely human capability of speech and language. And in the process I hope we are opening some students' eyes in surprise, as mine have been opened again and again over the years, as we uncover another new wonder of anatomy, or psychology, or cognitive ability – something more that illumines the wonderful way that God has made us capable of speech.

Now here's an adage worth remembering, because it applies not only here but in many areas of life. It's from Martin Luther who said, "Sinful people take the best things of God, and turn them to the worst use."[1] If ever anyone in pride dared to consider himself not a sinner, if he said to himself, "Let's see, I can't think of any sin I committed today..." – that person should just consider his own mouth.

Would you dare to do it yourself? Check the sins of **your** mouth? Boasting, lying, putting someone down, expressing contempt for someone, gossip, shading the truth, making excuses for wrong acts, making **lying** excuses for wrong acts, rationalizing sin, tempting someone else into sin, cursing, using God's name carelessly, disrespecting parents, disrespecting teachers, foul language, attributing bad motives to someone, trash talk, dirty jokes, unkind ethnic jokes, bullying, making fun of someone. I'm going to stop the list now or we could be here into the next class hour. Just tell me which of these things you have **never** done. There won't be many. If you're like me, there won't be any.

---

[1] Heidelberg Disputation, thesis 24, paraphrased.

And please don't think these sins aren't serious, that they are "just words" or some sinful excuse like that. These are grievous damning sins. They **will** send someone to hell.

No, more accurately, they **did** send someone to hell. These sins of your mouth and mine damned Jesus to death and hell in our place. By that sacrifice of love he washed away all our sins, and among them he washed out our mouths. He left them clean. Jesus left our mouths holy, perfect in God's eyes. God chose to put those sins of our mouths on Jesus where he paid the punishment for them on the cross. Instead God chose to look on us as if the words of his Son, words of kindness and gentleness and love – he looked on those words of Jesus as if they were ours. In the second verse I read, we learn that we are set, "*sealed for the day of redemption.*" We are forgiven! We are bound for Heaven!

Now, he says, live up to it. He says, "*Do not grieve the Holy Spirit of God, with whom you were sealed for the day of redemption. Do not let any unwholesome talk come out of your mouths, but rather only what is helpful for building others up according to their needs, that it may benefit those who listen.*"

I don't know what your future holds, where your life will take you. But in this September of 2009, God has put you here at Bethany Lutheran College, a place where every day in chapel, and every night online,[1] you can be reassured and encouraged by God's Word. What a wonderful opportunity, what an ideal workshop we have here in which to practice what this Word of God encourages us to do. Don't wait! No need to put it off. Start today to look for opportunities to use God's wonderful gift of language and speech to speak what is helpful for building others up according to their needs, that it may benefit those who listen.

That's what Jesus did, all his life. Let Jesus do the same, now, through your mouth.

†

---

[1] These were the days when an "Evening Bells at Bethany" devotion was on the campus cable channel each evening.

23 September 2009

God's Food Service

INI

How do you like the food service? No, not that one over there, the one here in this room. Today's message, according to the worship folder, is "God feeds us." Focus your attention please, for a few minutes on how God feeds us here, and over there, and in fact everywhere. The words "God feeds us" represent God's total care for us.

As you hear the words of Jesus before us this morning, feel how our Lord, as he talks about God's total care, is nudging us, nudging...nudging...toward what?

> No one can serve two masters. Either he will hate the one and love the other, or he will be devoted to the one and despise the other. You cannot serve both God and Money. Therefore I tell you, do not worry about your life, what you will eat or drink; or about your body, what you will wear. Is not life more important than food, and the body more important than clothes? Look at the birds of the air; they do not sow or reap or store away in barns, and yet your heavenly Father feeds them. Are you not much more valuable than they? Who of you by worrying can add a single hour to his life? And why do you worry about clothes? See how the lilies of the field grow. They do not labor or spin. Yet I tell you that not even Solomon in all his splendor was dressed like one of these. If that is how God clothes the grass of the field, which is here today and tomorrow is thrown into the fire, will he not much more clothe you, **O you of little faith**? So do not worry, saying, "What shall we eat?" or "What shall we drink?" or "What shall we wear?" For the pagans run after all these things, and your heavenly Father knows that you need them. But **seek first his kingdom and his righteousness**, and all these things will be given to you as well. Matthew 6.24-33

The main message is clear, of course – God the Father is caring for us, so don't worry about food or clothing. Well, I don't think many of us do that. I look out at you now and I don't see any starving people. Nobody is wearing rags – at least not out of necessity. Does that mean Jesus' words don't apply much to us? Of course not.

There are several kinds of sinful worry. All of them emerge from lack of faith – Jesus says, "*You of little faith.*" One kind of worry is **lack of faith** plus **desperation**. While we may fall into that once in a while, that's not our usual kind. For us, our daily kind of sinful worry is **lack of faith** plus **selfish**

desires. Our "worry" is more of the selfish kind – "Can I get what pleases me?" We complain about food, not because we're starving but because it's not what pleases us most. We're concerned about clothing not because we don't have any but because what we have is not the latest or coolest. Go down the list of things in your life that occupy your mind, your energy, your attention. Isn't the focus too often on "what pleases me"?

In these verses Jesus is nudging us toward maturity – Christian maturity. He is saying "Grow up!" Don't hear that as a scolding, but as encouragement from someone who sincerely wants you and me to be happy. "Grow up in your Christian maturity," he's telling us. That's not spoken as older person to younger ones, but to everybody. There are people your age who are exceptionally mature Christians, and some my age who are not. And we all can grow.

Jesus gets straight to the central question of Christian maturity: what are we seeking first? His answer: it should be the Kingdom of God and his righteousness. Christian maturity starts with God's righteousness. That's the sinless condition earned by Jesus as he lived his life in perfect obedience to God, and then placed that sinless condition, that "righteousness of God" upon us like a clean robe. At the same time he removed our sin by paying the penalty we owed for our unrighteousness, when he suffered death, the wages of our sin, on the cross. Our sins are forgiven. This righteousness of God, ours through Christ's work, has placed us in his Kingdom. We are in the Kingdom of God.

Then Jesus says, now seek that Kingdom, do that first. That is, pay attention to your place in the Kingdom. What is that place? What is your role in the Kingdom of God? Ask yourself: What am I here for? Why did God redeem us and put us here? Was it so we could get the best food that pleases us? If the answer is **no**, then why do we pay so much attention to that? Why did God redeem us and put us here? Was it so we could wear the latest fashions? If **no**, then why do we put so much effort into that? Why did God redeem us and put us here? So we could play with the latest gadgets, or party hard? Go down the checklist of where you put your attention, effort, money, and consider: is that why God put you here? If for a lot of those things the answer is **no**, then listen to Jesus urging: seek first the Kingdom of God! Put your attention and effort into why God redeemed you and put you here.

And then all those other things, the things we really need? Notice that Jesus doesn't say "They'll take care of themselves" – that's too accidental. He says, "God will take care of them." God himself! *"All these things will be given to you as well."*

Realize that! Let your faith grow to encompass not only your trust in Jesus for our salvation, but also the realization that **when you devote yourself to why God wants you here, God will feed you with all good things.** Live that realization actively the rest of this morning, and rest of today, and all your life. Then you have moved closer to the Christian maturity that Jesus wants for us, that will bring us real happiness.

We pray: Heavenly Father, we **do** worry, even though we are mature Christians, about a friend in Iraq or Afghanistan, a family member who is ill, how we will make it in school, or after school. For these failures of faith we ask forgiveness. Look on us as having the faith of Jesus, whose trust in you never wavered though he faced trouble and death for us on the cross. And then help us to **work hard in contentment, seeking first your kingdom,** certain that you love us, will surely feed us, and care for us in all things. We pray it in Jesus' holy name. Amen.

†

November 3, 2009

Lord of the U-Turn

INI

Among the happy moments in life are the times we walk out of the doctor's office after a checkup in which we are found fully healthy. Nothing wrong. Nothing to worry about, till the next checkup. The relief of that moment is surpassed only by the time we walk out of the dentist office. No cavities. Nothing to worry about till the next checkup.

But happy moments like those are always tempered by a nagging awareness. Some day, there **will** be a less pleasant visit. Some day the doctor **will** find something wrong. It might even be something that won't heal, something chronic, like diabetes, or MS – something that will afflict us for the rest of our lives, and we just have to learn to live with it. Sooner or later it will be something that won't heal, and we can't live with it. That discovery in the doctor's office might be delayed, but the only way to avoid it is by an earlier catastrophe. One way or the other, we will die.

I won't discount the sadness that always accompanies death. But we **do** address it with the faith worked by God's Word in passages such as this before us this morning:

> Then I heard a voice from heaven saying to me, "Write: 'Blessed are the dead who die in the Lord from now on.'" "Yes," says the Spirit, "that they may rest from their labors, and their works follow them."
> Revelation 14.13

Our Lord Jesus has been given many names in Scripture. This morning may I give him perhaps a new one? I'll call him Lord of the U-turn. That's a good name because Jesus turns things around.

Jesus reverses the effects of sin!

Remember the curse our first parents Adam and Eve earned by their sin? How mankind would have to work and sweat to wrest food out of the ground? Jesus for a few moments reversed that curse when he fed 5000 people out of a few loaves and fishes. John 6.10 He turned that curse around.

Does sickness strike even those in the strength of youth, and do we encounter more and more frailties as we age? Jesus went about healing, restoring to strength and health. He faced deterioration and turned it around.

Do people die? Remember that funeral procession for the widow's son coming out of Nain? Jesus raised that boy back to life and turned the procession around. Luke 7.11f. And then he turned around death itself for good when he submitted to it himself, and broke free from the grave in his Easter morning resurrection.

Jesus turns things around. He turns **us** around, because in his death he suffered punishment for **our** sin and puts on us who believe in him the white robe of his righteousness. We were marching to hell – he turns us around toward Heaven. We were marching to death – he turns us around to life. *"Blessed are the dead who die in the Lord from now on. Yes, says the Spirit, and they will rest from their labors, and their works follow them."*

Notice, the works follow – they don't go ahead. Our works are not our ticket into Heaven. Jesus provides the ticket, and it's free – free to **us**, but not to him. He paid for our ticket on the cross. And that turns our works around. When we depend entirely on Jesus for that ticket, the good things we do as believers are not selfish, not to earn points for selves but rather to show love and thanks to God by showing love to each other. Since those good things we do as Christians are empowered by Jesus, they are turned around; they really aren't **our** works anymore, but they are Jesus' works through us.

And so we arrive in Heaven surrounded by what Jesus did, wearing **his** white robe in a cloud of **his** good works. We can't enter Heaven any other way. We wouldn't want to enter Heaven any other way than surrounded by what Jesus did for us.

When we think of resting from our work, we think vacation. We certainly look forward to vacations. At some point in your life you'll decide on a favorite vacation spot. I know some who like Glacier National Park and go there as often as they can. For us, it's a time-share in Florida on a beautiful Gulf Coast beach. Isn't it delicious after a hard semester and a tough year to look forward to going to that vacation spot, to arriving, and just relaxing, with no cares or worries for a while?

But the fun is always tempered by the realization that it will end. The first day of the vacation week is great because seven whole days stretch before you. Then by Wednesday you're thinking, my goodness, is it half gone already? By Friday, it's only one day, one night left before it's over. And then it's over.

But not Heaven. There the rest will never end.

We look forward to it. We pray for it. In church, as part of the liturgy we often sing, *"Lord let your servant depart in peace."* Since we usually sing it at the end of the service, for a long time I thought depart meant just to go home. Well, it really does mean go home, but in a more profound sense. It means to die. The words were first spoken by aged Simeon as he held the baby Jesus in his arms. Remember, he had been promised he would not die before he saw the promised Savior. Now he held the baby, and was content to die, so he prayed, *"Lord let your servant now die in peace, according to your word. For my eyes have seen your salvation which you have prepared before all people."* Luke 2.29f.

At the end of our chapel services here, we often hear the words "Depart in peace." Certainly that means, walk out of chapel with the contentment of knowing that, through Jesus' work, your sins are forgiven and you have peace with God. But it means more: it means, know that you are ready to die. If the Lord calls you today, you are ready. You are at peace, confident in this promise before us this morning.

If you remember the relief you felt walking out of that clinic, knowing you were healthy, or cavity free, or you've known the pleasure of starting a vacation week of rest, then you can begin to imagine what it will be like walking into Heaven, surrounded by that cloud of what Jesus did: free from sin at last, free of physical infirmities, free of the fear of death, starting an eternity of rest thanks to the love of God in our Lord Jesus. Truly blessed are the dead who die in the Lord.

†

December 2009

Our Journey in One Verse

INI

If you watch sports on television, I know you've seen it in the stands, maybe behind the end zone, somebody holding up a sign that says, "John 3.16." It's good I suppose that they are willing to show they are Christians and it's a great verse, of course – the Gospel in a sentence: *God so loved the world* etc. But if I were inclined to hold up a sign at a football game (I'm not), I'd rather use instead the verse before us this morning also from the inspired pen of John. It tells the whole story of our Christian lives in 2½ verses. It tells of

> the mercy of God the Father
> the atonement by God the Son
> our sanctification by God the Holy Spirit

It tells how we enter the Christian life, what we do while there, and most of all, it tells where it will finally bring us. It's about the great trip, the journey that lies before each of us. It tells about going to Heaven. Listen to this wonderful text in Revelation chapter one:

> To Him who loved us and washed us from our sins in His own blood and has made us kings and priests to His God and Father, to Him be glory and dominion forever and ever. Amen. Behold, He is coming with clouds, and every eye will see Him, even they who pierced Him. And all the tribes of the earth will mourn because of Him. Even so, Amen. Revelation 1. 5-7

The saddest stories of all history, literature and film are those of lost opportunities. How sad that the young couple that could have found each other as soulmates passed up that opportunity to talk with each other that would have sparked a life-long love. How sad that so many who have heard of Jesus and even know his name have rejected him and have passed up the opportunity to receive the salvation he won for them. When Jesus comes again in the clouds all they can do is wail and mourn. Their chance is gone, the opportunity is past.

God has no pleasure in their anguish. But so it must be. There must be accountability, there must be consequences or there is no morality. Nor should we take pleasure in the mourning of those who are lost. We all fall short of God's glory. We can only thank the Holy Spirit who came to us through God's Word and taught us of him who loved us and washed us from our sins in his own blood, then moved our cold hard hearts to believe it and so be saved.

That's how we entered our Christian lives – washed clean of our sins in Jesus' blood, brought to faith in Baptism by the Holy Spirit where we now enjoy the privileges of our new relationship with God won by Jesus Christ. He has (we read) made us kings – John wrote this at a time when few lived as kings. He has made us priests – again written at a time when only a few were considered to have direct access to God. The full meaning of our Christian lives as kings and priests we'll leave aside this morning, since it is explored daily here in chapel.

The main focus here is that great journey. It's the hope we have been given, grounded in the work of Christ and in the promise of his coming again to end this present age and bring us to himself in Heaven. That is our sure Christian hope.

How will you greet Jesus when he comes? Do you have it planned? The custom in the Old Testament when meeting royalty, certainly when encountering God, was to fall flat on the ground, face down. We don't have such a custom in our culture. We'd just step forward and shake hands. What is your plan? You should have a plan. It's a measure of his love for us, I think, that Jesus doesn't seem to require that we greet him by falling down before him. In the Gospel reading last Sunday, Jesus said, when you see the signs of the end, lift up your heads! Luke 21.28 And a bit later he added, be always on the watch, and pray that you may be able to escape all that is about to happen, and that you may be able to stand before the Son of Man. v36

More important than how we greet him will be our reflexive response when he appears, when all the world will see him coming in a cloud. Where will you be, what will you be doing? Will you be in a place, doing a thing where your reflexive response will be "Oh no!"? What a terrible opportunity to miss, if we must join those who wail and mourn. Or will you be ready so that your reflexive response will be "Oh Yes!"?

Yesterday we sang a hymn that asked the question: "O How Shall I Receive Thee?" Over the years, the Bethany choir has sung a beautiful arrangement of that hymn. Its last stanza sums up the reading before us this morning. Let it be our prayer:

> He comes to judge the nations, a terror to his foes,
> A light of consolations and blessed hope to those
> Who love the Lord's appearing. O glorious Sun, now come.
> Send forth thy beams so cheering and guide us safely home.

Live out that hope and you won't need to hold up a sign to show others you are a Christian.

†

August 23, 2010
In Good Shepherd Chapel
for the Bethany Lutheran Theological Seminary Opening Service

Don't Lose the Cross

INI

7 Dear friends, let us love one another, for love comes from God. Everyone who loves has been born of God and knows God. 8 Whoever does not love does not know God, because God is love. 9 This is how God showed his love among us: He sent his one and only Son into the world that we might live through him. 10 This is love: not that we loved God, but that he loved us. 11 Dear friends, since God so loved us, we also ought to love one another. 12 No one has ever seen God; but if we love one another, God lives in us and his love is made complete in us. 1 John 4.7-12 NIV1984

This is **not** our text.

The text before us this morning has vanished. I had planned to speak to you today on these words from 1 John 4.10: *"God sent his Son as an atoning sacrifice for our sins."* But if you look at these verses from 1 John printed out on the front of your worship folder [and above], and examine verse 10, you won't find those words. They have vanished.

It's not that they aren't important words. In fact, in the middle of a discussion of God's love for us, they are the most important words of all. These words capture the essence of God's love for us. How could they vanish?

That's what my wife and I wondered last spring when we attended the funeral of a relative, a member of a family very dear to us who are not of our fellowship. The funeral was held in a mainstream Protestant church, and the officiant chose these verses from 1 John on which to base her sermon. She read these verses as they appear on the front of your worship folder. It sounded odd when she read them, and I confess I had to look up the verses in the pew Bible to check out why. It quickly became clear as it will to you if you look at these verses on the **back** of your worship folder. There verse 10 reads: *"This is love: not that we loved God, but that he loved us and sent his Son as an atoning sacrifice for our sins."* She had left out these words from verse 10: **and sent his Son as an atoning sacrifice for our sins.** They had just vanished.

Without those words, then, she could make the point of her sermon: we all loved the departed one very much, and it was our love that would keep him alive for us in our memories. That was it.

Funerals are invariably sad occasions. Jesus himself wept at one. John 11.35 But a funeral without Jesus – in fact, a funeral in which Jesus and his salvation work for us were deliberately and purposely left out – is nothing but depressing.

Seminarians, young students of the Word, you are being called to prepare to bring to the world this very message: *God sent his Son as an atoning sacrifice for our sins.* As it has been said for generations among Bible-believing Lutherans: we preach Christ, and him crucified.

I had another soul-searching experience early this summer. I received an email from a former student, a Bethany graduate, who wanted my advice. She wanted to know if I would encourage her to leave the Lutheran faith in which she had been brought up and join the United Church of Christ. She explained why she was so attracted to that church: they are so loving, she said, and they welcome everybody. I felt like shouting back: we're loving too! And we are. But I wondered why, after spending four years at our school and many hours in my class, she hadn't noticed that.

I exchanged numerous emails with this young woman. I tried to engage her on the importance of sound doctrine. I had recently written a short screenplay dramatizing Luther's wonderfully Biblical and Christ-centered presentation at the Heidelberg Disputation in 1518. As you recall, at the Heidelberg Disputation, which occurred only a few months after he nailed the famous theses to the church door in Wittenberg, Luther displayed a remarkably mature theology. The young woman seemed much interested in the script I sent her but one of her first comments was this: there is too much about the crucifixion in there.

There it is again, isn't it? Not only do the verses describing the atoning sacrifice of Christ vanish, but the crucifixion itself is wished away.

There is no room here for us to be smug. We have our own habits of mind that tend to do the same thing. Too many times in our own lives, we make Christ's crucifixion, his atonement too little a thing. When our preaching fails to center on Christ's payment for our sins, that atonement starts to vanish. When we worry about money or health or all the problems that life places before us, Christ's atonement starts to vanish. When we get stressed by our workload and annoyed by what we must do to prepare ourselves to preach the atonement, the atonement starts to vanish. We too need to focus on Christ on the cross. Especially when the guilt of our sins starts to overwhelm us, and we are overcome by our own shortcomings and weaknesses, and we fear we may never be effective shepherds of the Lord's flock, that's when we need most of all to focus on this verse and not let it vanish for us: *God sent his Son as an atoning sacrifice for our sins*. Our sins are forgiven.

That's the message to which we cling, by the Spirit's power, and it saves us and strengthens us and encourages us and motivates us. *God sent his Son as an atoning sacrifice for our sins*.

That's the message you are preparing to take out into the world, as the Lord's ambassadors.

It's the message that empowers the waters of Baptism. It's the message that finds embodiment in the bread and wine of the Lord's Supper. Don't ever let that verse vanish but make its message prominent in your life and in your preaching and teaching. God sent his Son as an atoning sacrifice for our sins. In that message is your purpose. In that message is the power of God.

SDG[1]

We pray:

Heavenly Father, we thank you for sending your Son to be an atoning sacrifice for our sins. Lord Jesus, we thank you for willingly submitting to your Father's will and offering yourself as the atoning sacrifice for our sins. O Holy Spirit, we thank you for calling us to faith in this atoning sacrifice. Empower us as we prepare to bring this saving message boldly to all those for whom this sacrifice was made. We ask this in the name of the atoning one, our beloved Savior. Let his saving work never vanish from our hearts or from our lips.

AMEN.

---

[1] My sermon notes always ended with "SDG," which stands for the Latin phrase, *soli Deo gloria*, meaning "To God alone be the glory."

October 10, 2010
At Peace Lutheran Church, North Mankato,
and also at Resurrection Lutheran Church, Winter Haven, Florida

Lord Increase My Faith!

INI

Please join me in the most wonderful prayer one can pray. It was prayed by the disciples in our Gospel reading. It's just four words long:

Lord increase my faith. Amen Luke 17.5

Today we consider faith. When I taught seminary students about sermon-making in homiletics class I used to caution them about preaching about faith. I told them, if you aren't careful you could turn people inward and focus them on their inner condition. You could make faith seem like something we must do to earn merit with God. Now, it is important for a Christian to understand faith's role in their lives. So I will take my own advice and speak cautiously to you this morning about faith. I'll first direct your attention to faith, and then I will direct your attention away from faith.

Today, I'll use all of the Scripture readings for this Sunday, printed on the back of your worship folder,[1] and look for what in particular these readings tell us about faith in Jesus. Of course, we're not talking about faith by itself – people have faith in all kinds of things. But the Bible, the message of God for us, teaches about **faith in Jesus our Savior**. Let me summarize in advance what we will find:

That faith in Jesus gives us life.

That faith in Jesus fills our life.

Look first at the last verse of the first reading: "**The righteous will live by his faith.**" Habakuk 2.4 St. Paul quotes this Old Testament passage in his letter to the Romans. That's the book in which he addresses the biggest question of life: how can we stand before God?

---

[1] For in the gospel a righteousness from God is revealed, a righteousness that is by faith from first to last, just as it is written: "**The righteous will live** by faith." Romans 1.17

Clearly no one is justified before God by the law, because, "**The righteous will live** by faith." Galatians 3.11

I have been reminded of **your sincere faith**, which first lived in your grandmother Lois and in your mother Eunice and, I am persuaded, now lives in you also. 2 Timothy 1.5

How long, O LORD, must I call for help, but you do not listen? ... but the **righteous will live** by his faith. Habakuk 2.4

To stand before God means we can live – live forever. To stand before God we must be righteous, sinless, holy. Righteous before God means we can live! How can we stand righteous and sinless before God? St. Paul answers that important question by quoting this Old Testamnt passage: *"The righteous (just) shall live by faith"* – faith: that humble, steadfast reliance in God, based on God's Word and promises.

That's not natural for us. Our natural state is the opposite: unbelief, and unbelief is the biggest insult to God. Have you ever told the truth and not been believed? Then you know yourself how insulting is the feeling of not being believed. St. Paul, as he writes to the Romans, explores the effects of unbelief. He speaks of how God's anger is being revealed against all the wickedness and godlessness around us, and in fact, when we are honest with ourselves, the wickedness and godlessness that so often still wells up within us.

The apostle supplies us with a pretty awful list and yes, I'm on it, and so are you. He says,

> They have become filled with every kind of wickedness, evil, greed and depravity. They are full of envy, murder, strife, deceit and malice. They are gossips, slanderers, God-haters, insolent, arrogant and boastful; they invent ways of doing evil; they disobey their parents; they are senseless, faithless, heartless, ruthless. Romans 1.29-31

That's quite a list. And please don't rush to the excuse that you haven't done **all** those things. If you've done **one** you are no longer righteous and sinless. The apostle has described our natural condition and it doesn't lead to life. It leads to death, now, soon, and throughout eternity. How shall we be rescued? How can we **live**? The prophet answers (and St. Paul echoes) *"The righteous will live by his faith."*

Notice, it is not by our deeds, or any good works, or keeping God's rules that we live. St. Paul quotes this Old Testament passage again in his letter to the Galatians. He says

> Clearly no one is justified before God by the law [keeping God's rules], because "The righteous will live by faith." Galatians 3.11

Keeping God's rules can never win us life because we can't keep God's rules perfectly. If we sin once, we are no longer sinless. God's rules, the Law, curses us, and condemns us to death.

But thanks be to God, as St. Paul goes on to write to the Galatians

> Christ redeemed us from the curse of the law by becoming a curse for us, for it is written: "Cursed is everyone who is hung on a tree." Galatians 3.13

There it is, the beautiful, precious good news, the Gospel. Jesus Christ hung on the tree of the cross bearing all of our sins, and the sins of the whole world. He paid there the penalty we owed God and for Christ's sake, God considers our penalty paid in full. We are in God's eyes, sinless and righteous. Our sins are forgiven. And that gift becomes ours – yours and mine- by faith. When we believe it, we have it.

Even that faith is a gift from God. The Holy Spirit moves us to trust in the salvation won for us by Jesus Christ on the cross. And then we have it. That is how faith in Jesus gives us life. Jesus' sacrifice for us makes us righteous. That righteousness is ours when we believe it. And we can stand before God and live. *"The righteous will live by his faith."*

Now let's look further into these readings and see how our faith in Jesus not only gives us life, but also fills our lives. We'll see that faith doesn't necessarily make our lives easy. But it does make them thoroughly and fully Christian.

No, not necessarily easy. Faith-life is not sugar coated, contrary to how some TV preachers would mislead you to believe that faith guarantees wealth and health.

In our second Bible lesson for today, Paul speaks about his suffering for the Gospel. Faith doesn't prevent suffering but it does mean we don't have to be ashamed of it, because with Paul we can say in suffering, *"I know whom I have believed, and am convinced that he is able to guard what I have entrusted to him for that day."* 2 Timothy 1.12

It's not necessarily easy. In our first lesson, the prophet wails a deep cry from the bottom of his soul: *"How long must I call for help, but you do not listen?"* Habakuk 1.2 The inspired Psalmist called out the same lament, *"how long?"* more than a dozen times. There is an entire inspired book of the Bible called *Lamentations.*

But these are not wails of complaining, or grumbling against God. It takes faith to wail like this. It's what one writer called "being brutally honest with God" and it shows faith: that is, confidence that the Lord is truly concerned, and hope that he will do something. The people Jesus himself commended for their faith were never prosperous and trouble-free. It was the poor, sick, and troubled who were blessed by their faith, who remained confident that God's answer is coming.

Where else does faith in Christ fill our lives? There are times of the miraculous, the surprising, as if we were by faith to re-plant mulberry trees into the middle of the lake (as in the third reading Luke 17.6). Now don't puzzle if you can't right now replant a tree in a lake. You could if it served God's purpose, but God's purpose is not to show off or to do magic tricks. Jesus gives us this fanciful example to show that with God there are no impossibilities.

And so history records many surprising events due to faith. In Hebrews 11, we find the famous list of heroes of faith: Noah built an ark, Abraham left his home for an unknown land, Moses left the wealth of Egypt and remained true to his people, Joshua brought down the walls of Jericho, Samson, David, the prophets, the martyrs who gave their lives. Hebrews 11. 7f. Certainly God is capable of miraculous responses to **our** faith.

But far more often, faith in Jesus fills the Christian's daily life in more ordinary ways. As when, like in second reading in which grandmother Lois, and mother Eunice taught their faith to young Timothy 2 Timothy 1.5 we pass our faith down to our children and grandchildren, trusting in God's promise: *"Train up a child in the way he should go, and when he is old he will not depart from it."* Proverbs 22.6

Look further in these readings: (at the beginning of the third reading) we can forgive others multiple times because in faith we know we are forgiven; (at the end of the third reading) we can lead a contented Christian life, knowing that our works of service are nothing special to be proud of, or depend upon, but we depend in faith entirely on the work of Jesus for us. These are ordinary effects of faith in the three readings. Can we also see faith operating elsewhere in our lives? I know we can. Consider:

By faith in Jesus...

> We get up in the morning to face a tough day, knowing God is with us.
>
> We unload our sins at night onto Jesus' cross, and sleep at peace with God.
>
> We see the fall leaves in colorful splendor, say thank you Lord.
>
> We come here to church to worship.
>
> We support a pastor and his ministry with friendship, encouragement and money.
>
> We bring our children to Baptism.
>
> We bring our children here for instruction, passing on our faith as Lois and Eunice did.
>
> We support our Christian schools, Sunday school, elementary, high school, and college.
>
> We plan ways to help people in need.
>
> We fight the sin that tempts and oppresses us.

All this we do by faith in Jesus.

In good times, by faith we offer prayers of joy. In troubled times, by faith we also offer prayers of joy.

We sing a hymn in our minds as we get wheeled into surgery.

We shake off the dread of death, confident that we rest in our Savior's arms, and that his angels will carry us to Heaven.

You can continue the list of ways faith in Jesus fills your life and see how all we do starts with our confidence that, in Christ, God is gracious. In Christ, God's intention for us is peace and good, and abundant life now and in eternity.

I have been directing your attention to faith. It's time for me quickly to direct your attention away from faith. We started a few minutes ago joining the disciples in prayer, *"Lord increase my faith."* Do you want stronger faith? Then don't look inward, don't try to gauge or measure the level of your faith. Instead, look outward. Look at Jesus and his cross. Look at Jesus brought to us in the Word. Bring your children to Baptism and remember your own Baptism where you were buried with Christ and with him will rise again to new life. Come to the Lord's table and receive there the body and blood of Jesus.

That's how faith increases. That's how our faith in Jesus gives us life. That's how our faith in Jesus continues to fill our lives. Lord, increase our faith today, through your Word and Sacraments. Amen.

†

Why You Are in College

INI

Why are you in college? I think the reading before us is about that. Let's see. It's from St. Paul's letter to the Colossians chapter two:

> So then, just as you received Christ Jesus as Lord, continue to live in him, rooted and built up in him, strengthened in the faith as you were taught, and overflowing with thankfulness. See to it that no one takes you captive through hollow and deceptive philosophy, which depends on human tradition and the basic principles of this world rather than on Christ. Colossians 2:6-8

Remember the clothing fads from when you were a kid? Something everybody had to wear in grade school, or even in high school? A certain kind of shoelaces, bracelets, jeans? I'm embarrassed to tell you this, but one year when I was in high school, all the guys had to wear gold cords – we all went out to buy gold colored corduroy slacks, and we wore them around school. It must have looked very strange.

Remember those toy fads that went by so fast? My kids went through the new ones each year. Maybe you are too young to remember the pound puppies, strawberry shortcakes, and cabbage patches, but you had some others of your own. There's a tremendous attractiveness, a magnetism when these fashions and fads "go viral." Everybody has to get in on them.

These toy and fashion fads are pretty harmless, even if expensive. St. Paul in our reading is talking about fads that are not harmless. He's talking about "hollow and deceptive philosophies," ways of thinking and living that are very popular all around us, but that can take us captive, that can rob us of our faith, and of our salvation.

Some of these are very close to your experience. I know you have felt their tug. They are so common all around us that St. Paul calls them "basic principles of this world." Most common is the idea that man is god. This goes all the way back to the Tower of Babel. This notion that we don't need God so we can imagine God doesn't exist, is preached with great energy by the atheists and agnostics these days. The idea that human beings are their own savior is so tempting that it even finds its way into nearly every religion, where they teach that what **we** do (not what God does for us) determines our destiny.

There's also the widely popular temptation to serve yourself first. What's the slogan? "Look out for number one!" This is the basis for the greed that permeates our culture, and for believing that money-making is the highest value of life. Some say increasing your earning power is why you go to college. Could that be why you are in college?

And then there's the temptation all around us of fun and pleasure as the highest value of life. "Just do it," we hear. "If you really loved me you would," we might hear. Those ideas are popular all around us. I hope that's not why you are in college.

There are other philosophies – some call them worldviews – and a long list of "isms" like modernism and post-modernism and many others, supported by what St. Paul calls "fine sounding arguments" – not good arguments, even by human standards, but they're fine sounding. I hope you are learning to become interested in these philosophies, world views, aspects of popular culture. I hope you want to recognize them as what they are: passing fads of thinking and acting. Study them and compare them with the real standard for evaluating all ideas: God's Word. Learning to sort out the good from the bad, learning to avoid becoming captured by any dangerous ideas – that's called discernment. It's a part of wisdom. I hope that's one of the main reasons you are in college.

Paul tells us why: we are different. We are changed. He reminds us of what has happened to us: *"You received Christ Jesus as Lord,"* he says. What a special wonderful blessing, that God found us with the message of Jesus, and of what Jesus did for us, how he paid for our sins there on the cross and made us friends once again with God. What a special wonderful blessing that God reached out to you and me and adopted us in Baptism and made us into believers in Jesus. Our sins are forgiven!

Now stay rooted! Like a solid tree, let your roots grow firmly into the rock of Christ, *"rooted and built up in him, strengthened in the faith as you were taught, and overflowing with thankfulness."*

Abounding, overflowing with thankfulness! Have you been doing that? Abounding in thankfulness to God? Do you know how to do that? It's worth some attention, some effort. Abounding in thankfulness to God. Give some thought to how you can do that. Maybe that's why you are in college.

†

September 7, 2010

Today, Only Thank You

INI

About seven years ago the Bethany Debate Team attended some tournaments in Belgrade, Serbia, one of the Balkan countries recently torn by war and ethnic cleansing. One evening, after a day's competition, students from a variety of countries gathered for a party. As they enjoyed each other's company, joining in a snake dance around the room, one of the coaches said in my ear: "Two years ago, their parents were shooting at each other."

Today in chapel we celebrate some pretty wonderful things by remembering some pretty terrible things. It's a wonderful thing that you could walk to chapel this morning without even thinking that those brick colonnades in front of the library and Old Main would make important protection, where you could duck for cover against sniper fire. A few years ago where we were debating, and right now in Afghanistan, and in parts of Iraq, those sniper worries are on the top of the minds of many people as they walk down any street.

It's a wonderful thing that you can go to your residence hall tonight and go to sleep, without fearing that a gang of thugs from nearby Eagle Lake or St. Clair will come sweeping through the campus with no police to stop them, raping and maiming and killing apparently for the fun of it. Right now, at this very moment in Darfur and Congo, central Africa, where it is night, young women are lying awake with just such a fear, because it has already happened there many times.

It's a wonderful thing that you can afford a college education – well maybe just barely in some cases, but here you are. Right now, in Liberia, and Haiti, and Gaza, and Zimbabwe and dozens of other countries around the world, more than half the population is living below the global poverty line which is defined as earning one U. S. dollar a day.

We come to chapel each day to worship God. One of the most important functions of worship is simply to say thank you, and to celebrate the blessings God showers upon us. That's what happens in our reading today, three verses from Psalm 147.

The entire Psalm is a celebration.

> [You'll hear more about this psalm next week if you tune in to *Evening Bells at Bethany*, the short nightly devotion on the BLC website designed to send you to sleep with thoughts of God's

Word in your head. Evening Bells is a good bedtime habit to cultivate while you are here at school. It starts tonight.]

This entire psalm is a celebration. It contains no complaints, it asks for nothing. It is simply an outpouring of gratitude. While our loving God invites us to ask him for things, and even promises to listen to our complaints, it is often best on some occasions simply to say thank you. That's what we are doing this morning.

The three verses from this psalm before us today focus on three blessings: protection, peace, and prosperity. Listen to these words:

> Extol the LORD, O Jerusalem; praise your God, O Zion, for he strengthens the bars of your gates and blesses your people within you. He grants peace to your borders and satisfies you with the finest of wheat. Psalm 147:12-14

Protection: "*He strengthens the bars of your gates and blesses your people within you.*" We don't have to duck sniper bullets on the BLC campus.

Peace: "*He grants peace to your borders.*" We don't have to fear raiders from St. Clair or Eagle Lake.

Prosperity: "*He satisfies you with the finest of wheat.*" We get by very nicely on more than one U. S. dollar per day.

This is a moment to realize: let's not take these temporal blessings from a loving God for granted.

We can do the same for spiritual blessings.

Protection: Last spring I taught for six weeks in China, a country where, if we held a gathering like this one here this morning, about now the police would come in – and the police would not be our friends. They would take down the names of each one of us, tell you to go home, and they might take the leader with them.

Thank you Lord for the freedom to worship.

Peace: That's what we receive when we gather around God's Word and worship as we are here this morning. "*Peace on earth*" is the message proclaimed by the angel choir on that first Christmas, Luke 2.14 as Jesus Christ, the Son of God, entered our earthly existence in a special way. He put on flesh and blood, and became a human creature, like us except with no sin. By his innocent death on the cross, he satisfied our moral debt before God – our sins are forgiven! – and he made us God's friends. Where we had been at war with God, Jesus brought us peace.

Thank you Lord for making peace between us and God.

Prosperity: Here at Bethany we have opportunities to indulge in the riches of God you can find in few other places. We have chapel for worship, "Evening Bells" for nightly comfort, classes where we plunge into God's Word in depth, other classes where every subject is related to God's word and will, and abundant opportunities to grow in our faith and in our love and service to each other. People who have graduated from Bethany, again and again, report to us: this is what they miss most about Bethany.

Thank you, Lord, for your Spirit who enables us to prosper here in your Word.

Protection. Peace. Prosperity. Temporal blessings and eternal blessings.

Today we have no complaints. We ask for nothing. We say only, Lord, thank you.

†

September 30, 2010

Working in Blessed Slavery

INI

Today I want to urge you to enjoy your slavery, because slavery is freedom.

Now, words like that are more than odd. They sound sinister, even Orwellian. You would expect to hear them only from the lips of a profound cynic, or even an evil tyrant. But in our Scripture reading this morning, they are words coming, through the inspired apostle, from a kind and loving God. Follow with me, please, these words before us from St. Paul.

> But thanks be to God that, though you used to be slaves to sin, you wholeheartedly obeyed the form of teaching to which you were entrusted. You have been set free from sin and have become slaves to righteousness. Romans 6.17-18

Slavery. It has taken many forms throughout history, but all have in common what is captured in the phrase, involuntary servitude. Paul is telling us here something central to the human condition. Everyone is a slave to something. You and I are too. The question is, to what?

Paul says, you **were** Slaves to sin. We were born into that, we didn't choose it. But our natural selves seem to want it. It's easy for our natural selves to turn ourselves over to sin. You know of people who have done this, people in the news do it, celebrities and leaders do it. We see people around us do it and they become shipwrecks of persons.

That natural tendency is still strong in us too. Even as Christians, we still have what Scripture calls the Old Adam, this natural sinful nature that wants to sin. You feel it every day and so do I. This entire chapter of Paul's letter to the Romans deals with these urges to sin even in Christians. He has just explained so beautifully and plainly the forgiveness we have through the grace of God in Jesus Christ and then he begins this chapter by posing this question: "*What shall we say, then? Shall we go on sinning so that grace may increase?*" Romans 6.1

The fact that this question even arises shows how deep is our natural slavery to sin. Even when we hear about the forgiveness and grace of God, our old self schemes and says to itself, great now that means I can sin more and be forgiven more! So the apostle has to chop that thought off. "*By no means! God forbid!,*" he says. "*We died to sin; how can we live in it any longer?*"

Do you see how sneaky and insidious is our natural slavery to sin? There is that part of us that still wants to do it more and more. But God urges us here through the inspired apostle: don't give in to that! That was before. Now we are changed. Now, he says, we are slaves to righteousness.

Now that's an involuntary servitude too. We didn't will that or choose it. Yesterday we heard how God chose you and me as bricks in the wall of the Church of God built on the cornerstone of Christ. Ephesians 2.20 The bricks didn't choose themselves. We confess how it happened in Luther's explanation of the third article of the Apostles' Creed:

> I cannot by my own reason or strength believe in Jesus Christ, or come to him, but the Holy Ghost has called me by the Gospel, enlightened me with his gifts, sanctified and kept me in the one true faith.

Like the Romans to whom Paul wrote, we too by the power of the Spirit have *"obeyed from the heart that form of teaching to which you were delivered."*

That form of teaching is, of course, the "one thing needful"[1] which we celebrate so often in this chapel, the saving Gospel of Jesus Christ. To obey that from the heart is to grasp by faith the work of Christ for us, faith in his good life which God now credits to us and faith in his innocent death paying the full penalty for our sins.

Playing with the words "slavery" and "obedience" Paul calls faith in Christ *"obeying from the heart"* the teaching of the Gospel, which he says leads us to a new slavery, one he calls *"slavery to righteousness."* You learned long ago, I think, what righteousness means to Paul. It's not something we earn, not something we do but something given to us. As we read just a few verses further in this same chapter: *"The **gift** of God is eternal life, through Jesus Christ our Lord."* Romans 6.23 When the Gospel seizes our lives, when we know and trust that our sins are forgiven, when we become slaves to righteousness, that, says Paul, is freedom – freedom from having to sin, even freedom from having to "not-sin," because our salvation depends not on what we do, sinning or not sinning; we are saved entirely by what Christ did for us.

This is who we now are, through faith in Christ. When we were slaves to sin, Satan worked through us and we did evil works, leading to death. Now that we are slaves to righteousness, Jesus works through us and we do good works, leading to eternal life.

That's not a bad addiction is it? – doing good through the power of Christ in us. That slavery, to righteousness, is freedom. Work at it! And enjoy it!

†

---

[1] The motto of Bethany Lutheran College based on Luke 10.42.

December 2010

Life and Death at Christmas

INI

The sight of your good friend lying injured in the middle of the basketball court has a profound effect on your enjoyment of the game.

You may have been thoroughly caught up in the excitement of the game and the anticipation of victory. But if your player friend is suddenly brought down with what might be a career-ending injury, your concern for the victory goes quickly into the background. And if on closer inspection you notice that the injury was to the neck and might even be life-threatening – well then you suddenly lose interest in the entire sport. There is something about a life-and-death situation that quickly brings our activities into perspective, makes us realize what is really important.

Jesus does something like that in our reading today. He comes into our busy lives where we are preoccupied with so many things with a message of life-and-death seriousness. This Jesus, whom we like to picture as kind, smiling, a gentle friend, is suddenly exceedingly grim. His stern manner by itself is enough to compel our attention as he describes happenings yet to come, happenings which, if they were to befall us – I should say **when** they befall us – are certain to put into perspective such minor things as team records, semester grades, friends, school plans, and other such matters that preoccupy us. For Jesus is talking about life and death. Listen:

> "Just as it was in the days of Noah, so also will it be in the days of the Son of Man. People were eating, drinking, marrying and being given in marriage up to the day Noah entered the ark. Then the flood came and destroyed them all. It was the same in the days of Lot. People were eating and drinking, buying and selling, planting and building. But the day Lot left Sodom, fire and sulfur rained down from heaven and destroyed them all. It will be just like this on the day the Son of Man is revealed. On that day no one who is on the roof of his house, with his goods inside, should go down to get them. Likewise, no one in the field should go back for anything. Remember Lot's wife! Whoever tries to keep his life will lose it, and whoever loses his life will preserve it. I tell you, on that night two people will be in one bed; one will be taken and the other left. Two women will be grinding grain together; one will be taken and the other left." "Where Lord?" they asked. He replied, "Where there is a dead body, there the vultures will gather." Luke 17.26-37

It's important to keep this life-and-death perspective in mind as Christmas approaches. Christmas of course is a time of joy; we're busy with preparations, friends and family, gifts, warmth, fun and celebration, as we welcome once again with joy this little baby Jesus into our world. But keep perspective on why Jesus came. This cute little baby, this sweet little child wrapped in swaddling cloths in the warm glow of the manger under angel-filled skies, this holy infant so tender and mild came to die.

He came to die for your sins and mine. While we sing in welcoming him, "O come, O come Immanuel, and ransom captive Israel," remember what the ransom price is: his own life! "Come," we are inviting him, "Come so that you can die for me!"

And he comes.

As poet-composer Jan Nelson wrote, taking us close to the Christmas stable,

> There in a bed of hay
> The little Christ child lay
> and he smiles, yes he smiles
> – though my debt he must pay –
> still he smiles, he smiles for me.

Athletic team records, grades, school plans all are important, but keep them in a life-and-death perspective, not to diminish them but rather to enhance them by realizing their true value in God's long-term plans for us. Certainly keep the joy in Christmas. Work hard on all the preparations and celebrating. Never feel guilty for being busy at Christmas; it's our way of celebrating Christ's birth. But keep a life-and-death perspective on the joy, not to diminish it but to increase it by focusing on its true cause.

Christmas is about life and death. Jesus' death, our life.

†

August 7, 2011
At Peace Lutheran Church, North Mankato

Sharing Hope with Creation

INI

How will you greet the Lord Jesus when you see him? Have you planned that? It will happen, you know, when you and I arrive in Heaven. And it won't be just some kind of vague meeting of spirits. The Bible teaches that Jesus took his human body up into Heaven. His disciples saw it go. And the Bible teaches that you and I in our bodies will rise from death as Jesus did and that (as Job proclaimed) in our flesh we will see God.

So I ask again: how will you greet the Lord Jesus when you see him?

The Old Testament way was to fall down. In those cultures, a person greeted someone greater – a king, certainly God – by falling face down to the ground. Is that what you will do? That's not our culture. Sometimes in church we kneel in the Lord's presence. Asian cultures today bow when greeting. We shake hands – is that what you will do? Walk up to Jesus and shake his hand? That seems not special enough. Maybe it's worth giving some thought if only as part of our anticipation, our eager anticipation of Heaven.

In today's epistle reading we find that we humans are not the only ones eagerly anticipating Heaven. We share that longing and that hope with all of creation.

> I consider that our present sufferings are not worth comparing with the glory that will be revealed in us. The creation waits in eager expectation for the sons of God to be revealed. For the creation was subjected to frustration, not by its own choice, but by the will of the one who subjected it, in hope that the creation itself will be liberated from its bondage to decay and brought into the glorious freedom of the children of God. We know that the whole creation has been groaning as in the pains of childbirth right up to the present time. Not only so, but we ourselves, who have the firstfruits of the Spirit, groan inwardly as we wait eagerly for our adoption as sons, the redemption of our bodies. For in this hope we were saved. But hope that is seen is no hope at all. Who hopes for what he already has? But if we hope for what we do not yet have, we wait for it patiently. Romans 8.18-25

So let's talk this morning about **Sharing with creation our hope in the Lord.** We'll first observe why we need this hope, because

1. Together with creation, we suffer sin's burden.

And then we'll recall what we hope for, that is,

2. Together with creation we patiently await our full freedom.

We all know well the burden of sin. Remember how the Bible tells us what God gave us and what we lost. The universe, we read in Genesis, was created "very good." When something is very good in God's eyes, it is very good indeed. Creation was good physically, beautiful and harmonious, and it was good morally. Everything was conforming to God's will and pleasing to him. Human beings, too, Adam and Eve, were created very good, physically and morally. They were created in what the Bible calls the image of God, wonderful in intellect and knowledge, physically strong and morally straight.

But then sin came. Our first parents yielded to Satan's tempting voice. God's simple and only test by which they could continually show their love for him, "Don't eat from that one tree," they failed and plunged themselves and all creation into sinfulness. That wonderful image of God was lost. The glowing intellect was dimmed. We still have some capacity for thought and knowledge, but it comes with hard study and we are easily deceived. Our physical strength is limited and as we age it becomes feeble, finally unto death. The most profound loss was moral. Human desires and choices were turned entirely to sin, to selfishness, to pride, to evil. We had no capability whatever to do good in God's eyes and were doomed to punishment, to death, here on earth and eternally.

What a devastating loss! The effects of sin were so profound that they impacted not only the sinners, human beings, but all creation. The whole universe was dislocated by sin, made subject to frustration, the apostle says – that is, creation could no longer fulfill its creative function. It was no longer able to be what God first intended it to be. And so there came tornadoes, hurricanes, earthquakes, tsunamis, drought, and floods.

We can still tell that nature is a creation of God. We can still see, as Dr. Dau points out in his wonderful introduction to the Law and Gospel lectures of CFW Walther, that this is a "moral universe":

> *This world was not made to sin in; even the laws of nature resist the effort to sin, and the brute and inanimate creatures rebel, as it were, against being pressed into service to sin. Man finds out that it is really more proper, easier, and more advantageous not to sin in a world like ours, and that under existing conditions a person invariably makes life here hard for himself and others by sinning. Fully to suit sinners, the world would have to be made over again.[1]*

---

[1] C. F. W. Walther, *The Proper Distinction Between Law and Gospel*, introduction by Theodore Dau, p.vi.

Creation can still be good and lovely; when we work honestly with nature it produces food and resources for us, and while it takes effort, our gardens become bountiful with vegetables and beautiful with flowers. But where sin touches nature, it becomes ugly and destructive. Today's prevailing sin might well be materialism and greed. Everything we encounter – advertising, celebrity worship, politics – seems to glorify selfishness and maximize and reward greed. And when human greed touches nature, it makes things ugly. Have you been to the Pacific Northwest in our country to see the beautiful forests clear-cut away to leave mile upon ugly mile of bare tree stumps? Have you driven through the Rocky Mountains and noticed the rugged beauty of the cliffs marred by slag heaps, mining waste just left there, running down the mountainsides like teardrops? Have you flown over the Appalachians in the east to view the mountain-top removal methods of mining that destroy not only beauty but wildlife and fish as the toxic waste washes down through the mountain streams? I know you have seen photos of animals caught in the oil spills. And maybe you've read that, because of money, the earth's rainforests are being cut back every year by an area equal to the state of South Carolina, and that if this continues, the earth's rain forests, and their abundance of species of wildlife, will be entirely gone in 100 years? Yes, today, perhaps even more than when the apostle wrote, creation is groaning, as in the pains of childbirth, because of sin.

We feel that burden too, individually. We run down, as we age, with sags and bulges and memory loss and bad knees. And we struggle continuously with our own sin.

I get tired, don't you? of struggling against pride, and self-centeredness, and envy, and lust, and greed, and laziness, and all those other sins that assail us. We sigh to ourselves because of our lives in a sinful world, in these sinful bodies, and we grieve when we see the effects of sin in the lives of those we love. We try hard to make things better for them; sometimes we can make things a little better but sometimes we just can't fix things no matter how hard we try.

My, this has been a dreary and disheartening sermon so far, as we observe that, together with creation, we suffer sin's burden. But remember our theme: **Sharing with creation our hope in the Lord.** God has for us this wonderful gift: **hope** – that is, the **confident expectation of promised blessings.** These blessings are not now visible to us. But hope is much more than a **wish**. God is not asking us to wish for something too good to be true, something that is unlikely to happen. This blessing is real; it has already been won for us by God's Son Jesus Christ.

Yes, all creation was dislocated because of sin and all humankind was condemned because of sin. But God in his love did not leave us in that dreary condition. He entered into this ruined creation and became himself a fully human being, though without sin. God lived a life in this fallen world, was tempted to sin as all of us have been, but never yielded. God suffered under the wickedness of sinful men and was innocently put to death. Jesus Christ, God himself, fulfilled God's plan to rescue us and all creation from sin. In his love and grace, to remove sin's curse, God transferred all of our sins onto Jesus and transferred all of Jesus' innocence onto us. When Jesus died on that cross God counted all sinfulness paid for in full. Then Jesus rose again from death to show us that God's great rescue plan was accomplished, that our sins are gone, that death and decay have been replaced by life, and those who trust in God's rescue have its benefits, the sure hope of everlasting life in Heaven.

The apostle Paul tells us here that creation believes it. All nature looks forward to that future day when hope is fulfilled. What will that be like? The Bible's descriptions of Heaven aren't fully detailed; they can't be, because they are so far beyond our capability to understand. Paul says at the start of our reading that we can't fully comprehend what it will be like: "Our present sufferings are not worth comparing with the glory that will be revealed in us." The Bible can't reveal everything about Heaven but it tells us just enough to make us certain that we want to be there. What does this reading tell us about what we together with creation patiently await?

It says we will together enjoy a *"glorious freedom."* It says frustration will be removed, that is, finally nature can be fully what God intended. And the same for us: finally **we** can be fully what God intended. Will I be different when free from sin? Certainly! Now, because of sin I can't even be what *I* want to be, let alone what God wants me to be. But then, we can be fully who God intended. We can be what God has made us through his loving creation and loving redemption and loving sanctification. That's what it means to be adopted as God's "sons," to enjoy the redemption of our bodies, release from sin and mortality.

Elsewhere in Scripture we read more about Heaven. In John's Gospel, we have that wonderful promise of Jesus, *"In my Father's house are many rooms; ...I go to prepare a place for you."* John 14.2 We'll have a wonderful place to live! In Revelation we read that in Heaven death has been completely replaced by life. A river of clear (unpolluted) water runs through Heaven. There will be a new earth. That's the redemption of creation. Everything that troubles us will be healed. Everything will be fixed. And it says we will reign, that is, we will be actively busy in management, in service to God and others and it says we will see God's face. Revelation 22.4

Yes, we will meet Jesus. That brings us back to our opening question: how will you greet him? Fall to the ground? Kneel? Shake hands? We know that Jesus took little children right up onto his lap. He tells us that the Good Shepherd picks up the lost sheep and carries it to safety. We know that throughout our lives we have been kept safe in Jesus' arms. When I meet Jesus, I think I'll probably bow down in humble gratitude, but then (do I dare it?) I'm looking forward to a hug.

Certainly, together with creation, we suffer sin's burden. But also, together with creation we patiently await our full freedom in the redemption won for us by Jesus Christ. And so with all creation we share our hope in the Lord.

†

September 8, 2011

Be Changed

Have you heard any good news lately? A favorite relative had a baby? Your team won a close game? You passed the history exam? We love good news. What's the greatest, best news you ever heard? Since we're in chapel, you probably expect me to say that the answer should be the Gospel. That very word means good news. You are right: it should be.

Do you know that? Do you feel that? When the Gospel comes to mind, does it fill you with joy and confidence? Does it cast away all fear? Does it do that, even when you are not in chapel or in church? Even after you've heard it for the hundredth, the thousandth time?

You know in your head, I am sure, why the Gospel **should** be the best news you have ever heard. It's the assurance that the almighty God, Maker of heaven and earth, knows you personally, loves you personally, and has at great cost to himself assured your well-being, both now and for all eternity. The Gospel is the message that purely out of his grace, his love that we did not deserve, God has selected you by name, has placed your sins on the back of his only Son, Jesus Christ, whom he sent to bear the torments of hell and suffer death in your place, so that you might be saved from that fate which you deserved (and I deserved). By that act of love, God bought you so you could be **changed** from what you were, his degenerate enemy, to what you were meant to be, his holy child, in his blessed and joyful company forever.

Your sins are forgiven! God has by his gracious acts changed you and me from sinful to sinless. My message to you this morning is this: You are changed – so be changed.

I draw this message from a profound Bible text that is set before us this morning. It's from the middle of a psalm composed by David. The Bible introduces this psalm by observing, "Then David spoke to the LORD the words of this song on the day when the LORD had delivered him from the hand of all his enemies and from the hand of Saul." It's a triumphant song as it describes the way the Lord works. Here are David's words:

> With the merciful You will show Yourself merciful;
> With a blameless man You will show Yourself blameless;
> With the pure You will show Yourself pure;
> And with the devious You will show Yourself shrewd.
> You will save the humble people;
> > But Your eyes *are* on the haughty, *that* You may bring *them* down.
> > For You *are* my lamp, O LORD; The LORD shall enlighten my darkness.
>
> 2 Samuel 22. 26-29

There are many sermons in these words but this morning let me simply observe that they talk about how God deals with humankind, and more specifically, what he expects of us, who know and appreciate the best news ever. Again, in sum: You are changed – so be changed.

You and I were selected by God and brought to faith by the power of the Holy Spirit through Baptism and hearing his Word. That's how we were changed. As believers we are not what we were. Instead we are God's children, bound for Heaven. But we are not in Heaven yet. While we travel there through this life, God wants his saving work for us to make a difference in what kind of people we are now. We see that many places in Scripture, as in the precious Lord's prayer, *"Forgive us our trespasses, as we forgive those who trespass against us."* Matthew 6.12 Believers are to be changed, not to bear grudges or seek revenge, but to forgive. Jesus described to us the day of judgment, where the goats are sorted out for destruction while the sheep are gathered into heavenly bliss; the standard for judgment is the deeds believers performed as a result of their faith:

> Then the King will say to those on his right, "Come, you who are blessed by my Father; take your inheritance, the kingdom prepared for you since the creation of the world. For I was hungry and you gave me something to eat, I was thirsty and you gave me something to drink, I was a stranger and you invited me in, I needed clothes and you clothed me, I was sick and you looked after me, I was in prison and you came to visit me." Matthew 25.34-36

This is what David is praising in the reading before us. When we are changed by God, we begin to learn to do those things that please him, the things that characterize his children.

God changed us, so be changed. Be what God intended us to be! Merciful! Blameless! Pure! Humble! And then, as the psalmist assures us: O Lord...

With the merciful You will show Yourself merciful;
With a blameless man You will show Yourself blameless;
With the pure You will show Yourself pure;
And with the devious You will show Yourself shrewd.
You will save the humble people;
> But Your eyes *are* on the haughty, *that* You may bring *them* down.
> For You *are* my lamp, O LORD; The LORD shall enlighten my darkness.

We know the best good news ever! Jesus has placed us beside him in a walk to Heaven. Now walk with him.

†

Sunday, May 20, 2012
At East Seoul Canaan Lutheran Church, Seoul, South Korea
Preached in English, with translator Pastor Young Ha Kim

Meeting Jesus in Heaven

INI

When you see our Lord Jesus, how will you greet him? Have you planned that? It will happen, you know, when you and I arrive in Heaven. We will meet Jesus. And it won't be a meeting of ghosts or spirits. The Bible teaches that Jesus took his human body up into Heaven. His disciples saw it go. And the Bible teaches that you and I in our bodies will rise from death as Jesus did and that (as Job said) in our flesh we will see God. Job 19.25f.

So I ask again: how will you greet the Lord Jesus when you see him? The Old Testament way was to fall down. In those cultures, a person greeted someone greater, a king, certainly God, by falling face down to the ground. Is that what you will do? That's not our culture. Sometimes in church we kneel in the Lord's presence. In the U. S. we shake hands – that seems not special enough for meeting God. In Korea we bow when greeting – is that what you will do? Walk up to Jesus and bow? Maybe it's worth giving some thought if only as part of our eager anticipation of Heaven.

Christians love to think about Heaven. We know it's real because God tells us it is in Scripture passages like the one before us this morning. These Bible verses are taken from the book of Revelation where God is giving John the apostle a glimpse of Heaven.

> After this I looked and there before me was a great multitude that no one could count, from every nation, tribe, people and language, standing before the throne and in front of the Lamb. They were wearing white robes and were holding palm branches in their hands. And they cried out in a loud voice:
> > "Salvation belongs to our God, who sits on the throne, and to the Lamb."
> All the angels were standing around the throne and around the elders and the four living creatures. They fell down on their faces before the throne and worshiped God, saying: "Amen!
> > Praise and glory and wisdom and thanks and honor and power and strength be to our God for ever and ever. Amen!"
> Then one of the elders asked me, "These in white robes – who are they, and where did they come from?" I answered, "Sir, you know." And he said, "These are they who have come out of the great tribulation; they have washed their robes and made them white in the blood

of the Lamb. Therefore, they are before the throne of God and serve him day and night in his temple; and he who sits on the throne will spread his tent over them. Never again will they hunger; never again will they thirst. The sun will not beat upon them, nor any scorching heat. For the Lamb at the center of the throne will be their shepherd; he will lead them to springs of living water. And God will wipe away every tear from their eyes." Revelation 7.9-17

Some people have said this picture of Heaven sounds boring. They say it would be boring to stand around singing for eternity. Well, remember that some people love to sing. And God promises that Heaven is far more wonderful than here. If you love to sing here, if you love music, in Heaven music will be far more beautiful and fun. Everything will be far more wonderful there. Think of what you enjoy here as a Christian. It will be far more wonderful there. Do you enjoy <u>nature</u>? There will be a new earth that is more wonderful than this one. Enjoy sports and activities? You will be more skillful in Heaven. Enjoy <u>learning</u>? There will be far more knowledge to explore in Heaven. Enjoy <u>relationships</u>? They'll be much richer in Heaven, especially with Jesus. Imperfections – yours, those of your loved ones – will be gone since sin and its effects are removed. You will be restored to what God intended you to be. Is your enjoyment here smaller because (as the saying goes) "all good things must come to an end"? Not in Heaven. Good things there will go on forever.

It's great fun to explore what the Bible says about Heaven. But the verses before us address a key question for us now: How do we get there?

You know there are many ideas out there about how to get to Heaven and all of them are mistaken except this one described here. Some people (believe it or not) think suicide bombers go to Heaven – terribly mistaken! Some people believe that everybody goes to Heaven – terribly mistaken. Some people believe that good people go to Heaven, or at least people who try to be good – terribly mistaken, because nobody can be good enough to achieve God's requirement of perfection.

These verses teach us there is one way, and only one way: "*These are they who have come out of the great tribulation; they have washed their robes and made them white in the blood of the Lamb.*"

When we read these verses, it's easy to think John is looking at "those people," that bunch of people over there in white robes. But it's not about that bunch of people over there, it's this bunch right here. It's us. When we read these verses, it's easy to think it's about a big mass of people with no faces. But it's not a faceless mass of people. It's individuals, it's the one lost sheep for whom the Shepherd left the 99 to go seek out and find. Luke 15.4 It's the ones the Lord knows by name. John 10.3 It's you and I.

You and I have been washed in Jesus' blood. Our sins were placed on Jesus' back on the cross and the punishment for our sins is paid in full. That Lamb of God there on the throne took away the sins of the world; that includes **your sins and my sins**. Jesus' perfect life of obeying God has been credited to **us.** The Holy Spirit came to **you** in your Baptism and made you a believer. The Spirit comes again and again in His word to **you** and the Holy Spirit comes to **you** in the Holy Supper to strengthen **your faith.**

By God's grace You are one of those in John's vision of Heaven, one of those who has **washed their robes and made them white in the blood of the Lamb.** And so am I. If the Apostle John looked closely at that crowd in white robes, he would have seen your face there, and mine, faces filled with joy, with tears wiped away by our Lord Jesus himself: *"For the Lamb at the center of the throne will be their shepherd; he will lead them to springs of living water and God will wipe away every tear from their eyes."*

Yes, we **will** meet Jesus. That brings us back to our opening question: how will you greet him? Fall to the ground? Kneel? Shake hands? Bow? We know that Jesus took little children right up onto his lap. Mark 10.16 He tells us that the Good Shepherd picks up the lost sheep and carries it to safety. Luke 15.5 We know that throughout our lives we have been kept safe in Jesus' arms. When I meet Jesus, I think I'll probably bow down in humble gratitude, but then (do I dare it?) I'm looking forward to a hug.

†

September 15, 2012

Does God Like You?

INI

What do you suppose God thinks about you? Is God pleased with you? Disappointed in you? We know that God loves you, but does God **like** you? Listen to these words from God:

> If you call on the Father, who without partiality judges according to each one's work, conduct yourselves throughout the time of your stay here in fear; knowing that you were not redeemed with corruptible things, like silver or gold, from your aimless conduct received by tradition from your fathers, but with the precious blood of Christ, as of a lamb without blemish and without spot. 1 Peter 1:17-19

This is a passage clearly directed to us, to Christians, to those who "*call on the Father.*" And it does **not** suggest we should consider ourselves God's favorites. In fact, it says we should conduct ourselves throughout our lives in **fear**. Fear of what? Fear of falling back into the "*aimless conduct received from our ancestors.*" What's been handed down from them? An aspect of human nature that goes all the way back to our very first parents, Adam and Eve. The essence of that very first sin still dwells in our nature. It's **the desire to be our own god.** That sinful desire attacks everyone, but Christians in a special way: **We start to think God must be pleased with us because of what we do.**

First, we start to dismiss the seriousness of our own sins. We can start to think that our sins aren't "so bad" since we're Christians, that God kind of looks on a Christian's sin more lightly. No, this Bible verse says God judges impartially. My envy is as bad as an unbeliever's envy. My lust is as bad as a pagan's lust. Your gossip is as bad as anyone else's. Your and my failure to fear, love, and trust in God above all things (that's the First Commandment) is as bad as any idol-worshipping heathen's. God judges impartially.

But something in the back of our head still says, look what I can do. Maybe I can butter up God, like I can professors. If I show them I'm a good student, sit in the front of the class, actually do the homework, take part in discussions, then they'll notice me, and like me, and I'll become a favorite. I hope that you actually do all those things for professors. It doesn't work with God.

But wait! Don't we Christians do good things? Don't we actually serve God? Don't we come to chapel? Try to avoid sin and live a God-pleasing life? Help people in need? Pray? Don't we try to choose a profession in which we can serve God by serving others? I hope so.

But consider the nature of the good things we do. Luther said, in the Heidelberg Disputation, that we should do good works in the awareness that they could actually be deadly sins. Deadly sins! The good things we do could condemn us to hell! How could that happen? That can happen when we start to depend on our works, instead of on Jesus, to please God. When we look with pride on what we do for God, we've become our own god. When we hold up anything we do before God and think, now God must accept me, we have replaced Jesus with ourselves, and become our own god.

This reading from Scripture emphasizes that there is only one thing that makes us acceptable to God: a **redemption**. It's not that all we need is a little break. It's not that we need only a chance. We need a **rescue**! We were bought, not because we had any value but entirely because of God's grace. God chose to love us, so he bought us, and not with any small price, or even any big price of silver or gold, but with the precious blood of his innocent Son.

Some of us here – perhaps many in the future – have enjoyed the blessing of a new baby arriving in your family. Then you know love. Love for husband or wife is very special, certainly. But love for that baby, **your** baby, is different. It's consuming. You can look at that child sleeping (somehow they are easier to love when sleeping) and think, my child, my baby – how could I love anything more that this? Your parents looked at you like that. God, with a love far more profound than any human mother or father could muster, loved his Son Jesus like that. But still God gave him, let him die to purchase you and me.

So, does God like you? Answer this question yourself this way. Say this to yourself: the Holy Spirit has called me, and opened my heart to believe in Jesus as my Savior. And now when God looks at me, he sees Jesus. Yes, God does see my sins, my many sins. and he judges them impartially as terrible, damning sins. And then he puts them on Jesus, who pays their penalty on the cross and takes them away. Jesus says, "Put it on me." The lamb without spot or blemish becomes bloody and dies. That's what God now sees when he looks at us.

And when God looks at us and sees us doing good things, then too he sees Jesus. He sees that life Jesus lived perfectly pleasing to God, which he now credits to us. He sees Jesus at work in us, empowering us to please God. It's all Jesus. It's none of us. And when God sees Jesus in us, certainly he not only loves us but likes us.

†

March 5, 2013

Church vs. Bully

INI

We hear much talk these days about bullying, especially in schools. While the focus on it is new, the phenomenon is not. One might argue that all of history is a story of the biggest bullies of each era – the Medes and Persians – Romans – Huns – Ottomans – Nazis – empire builders – on and on. That explains the longing and appreciation for a good king, one who had the power to fend off external bullies and enable everyone to enjoy a peaceful life.

There are lots of definitions of bullying out there these days, but they all have a few characteristics in common, especially these three: the bully means harm, the bully is unrelenting and persistent, and the bully is trying to gain power over his victim. Listen to Jesus speak of a bully:

> He said to them, "But who do you say that I am?" Simon Peter answered and said, "You are the Christ, the Son of the living God." Jesus answered and said to him, "Blessed are you, Simon Bar-jonah, for flesh and blood has not revealed this to you, but my Father who is in heaven. And I also say to you that you are Peter, and on this rock I will build My church, and the gates of Hades shall not prevail against it.
> Matthew 16.13-19

Here Jesus is talking about spiritual bullying, and how we are protected from it. He speaks of the "Gates of Hades," the abode of the dead. When ancient cities had to be protected with walls, the gates were the most vulnerable spots, so they got extra protection, making them instead the most powerful spots. More than that, the gates were the places from which the power of the city went forth, to attack others. So "the gates of hell" represent the utmost power of Satan, ruler of the eternally dead, the sworn enemy of us all, the deadliest bully ever. Certainly the Devil's actions represent bullying behavior in those same three ways: he means our harm, he is after us repeatedly, and he is trying to gain power over us.

There are a couple of ways his bullying differs from ordinary bullying. One is that his bullying does not always at first distress us. In fact, he at first makes what he does to us look pleasant, even desirable. That leads to the second difference between the Devil's bullying and ordinary bullying: the Devil has an ally **inside us.** There is something in us (the Bible calls it the "old Adam") that wants to cooperate in the bullying. That makes us complicit in it. In our thoughts, words, and actions we cooperate in our own bullying and that makes us responsible and guilty.

But despite these differences, the Gates of Hell are true bullies. Satan means to harm us, to deliver us out of the realm of God's love and into eternal shame and suffering. And his acts against us are repeated and persistent. What can protect us from this bully? What can protect us from the Gates of Hell?

We are told that one of the ways to protect yourself from an ordinary bully is to find a good and supportive group of friends. Jesus says here that on Peter's confession he is going to build his Church, a community of those who believe in him, a community so strong that the Gates of Hell will never overcome it.

This is the first recorded mention by Jesus of his Church, a good and supportive group of friends whose strength against the bully comes from the foundation on which it is built: that Jesus is the Christ, the promised Messiah, the true Son of God, second person in the Holy Trinity who was sent by the Father into this world with a mission: to save us by his substitutional perfect life in our place and by his sacrificial death bearing all of our sins.

We see especially in this text how he saved us by his glorious resurrection when he literally burst out of the Gates of Hell, death that was trying to hold him in. By doing that, destroyed their power. That Easter event assures us that all of our sins are fully forgiven and that we too will enjoy an Easter resurrection to eternal life. All this is encompassed in these words of Peter's confession: Jesus is the Christ, the Son of the living God. All who believe that truth are brought into our Lord's Church where we find protection, where we find strength in the Word and Sacraments, where we find support in the fellowship and encouragement of fellow believers. There we find defense against the bullying of Satan.

So let me invite you again this morning: appreciate the Church, appreciate your fellow believers. Continue coming to chapel. Join in the community of believers on this campus. Enjoy the family of believers in local congregation you attend on Sunday. Realize the connection you have with other Christians around the U. S. Recognize that you have brothers and sisters in the faith around the world. Pray for your Christian family members in far away parts of our planet who must worship in small groups or even in secret. Rejoice in your connection with your believing parents, grandparents, yes great-grandparents who have already gone from the "Church militant" here on earth to the "Church triumphant" in Heaven. Recognize **your connection** with the believers of history, the Christians of the Reformation who heard Luther preach, the dwellers in the Roman Empire in North Africa who heard Augustine preach, the residents of Asia Minor and Greece and Rome who heard Paul preach. Know that you are one in faith with Mary and Joseph and aged Simeon who held the Savior in their hands. Believe along with Isaiah and

Elijah and King David and Joseph and Abraham, Noah and Eve, all of whom believed, as we do, in the Messiah, the anointed one, the Christ, the Son of God.

What a membership we have, in **the Church**, built on this rock, this fact, that (in Peter's words) Jesus is "the Christ, the Son of the Living God." The Gates of Hell will never prevail against it.

Prayer:

> Though devils all the world should fill, all eager to devour us,
> We tremble not, we fear no ill, they cannot overpower us.
> This world's prince may still scowl fierce as he will,
> He can harm us none. He's judged, the deed is done.
> These little words can fell him:
> Lord Jesus, I believe that you are the Christ, the Son of the living God.

> Amen.

†

November 27, 2013

Wedding service[1] for
Beka and Steve

INI

Relatives and friends, Aria, Owen, and Hunter, especially Beka and Steve:

How would you like to be dropped from a low-flying helicopter into a huge pile of marshmallows, whipped cream, and chocolate syrup? Would that be a happy time? **That's something like what all of us feel on a day like this,** when we celebrate God's wonderful blessing of marriage. It's like God is dropping you into a delicious celebration of his love, and his gifts, and his blessings.

For your wedding text you chose a verse that captures some of those blessings, which he has prepared for all of us, but apply in a special way to marriage.

> Be completely humble and gentle; be patient, bearing with one another in love. Make every effort to keep the unity of the Spirit through the bond of peace. Ephesians 4.2-3

Here are at least three big marshmallows of God's blessings: Look at main words: **love, unity, peace.** Wonderful blessings, especially since with each one, God **created** it, God **restored** it, and God **brings it to life** in us.

God created **love.** God **is** love: unselfish giving for the good of the loved one. In love he **made** us; knowing all that is good for us and supplying it. In love he **redeemed** us; unselfishly giving his Son. In love he **called us to faith** in him, filling our greatest need, to be close to him now and forever. God blesses us with love.

God created **peace.** Especially after human sin broke the bond between us and God and made us his enemies, it was entirely God (not us) who devised the plan to restore peace. The angels sang about it at Christmas when Jesus came to do his work, living in our place the life we should have lived, dying in our place the death we deserved, and rising again to assure us of God's forgiveness. God blesses us with peace.

God created **unity.** At creation humanity was one with God in hearts and minds. Now through the Holy Spirit we are restored to oneness with God in hearts and minds by Baptism and the Word. God blesses us with unity.

---

[1] I was privileged to conduct the ceremony when our dear daughter Beka married our dear son-in-law Steve Matthes.

So it should be no surprise that God who created love, peace, and unity should also have created **marriage,** the **best place on earth** for love, peace, and unity to be found.

It's not always perfect, because of sin. We soil the marshmallows and dirty up the whipped cream. Consider the **opposite** of what Paul urges. He says be **humble** – how often doesn't pride rear up and divide married couples from one another? He says be **gentle** – how often do our words and behavior become rough and bruising? He says be **patient** – impatience is a form of selfishness, putting **me,** my time, my interests before yours – oh, that's too frequent.

That's why Paul has to urge the remedies: be **humble, be gentle, be patient.** It's Jesus, talking to us through the apostle. Jesus in his redeeming love says to us, I was **humble** for you; now let my love make you humble too. I was **gentle** for you; now let my love make you gentle too. I was **patient** for you; now let my love make you patient too.

What a fine Bible verse for a marriage! God created **peace**, restored it in Jesus Christ, and empowers it in marriage. God created **unity**, restored it by the Holy Spirit in Word and Sacrament, and empowers it in marriage. God created **love**, demonstrated its depth on the cross, and empowers it in marriage. God created marriage, **your** marriage. May yours always be heaped up with the marshmallows and whipped cream of God's blessings.

†

December 2013
Reworked from Trinity Chapel in September
for Resurrection Lutheran Church, Winter Haven, Florida

Fear not!

INI

What an experience those shepherds had that first Christmas night! It's easy to wonder how they felt, how their emotions went from being "**sore afraid**" to **amazement** at the angels' song, to **excitement** as they ran to the manger, to **awe** as they viewed their Savior, a baby, to **great joy** as they spread abroad the news of this birth.

I wonder if, as shepherds and as believers in the promises of the prophets, they realized their special connection to this baby – that he too was to be a shepherd, **the Good** Shepherd. They recognized a theme in the angels' song that echoed a song from the psalms they must have known, the psalm we too know well, the one that assures us *"the Lord is our Shepherd, we shall not want for anything."*

Let me read one verse from that psalm, and then the angels' announcement.

> Yea, though I walk through the valley of the shadow of death,
>> I will fear no evil;
>> For You are with me;
>> Your rod and Your staff, they comfort me. Psalm 23.4

> Then the angel said to them, "Do not be afraid, for behold, I bring you good tidings of great joy which will be to all people. For there is born to you this day in the city of David a Savior, who is Christ the Lord. ... And suddenly there was with the angel a multitude of the heavenly host praising God and saying: "Glory to God in the highest and on earth peace, good will toward men!" Luke 2.10 and 13

Did you notice the common theme? First, both say **don't fear**. Second, they proclaim **comfort and peace**. Let's talk about each.

So, what are you afraid of? I know that sounds like a crazy dare. Betcha can't ride your skateboard on top of a moving semi! Betcha can't eat this bug! What are you afraid of?

But I'm asking it as a serious question: What do you fear? Some might reply bravely, I'm not afraid of anything. But you probably are. In that certain situation, you will feel fear. Afraid of spiders? Bats? Tornados? All of the above? Afraid of losing someone's love? Afraid of losing your memory? Afraid of falling? Cancer? Death?

Whenever any fear assails us, this is the passage to recall:

> Yea, though I walk through the valley of the shadow of death,
> > I will fear no evil;
> > For You are with me;
> > Your rod and Your staff, they comfort me.

It's human nature to fear things. Maybe that's why one of the strongest themes running through the entire Bible deals with our fear. The word translated fear (with the meaning be afraid) appears in nearly every Book of the Bible, more than 100 times and the word "afraid" another 216. The repeated message from God: **fear not** – don't be afraid! Want a sampling?

> And the LORD appeared to Isaac the same night and said, "I am the God of your father Abraham; do not **fear**, for I am with you. Genesis 26.24

> Be strong and of good courage, do not **fear** nor be afraid; for the LORD your God, He is the One who goes with you. He will not leave you nor forsake you." Deuteronomy 31.6

> For I, the LORD your God, will hold your right hand, saying to you, "**Fear** not, I will help you." Isaiah 41.13

And so on throughout the Old Testament. And then the words of our Lord himself:

> Do not **fear**, little flock, for it is your Father's good pleasure to give you the kingdom. Luke 12.32

> Peace I leave with you, my peace I give to you; not as the world gives do I give to you. Let not your heart be troubled, neither let it be **afraid**. John 14.27

There Jesus is echoing the message of the angels on Jesus' birthday, when he speaks of both peace and fear:

> Then the angel said to the shepherds, "Do not be afraid, for behold, I bring you good tidings of great joy which will be to all people. For there is born to you this day in the city of David a Savior, who is Christ the Lord." Luke 2.10-11

And then the chorus of angels sang, "peace on earth, good will to men." Luke 2.14 And the angels again on Jesus' resurrection day:

> But the angel answered and said to the women, "Do not be afraid, for I know that you seek Jesus who was crucified. He is not here; for He is risen." Matthew 28.5

If there is any lesson we should learn from Scripture, it is not to be afraid of anything for (as we read here) our Good Shepherd, Jesus, keeps us safe always **in life and in death.**

Wait, did I say also in death? Isn't death the greatest of evil? Isn't it sensible to be afraid of death? For others, probably so, but not for Christians, not for those who confidently follow their Good Shepherd even through the valley of the shadow of death. Even there we fear no evil for our Lord guides us with his rod and staff, the protecting and sustaining power of his Word and Sacraments, convincing us as he did St. Paul of this powerful truth: *"For me to live is Christ, to die is gain."* Philippians 1.21

What, after all, makes death so scary? It's the innate human awareness that death is punishment for sin, that death brings us to an accounting where we stand before a holy and just God blotchy and putrid because of our offenses against him, deserving eternal punishment. That's what makes death something to fear.

But remember what Christ has made of death. By his dying to pay for our sins, we who believe in him stand before God clothed in Jesus' holiness. Our sins are forgiven. There is now no condemnation for those who are in Christ. Romans 8.1 He has taken from death its power over us. O death, where is your sting? 1 Corinthians 15.55 Death now is only a scary mask; only the frightful appearance is left but no substance. Luther said death is now like a dead snake, scary and ugly looking but it has no power. It's our Lord who has the kingdom and the power and the glory.

Does our Lord's power protect us only from little fears? From spiders and bats? Does he protect us only if things don't get too bad? No, he protects us against the worst. He protects us in the valley of the shadow of death. He himself went into the worst, into death and hell, so we would never have to. We can say with the inspired writer,

> For if we live, we live to the Lord; and if we die, we die to the Lord. Therefore, whether we live or die, we are the Lord's. For to this end Christ died and rose and lived again, that He might be Lord of both the dead and the living. Romans 14. 8

Isn't that the second great Biblical theme in this verse? **Comfort** that comes from the **peace** announced by the angels to the shepherds, peace restored between God and humankind. As God said to Isaiah,

> **"Comfort**, yes, **comfort** My people!"
> Says your God.
> "Speak **comfort** to Jerusalem, and cry out to her,
> That her warfare is ended,

> That her iniquity is pardoned;
> For she has received from the LORD'S hand
> Double for all her sins." Isaiah 40.1-3

And the psalmist:

> Yea, though I walk through the valley of the shadow of death,
>> I will fear no evil;
>> For You are with me;
>> Your rod and Your staff, they comfort me.

And the angels:

> Fear not –
> Glory to God in the highest, and on earth, peace.

I think that the Christmas shepherds knew they were meeting their Good Shepherd. They knew their Bible. They knew the Savior would come and they rejoiced when his coming was announced to them. We too have rejoiced again this Christmas season; we have put away our fear, and basked again in the comfort and peace that comes from being in the care of our Good Shepherd.

†

February 16, 2014
At Peace Lutheran Church, North Mankato

Our Lord of the Light (Switch on)

INI

Click on. Click off. How many times do we do it every day? Electronic devices, appliances, especially light switches. It starts early in life. It's one of the first things that fascinates babies. My children and grandchildren learned this early. Among their first words were "on" and "off."

Today we're going to learn from all three Scripture readings, that the light switch provides a lesson in God's truth. We'll appreciate Our Lord of the Light (Switch on):

We see it in today's readings; we see it in jesus' words and work.

While we'll draw from all three readings, we first read again Jesus' words:

> Again, you have heard that it was said to the people long ago, "Do not break your oath, but keep the oaths you have made to the Lord." But I tell you, do not swear at all: either by heaven, for it is God's throne; or by the earth, for it is his footstool; or by Jerusalem, for it is the city of the Great King. And do not swear by your head, for you cannot make even one hair white or black. Simply let your "Yes" be "Yes," and your "No," "No"; anything beyond this comes from the evil one. Matthew 5.21-37

These words close the Gospel reading. "Yes" or "no." That's a formula for telling the truth, isn't it? We are to speak what is true, not false. There is to be nothing in between. We can't mix yes and no together, they are opposites. We shouldn't mix true and false together. If we try to do that we create "half-truths" and they are misleading. Yes yes and no no. This two-thousand-year-old wisdom from Jesus is quite modern. We call it binary digital.

Pardon me for getting technical here. I'd like to explain binary digital a bit more. You've heard the term digital a lot I'm sure. It's the basis for all our computers, phones, tablets, games, TVs, appliances and whatever not? Digital means there is a distinct difference between items, with nothing in between. For example, our alphabet is digital: A is A, B is B, all the letters are distinct from one another. There is nothing in between A and B, nothing mostly A but a little B, it's all one or all the other. Nothing A with a little B mixed in. There is a distinct difference between items. Our alphabet is 26-fold digital, with 26 choices. Your computer and all those other things run on binary digital. "BI" means two, just as "Bicycle" has two wheels. Binary means only two choices; it's a light switch: on or off. I'm not talking about one of those wimpy dimmer switches, but a snap switch: all on or all off.

Let me be clear: not everything in life is binary digital, all black or all white. As we puzzle our way through the many questions that life throws at us, we deal with many shades of gray, many unclear distinctions. We may have to make many compromises. But here's the point of **all our readings** this morning: **where God's plan for our salvation is concerned, it's binary digital**. It's two states, two conditions, and only two, with nothing between.

Our Lord is a Lord of the light switch.

That should be no surprise to us about God. Binary digital began at creation, when God threw the great cosmic light switch and said, "Let there be light." Genesis 1.3 and at that instant came into being not only visible light (that's far far too small a thing) but also all of what we call the laws of physics, the laws of nature, the structure of the universe, the periodic table, the electromagnetic spectrum, the Fibonacci series, the structure of the atom, and if there are strings and a Higgs boson, all that makes the world as we know it, much of it we don't yet know, all that made the about-to-be-created world possible. It was OFF, and an all-wise God turned it all ON in an instant. Click ON. And, we must certainly agree when we read, it was good.

We find binary digital not only in the physical, but also in the moral universe. Look again at our Old Testament reading for today:

> This day I call heaven and earth as witnesses against you that I have set before you life and death, blessings and curses. Now choose life, so that you and your children may live. Deuteronomy 30.19

Only two states. Choose life or death. They don't mix. It's binary digital.

We find it, too, in today's Epistle reading. This time it's a distinction between the so-called "wisdom" of the world and the wisdom of God, between human words and the Holy Spirit's words. Listen again:

> We do, however, speak a message of wisdom among the mature, but not the wisdom of this age or of the rulers of this age, who are coming to nothing... [these two wisdoms are separate, digital, not to be mixed] ... as it is written: "No eye has seen, no ear has heard, no mind has conceived what God has prepared for those who love him" – but God has revealed it to us by his Spirit... This is what we speak, not in words taught us by human wisdom but in words taught by the Spirit, expressing spiritual truths in spiritual words. 1 Corinthians 2.6-9

So the Apostle is telling us, there are only two systems of knowledge about spiritual things. They don't mix. Now of course we respect and study the great bodies of knowledge, of science and history and literature and all the other branches. We have teachers and students examining all these things at

Bethany Lutheran College. But the "wisdom" of the world spoken of here is about our salvation. And there are only two systems; they don't mix.

What is this wisdom of the world? Look at what the world believes about salvation. First leave aside those who don't believe there is a God at all; the Bible calls them "fools." Psalm 14.1, Psalm 53.1 Every religion in one way or another believes that it is by what we do that we please God and reach a happy after-life. Even many Christians believe that: be good, they think, and God will take you into Heaven. Or at least try to be good some of the time and God will overlook the rest. The popular belief is even that **everybody** goes to Heaven. That's what Paul condemns here as the wisdom of the world.

But the true wisdom, the wisdom from God, says: no, the two "wisdoms" are distinct, they don't mix. He describes the wisdom of God as a mystery now revealed: God's plan. And guess what? It turns out to be binary digital.

We've seen binary digital in today's Old Testament and Epistle readings. Now let's look at it in Jesus' words and work. We have some of Jesus' words in our Gospel reading:

> You have heard that it was said to the people long ago, "Do not murder, and anyone who murders will be subject to judgment." But I tell you that anyone who is angry with his brother will be subject to judgment. Again, anyone who says to his brother "Raca" is answerable to the Sanhedrin. But anyone who says, "You fool!" will be in danger of the fire of hell. Therefore, if you are offering your gift at the altar and there remember that your brother has something against you, leave your gift there in front of the altar. First go and be reconciled to your brother; then come and offer your gift. Settle matters quickly with your adversary who is taking you to court. Do it while you are still with him on the way, or he may hand you over to the judge, and the judge may hand you over to the officer, and you may be thrown into prison. I tell you the truth, you will not get out until you have paid the last penny. You have heard that it was said, "Do not commit adultery." But I tell you that anyone who looks at a woman lustfully has already committed adultery with her in his heart. If your right eye causes you to sin, gouge it out and throw it away. It is better for you to lose one part of your body than for your whole body to be thrown into hell. And if your right hand causes you to sin, cut it off and throw it away. It is better for you to lose one part of your body than for your whole body to go into hell. It has been said, "Anyone who divorces his wife must give her a certificate of divorce." But I tell you that anyone who divorces his wife, except for marital unfaithfulness, causes her to become an adulteress, and anyone who marries the divorced woman commits adultery. Matthew 5.21-32

How often have you thought, as I have when listening to the "Gospel" readings for which we stand up every Sunday, where is the Gospel, the good news, in a reading which, like this one, contains tough tough Law? How do you feel when you hear Jesus talk like this?

It makes me squirm. What can we make of this, when our Lord teaches detailed tough Law? Here's one thing: **it is God's Law**: don't water down the Law of God, as Jesus said was being done by teachers of his day.

How do we do that today? By thinking my sins aren't too bad. By thinking well it's all forgiven anyway, no big deal. By adjusting God's Law to our benefit. Here comes our Old Testament reading again: it's binary digital, one or the other, life or death. Every disobedience is a choice of death and hell. There is no mixture of life and death. Jesus, a few verses after our reading summed it all up: "*Be perfect, as your Father in heaven is perfect.*" Matthew 5.48 We call Jesus "Lord" for a reason: he is to be obeyed. There is a place in our lives for repentance – Luther says we should do it daily. There is a reason why, right after the pastor pronounces our sins forgiven on Sunday morning, we sing again, "Lord have mercy upon us."

But now let's draw on the Wisdom of God spoken of in the Epistle reading. The mystery now revealed teaches us more about what was going on when Jesus spoke those words of Law. Jesus is showing us here that he knew the Law of God. He knew it inside and out. God's expectations for us were perfectly clear to him. Why is that a comfort to us? He tells us himself, in words a few verses prior to our reading:

> Do not think that I have come to abolish the Law or the Prophets; I have not come to abolish them but to fulfill them. I tell you the truth, until heaven and earth disappear, not the smallest letter, not the least stroke of a pen, will by any means disappear from the Law until everything is accomplished." Matthew 5.17-18

Even as he taught God's Law, Jesus was fulfilling God's Law in our place. And since he knew it so thoroughly, we can be assured that he fulfilled it exactly and completely and thoroughly. His perfect obedience is now credited to us.

> For all have sinned and fall short of the glory of God and are justified freely by his grace through the redemption that came by Christ Jesus. God presented him as a sacrifice of atonement, through faith in his blood. Romans 3:23-25

This is the Gospel that does not make sense to the worldly mind: "*The saying is trustworthy and deserving of full acceptance, that Christ Jesus came into the world to save sinners, of whom I am the foremost.*" 1 Timothy 1.15 Listen to the Baptizer John point to this Jesus, the "*Lamb of God, that takes away the sin of the world."* John 1.29 Hear St. Paul writing that *"God was in Christ, reconciling the world unto himself, not counting their sins against them."* 2 Corinthians. 5:19 Hear St. Peter proclaim that *"Christ died for sins once for all, the righteous for the unrighteous, to bring you to God."* 1 Peter 3.18 *"In him we have redemption, the forgiveness of sins."* Colossians 1.14 *"In him we have redemption through his blood, the forgiveness of sins, in accordance with the riches of God's grace."* Ephesians 1.7

Here is why it is a comfort to us, even when Jesus strongly emphasizes God's Law in his teaching: he **knew** God's Law in every detail, he **kept** God's Law in every detail for us. When Jesus said on the cross *"it is finished"* John 19.30 it meant our status has changed, not just shifted a little, but totally changed. A huge **click on**. We were God's enemies – click – we are now God's children. We were sinners – click – now we wear the holiness of Christ. That's why it's a highlight in the life of a pastor to conduct a Baptism, a highlight in your life every time you witness a Baptism: the moment we are baptized – click – that child is switched on, moved from death to life. And it remains a comfort in every situation in life. God's light switch for us is **on**, as he promises, *"I will never* (Greek "never never not ever!") *leave you or forsake you."* Hebrews 13.5

Our everyday light switches seem easy. Click on, click off, nothing to it. But behind that apparent ease lies a great deal of infrastructure, lots of clever inventions over many decades, the power plants, the electrical grid, the maintenance, the wiring in your house – we only appreciate it when there's a power outage and we're without it. In a much more profound way, our salvation might seem too easy – it's by grace, it's a gift! What's hard about accepting a gift? Yet what went into preparing that gift? A history of the world over many centuries, starting with the first sin and the first promise of a Savior, through all the patriarchs and prophets, and the census that brought Mary and Joseph to Bethlehem for a prophesied birth. That perfect life Jesus led even while teaching the Law he was fulfilling, his sparkling and wonderful life of love and doing good, his ugly and agonizing death making payment to God for all of our sins, the triumphant resurrection to assure us that his work for us was fully effective and acceptable to God. And then the Word and Sacraments that brought the Gospel message to us. And finally the Holy Spirit created faith in our hearts. All this so that in your life, click on!

There is no other click.

Thanks be to God.   †

The people that walked in darkness have seen a great light: they that dwell in the land of the shadow of death, upon them hath the **light shined**. Isaiah 9.2

February 27, 2014

Which Soil Am I?

INI

OK, let me tell you what is really going on here in this room this morning. No, better still, let Jesus himself explain what is going on here in chapel this morning and every morning, and how that maps onto your entire life. One day, Jesus told this story:

> Behold, a sower went out to sow. And as he sowed, some seed fell by the wayside; and the birds came and devoured them. Some fell on stony places, where they did not have much earth; and they immediately sprang up because they had no depth of earth. But when the sun was up they were scorched, and because they had no root they withered away. And some fell among thorns, and the thorns sprang up and choked them. But others fell on good ground and yielded a crop: some a hundredfold, some sixty, some thirty. He who has ears to hear, let him hear!" Matthew 13.3-9

This may be the very first parable that Jesus told so far as we can tell. Even if it was not, it could stand as the very first parable in importance because it covers all of our Christian living – or the total lack thereof. Perhaps its importance too is reflected in the fact that Jesus explained its meaning, something he didn't usually do with parables. This is our reading for this morning:

> <u>Therefore</u> hear the parable of the sower: When anyone hears the word of the kingdom, and does not understand it, then the wicked one comes and snatches away what was sown in his heart. This is he who received seed by the wayside. But he who received the seed on stony places, this is he who hears the word and immediately receives it with joy; yet he has no root in himself but endures only for a while. For when tribulation or persecution arises because of the word, immediately he stumbles. Now he who received seed among the thorns is he who hears the word, and the cares of this world and the deceitfulness of riches choke the word, and he becomes unfruitful. But he who received seed on the good ground is he who hears the word and understands it, who indeed bears fruit and produces: some a hundredfold, some sixty, some thirty. Matthew 13.18-23

You're already doing what this story invites you to do: you are hearing the Word. Do you wonder into which of these four categories you fit? If I were still teaching screenwriting, I'd adopt this as an assignment: write a short screen play about someone who fits into each of these categories. It wouldn't be hard to do; any of you could do it since I'm sure we each know somebody who fits into each one, and we could just write their stories.

The person closest to us who fits into each category, of course, is **ourselves**.

That's true, isn't it? It's not a question of which category we fit in. It's a question of realizing that at one time or another we fit into all of them. Look at the enemies of the Word the parable mentions: they are in ourselves. They **are** ourselves.

Consider the first, where the seed of God's Word falls on the pavement so that the Devil just picks it up before it has any effect at all. I don't know if Luther invented the cliché but he used it about these people: "In one ear and out the other." Don't tell me you've never sat here in chapel where God's precious Word is being proclaimed and you didn't even listen, your mind was miles away. Don't blame birds for snatching away the seed. It's we who give them the opportunity.

How about the second situation, where the seed falls on rocky ground, springs up quickly, then when trouble or persecution comes, it withers away because there is no root. Yes, I proclaim myself a Christian and rejoice in it. But wait! Now I'm out with the gang and suddenly it occurs to me: "You mean now I have to **live** like a Christian? Won't my friends laugh at me?" And suddenly the Word of God means nothing. It has withered away. It dies.

And in the third case, where the thorns and thistles choke out the Word. It's no accident that Jesus identifies the thorns and thistles together as "cares of this world (worrying) and the deceitfulness of riches (money)" because the two so often go together. If your main goal in life, your main reason for getting an education is to make a lot of money you are risking letting those thorns and thistles chokes out the Word.

I promised at the beginning that this would be Jesus' explanation of what was going on here right now. This **is** what's going on here right now. God's Word is falling on you like seed right now. How's the ground? And how does it become good soil?

When all those bad things happen, it's our fault. But the good soil? That's God's doing. The Holy Spirit comes to us in the Word and creates the good soil in us, purely by God's grace in Christ. The Word of God itself, with its power, pounds on the rocks of unbelief in our hearts, and cracks and crumbles it into good fertile soil.

So then, what is going on here in Chapel this morning and every morning? You listen to God's word proclaimed here. You hear God's Law, what God demands of us, and look into it, see your sin, and repent of it in sorrow. You hear God's good news, the Gospel, and understand how Jesus Christ, God's own Son, spent his entire life living in perfect obedience to God's requirements and that he did that in our place. You understand that he then went into death on the cross, not because he deserved the punishment of death for his own sins because he had none, but because he was bearing our sins and our punishment in our place. And you believe that through faith in Jesus we are washed clean of our sins – they are all forgiven – and we have been made God's own beloved children, heirs of eternal life with him in Heaven. And you trust that Word of God. When all this happens, you know that the Holy Spirit has worked, that the seed of the Word has made you into good soil.

And you will – no, let me rather say, you **are** bearing fruit many-fold. Do you see it in your life? Do you see how this parable describes what is going on here and how what happens here in chapel and in church and in Bible study in your classes and in your room – how this maps onto your entire life, a life of bearing fruit?

Listen to the Apostle Paul describe your life:

> But the fruit of the Spirit is love, joy, peace, longsuffering, kindness, goodness, faithfulness, gentleness, self-control. ... And those who are Christ's have crucified the flesh with its passions and desires. If we live in the Spirit, let us also walk in the Spirit. Galatians 5:22-25

Indeed. Let us hear the Word as good soil and then walk in the Spirit.

SDG

Prayer: Blessed Lord, who has caused all Holy Scriptures to be written for our learning, grant that we may in such a way hear them, read, mark, learn, and inwardly digest them, that by patience and comfort of your holy Word we may embrace, and ever hold fast the blessed hope of everlasting life, which you have given us in our Savior Jesus Christ, who lives! and reigns with you and the Holy Spirit, ever one God, world without end. Amen.

†

May 14, 2014
In the Good Shepherd Chapel
for the vicar workshop at Bethany Lutheran Theological Seminary

Resting in Jesus' Arms

INI

People were bringing little children to Jesus to have him touch them, but the disciples rebuked them. When Jesus saw this, he was indignant. He said to them, "Let the little children come to me, and do not hinder them, for the kingdom of God belongs to such as these. I tell you the truth, anyone who will not receive the kingdom of God like a little child will never enter it." And he took the children in his arms, put his hands on them and blessed them. Mark 10.13-16

We think of this incident most often as an illustration of Jesus' love of children. We cite it as a proof text in support of infant Baptism, and it's part of our liturgy when we baptize babies. All of that is appropriate.

When we move past the important dogmatics, and start to embrace the moment of this incident, we can put ourselves in the place of the disciples and feel their officiousness as they try to protect their Rabbi from the disturbance of these annoying moms and their kids, and then their chagrin at being chastened by the Lord.

But we might want even to move past the disciples and put ourselves in the place of those children. Can we today view this incident as these children? What must it have been like to be in the very arms of the Savior and to be blessed by him?

Jesus himself describes those children: they had a very special faith, a child-like faith. If you have children, you've already pondered the faith of an infant, the willing complete dependence of a toddler on their parents. Notice Jesus didn't cite the faith of a teenager, that's much different as you know. But a little child has unquestioning trust in where his nourishment will come from, where her protection is, who has the strength that he doesn't have, who will guide her safely or find him when he gets lost – trust in who will do everything to assure the child's future. A child is most content just **resting** in the arms of mommy or daddy.

It's the same theme as captured in the window you've enjoyed daily in this chapel[1] or in the rendition on your handout from Peace Kissimmee where I worshipped 10 days ago – a real resting in the arms of the Lord.

---

[1] The Good Shepherd window is reproduced on the back cover.

Good Shepherd window at Peace, Kissimmee FL

Let me suggest to you today that those aren't some other children. They are us. What was it like for those kids to be blessed by the Lord himself? Just like you and I have been blessed by the Lord himself. Let me urge you today on the basis of this text to rest your ministry (and yourself and everything in your life) in the arms of the Lord.

Rest your children in the Lord's arms. When the Lord blesses you with children he gives you a great pleasure, and a great challenge. With children come times of unsurpassed joy and unsurpassed anxiety and sorrow. If you have children you've already placed them into the Lord's arms in Baptism, just as you were placed there. And while you will work hard at raising your children – resting isn't laziness; remember the parable of the talents; to whom much is given, much is expected – in those times of greatest joy and greatest distress you will want simply to leave your children in the Lord's arms with unquestioned trust.

Rest your family in the arms of the Lord. Your wife is your greatest earthly blessing from God. What comfort, joy, and pleasure to have a helper fitting for you. At the same time, tensions can sometimes build up when misunderstandings arise in a marriage, or when illness strikes. And while you will work hard at your marriage relationship – rest is not laziness; *"to whom much is given, much is expected"* Luke 12.48 – in those times of greatest joy and greatest distress you will want simply to rest your wife in the Lord's arms with unquestioned trust.

Rest yourself in the arms of the Lord. We strive, under the Holy Spirit, to realize our best selves, the New Man, to put down and drown the Old Adam.

We struggle against our sins every day and too often just fail. When sickness or other challenges erupt we might reach the point of wondering if God is even there. That's especially the time you will want simply to leave your self in the Lord's arms and bask with unquestioned trust in the forgiveness of all your sins he won for you and me on the cross.

Rest your ministry, your flock in the arms of the Lord. To be responsible for souls! What a challenge, what a burden! What a joy when our faithful administering of Word and Sacrament is blessed by the Holy Spirit according to his promise. But it can be hard. Money can be scarce, appreciation rare, opposition relentless, sermons never easy. You learn the most difficult problems that burden your people and find yourself bearing them on your own shoulders. You're going to work hard at serving your congregation – rest is not laziness; "*to whom much is given, much is expected.*" In those times of greatest joy and greatest distress you will want simply to entrust your flock to the Lord's arms.

All this you can do with childlike confidence ...

- in your own salvation won by the blood of Christ,
- in the power that God will supply to meet all your challenges and needs,
- in the mansions of heaven our Lord is preparing for us.

You can rest your ministry in the arms of the Lord.

You all know Luther's sacristy prayer. It's often posted there in the sacristy for you to pray at the moment of your most important service: as you go out to preach the Word and administer the Sacraments. It invites us to put all our trust in God, to rest our ministry in his arms. Let us rise and pray it together.

> Lord God, you have made us to be pastors in your church. You see how unfit we are to undertake this great and difficult office, and if it were not for your help, we would have ruined it all long ago. Therefore we cry to you for aid. We offer our mouths and our hearts to your service. We desire to teach the people. And for ourselves, we would learn evermore and diligently meditate on your Word. Use us as your instruments, but never forsake us, for if we are left alone, we shall easily bring it all to destruction. Amen.

†

The Sixth Sunday After Trinity, July 27, 2014
At Bethany Lutheran Church, Princeton MN

God's Gracious Pivotal Moments

INI

A while ago Jason Kidd, a very good professional basketball player, was traded to the Dallas Mavericks, a team that was not doing well at all. He thought he was going to make a big difference, and he famously said, "We're going to turn this team around 360 degrees."

Now you kids here know enough math to tell us what is wrong with saying that. You know that 360 degrees is a full circle, don't you? So if you turn around a full circle, 360 degrees, you end up going in the same direction you were before. I hope what Mr. Kidd meant was, "We're going to turn this team around 180 degrees." That would mean, the team was going in a bad direction, we're going to turn it in the opposite direction.

As we continue the series of sermons Pastor Gernander started on the book of Acts, we come to this portion of God's Word that describes one of the most dramatic 180-degree turn-arounds of all time, the conversion of Saul, who later would be known as the apostle Paul. You heard it in the second reading a while ago. It's a long reading, so I won't read it all at once again now, but rather in bits and pieces as we examine today's theme:

God's gracious pivotal moments

A pivot is a turnaround of 180 degrees, and we'll see first **how** God graciously pivoted Saul, and then **why** God graciously pivoted Saul.

As we examine God's dealing with Saul (I'll call him Saul or Paul because it's the same person), we'll notice that God pivots us in the same way. Oh, there are some differences between what happened to Paul and what happened to us, but the differences are not important. What is important is how God pivots us in the same way that he pivoted Paul. Let's list the ways that we and Paul are alike in being graciously turned around by God.

First item on the list: **God saw how much Paul needed to be turned around, and he sees how much we need to be turned around**. This Saul in our reading was a truly terrible person.

> Acts 9.1-2 Meanwhile, Saul was still breathing out murderous threats against the Lord's disciples. He went to the high priest and asked him for letters to the synagogues in Damascus, so that if he found any there who belonged to the Way, whether men or women, he might take them as prisoners to Jerusalem.

The believers in Jesus had good reason to fear Saul. He was an activist. He was rabid. Remember when Pastor Gernander preached about martyrs? He told you about the first martyr who died for the Christian faith, Stephen. Well, this Saul was there when Stephen was killed. We read in the 7th chapter of Acts,

> Acts 7.58 [The people] dragged [Stephen] out of the city and began to stone him. Meanwhile, the witnesses laid their clothes at the feet of a young man named Saul.

> Acts 8.1 And Saul was there, giving approval to his death.

Now Saul wasn't content only to watch a Christian be killed. He took the initiative to go to the authorities, and get official permission to go to Damascus, find all the Christians he could, and bring them back to Jerusalem as prisoners, possibly for more executions. Saul certainly needed a pivot. God saw that this wicked man needed to be turned around.

First item on the list again: God saw how much Saul needed to be turned around. Are we like Saul in that way? Did God see how much you and I needed to be turned around? We thank God that he did. We'll see that even more with the second item on the list, **God showed Saul, as he shows us, that we need to pivot**.

Here's how it happened to Saul. With a flash of light **God broke into Saul's life.**

> Acts 9.3 As he neared Damascus on his journey, suddenly a light from heaven flashed around him. He fell to the ground and heard a voice say to him, "Saul, Saul, why do you persecute me?"

In this powerful way, Saul was brought face to face with his own sin.

> Acts 9.5 Saul asked, "Who are you, Lord?" He replied, "I am Jesus, whom you are persecuting."

Saul wasn't just persecuting believers. He was persecuting Jesus. He was an enemy of God. Jesus made clear to Saul his need to turn around.

God did that to you and me, too, didn't He? Not in so dramatic a way; there was no flash of light that threw us to the ground. But we have heard the voice of God, haven't we, in God's Law. We did learn, each of us, the Ten Commandments, that concise summary of God's will, and as we honestly measured our lives against that standard of perfection, God shows us how far short we have fallen. Jesus pointed out to Saul that his actions weren't just hurting other people, but they were hurting Jesus. In the same way, each and every sin we commit, every evil thought, every unkind word, every selfish action of ours is another stab of pain as Jesus suffered for those sins on the cross. God breaks into our lives, too, with his Law, making it clear to us that we were heading to hell, and needed to pivot.

It's good for us to realize **how unable we are to please God by ourselves**. God made that clear to Saul.

> Acts 9.8-9 Saul got up from the ground, but when he opened his eyes he could see nothing. So they led him by the hand into Damascus. For three days he was blind.

How helpless is the feeling of a person used to seeing, who suddenly becomes blind. Saul, who a few moments earlier had been leader of a powerful police force, now had to be led by the hand. It was good for him, and for us, to realize that we by ourselves could never turn ourselves around from heading to hell. We were, as Scripture teaches, dead in our trespasses and sins. A dead person can't turn around by himself. Saul needed God to break into his life and pivot him, and so do we.

So let's continue our list:

First God **saw our need to pivot**, then he **showed us** our need to pivot, that brings us to the next item: **God pivots us**. He sets us on a new direction. We read again about Saul:

> Acts 9.5 Saul asked, "Who are you, Lord?" He replied, "I am Jesus, whom you are persecuting, Now get up and go into the city, and you will be told what you must do."

Saul may have been completely helpless, but Jesus had it all planned out. And we too are completely helpless to turn ourselves around, but Jesus has it all planned out. He has already prepared a path to our salvation and he puts us on that path. With us, as with Saul, it involved a human messenger to bring us God's Word, and with Baptism.

> Acts 9.10 In Damascus there was a disciple named Ananias. The Lord called to him in a vision, "Ananias!" "Yes, Lord," he answered. The Lord told him, "Go to the house of Judas on Straight Street and ask for a man from Tarsus named Saul."

Ananias had heard of Saul and what he had done, but the Lord reassured him that Saul was not to be feared. He went to Saul as the Lord told him to:

> Acts 9.17 Then Ananias went to the house and entered it. Placing his hands on Saul, he said, "Brother Saul, the Lord Jesus who appeared to you on the road as you were coming here has sent me so that you may see again and be filled with the Holy Spirit." Immediately, something

like scales fell from Saul's eyes, and he could see again. He got up and was baptized.

Here it is, in Saul, just as it is for us: God's entire plan to pivot us, to turn us away from destruction and back to him. How significant it is that the One dealing directly with Saul, as with us, is Jesus himself. God did not send an angel to that road to Damascus, but there was the very Son of God carrying out this whole plan. Ananias said, "Brother Saul, the Lord Jesus who appeared to you on the road as you were coming here has sent me." This is the One who came into the world born a Baby at that first Christmas, who lived a life totally pleasing to God, who with his undeserved death transferred that perfect life to our account, even as he took on himself the guilt and punishment we deserved for our sins. By Jesus' sacrifice, our sins are forgiven. This is Jesus, whose life, death, and resurrection prepared the way for us, created this new path to Heaven. He came personally to Saul to turn him around and place him on that new path, just as he comes to us personally in the Sacrament of the Altar with his holy body and blood to assure us again and again that our sins are forgiven. Jesus had it all planned out for Saul, as he does for us. For Saul he sent a messenger, Ananias, with his Word. For you he sent Pastor Gernander, or some other pastor, with his Word. We read about Saul, "*He got up and was baptized.*" You too were baptized. That, in fact, was your gracious pivotal moment. That's when you were washed clean from your sins, when God turned you around, when you were buried with Christ into his death in your Baptism, so that like him, you and I too can rise to a new life, one that began with your Baptism, continues every day, and lasts through eternity.

All that is **how** God supplies us with his gracious pivotal moment. As with Saul, God sees our need to pivot, he shows us our need to pivot, he breaks into our lives and through Baptism sets us on the path to salvation he has prepared for us.

But these Bible verses teach us not only how God pivots us, but also **why**.

You know why: God loved Saul so much, God loved you and me so much, God so much "*loved the world that he gave his only begotten son, that whoever believes in him should not perish, but* [be pivoted around and instead] *have eternal life.*" John 3.16

But we can learn more here about why God pivoted Saul, and you and me. God had a loving purpose for Saul.

Acts 9.15 The Lord said to Ananias, "Go! This man is my chosen instrument to carry my name before the Gentiles and their kings and before the people of Israel. I will show him how much he must suffer for my name."

As you continue your study of the book of Acts you will see again how much the apostle Paul did suffer for Jesus' name. How grateful we are that God appointed him to *"carry Jesus' name before the Gentiles,"* because that's us, you and me. How precious that God speaking through this apostle has placed into our lives assurances like these:

In his letter to the Romans: *"For all have sinned and fall short of the glory of God, and are justified freely by his grace through the redemption that came by Christ Jesus."* Romans 3.23

In his letter to the Ephesians: *"For by grace you have been saved through faith, and that not of yourselves; it is the gift of God, not of works, lest anyone should boast."* Ephesians 2.8

And in his letter to the Romans: *"For I am persuaded that neither death nor life, nor angels nor principalities nor powers, nor things present nor things to come, nor height nor depth, nor any other created thing, shall be able to separate us from the love of God which is in Christ Jesus our Lord."* Romans 8.28f.

Of course we could go on and on. If you would list all of your favorite Bible passages, probably more than half of them will have come from God through the apostle Paul.

Once Paul was pivoted, he wasted no time starting on his new path of service to the Lord.

> Acts 9.19 Saul spent several days with the disciples in Damascus. At once he began to preach in the synagogues that Jesus is the Son of God.

> Acts 9.22 Yet Saul grew more and more powerful and baffled the Jews living in Damascus by proving that Jesus is the Christ.

Paul was an immensely talented man, and he immediately put to use the gifts God had given him. What's your gift? It might or might not involve directly witnessing to others about Jesus, proving that he is the Christ. But listen to what impressed people the most about Paul:

> Acts 9.21 All those who heard him were astonished and asked, "Isn't he the man who raised havoc in Jerusalem among those who call on this name?"

People noticed that Paul was pivoted. They were astonished and impressed.

That can be one of your most useful services to the Lord as well; that people will notice, "here is a person who has been set on the path to Heaven." They will see in your life and mine how Jesus has graciously broken into our lives, turned us around, and set us on a path of serving him by serving others, on our way to eternal life with our Lord in Heaven.

So keep on serving with **your** talents, whatever they are, and wherever God has placed you:

- care for your aging parents or grandparents
- cope with your sickness, or that of a loved one
- raise your kids
- study hard in school
- work hard at your job
- be the best dad/ mom /kids you can be
- keep praying for everyone
- take on any challenge life gives you

Do it all with an inner joy from knowing that God loves you so much he sent his Son to forgive your sins, to pivot you, turn you around 180 degrees, and put you on this wonderful path to Heaven.

†

October15, 2014

God Equips Us for the Battle

INI

I'm glad you made it safely to chapel this morning. Did you worry about that? As you left your room this morning, did you watch for an IED along the sidewalk that might cripple or kill you? Did you worry that, as you crossed the plaza, a rooftop sniper might pick you off? You know, of course, that around the world there are many places where such dangers are a daily concern. We should thank God for the blessing that we do not live in a war zone.

Or should I say, "**That** kind of war zone." In today's reading, the Apostle reminds us that we do live daily in danger of the worst kind of sneaky attack, an attack of the Devil.

> Finally, my brethren, be strong in the Lord and in the power of His might. Put on the whole armor of God, that you may be able to stand against the wiles of the devil. Ephesians 6.10-11

Do you remember, as a little kid, hearing that scary Bible passage about the lion?

> Be sober, be vigilant; because your adversary the devil walks about like a roaring lion, seeking whom he may devour. 1 Peter 5.8

That image, of the roaring lion wanting to eat me up truly caught my attention and fired my imagination. Maybe yours too. As we grow older, the image becomes less scary. After all, it is only a simile. But we should not become less wary because the words before us emphasize again the "**wiles**" of the Devil. The word in Greek is the one from which we get our English word "method." The devil is not careless or haphazard in his attacks on us. He schemes. He knows your weakness, as he does mine. He knows exactly what can get you to sin, exactly when to put that lure in front of you – maybe at night, or when nobody is looking, or when you are distracted. And that's when he does it, suddenly, unexpectedly. He can explode his temptation IED as you leave your room or snipe at you with a sin as you cross the plaza. He is both powerful and sneaky and alone we would be easy prey. "With might of ours can naught be done," wrote Luther the poet; "soon were our loss effected."

But we have a champion on our side. "For us fights the valiant one, whom God himself elected." Jesus Christ it is, Lord of Hosts in whom we find the strength we need, what in our reading is a triple force: "*Be **strong** in the Lord and in the **power** of his **might**.*" Three different Greek words, translated with three different English words: strength, power, might. These are not just empty words of encouragement, like "hang in there, good luck."

To enable us to be strong God gives us the equipment, the weapons. A few verses after our reading, they are listed:

> Stand therefore, having girded your waist with **truth**, having put on the breastplate of **righteousness** and having shod your feet with the preparation of the **gospel of peace**; above all, taking the shield of **faith** with which you will be able to quench all the fiery darts of the wicked one. And take the helmet of **salvation**, and the sword of the Spirit, which is the **word of God.** Ephesians 6.14-17

Those are the weapons:

- Truth, which we have in God's Word;
- Righteousness, God's gift of justification, declaring that our sins are forgiven, and we are righteous;
- Gospel, the news of how Jesus won that forgiveness for us
  - With an exemplary life offered to God as if it were ours, and
  - In his sacrificial death by which he bore the punishment of all our sins – the Gospel;
- Faith, by which we grasp and receive all those benefits;
- Salvation, our free gift of grace;
- And the Word of God, which brings all this power to us.

This is not a battle we need to fight in fear. With these weapons we can't lose! So we can wield these weapons with joy. The joy we receive from God's weapon supply can itself become another weapon. When we are filled with **joy** in God there is no room for the devil's supposed false fake joys to tempt us.

I invite you to do two things with these weapons: personalize them and specify them.

We need to personalize God's promises. For example, we all know the passage, "*God so loved the world...*" John 3.16 Let's include ourselves personally in that passage: "God so loved **me**, God so loved **you** that he gave his only begotten Son, so that when you and I believe in him, you and I will not perish, but have eternal life."

Soon we will be singing again at Christmastime, "Joy to the World, the Lord is come."

Personalize the hymn: "Joy to you, joy to me, the Lord Jesus has been born to be our Savior." Use the gift of joy – if you find your joy in the Lord and the Gospel, the devil won't be able to lure you with his supposed false fake joys.

Joy to **you**! You have the weapons: Truth, Righteousness, Gospel, Faith, Salvation, and the Word of God. Now specify them, that is, make them specific. These are not just abstractions, just metaphors. The truth, the Righteousness, the Gospel, all the others: What specifically do they bring to **you**?

"God's own child, I gladly say it, I am baptized into Christ!" ELH 246 Sing it with joy every morning as you leave your room to push away the devil's IED. Come to the **Lord's table** to receive, in his body and blood, the forgiveness of your sins; you approach in repentance, you depart in **joy**. You have **daily chapel**, speakers always reminding you of the Gospel. Leave here every day with joy. You have a **calling** – faculty members your calling is wonderful; fill it with joy. All of you: you have a purpose in life. You have a heavenly Father eager to **hear your prayers**; talk with him with joy. You have the promise that God will **help you through** whatever is worrying you; bring problems not with worry but with joy.

You have a wonderful future, now and forever, when the warfare is finally over, all danger is past, and lasting peace and **joy** will come in Heaven. You are loved by God, Jesus died for you, your sins are forgiven. Joy to the world. Joy to you!

†

December 28, 2014
At Resurrection Lutheran Church, Winter Haven, Florida

God's Favorite Christmas Words

INI

Christmas is a wonderful time for words. Words carry our holiday greetings; we say "merry Christmas, happy New Year" and reply "Same to you!" Words in holiday letters update our friends and relatives about family happenings. And of course we turn again to the words of Scripture to hear again the beautiful story of the first Christmas: "*And it came to pass in those days there went out a decree from Caesar Augustus ...*" Luke 2.1 Just hearing those words again warms our hearts, and takes many of us back to childhood when we memorized them and recited them in church at a children's Christmas service. The heart of that story was the message of the angel to the shepherds out in the field. Those words will be the Bible portion that we focus on this morning:

> And the angel said unto them, Fear not: for, behold, I bring you good tidings of great joy, which shall be to all people. For unto you is born this day in the city of David a Savior, which is Christ the Lord. Luke 2.10-11

We all enjoy the words surrounding Christmas, especially since so many of them appear in beautiful poetry and hymns and carols. I can't help believing that just as we enjoy those poetic Christmas expressions, they must also be among God's favorite words. Let's use this sermon, on the first Sunday after Christmas, to recall some of them together, shall we?

First there is the proclamation: how God must have delighted in it, announcing that his plan from the beginning of the world, indeed, his plan from eternity, was finally coming to pass. The proclamation of the angel might well be God's favorite Christmas words. That proclamation was celebrated in the traditional English carol, "The First Noel." Nobody knows who wrote it; it emerged in the 17th century, more than 300 years ago. Nobody is even sure where the word "noel" came from. It was French but might have come from the Latin *natalis* meaning birth, or from *novella* meaning new. But it's plain that the word refers to the good news from the angel that Jesus has come. Is anyone here old enough to remember a newspaper boy standing on a corner selling newspapers by shouting, "Extra extra, read all about it!" Nobody does that anymore, but that's what this refrain sounds like: "News news, news, the King of Israel is born today!" "Noel, noel, noel, noel, born is the king of Israel!" The proclamation by the angel of Jesus' birth might be God's favorite Christmas words.

What about the names of Jesus? We give a lot of thought to naming our children, looking up lists of baby names in books, and considering names of parents and grandparents, and once we choose a name for our baby, we consider that name precious. God must love the names he gave his Son. They are all so meaningful. Of course, the Angel told Mary what to name him: *"And, behold, thou shalt conceive in thy womb, and bring forth a son, and shalt call his name Jesus."* Luke 1.31 In Greek Ἰησοῦς Ye-sous; in Hebrew יֵשׁוּעַ Yeshua. It means "God Saves."

But there are other names given him in Scripture. How many can you think of? A favorite of everyone must be "Immanuel." The Old Testament prophet Isaiah first used it: *"Therefore the Lord himself will give you a sign. Behold, the virgin shall conceive and bear a son, and shall call his name Immanuel."* Isaiah 7.14 That name is a combination of two Hebrew words: עִמָּנוּ "immanu" which means "with us," and אֵל "El" which is a word for "God."

That name, and others, are celebrated in the hymn "O come O come Emmanuel." Like the "Noel" hymn, nobody knows who wrote this hymn; it's even older than "Noel" and comes from a Latin hymn sung in the 12th century. Each stanza in this hymn invokes a different name for Jesus. The first notes how much we need "God with us." Ever since Adam and Eve sinned and were sent out of the Garden of Eden, exiled from Paradise, we all like them would have been separated from God, lost and alone in our sins. In our exile we need the ransom ["redemption"] Jesus came to provide:

> O come, O come, Emmanuel, and ransom captive Israel,
> That mourns in lonely exile here until the Son of God appear.

The second stanza calls Jesus "Wisdom." This is what we read about Jesus as he grew up: *"And the child grew, and waxed strong in spirit, filled with wisdom: and the grace of God was upon him."* Luke 2.40 Listen to how this Wisdom teaches us about the plan of God for us, how Jesus sets everything in order, and shows us how our faith in him is the path to Heaven:

> O come, Thou Wisdom from on high and order all things, far and nigh;
> To us the path of knowledge show and cause us in her ways to go.

In stanza three Jesus is named the "Desire of Nations." The Old Testament prophet Haggai used those words to describe Jesus: *"And I will shake all nations, and the desire of all nations shall come: and I will fill this house with glory, says the LORD of hosts."* Haggai 2.7 And shouldn't all nations desire what Jesus brings?

> O come, Desire of nations, bind all peoples in one heart and mind;
> Bid envy, strife, and quarrels cease; fill the whole world with heaven's peace.

The next stanza names Jesus a "Dayspring," an old poetic word for "dawn," the time when the "day springs up" in the morning. Before John the Baptizer was born, his father Zacharias could not speak for a while, but when his son was born and named "John," he could speak again, and in his song of praise he said this: *"The dayspring from on high has visited us to give light to them that sit in darkness and in the shadow of death."* Luke 1.78-79 Imagine how dark, sad, and gloomy our lives would be if all we had to look forward to was death. So we sing to Jesus:

> O come, Thou Dayspring, come and cheer our spirits by thine advent here;
> Disperse the gloomy clouds of night and death's dark shadows put to flight.

Then there is this name: "Rod of Jesse." Jesse of course was the father of King David. He is pictured as the tree trunk from which a firm branch would grow, a powerful stick or club of wood symbolizing great power. Isaiah said, *"And there shall come forth a rod out of the stem of Jesse, and a Branch shall grow out of his roots: and the spirit of the LORD shall rest upon him, the spirit of wisdom and understanding, the spirit of counsel and might, the spirit of knowledge and of the fear of the LORD."* Isaiah 11.1-2 And so we sing, trusting in Jesus' great strength for us:

> O come, thou Rod of Jesse's stem; from every foe deliver them
> That trust thy mighty pow'r to save, and give them vict'ry o'er the grave.

Finally there is the stanza about the "Key of David." A key can unlock a door and can lock it up again. Isaiah wrote this about God's servant Eliakim the son of Hilkiah: *"And the key of the house of David will I lay upon his shoulder; so he shall open, and none shall shut; and he shall shut, and none shall open."* Isaiah 22.22 That same verse is quoted later in the Bible Revelation 3.7, not about Eliakim but about Jesus, who unlocks for us the door to heaven:

> O come, thou Key of David, come, and open wide our heav'nly home;
> Make safe the way that leads on high, and close the path to misery.

The many names of Jesus must be some of God's favorite Christmas words.

The setting of that first Christmas has also inspired so many beautiful descriptions of what was probably a very stressful scene. Mary was about to have a baby, and they couldn't find a place to stay. How many places must they have asked before someone finally said they could go into the cattle stalls? All this is recorded by St. Luke with just these few simple words: *"She laid him in a manger, because there was no room for them in the inn."* Luke 2.7

A woman named Cecil Frances Alexander wrote a series of hymns for children to illustrate various parts of the Apostles' Creed. For example, on the phrase "suffered under Pontius Pilate" she wrote "There is a Green Hill Far Away." On the phrase "conceived by the Holy Ghost, born of the Virgin Mary," she wrote the following:

> Once in royal David's city stood a lowly cattle shed, where a mother laid her baby in a manger for His bed. Mary was that mother mild, Jesus Christ her little Child.

> He came down to earth from heaven Who is God and Lord of all, and his shelter was a stable, and His cradle was a stall.

> With the poor and mean and lowly lived on earth, our Savior holy.

I don't know if the manger was in a stable shed; more likely it was in a cave, since that is what the geology of Bethlehem was like. And while we in America celebrate Christmas in wintertime hoping for snow (a "white Christmas"), it's pretty certain there wasn't any snow at that first Christmas in Palestine. Still we love the words of the poet Christina Georgina Rossetti. She was born in 1830, educated at home, and though she wasn't a hymn writer, she was a poet. While it wasn't really cold winter where Jesus was born, we can consider the world into which he was born as cold, frozen and hard with sin. She wrote:

> In the bleak midwinter, frosty wind made moan, earth stood hard as iron, water like a stone; snow had fallen, snow on snow, snow on snow, in the bleak midwinter, long ago.

> Our God, heaven cannot hold him, nor earth sustain; heaven and earth shall flee away when he comes to reign. In the bleak midwinter a stable place sufficed the Lord God Almighty, Jesus Christ.

> Angels and archangels may have gathered there, cherubim and seraphim thronged the air; but his mother only, in her maiden bliss, worshiped the beloved with a kiss.

> What can I give him, poor as I am? If I were a shepherd, I would bring a lamb; if I were a Wise Man, I would do my part; yet what I can I give him: give my heart.

And that's how it is at Christmas: when the Holy Spirit brings into our hearts the news of a Savior, we are moved to give those hearts back to him.

Maybe words about the setting of Christmas are God's favorite Christmas words.

A favorite theme of Christmas hymn writers has been the contrasts of the Incarnation, the almighty God taking on human flesh and becoming a tiny helpless baby. One of my favorites is a little-known hymn by William Walsham How (he died in 1897). Notice the contrasts between the first half and second half of each stanza:

Who is this so weak and helpless, Child of lowly Hebrew maid,
Rudely in a stable sheltered, coldly in a manger laid?
　　'Tis the Lord of all creation, Who this wondrous path hath trod;
　　He is God from everlasting, And to everlasting God.

The next stanzas remind us that Christmas isn't just about a cute little baby – although I am sure Jesus was a cute little baby. But remember what this baby came to do. He came to live a life of perfect obedience to God, something we couldn't do so he did it in our place. And then he came to die, paying the penalty we owed God for our sins. That's why, when God now looks at us, he sees us as Jesus made us: since our sins are forgiven, God sees us as sinless and holy as Jesus was. So we sing:

Who is this, a Man of Sorrows, walking sadly life's hard way,
Homeless, weary, sighing, weeping over sin and Satan's sway?
　　'Tis our God, our glorious Savior, who above the starry sky
　　Now for us a place prepareth, where no tear can dim the eye.

Who is this? Behold Him shedding drops of blood upon the ground!
Who is this, despised, rejected, mocked, insulted, beaten, bound?
　　'Tis our God, who gifts and graces on his Church now poureth down;
　　Who shall smite in holy vengeance all His foes beneath His throne.

Who is this that hangeth dying while the rude world scoffs and scorns,
Numbered with the malefactors, torn with nails, and crowned with thorns?
　　'Tis the God who ever liveth 'mid the shining ones on high,
　　In the glorious golden city, reigning everlastingly.

And because of his dying, by which he paid for our sins, we know that we will share that life with him everlastingly.

For many of us, our favorite Christmas words are the prayers we find in the Christmas hymns. How many of us memorized these when we were children, and still pray them regularly? Martin Luther wrote "From Heav'n Above to Earth I Come" as a pageant, a play to be acted by his children. But many of us especially remember this stanza:

Ah, Dearest Jesus, holy Child, make Thee a bed, soft, undefiled
Within my heart, that it may be a quiet chamber kept for Thee.

Martin Luther is often given credit for writing the carol "Away in a Manger." But this third stanza, a beautiful prayer, was added by John Thomas McFarland (who died 1913, almost exactly a hundred years ago).

Be near me, Lord Jesus, I ask Thee to stay close by me forever, and love me, I pray.

> Bless all the dear children in Thy tender care and take us to Heaven to live with Thee there.

You've seen the theme for this sermon: God's Favorite Christmas Words. What you've heard so far are my own favorite Christmas words, and I'm sure some of your favorites too. What words might actually be **God's** favorite Christmas words? I'd like to speculate, knowing the great love that God showed us in sending his Son into the world that night, that his favorite Christmas words were six of those spoken by the angel to the shepherds, recorded by St. Luke in his Christmas chapter, chapter 2. I'm speaking of the six words in a row at the end of verse 10 and the start of verse 11.

From Luke 2:10b "to all people" in the Greek language: παντὶ τῷ λαῷ
From Luke 2:11a "for unto you" ὅτι ε τέχθη ὑμῖν [literally, "for born unto you"]

You see, the news wasn't just that a child was born, or even that a special child was born; this child was born "unto you," that is, **for us.** The plan wasn't just to help a few people; it was **for all people**. God in his great love **for us**, and **for all people**, was carrying out his plan **for us**, and **for everybody**!

It wasn't a new thought of course. Centuries before it happened, the prophet Isaiah emphasized the same message in a passage often quoted at Christmas time, and set to music so beautifully by George Frederick Handel in his marvelous oratorio, *Messiah*: *"For unto us a child is born, unto us a son is given: and the government shall be upon his shoulder: and his name shall be called Wonderful, Counselor, The mighty God, The everlasting Father, The Prince of Peace."* Isaiah 9.6

It's a thought picked up again in our Christmas songs such as in *The First Noel*, the first song we spoke of earlier. We don't often sing it through to stanza six, but if we did we'd find this thought there, in the first line.

> Then let **us all** with one accord sing praises to our heav'nly Lord,
>   That hath made heav'n and earth of naught,
>   and with His blood mankind hath bought.
> Noel, noel, noel, noel, born is the King of Israel

For all people. For unto you. Those might be God's favorite Christmas words. They certainly are mine.

†

April 15, 2015

Written for You

INI

Have you ever been "jumped" by a Bible passage? You can't be a student of Scripture for long – I know you all are – before a sentence jumps out at you and grabs you and you are in awe of the message and its meaning for your life. Consider the words before us this morning, from the final chapter in John's Gospel in which he reports to us about the resurrection; then at the end are these words:

> And truly Jesus did many other signs in the presence of his disciples, which are not written in this book; but these are written that you may believe that Jesus is the Christ, the Son of God, and that believing you may have life in His name. John 20:30-31

It might not be much of an exaggeration to say about these verses: It's all here, God's entire plan, in a few short words. The key doctrines are all there. Keep your worship folder in front of you, we're going to look at the words.

"These things are written so that..." Here we have the **necessity of revelation**. Do we Christians take the Bible for granted? Imagine this world without Scripture! How little we would know about God! How lost we would be! Here is God's gift to us: he made a plan to save us, he carried out that plan in the life, death, and resurrection of his Son Jesus, and then, to reveal it to us who weren't there to witness it, **he had it written down.**

Here too is taught the **sufficiency of Scripture.** "*...which are not written in this book; but these are written...*" God hasn't told us everything. We don't need to know everything. That's something to remember in many parts of our lives. We may not understand all of God's ways in our life, but we don't need to know everything. What has been written is enough! Lutherans use the phrase *sola Scriptura* – Scripture alone; from what has been written, we can believe.

That is God's purpose in this writing: "*these are written that you may believe.*" Believing is all that's needed. Lutherans use the phrase *sola fide* – faith alone.

But faith is not empty, not without an object. After all, many people believe things that are false. These things are written so we may believe what is true: "*...that Jesus is the Christ, the Son of God....*" These words encapsulate the **person and work of Jesus:** that he is the Christ, the Messiah, the Savior promised from the earliest days of history; that he is the very the Son of God, whose innocent death on the cross was so precious that it paid for the sins of the whole world – that includes yours and mine – who had the power to burst the chains of death on Easter morning.

That, then, is the purpose of God's gift of this writing: That we may **know** who Jesus is, and more than that, **believe** that this is who he is. When this work of God creates that belief, we are changed: our sins are forgiven, and we have "*life in his name.*"

"*Life in his name!*" We've celebrated Jesus' Resurrection and been reassured that for us too death is a doorway to life. But it's not just a future thing, precious as that is. **We have that Life now.** Look at the words: when you are believing (as you are now), "*...believing, you may have life in His name.*" That's what we have now: life in his name.

Realize the power of your life in this name.

Peter said to the man who could not walk: "*In the name of Jesus Christ of Nazareth, walk.*" And he did. Acts 3.6

Once St. Paul became so troubled by a woman with an evil spirit that he turned around and said to the spirit, "*In the name of Jesus Christ I command you to come out of her!*" At that moment the spirit left her. Acts 16.18

St. Paul proclaimed that "*at the name of Jesus every knee should bow, in heaven and on earth and under the earth.*" Philippians 2.10

This powerful name makes a difference in lives, in **your** life, because your life, now, is in his name. Jesus has put his name on you. It happened at your Baptism. The Holy Spirit in your Baptism worked faith in your heart, you became a believer, "*...and that believing, you ... have life in His name.*"

We've looked at several parts of this wonderful passage. Here is the last and best thing about this verse: The word we see there twice: see it? the word "*you.*" This time it doesn't say "many people" have life, but **you.** You are in this verse. Read it with me out loud, starting from "these are written"; "*these are written that **you** may believe that Jesus is the Christ, the Son of God, and that believing, **you** may have life in His name.*"

Let's do it better than that; let's read it one more time, this time, instead of the word you, **say your first name**: "*these are written that NNN may believe that Jesus is the Christ, the Son of God, and that believing NNN may have life in His name.*"

Through what is written here, God has reached out and grabbed you. Thanks be to God.

†

May 13, 2015

Missing Chapel but Not Church

INI

We've celebrated Jesus' resurrection. Tomorrow we celebrate his Ascension. Will we ever in this life fully grasp what these two events mean for us? Listen to St. Paul's prayer:

> (May the God of our Lord Jesus Christ give you understanding... that you may know) what is the exceeding greatness of His power toward us who believe, according to the working of His mighty power which He worked in Christ when He raised Him from the dead and seated Him at His right hand in the heavenly places, far above all principality and power and might and dominion, and every name that is named, not only in this age but also in that which is to come. And He put all things under His feet and gave Him to be head over all things to the church, which is His body, the fullness of Him who fills all in all. Ephesians 1.20-23

In a few days – hours, really – this chapel will be moving out of your life, for some a little while, for others a long time. Will you miss it? I would. I love this chapel for many reasons: its organ, spaciousness, artwork. It took me a while when I watched it under construction 20 years ago. I first thought the architecture was strange and senseless but I came to understand it and admire it greatly. When I taught Visual Communication I would bring the class here to discuss the artwork, the genius of the lighting, how the morning sunlight streams in, casting colors on the floors, walls, pillars; the concerts held here, the messages of the choirs, the chapel services where you are daily offered strength and hope and courage and forgiveness through Jesus Christ our Savior.

Graduates soon-to-be: will you miss it? I am blessed to be able to come back from time to time. It's only a slight exaggeration to say I wish I could be here always – if not here, in church somewhere, where God's Word is faithfully presented.

Don't you treasure this too?

Consider the assurance offered here that God loves us. It's so easy to say, so often said, yet so profound beyond all telling! And God looks after each of us as an individual person and in every tiny detail: Jesus said not a sparrow falls without the Father knowing it. Matthew 10.29 Jesus said, even the hairs of your head are counted. Matthew 10.30 He assures us that he knows you by name. John 10.3, 14, Revelation 3.5. He washed you clean of sin when you were named at your Baptism. He comes to you and me individually and in person in the

Sacrament. He hears your prayers. He forgives your sins; the penalty for each of them was paid on the cross. He sent you his Spirit by his Word. He made you a member of his Church, the communion of saints, the company of believers.

Jesus is Immanuel, God with us – he is in us, and we in him. That's the "narrow view," and it is tremendously comforting.

In today's reading, the apostle pulls back the camera, as it were, and presents a broader view, a world-wide, universe-wide view and it is in its way even more comforting. For where is that Jesus now, who is with us and within us? We read again,

> He is raised from the dead by the mighty power of God And seated at God's right hand, far above all rule and authority, power and dominion, and every title that can be given, not only in the present age but also in the one to come.

Just as Jesus said before he ascended into Heaven, "*All power is given to me in heaven and in earth*," Matthew 28.18 And we read, "*And God placed all things under his feet and appointed him to be head over everything –[and note this]– for the church, which is his body, the fullness of him who fills everything in every way*." Ephesians 1.22

If that narrow view, Christ with us as individuals, gives us comfort, consider this broad view: Christ is the all-powerful head of his Church, his Body, and we are in that Church, members of that Body. That powerful Head supplies his Body with no less than "*the fullness of him who fills everything in every way*." That includes all spiritual gifts and graces: wisdom, goodness, truth and holiness, for through his work our sins are forgiven; we are without blame before God the Father. As St. John says, "*Of his fullness have all we received, and grace for grace*." John 1.16

Will you miss this chapel? I expect you will. But remember, even though you may be leaving this chapel for a while you are not leaving Church. You are always in Church! You are always taking what is offered here in this chapel with you this summer and into your future. You can turn to the Word every day, as we do here, and find comfort in knowing that Jesus your Brother reigns over all things from Heaven for the benefit of his Church, you and me. Enjoy knowing God's power in your life as you do God's work, which we are appointed to do in all our lives. For you and I, we are the Church, the body of Christ who rules all.

†

August 29, 2015
In the Good Shepherd Chapel
for the Bethany Lutheran Theological Seminary Opening Service

Preparing the Nets

INI

It's a bitter-sweet topic as summer ends, but let's do it. Let's talk fishing – with special attention to the tools. The two verses before us are from the familiar story of the calling of the first disciples, which reads as follows:

> One day as Jesus was standing by the Lake of Gennesaret, with the people crowding around him and listening to the word of God, he saw at the water's edge two boats, left there by the fishermen, who were washing their nets. He got into one of the boats, the one belonging to Simon, and asked him to put out a little from shore. Then he sat down and taught the people from the boat. When he had finished speaking, he said to Simon, "Put out into deep water, and let down the nets for a catch." Simon answered, "Master, we've worked hard all night and haven't caught anything. But because you say so, I will let down the nets." When they had done so, they caught such a large number of fish that their nets began to break. So they signaled their partners in the other boat to come and help them, and they came and filled both boats so full that they began to sink. When Simon Peter saw this, he fell at Jesus' knees and said, "Go away from me, Lord; I am a sinful man!" For he and all his companions were astonished at the catch of fish they had taken, and so were James and John, the sons of Zebedee, Simon's partners. Then Jesus said to Simon, "Don't be afraid; from now on you will catch men." Luke 5.1-10

When Jesus approached this important scene, the fishermen were taking good care of the main tool of their trade, their nets. Nets weren't the only means of fishing back then; when Jesus told Peter to fetch a coin to pay taxes he told him to cast in a hook. Matthew 17.27 But for commercial fishing, catching fish in volume, making a living from it – **serious** fishing – there had to be nets. Without the nets, there was no trade, no occupation, no income. So the nets had to be cared for.

Nets can't have been cheap. They may have been the most expensive occupational investment, possibly more than boats which were easier to get. And there was no strong nylon weave back then. Egyptian nets of the day were made of water reed fibers, others from the fibers of date palms, grass, or papyrus. A good load of fish could start to tear the net (verse 5). As Mark recorded this incident, the men were not just washing, they were mending their nets.

But Jesus called them, inviting them to catch **men** not fish. And they left their nets and followed him.

To catch fish, they used nets. In "catching men" what is the main tool of the trade without which there is no success? Of course, it's the Word of God and the visible Word of God, the Holy Sacraments – what we call the Means of Grace. That's a man-catching net made not of crisscrossing strands of rope, but these two strands woven together: **objective justification** and **Christ's institution** – objective justification, the work of Christ to pay fully for the sins of the entire world, and then his institution, his commands to "preach the Gospel," "baptize them," "take eat and drink."

At the side of the Galilee Lake there was a time for fishing and a time for preparing the tools, washing and mending the nets. Here, in the Seminary, is when you prepare the tools, when you wash the net of the Means of Grace.

In the field of **Biblical Theology** you study the Gospel itself embodied in the Word throughout Scripture – that God was in Christ reconciling the world unto himself, and that the Holy Spirit wants this forgiveness both offered and conveyed to all people through the Means of Grace.

In **Systematic Theology** you are learning how the Means of Grace, the Gospel and Sacraments, are correctly and properly understood, and you are learning how to defend the purity of Scripture's teachings about the Gospel and the Sacraments against the distortions of sectarianism and fanaticism.

In **Historical Theology,** you are learning how the good news was foretold in early history of the world, proclaimed in the life of Israel, fulfilled in the incarnation, perfect life, atoning death, and justifying resurrection of our Lord Jesus, and proclaimed by the apostles. You are celebrating how the Holy Spirit employs the Means of Grace to create his Church throughout the world and especially in the train of events leading to our particular fellowship.

In **Practical Theology,** you are learning how the Holy Spirit will work through you as you rightly divide the Word of Truth and administer the sacraments as the Lord instituted them.

Seminary years (believe it or not) pass quickly. They are important years, a time for preparing the tools provided us by none other than God the Holy Spirit. Like Peter, we know we are not worthy but through God's love we have our Lord's grace – your sins are forgiven! – and we have our Lord's call.

So let's get the school year started, washing our nets, getting them ready with the Holy Spirit's power to catch men.

†

[Themes in this sermon appeared in 2004, urging appreciation of our spiritual heritage – see *With the Strength God Gives Me* (2017), p. 143. A decade later they are substantially re-worked here into a Mission Festival sermon.]

September 27, 2015
At the Norwegian Grove and Norseland Lutheran Churches

Our Song of Praise for All the World

INI

It's so good to be here, to see you here, but I have a question: why are you here this morning? Even if it's only to hear this beautiful reading before us from 2700 years ago, it will be worth the trip:

> In that day you will say: "I will praise you, O LORD. Although you were angry with me, your anger has turned away and you have comforted me. Surely God is my salvation; I will trust and not be afraid. The LORD, the LORD, is my strength and my song; he has become my salvation." With joy you will draw water from the wells of salvation. In that day you will say: "Give thanks to the LORD, call on his name; make known among the nations what he has done, and proclaim that his name is exalted. **Sing to the LORD, for he has done glorious things; let this be known to all the world.** Shout aloud and sing for joy, people of Zion, for great is the Holy One of Israel among you." Isaiah 12.1-6

This reading answers the question, why are you here this morning? Oh, you might say, we are here for mission festival and that is commendable. Mission festivals have seemed to disappear lately. I remember the mission festivals when I was a child. There was a morning service, and then a potluck, and then an afternoon service. It was always in August, and before air conditioning very hot. Stained glass church windows aren't designed to open for a breeze, and during the sermon everyone was waving an insurance company fan on a stick to keep cool. Many places don't have mission festivals anymore. You still have a mission festival: that's good, and that's why you are here.

There is another way to answer that question. You can say, I am here because

- A bell rang on the door of Sorenson's dye shop in Oslo, Norway, 174 years ago, that's why I'm here this morning. Or farther back,
- Gorm the Old made a deal about Harold Bluetooth;
- An idea came into an English schoolboy's mind more than 1300 years ago;
- A ship sailed from Troas across the Aegean Sea to Neapolis in 53 AD;
- Jesus Christ died on the cross.

All these events may at first seem unrelated, but they are all captured in this song of Isaiah: **Sing to the LORD, for he has done glorious things; let this be known to all the world.**

Today we'll talk about **OUR SONG OF PRAISE FOR ALL THE WORLD.**

It started, of course, with the most important item on our list: **Jesus Christ died** on the cross. Way back in eternity God knew you and me. He loved us. He wants us be with him forever. But we had strayed away from God; by our sins, we had made ourselves unfit to be anywhere near a holy God. We can't make ourselves worthy to be with God no matter what we do. Because of our sins, we deserve to die, we deserve to be sent far away from God forever. That is hell.

To accomplish his loving plan for us, God the Father had to rescue us. He had to sacrifice his only Son to rescue us. Christ Jesus, God the Son, came into this world as a human being and lived a life completely free from sin. So he didn't deserve to die but he did so anyway, because he took **our sins** onto himself and paid on the cross the penalty for sin we owed. He died in our place. That is how Jesus removed our sin from us and made us clean and worthy to be with God for all eternity. "*It is finished!*" he said as he died on the cross. John 19.30 There is nothing more for us to do; Jesus did it all. When we believe in him, we have what he won for us – life with God, now and forever.

Jesus finished the work of saving us many centuries ago. We still need the work of God the Holy Spirit to assure that God's saving Word would reach us, so that we could know about Jesus and believe in him. Remember all those odd stories from a moment ago? Each of them was a piece of the Holy Spirit's work to bring us here this morning. Each was a verse from the song of Isaiah:

> **Sing to the LORD, for he has done glorious things;**
> **let this be known to all the world.**

Remember the ship sailing from Troas to Neapolis in 53 A.D.? It carried the Apostle Paul to Greece. The church, which till then had been confined to Asia, was now in Europe, a step closer to us. That was a mission trip:

> **Sing to the LORD, for he has done glorious things;**
> **let this be known to all the world.**

Remember that idea in an English schoolboy's mind some 1300 years ago? In A.D. 718 that young man named Boniface decided his calling was to leave his native Devonshire and preach the Gospel in Germany. Through his work the Word spread into central Europe, where the Reformation would begin. That was a mission trip:

Sing to the LORD, for he has done glorious things;
let this be known to all the world.

Remember Gorm the Old? He was King of Denmark and arranged to bequeath his throne to his son Harold Bluetooth. Gorm's wife Thyra had taught her son about Jesus, and many years later Harold, the first Christian Danish king, sent missionaries into Norway. Now the Gospel had reached the home of this congregation's spiritual ancestors. That was a mission trip:

Sing to the LORD, for he has done glorious things;
let this be known to all the world.

That bell ringing on the door of Sorenson's dye shop in Oslo 174 years ago signaled the entrance of a man named J. W. C. Dietrichson. Their conversation turned to missions. Sorenson offered to pay the fare for Dietrichson's first trip to America. Because of that offer, you and I are here in this church today. Dietrichson's first services in America were held under two oak trees near Koshkonong in Wisconsin. That was a mission trip:

Sing to the LORD, for he has done glorious things;
let this be known to all the world.

The theme for this sermon is not **ISAIAH'S** SONG OF PRAISE FOR ALL THE WORLD. It's **OUR** SONG OF PRAISE FOR ALL THE WORLD. What about you and me in the stories of the future? Can you and I help to continue this 2700-year-old song of Isaiah, to continue bringing the news of God's glorious acts to all the world?

"All the world" is very big – seven billion people. The Lord has given us some special blessings: mission workers, yes – a great blessing but not enough to reach seven billion people. Today God has given us another special blessing: the gift of technology, ways of reaching vast numbers of people. At Bethany we have an organization called the *Christ in Media Institute* dedicated to using technology to reach out with the Gospel. As its director, I've become aware of interesting situations around the world. The reading before us reminds me of three such situations.

Here is one: We read, *"I will praise you, O LORD. Although you were angry with me, your anger has turned away and you have comforted me."* Right now in India, members of our church there are learning how to show Gospel messages to others on their cell phones. Imagine a young man there brought up in the Hindu religion. They have hundreds, even thousands of gods. This young man has a conscience assailing him. He thinks some god is angry at him and doesn't even know which one. A friend who is a member of our church there shows him a video on his cell phone about Jesus. He even transfers the video from his phone to his friend's phone, for him to watch and study whenever he wishes. The message is this: because of what Jesus did for us, dying on the cross to take away our sins, he knows (as we read from Isaiah) *"Although you were angry with me, your anger has turned away and you have comforted me."* That is a mission trip:

Sing to the LORD, for he has done glorious things;
let this be known to all the world.

Here is the second situation: We read *"Surely God is my salvation; I will trust and not be afraid. The LORD, the LORD, is my strength and my song; he has become my salvation."* Right now, in Mexico, some mission workers are teaching Bible lessons on the internet in an online school called *Academia Cristo,* "Christ's school." Imagine a farmer in rural Mexico whose daughter is very sick and he is worried. He gets a Bible lesson on his cell phone and even shows it on his TV. The lesson is the story of Jesus healing the daughter of Jairus, Jesus showing his power to save by healing someone very sick. *"Surely God is my salvation; I will trust and not be afraid. The LORD, the LORD, is my strength and my song; he has become my salvation."* That is a mission trip:

Sing to the LORD, for he has done glorious things;
let this be known to all the world.

Here is the third situation: We read *"With joy you will draw water from the wells of salvation."* Right now in Ethiopia several mission workers trained in our sister synod's seminary in Mequon are digging wells. They are in one of the massive refugee camps there containing people who have fled, many of them walking hundreds of miles to escape the violence and genocide in their home country of Sudan. The well provides the refugees with an essential of life, water, but they are also bringing them, on cell phones, the living water that Jesus spoke of to the woman at the well in Samaria, the news of God's rescue plan through Jesus. Those who believe in him, he said, will never thirst. *"With joy you will draw water from the wells of salvation."* That is a mission trip:

Sing to the LORD, for he has done glorious things;
let this be known to all the world.

We told stories of the past that brought God's glorious acts to us. There are many more stories that can be told of the present and the future, in Chile, and Colombia, and India, and Pakistan, and China, and Cameroon, and Ukraine, and so many other places. By supporting this work we are still singing the song of Isaiah, the same song that brought God's glorious things to us has become OUR SONG OF PRAISE FOR ALL THE WORLD.

In that day you will say: "Give thanks to the LORD, call on his name; make known among the nations what he has done, and proclaim that his name is exalted. Sing to the LORD, for he has done glorious things; let this be known to all the world. Shout aloud and sing for joy, people of Zion, for great is the Holy One of Israel among you."

Today for our further encouragement we will go back to how it started. At the Lord's Table this morning we cross all those generations, and years and centuries – we go back to the cross, where Jesus' body was broken, and his blood was shed for us. Thanks to that sacrifice and to all the mission trips that finally brought that good news to us, today in this meal Jesus is here and that's why we are here.

†

October 29, 2015
For the Reformation Vespers Service,
opening the annual B. W. Teigen Reformation Lectures

Life Built Around a Sentence

INI

Grace to you and peace from God our Father and the Lord Jesus Christ, who gave himself for our sins to deliver us from the present evil age, according to the will of our God and Father, to whom be the glory forever and ever. Amen. Galatians 1.3-5

Listen please to these words from St. Paul before us this evening:

> Therefore, since we have been justified through faith, we have peace with God through our Lord Jesus Christ, through whom we have gained access by faith into this grace in which we now stand. And we rejoice in the hope of the glory of God. Romans 5.1-2

On a distant planet far from earth a child finds a scrap of paper, on it strange writing. She shows it to her father who recognizes it as part of a much larger work and sets about finding someone who can read what is written there. Thus is set in motion a sequence of happenings that will eventually summon to that planet Christian missionaries from earth, because the words on that scrap of paper are from the Bible, from the letter of St. Paul to the Romans, the very words we have before us this morning. How that paper scrap got there, how they learned of its origin on Earth, how they summoned missionaries – all that I leave to your imagination, since this is a science fiction plot that emerged back in 2013 from a group discussion sponsored by the *Christ in Media Institute* about how to write a Christian science fiction film.

There is no question that this sentence is powerful enough to build a story around. This morning I'll assert that this sentence is powerful enough to build a **life** around.

The apostle, before these words appear, has concluded his proof from Scripture that we are set right before God, "justified," not by what we do, works, but simply by believing in what God has done for us. We are, he has shown, "justified by faith." Now with this sentence, he fairly bursts forth with the triumph of that fact. **JUSTIFIED!** His own word order here is a bit Yoda-ish perhaps, but this is what he says: "**JUSTIFIED we are by faith, therefore...**" and now what? Why, everything changes. Our entire lives are different now. Our lives can be built around that fact.

First, we have peace with God. What a change! When we were under the curse of sin, we could not have peace with God. We were enemies of the God whom we so often offended with sin. As a just judge, God had to condemn us.

But as a caring Father God loves us. By his act of justifying us, he changed our status. He removed our sin – your sins are forgiven. With sin gone, peace is possible; our state of enmity has become a state of reconciliation.

When we hear that peace proclaimed it invites our faith, it invites us to believe it. Indeed, it **causes** us to believe it and when we believe it we have it. We are justified by faith.

Who is responsible for such a profound change in our relationship to God? We have this peace with God "*through our Lord Jesus Christ.*" We owe it all to Christ, to his atoning sacrifice paying the punishment price for all our sins, and to the righteousness of his holy life which God now credits to us. That ugly thought you had this morning, it went onto Jesus and God punished him for it instead of you. That unkind word you spoke, that went on Jesus too. And those things you did that made you ashamed, Jesus took all of those onto the cross with him and he paid for them there in full – they are gone.

Then those wonderful things Jesus did – the way he loved his Father while we were cold and indifferent to God – God looks at us as if we did what Jesus did. The way he gave of himself to help others, while we are so self-centered – God looks at us as if we did what Jesus did. And since because of Jesus our sins are gone and his goodness is made ours, we have peace with God, a peace to build our lives around. From the moment of our Baptism when the pastor dismissed us from the font with "*the peace of God that passes under-standing,*" Philippians 4.7 until we pray with Simeon at life's end, "*Lord now let your servant depart in peace,*" Luke 2.29 "*we have peace with God through our Lord Jesus Christ.*"

But there is an "also" in this sentence. Justified by faith, we have not only peace with God but **access to grace**, to God's favor undeserved. We were not born into grace, but now Paul says because God has justified us, he invites us, brings us into his grace. And we **stand** in it, firm and safe, all our lives long. Between the Baptism just referred to and the departing from this life just referred to, God gives us this privilege through the writer to Hebrews:

> Let us then approach the throne of grace with confidence, so that we may receive mercy and find grace to help us in our time of need. Hebrews 4.16

A life of peace with God! A life of access to the power of God's wonderful grace in every need! Isn't that a life of rejoicing? We "*rejoice (Paul says) in hope of the glory of God.*"

No, The word "rejoice" is too weak. The word Paul uses has a public aspect to it. We are to do it **loudly**. Use the word **triumph** as in a parade of victory. We **show it off** – not ourselves, but our hope of God's glory. All our lives should make plain to anyone looking that we are justified by faith through Jesus Christ, that we have peace with God, that we have access to his grace and that we look forward to sharing God's glory.

This is indeed a sentence that we can build ... no rather, this is a sentence that **God has built** our lives around. Could only this sentence on a scrap of paper bring the people on that distant planet to saving faith? Well, it was, after all, only a "scrap" of knowledge about God's power to save that made Rahab of Jericho a hero of faith as confirmed in Hebrews 11. Luther's life was built around all of Scripture but if there was one sentence to sum up his life, it might be this one. The same can be said of many... I pray, **all** lives knowing that God has built our lives around this proclamation:

"Therefore, since we have been justified through faith, we have peace with God through our Lord Jesus Christ, through whom we have gained access by faith into this grace in which we now stand. And we rejoice in the hope of the glory of God." Romans 5.1-2

†

December 3, 2015

The Most Important Person in the World

INI

Remember the neighbor kid? A boy younger than you maybe down the block or road, or the little brother of a friend – do you remember that kid, have him in mind? Now imagine that boy some years later, grown up, an adult, maybe 30 years old, and you are sitting across from him in a restaurant. He looks you in the eye and says with all seriousness, "I am the most important person in the world." What would your reaction be? "Yeah, sure, I remember you when you were a little kid."

Maybe with this image in mind we can understand the reaction of some people to Jesus. One day near the beginning of his public ministry, he had been traveling around Galilee speaking in synagogues. We read about it:

> He came to Nazareth, where He had been brought up. And as His custom was, He went into the synagogue on the Sabbath day, and stood up to read. And He was handed the book of the prophet Isaiah. And when He had opened the book, He found the place where it was written: "The Spirit of the LORD is upon Me, Because He has anointed Me to preach the gospel to the poor; He has sent Me to heal the brokenhearted, to proclaim liberty to the captives and recovery of sight to the blind, to set at liberty those who are oppressed; to proclaim the acceptable year of the LORD." Then He closed the book and gave it back to the attendant and sat down. And the eyes of all who were in the synagogue were fixed on Him. And He began to say to them, "Today this Scripture is fulfilled in your hearing." So all bore witness to Him, and marveled at the gracious words which proceeded out of His mouth. And they said, "Is this not Joseph's son?" Luke 4.16-22

Did you notice those last words? Everybody in that synagogue knew what was going on there. First, they all knew who was the most important person in the world: the Messiah, the one God promised in Eden after the first sin, the one God promised again to Abraham and then Isaac and Jacob, the one King David sang about in Psalms, the one all the prophets said was coming. Those prophets had in fact described him, the one who was to come, in detail. Everyone in that synagogue that day knew that one of those descriptions of the most important person in the world, the Messiah, was in the prophecy of Isaiah, the very place that Jesus read from that day. Isaiah 61:1-3

And now here was a man standing in from of them saying, **That's about me.** I fit that description. I am the long awaited "most important person in the world," the Messiah.

Their reaction was much like ours might have been. Didn't I know you when you were a kid? They said, "Is this not Joseph's son?" Do you see their problem? This was Jesus' introduction, the Messiah's announcement about who he was, and they let their familiarity block their understanding. How can someone be so special, they thought, who is so ordinary?

What can we learn from their mistake?

The season of Advent has begun. It's an announcement of who is coming at Christmas, an introduction of the most important person in the world, the Savior. We all look forward to Christmas and exciting things like vacation, gifts, family, and celebrations. Of course we know the real meaning of the day, that part too easily becomes routine. We've heard the Christmas story many times. It's **familiar**, it's **ordinary**. The ordinary can blur our focus and be the enemy of our understanding.

May I encourage you today to **fight the familiar** this holiday season. Don't lose the astonishment of the Christmas story. Don't assume, oh I know enough about this Jesus. Go deeper into the Word, and let Jesus tell us more and more about who he is and what he's doing **for us.**

Listen again to his announcement:

"The Spirit of the LORD is upon Me, Because He has anointed Me to preach the gospel to the poor" "The poor" – that's us, who because of our sin are totally without righteousness:

"He has sent Me to heal the brokenhearted." "Those brokenhearted" that's us, people crushed by the weight of our sins.

"To proclaim liberty to the captives." "The captives" that's us, by nature the prisoners of Satan;

"And recovery of sight to the blind." "The blind" that's us, who by ourselves can't grope our way to Heaven; Jesus is talking about how he came to overcome all the effects of sin, our sin, by winning the forgiveness of sins through his life of obedience lived in our place and his atoning death died in our place. Through him, your sins are all forgiven.

Never cease being amazed; look afresh at this man at every opportunity. Find him in the **concerts,** study him in the weekly **Advent services**, enjoy him in **Sunday services** and special **holiday** services, treasure him in your **private devotions** in the Word. Remain startled at what he claimed, at what he did. Don't let it become ordinary. Renew your astonishment and your determination to learn more about this remarkable person, this most important person in the world, this Savior.

†

March 1, 2016

Caging That Lion

INI

You've been warned, haven't you? We've all been warned, in certain situations to be careful, watchful, alert. Our national motto has become "see something, say something." Young women especially are told, if you are out partying with people you don't yet know well, be alert, stay sober. So we're warned about many things because there are dangers out there. I guess it's the kind of world we live in today. And so it always was. Listen to St. Peter:

> Be sober, be vigilant; because your adversary the devil walks about like a roaring lion, seeking whom he may devour. Resist him, steadfast in the faith, knowing that the same sufferings are experienced by your brotherhood in the world. But may the God of all grace, who called us to His eternal glory by Christ Jesus, after you have suffered a while, perfect, establish, strengthen, and settle you. To Him be the glory and the dominion forever and ever. Amen. 1Peter 5.8-9

We know well this enemy, this "adversary," because he has gotten into our heads so often. This Bible description of him as a lion scared me as a little kid and scares me now. The psalmist knew lions from personal experience and he knew why they roar: because they are hungry! David wrote, "*Roaring lions that tear their prey open their mouths wide against me.*" Psalm 22.13

But the lion picture might not be the scariest image in Scripture. We all know about the snake, and how most of us feel about snakes. Perhaps the most frightening image comes from the incident reported in the Lenten history that we are reviewing again this season, when Jesus turned to Peter, who had been named "the Rock," the great apostle, the one who wrote the words before us, and Jesus said to him, "*Simon, Simon, Satan has asked to sift you as wheat.*" Luke 22:31 If Satan has such designs on Peter the apostle, what could he do to you and me? "Sift us like wheat?"

I don't need this morning to describe to you the temptations of Satan, the forms they take, the times they strike when we are most vulnerable. Should we be afraid? Yes, because there is real danger of being "devoured." The word means literally "to drink down." Being swallowed up by a lion means utter destruction and so we are warned.

But also **no**. Because we know from Scripture that Satan cannot touch those who are kept by the power of God through faith unto salvation. John writes in his first letter, "*We know that anyone born of God does not continue to sin; the one who was born of God keeps him safe, and the evil one cannot harm* *him."* 1 John 5.18 It's those who stray away that the lion is seeking; he walks about, looking eagerly after any lost sheep that may have wandered from the fold. That's why, when we fall, as we do so often, daily, we are called to repentance. We acknowledge our sins and flee again to the Word of promise, to Jesus.

Jesus did say to Peter, *"Simon, Simon, Satan has asked to sift you as wheat."* But went on to assure him, *"But I have prayed for you, Simon, that your faith may not fail,"* Luke 22:31 and he turned Peter to repentance. Jesus' prayer for us is more powerful than Satan and Jesus did more than just pray for us. As with everything we are supposed to do but fail, Jesus did it for us. Jesus was tempted by Satan and did not fall. He was tempted in the wilderness. He was tempted in the park the night before his death as he took onto himself all of our sins to pay their penalty before God. He was, we read, in every respect tempted as we are, yet without sin. Hebrews 4.14-16

So if Jesus resisted temptation for us, we don't have to? Is that right? Aha! See how sneaky Satan's temptations can be? I just spoke one from the pulpit in this chapel! No, certainly not.

We are to stay vigilant, to *"keep watch."* It's the same word Jesus used when he said the end of the world is coming unexpectedly like a thief in the night so **keep watch**! Mark 13.35 It's the word Jesus used to his sleepy disciples in Gethsemane. Matthew 26.40

And then he said **resist**! Don't give in – something we by ourselves have no power to do unless we do it *"firm in the faith,"* clinging to Jesus through his Word and to the promise written here: *"God of all grace...who has called you, will restore you, make you strong."* Look for that strength in the Word, in the Sacraments. Look for it here in chapel, in class, in the encouragement of your friends here at Bethany and your family at home. Look for it in what the Apostle here calls the *"brotherhood."* Through that Word, God who has already made you perfect through the work of Jesus – your sins are forgiven! – he will continue to perfect his work of grace in you and make you strong, firm and steadfast.

And especially look forward to Easter. Remember that word "devour"? It is the very same word Paul used in the great resurrection chapter: he writes, *"Death has been swallowed up in victory."* 1 Corinthians 15.54 There is the antidote to all the powers of the roaring lion: *"Death has been swallowed up in victory. Thanks be to God! He gives us the victory through our Lord Jesus Christ."* To him be the power for ever and ever. Amen.

†

April 2016

Because of Scoffers, Comfort

INI

Have you met the scoffers yet? Every Christian at some point will meet people who don't understand how anyone could be a Christian and might even try to make you feel silly for being a believer. How you deal with them will vary with the situation. But you should know that Jesus encountered such people too and in his response to them was a teaching that provides us with strength and comfort.

> The Jews gathered around him, saying, "How long will you keep us in suspense? If you are the Christ, tell us plainly." Jesus answered, "I did tell you, but you do not believe. The miracles I do in my Father's name speak for me, but you do not believe because you are not my sheep. My sheep listen to my voice; I know them, and they follow me. I give them eternal life, and they shall never perish; no one can snatch them out of my hand."
> John 10.24-28

So there was Jesus in the temple, and some unbelievers "gathered" – the word really means, surrounded him and pressed him. "If you are the Messiah, say so!" Now when somebody has told you something important and you insist that he tell you again, it's an insulting demand. Jesus answered as if he were tired of them. He had shown himself to be the promised Messiah again and again by word and deed. There were the great **I am** teachings: "*I am the light of the world*" John 8.12, and in this same chapter: "*I am good shepherd*" John 10.11,14, echoing God's own name "I Am" given to Moses from the burning bush. He said "*I and My Father are one.*" John 10.30 He had said "*Abraham saw my day and was glad.*" John 8.56 He had called himself Old Testament names for the Messiah, the Son of God John 10.36 as well as the Son of Man. Matthew 9.6 Nobody with sense could misunderstand what that meant. So Jesus was exactly right when he said, I told you already. But if his words weren't enough, Jesus said, look at the miracles, testimony that he indeed was who he said he was. These scoffers deserved a rebuke. I think Jesus said it sadly: "*You don't believe because you are not my sheep.*"

Though we can feel sorry for them, we can be thankful that the scoffers surrounded Jesus that day because Jesus followed his rebuke of them with precious words for us: "*My sheep listen to my voice; I know them, and they follow me. I give them eternal life, and they shall never perish; no one can snatch them out of my hand.*"

Some will twist even these wonderful words. Some would want to make this verse a burden, not a comfort. They turn this saying of Jesus into a condition, as if it read: **if** you hear my voice, then I will know you and **if** you follow me, then I will give you eternal life. But let's just really listen to Jesus' voice and find the greatest comfort in the words. He talks about those he calls "my sheep" by his gracious loving choice, that's you and me. Then with simple present tense verbs he describes what we his sheep do. Simple present tense verbs. It's not a conditional – if we do something then he does something. It's not a hypothetical – possibly this could be true or maybe not. It's a simple present tense description of those he calls sheep. He describes something that simply **is**; it's a gracious, loving, caring, comforting **description**.

You and I are his sheep. He knows us by name, fully, in all our sins and weaknesses. As his sheep, Jesus says, here is what we do: we listen to his voice, that's what we do. We attend to his Word, in Scripture, in Baptism where his voice says that it washes away our sin, in the Lord's Supper, where his voice assures us that this body and blood are shed for us for the forgiveness of our sin.

We follow him, that's what we do, obeying his commands, especially the will of his Father, which is to believe in him and trust him. And we search his Word to learn how to live in a way that doesn't disgrace him. That's what it means, to live a Christian life; we follow him.

And he gives us eternal life, that's what **he** does – another simple present tense verb. Not "might give," not even "will in the future give," but now and continuously he gives us eternal life. We have it now; we will enjoy it forever.

And then he says, we shall never perish. He uses the strongest possible negative here, a repeated negative, absolutely strong, as if to put it this way: they will not never ever no way perish, but rather, he concludes, I keep them safe in my hand. What a comfort, to think of Jesus' hand – his hand pierced for you and me on the cross as he paid there for all of our sins, forgave them, and freed us from the guilt and shame we deserve.

I look forward some day to taking Jesus' hand as he guides me across the threshold from this life to the joy of Heaven with him. But for now we rest in his hand for safety. Have you seen a little child who has found something precious – an injured bird, or a fuzzy baby chicken? She will cuddle that precious thing so carefully in her hands because at that moment it is her very favorite thing. You rest in Jesus' hand in the same way, precious and cherished, his very favorite thing, perfectly kept and protected.

Is it hard to imagine that you are Jesus' very favorite thing? **For what else but his favorite thing would he give his life?**

If scoffers ever surround you, deal with them as you will. But let their presence remind you of Jesus' words: "*You, my sheep, listen to my voice; I know you, and you follow me. I give you eternal life, and you shall never ever perish; no one can snatch you out of my hand.*"

†

September 8, 2016

The Way to Not Sin

INI

Were you raised by good parents? Then you heard it a lot: "Behave yourself." "Be good." Were you brought up a Christian? Then you heard the same from God. "Thou shalt, thou shalt not," in other words, don't sin. And it's not just stern orders. Neither parents nor God want to just sit back and judge you. Both your parents and God really want you to not sin.

So in this reading, God gives us some help: first some strategy about **how** not to sin and then some motivation: about **why** not to sin.

> Beloved, I beg you as sojourners and pilgrims, abstain from fleshly lusts which war against the soul, having your conduct honorable among the Gentiles, that when they speak against you as evildoers, they may, by your good works which they observe, glorify God in the day of visitation. 1 Peter 2. 11-12

There it is again: don't sin! That's a tough task – impossible in fact but here God is urging us to work at it. And he wants to help us do that first by telling us **how**, by giving us a strategy for avoiding sin.

He says, **abstain** from fleshly lusts. The word Peter uses for "abstain" involves **space**. Abstain here is not just a "no thank you" when a plate of sin is passed to you; it's a "get out of there!" It means, create a distance between you and sin. Do you remember the old joke? Someone phones a friend, says, I broke my leg in three places and the friend replies, you should stay out of those places. If it's part of your life that you sin in certain places, stay out of those places. If you're among people starting to gossip, say to yourself, help me Jesus, and leave. If you're in a compromising sexual situation, say help me Jesus and leave. Sometimes its physically leaving, sometimes its mentally leaving. When your thoughts go to a place of sin, say help me Jesus and take your thoughts elsewhere. By saying "abstain from fleshly lusts," God is giving us a strategy for doing just that.

But as important as the how is the **why**. Often we feel motivated by guilt. I'm not going to say that's bad. Sorrow for sin is the first stage of repentance. But the apostle gives us some different motivations, three of them here, three "why's" that we should not sin:

The first is **to protect your "soul"**; sinning, he says, is a war against your soul. And "war" is a good translation here. This isn't a fistfight, which is quickly over or even a single battle but a military campaign, planned and executed over a long time against a military-like objective. The goal of the enemy is to take your soul, your self, to take over your personality, to seize who you are, to take what is eternal about you and damn it to hell. Peter says, here's **why** to abstain from sin: to protect this essence of yourself.

There's a second motivation: **to take advantage of opportunity**. Opportunities are fleeting; they are there for a little while and then gone forever. There are few sadder happenings in life than missing an opportunity. You've heard the stories: I could have asked her to marry me but.... I could have told grandpa I loved him before he died but.... Peter says, we are like strangers and pilgrims, that is, we're just passing through, we're not here long. And he is telling us here that our Christian life, our life of doing good and not sinning, is an opportunity, a testimony to unbelievers. We can flip them. These people all around us who are likely to scoff and laugh and criticize us – they look at how we live and see not only that we avoid evil, but we do good. Then *"they may, by your good works which they observe, glorify God in the day of visitation."* Peter is saying, don't add another story of missed opportunity, "I could have shown them Jesus, but...."

Two strong reasons to abstain from sin: to protect our souls and to witness to others through our lives. But for the strongest why, we skip down the page past these verses before us to the end of the chapter where we read this:

> "[Jesus] Himself bore our sins in His own body on the tree, that we, having died to sins, might live for righteousness – by whose stripes you were healed." 1 Peter 2.24

There it is, the **only** way we can be free from sin. God, who wants us to be free from sin, knew that the only way we could be free from sin is if he lifted them off of us. And the only way he could take our sins from us would be to put them on his Son Jesus. That came first. It's done. Our sins are forgiven.

And then what? *"[Jesus] Himself bore our sins in His own body on the tree, that we, having died to sins, might live for righteousness."* Jesus is not only our Savior, Jesus is our motive. With his strength, in thanks to him, we can get out of those places where we sin, we can show Jesus to those around us by our lives, and we can fight the battles that seek to take our souls, knowing that in him that war has already been won.

> Let us ever walk with Jesus, follow His example pure,
> Flee the world, which would deceive us and to sin our souls allure.
> Ever in His footsteps treading, body here, yet soul above,
> Full of faith and hope and love, let us do the Father's bidding.
> Faithful Lord, abide with me; Savior, lead, I follow Thee.

†

October 3, 2017

Lifting Sisters and Brothers

INI

I'm speaking to you this morning on an extremely sensitive matter. Let's ease into it this way.

Remember when you were in grade school and sometime in August each year you'd go out maybe with your Mom or Dad and gather school supplies – a protractor (remember those?), a compass, a ruler, a bunch of pencils, some wide-lined notebooks, and if you were lucky, that big box of 64 crayons, and of course a new backpack to carry them in. That whole collection of supplies was to help you succeed in school.

God has given us a backpack full of supplies to help us succeed in our Christian lives. Chief among them are what we call the "means of grace," the Word of the Gospel and the Holy Sacraments by which God brings to us the news of what he has done for us all, and by which he brings us to faith in Jesus as our Savior. But there are other things in that backpack too, and this morning we focus on an important one: **each other!** St. Paul describes it:

> Brothers, if a person is caught in some trespass, you who are spiritual restore such a person in a spirit of humility, carefully watching yourself so that you are not also tempted. Bear one another's burdens, and in this way fulfill the law of Christ." Galatians 6:1-2

You all know about the fight we are in, the fight against sin. That's what the apostle is talking about here. You know about it because you wage that battle every day and so do I. In these verses God gives us first some insight and then some direction.

The insight is into how a Christian falls into sin. It says, we are caught, like it sneaks up on us from behind, often by surprise, in a trap set by the Devil. No Christian plans to sin. If someone plans to sin, he risks not being a Christian. But we get careless, we're not watching, and suddenly our old flesh surges up, and Satan attacks. Do you remember the last time it happened to you? It might be small at first, a "one time only" thing, we tell ourselves. But it's coming back. We might even start to plan doing it again. And then we're not Christian anymore. We are slaves to that sin, slaves to sin. It could happen to any of us. And think what we are then losing!

God says here, when that happens we can help each other. In that backpack of supplies God gives us to succeed in our Christian lives is **each other.** We don't have to fight sin alone; we can do it together.

You may notice in a Christian friend the burden of some sin. It's a burden, and it will show up. Suddenly they're troubled. They stop going to chapel. They start to avoid their old friends. And you know why, you know what they are doing, and it's wrong. God says, when you notice that, you have something to do. *"You who are spiritual restore such a person."* You, the believer in Jesus, have the Holy Spirit in you. The Holy Spirit can work **through you** to help, to restore your Christian friend. The word picture here is of setting a broken bone back into place, taking something that has become painful and useless, removing the pain, lifting the burden, and restoring the usefulness in your friend.

That's what is meant by *"fulfill the law of Christ."* You are acting toward your friend as Christ acted toward us. He saw us broken, useless, burdened by sin, headed for the eternal pain of hell, and he restored us. You hear about it every day here in chapel. In fact he restores us every day here in chapel when through the preaching of his Word God proclaims that for Jesus' sake your sins are all forgiven, when we hear again how his life and death and resurrection have mended our lives, made us God's children through faith in him, empowered us in this life and set us on the path to an unimaginably beautiful life to come.

All of that is the insight about how sin catches us. Now the direction. We know what Jesus did to restore us. Now he calls on us to restore one another to our proper place, to peace, and to usefulness.

First what if you are the one caught by a sin. It can happen to any of us. Pray that if that happens you will be approached by a Christian friend about it. Don't get defensive – that would be our first impulse, wouldn't it? It would be mine. "Who are you to tell me what to do..." No, this Christian friend is coming **at God's command** to restore you, to pull you back, to help you repent, turn around and mend your life before you become a slave to sin and no longer Christian. Hear this person's words gratefully. It's hard for them, but they are doing God's work in love for you.

But what if you are the mender? What if you see a friend being caught in a sin trap that is pulling them away from their Lord? It's hard to do. It's a very sensitive situation.

Talk to them. Don't be shy. You are doing it by God's command and with his strength. But do it carefully, humbly. There's no room for superiority, no accusation or condemnation, certainly no delight in finding fault in someone else, but with affection, gently, humbly, because you know yourself, and how easy it would be for you to fall into a sin trap too.

And remember the other items in your backpack. Use your supplies! Lead them back to the means of grace. Remind them of their Baptism, where that gracious water washed their sins away, where they were buried with Jesus and then raised to a new life with him, where God created them a new person that can be renewed in holiness every day. **Say to them, how can you throw your Baptism away?**

Invite them back to the Lord's table, where in repentance they can receive the body and blood of their Lord given and shed for them on the cross, and with them the forgiveness won by him. **Say to them, how can you turn away from such a gift?** Show them God's Word, both the Law and the Gospel, bring them back to chapel. Pray for them and pray with them.

We have quite a powerful backpack full of supplies to help us lead a successful Christian life, and one of the most important items in that backpack is you yourself. What greater purpose can you serve in this life than to help restore a Christian friend back to the path that leads them to Heaven? That is fulfilling the Law of Christ.

For that privilege, and the strength to carry it out, thanks be to God.

We pray:

Lord God the Holy Spirit, when we are caught by a sin, send us a Christian friend to restore us, and help us to receive that friend with gratitude and repentance. And when we see a friend caught by a sin, give us the strength and resolve to be your instrument, gently and humbly to restore our friend (for whom our Lord died) to the path of life. We ask this in Jesus' name. AMEN

†

September 7, 2017

Touch Him for Power

INI

Every human being has an intense and personal interest in healing. Right now, I suspect more than half the people in this room have a scratch, bruise, nick, or cut, or worse that they want to heal, that they expect to heal, in some cases that they hope to heal. It's a universal concern; nobody is left out of this.

Jesus devoted a lot of time to healing. There are many incidents recorded in the Gospels where Jesus healed someone and each of them is unique in its own way. Some he did by touching, some just by his word, some close up, others at a distance. Once he spit on the ground and made a little mud to apply in healing. We have a healing incident before us this morning. What made this one especially interesting? I know what it was for me. Let's read about it.

> Now a woman, having a flow of blood for twelve years, who had spent all her livelihood on physicians and could not be healed by any, came from behind and touched the border of His garment. And immediately her flow of blood stopped. And Jesus said, "Who touched Me?" When all denied it, Peter and those with him said, "Master, the multitudes throng and press You, and You say, 'Who touched Me?'" But Jesus said, "Somebody touched Me, for I perceived power going out from Me." Now when the woman saw that she was not hidden, she came trembling; and falling down before Him, she declared to Him in the presence of all the people the reason she had touched Him and how she was healed immediately. And He said to her, "Daughter, be of good cheer; your faith has made you well. Go in peace." Luke 8.43-48

Here's what has always caught my attention, and fascinated me about this one: Jesus said, "*I perceived power going out from Me.*" When Jesus heals, performs any of his miracles, he feels his power flowing out from him! I assume that happened whenever he performed a miracle. This time he healed somebody without intending it but he knew it happened because he felt the healing power flow.

We know all that because this patient, this woman, in effect, tried to steal a cure while Jesus was distracted with something else. He was on his way on another mission. Jairus, an important synagogue official, had come to him for help for his very sick daughter. On their way to his house a big crowd was following along and progress was slow. Then here comes this woman, weak and feeble in body after more than a decade of slow blood loss, a condition that rendered her not only physically weak but socially "unclean," to be avoided – anyone who touches her, anyone she touches would also be unclean. There she was, poor, having used all her resources unsuccessfully seeking a cure, unimportant, humble, shrinkingly timid.

But she had heard of Jesus and had a plan to get healed in secret. Sneaking her way through the crowd behind Jesus she carried out her plan. The healing part worked but the secret part went awry; he noticed! "Power had flowed out" from him. She was caught! Now the entire attention of the crowd, and of Jesus was focused on her, this timid, humble woman. Imagine her fear. Would he be angry? She had after all touched him, which supposedly made him unclean. So she fell down before him and now, with all the crowd focused on her, she confessed to everyone what had happened.

Of course, Jesus knew all along what had happened. So why did he stop, and single her out before the crowd? I think it was because Jesus had, beyond the cure, still more blessing for her. This meek and shrinking one was to become a bold confessor. Another gift of Jesus, the joy of witnessing was to be hers. So he called her "daughter," the only time recorded that he addressed a woman with this endearing term, and told her to go in peace.

Have you already applied this Scripture to your own life?

We have a debilitating, chronic condition too: our sin that will bring us to the grave and to eternal punishment. It's a condition that has no cure – except one. This woman turned to Jesus for her cure. She came to the Word made flesh.

We can't touch Jesus' garment for help but we can do much more. We can always go to the same Word of God. We can depend on the promise he made in our Baptism. In fact, we can touch him, take his body and blood into ourselves in the Holy Supper. With such simple things as hearing, eating and drinking, we are touching much more than the hem of his garment. And from the Word the power goes out; to each of us personally, it flows.

What is the power that flows to us from Jesus? His **righteousness**, the righteousness of God himself that he earned with his perfectly obedient life. That power flows to us, becomes ours. And his **forgiveness**, the forgiveness of God himself, won for us by Jesus on the cross. That power flows to us; God has forgiven all your sins.

Are we too unimportant? Do you think you might be the least important person in this room, not to mention in the world. Do you sometimes think Jesus is too busy to pay you attention? You know the universe is Jesus' concern and a host of angels surrounds him on his throne. How could he be concerned with you?

Remember this: on his way to deal with Jairus' daughter, interrupted, he paused to deal with one individual, to deal with this woman, weak and feeble in body , but sturdy in her purpose, intense in her desire to be whole, humble yet bold in her faith, modest yet confident in the power of the Word, effacing herself yet strong in Jesus, shrinking and timid but once healed wanting the world to hear, proclaiming to all what Jesus had done for her.

Be assured that when you or I meekly reach out in faith to Jesus he knows us personally, by name. His power – his righteousness, his forgiveness – flows to you. Even now, whatever your need, do more than touch a hem! Go to the Word from which his power flows to you. When you hear Jesus ask *"Who touched me?"* answer in faith "I did" and hear his benediction: *"Be of good cheer! Your faith has saved you. Go in peace."*

†

December 24, 2017
At Resurrection Lutheran Church, Winter Haven, Florida

God's History of the World

INI

Many years ago I preached a Christmas sermon entitled "What Is Christmas All About." That was on December 29, 1963, few days less than 54 years ago.[1] It focused on the contrast between the busyness and commercialism surrounding Christmas on the one hand, and the quiet solemnity of the birth in Bethlehem of the Savior of the world. It captured the theme well. Christmas is all about the coming of the Savior, just as Linus proclaimed in the Charlie Brown Christmas television show by reading the story from Luke chapter two. My sermon text that day was that same story in Luke chapter two.

But sad to say, my sermon back then contained an unfortunate theme often heard from pulpits at Christmastime, one I've recovered from with Judy's help. Back then I condemned, in pretty strong terms, all the "busyness" of the Christmas season as only a distraction from what Christmas is all about. Here's what I learned from Judy: Christian people – especially women – do a lot of work to celebrate Christmas. While it **could** become a distraction from the real meaning of Christmas, among faithful Christian women who love their Lord and appreciate what he has done for all of us, all that busy-ness is more likely not a distraction for which they should be scolded but a wonderful tribute for which they should be commended and thanked. They are teaching their families how to appreciate and how to celebrate and how to worship their Lord by serving others. Good Christian people do a lot of work properly to celebrate this wonderful birthday. It's a reflection of all the work God did; God did a lot of work to bring Christmas about.

That sermon long ago entitled "What is Christmas all about" was based on the familiar text of the Christmas story in Luke chapter two, specifically these words:

> For unto you is born this day in the city of David a Savior, which is Christ the Lord. Luke 2.11

Those words indeed capture the real meaning of Christmas. They focus in on the central message: it was the birth of our Savior. This morning, I'd like to use the same theme, "What was Christmas all about?" but with a different perspective provided by a different Bible text, one that pulls back and provides a broad view of Christmas set in the history of world, the history of

---

[1] It is in my previous book, *With the Strength God Gives Me*, p. 23.

God's entire salvation plan, a plan that encompasses all of history but centers on Christmas.

We have in this reading before us, in this final chapter of the Bible, a prophetic summary of the whole Bible, of God's entire plan of salvation – the history of the world, from God's perspective. It covers the past, present, and future. Listen as I read this remarkable passage:

> And he showed me a pure river of water of life, clear as crystal, proceeding from the throne of God and of the Lamb. In the middle of its street, and on either side of the river, was the tree of life, which bore twelve fruits, each tree yielding its fruit every month. The leaves of the tree were for the healing of the nations. And there shall be no more curse, but the throne of God and of the Lamb shall be in it, and His servants shall serve Him. They shall see His face, and His name shall be on their foreheads. There shall be no night there: They need no lamp nor light of the sun, for the Lord God gives them light. And they shall reign forever and ever. Revelation 22.1-5

I see Christmas all over these words. Do you? May I take you through this passage image by image?

It starts with the river. *"And he showed me a pure river of water of life, clear as crystal."* Water of life is an apt phrase because water means life; without water there is no life. This river flowing out of the throne of God is first the river of creation that started in Eden where God created life and our first parents. It flows on along a street, a pathway of history, the pathway of God's salvation plan from the beginning of the world until now. This is life water, this is Salvation Water, sparkling and crystal clear. For you and me it becomes most real in the water of Baptism – there is water truly creating life because (we read) it flows *"from the throne of God **and of the Lamb.**"*

When you picture in your mind the throne of God do you see a magnificent chair elaborately decorated? I'd suggest a different picture for the throne of the Lamb from which this salvation river flows. It's far better to picture a **manger** as the throne of God, far better to picture a **cross** as the throne of God, both much more magnificent than the most elaborately decorated palace. Those are the places from which God rules and from which he serves us.

This salvation river flows along this street, that is, along the ages of history, watering the trees.

Salvation history is full of trees. At the beginning was the tree of the knowledge of good and evil that fatally tempted Adam and Eve and ruined us all. Even more important was the tree that reversed that ruin. St. Peter wrote of it: *"He himself bore our sins in his body **on the tree**, so that we might* *die to sins and live for righteousness; by his wounds you have been healed."* 1 Peter 2.24

The tree of the cross is the tree of life! It brings us the 12s: this tree that brings us life bears 12 fruits in every one of the 12 months. Throughout history God worked out his salvation plan through the12 sons of Jacob, then through the 12 tribes of Israel, then the Gospel of salvation went out to the whole world through the 12 apostles and still does today.

And the purpose, the effect of the fruit? Healing, curing the separation wound between God and us due to our sin, ***"the healing of nations."*** Can't you hear the proclamation of the Christmas angel? *"I bring you glad tidings of great joy, which shall be to* ***all people."*** Luke 2.10 That's why the prophet can say, *"There will be no more curse."* St. Paul explained it: *"Christ redeemed us from the curse of the law by becoming a* ***curse for us****, for it is written: 'Cursed is everyone who is hung on a tree.'"* Galatians 3.13

And finally the prophet looks into **his** future and sees us, God's servants, the ones chosen and sealed with Jesus' name on their foreheads, the ones who believe in him, the ones who by faith have put on the sinlessness won for them by Jesus on the cross. Several times in Revelation the prophet describes the throngs of people in Heaven. Maybe this is the most well-known; describing a great crowd in white robes, the "host arrayed in white" of which the hymn sings, we read:

> These are they which came out of great tribulation, and have washed their robes, and made them white in the blood of the Lamb. Therefore are they before the throne of God, and serve him day and night in his temple: and he that sitteth on the throne shall dwell among them. They shall hunger no more, neither thirst any more; neither shall the sun light on them, nor any heat. For the Lamb which is in the midst of the throne shall feed them, and shall lead them unto living fountains of waters: and God shall wipe away all tears from their eyes. Revelation 7.14-17

Whenever you read in Revelation about the crowd in Heaven, don't think about them as "those people." **They are us.** If we could zoom in, we would see your face there, and mine, because by God's grace we are among those who have washed our robes in Jesus' blood by faith. Here is another description like that: *"His servants shall serve Him. They shall see His face, and His name shall be on their foreheads."* What about them? Or I should say, what about **us**? We read: *"They will serve him* (isn't that happening now?), ***and they shall see his face."*** Contemplate that!

Remember that profound Old Testament story when Moses asked to see God's glory? God said I will pass by and you can see my back but my face must not be seen, for no one may see my face and live. Exodus 33.18-23 But at the first Christmas with the proclamation of "good news of great joy" when God entered the world to carry out his plan to remove the curse, the shepherds looked down into the manger and gazed upon **the face of God.** The prophet says the curse is gone; our sins are forgiven; we shall see his face.

This is a good time to appreciate all that our wives, mothers, and daughters do during this season to help us celebrate the birth of our Savior. So much more we appreciate all that God did throughout all history to come into the world at just the right time so that he could take our sins away. God arranged the history of the world **in order to bring God's love to you**.

Read this remarkable passage before us today three times. Read it once as a description of the **entire history** of the world as God carried out his plan to save us. Read it a second time as a **description of us**, now, with his name on our foreheads, sealed as his chosen and forgiven ones as we serve him even now. And then read it as our hymn leads us to picture the **place of beauty and** light that by God's grace we will all enjoy, where Jesus who reigns there will bring us to reign with him in Heaven.

That's what Christmas is all about!

†

March 16, 2018

The Bread of Life

INI

Have you ever wondered, if you had been living at the time Jesus walked this earth, and heard His teachings from his own lips, would you have been his follower? It's easy for us – most of us have been Christians from infancy, since our Baptism – to say, surely I love Jesus, certainly I would have followed him. And yet there were people in that day who heard him and chose not to be his followers. In the words before us this morning from St. John's Gospel, we find a difficult conversation Jesus had with some people around him. And after that conversation, we read that some of them decided to leave, to *"walk with Him no more."* Here in the middle of that conversation are some of the words that these people found so hard, that caused them to walk away. Jesus said,

> I am the bread of life. Your fathers ate the manna in the wilderness and are dead. This is the bread which comes down from heaven, that one may eat of it and not die. I am the living bread which came down from heaven. If anyone eats of this bread, he will live forever; and the bread that I shall give is My flesh, which I shall give for the life of the world. John 6.48-51

Since the world began bread has been considered essential for life. That truth is embodied in our very language. Bread has been called "the staff of life." A person who provides all that an entire family needs is called its "bread-winner." The region of a country that is most prosperous is called the "breadbasket of the nation." Jesus taught us to pray, give us this day our daily bread, and Luther correctly explained that to mean "all that we need for this body and life." Bread is sometimes hidden deeply in our language. The word "companion," for example, comes from two Latin words: "cum" which means "with" and "panis" which means "bread." A companion is someone with whom we share our bread. Even the English word "lord," a title we give to our Lord Jesus, comes from the old Anglo-Saxon *hlāfweard*, meaning "loaf guard" or "bread keeper." Bread is essential. It sustains life.

When Jesus announced to these people "I am the bread of life," they heard two things – two things that made some of them turn away and leave him. Today let us hear the same two things and find in them reasons to stay.

First he said, *"I am."* In those words, the people listening to him heard a claim, that this man standing in front of them was saying he is God. They heard in those words *"I am"* an echo of Old Testament history, when God spoke to Moses from the burning bush and commanded him to go to Egypt to set his people free from slavery. Moses asked, who should I say is sending me, what is your name? And God replied, *"Tell them I AM is sending you; my name is I AM."* Exodus 3.14 So when Jesus said *"I am,"* as he did frequently in his ministry, people recognized he was claiming to be God.

And then when Jesus said *"I am the bread of life that came down from Heaven,"* they also recognized that he was expecting – in fact demanding total commitment to him.

So why did people turn away?

Well, God's demands are hard. You and I both know from experience, don't we, how hard it is to give up our sin. We know how hard it is to turn away from those precious things we consider so important in this life, our pursuit of money, of fame and popularity, of fashions, of gadgets. We know how hard it is to give up finding our own way to Heaven, to stop thinking "I'm a good enough person," "I come to chapel," "I can earn God's favor," "I'll get to Heaven because of what I do." It's hard to give all that up.

When Jesus says he is the bread of life, he is saying that for real life what we need is not anything in this world nor anything in ourselves, but what we need comes down from Heaven.

Jesus said many "I am's" in His ministry – *"I am the vine,"* John 15.5 *"I am the door,"* John 10.9 *"I am the good Shepherd,"* John 10.11,14 many others. This one, *"I am the bread of life,"* is one of the hardest because it requires us to depend fully on him. "Eat this bread" means to believe, not just intellectually, not just assenting in our head that something is true, but it means to depend on him, to commit our entire lives totally to him. And that's not natural. It's not natural to depend totally on Jesus, in fact it's impossible – for us.

It becomes possible only when it's the work of the Holy Spirit. The people in this room, and everyone hearing my voice this morning, has this unsurpassed blessing: we have been called by the Holy Spirit to eat this bread of life of which Jesus speaks. The Lord has opened our hearts to hear his message in his Word, so that we know our sin, so that we come to Jesus as poor, needy, wretched sinners, throwing ourselves on his mercy, believing that he alone can save us. The Holy Spirit has taught us that Jesus is the bread of life come down from Heaven, that this bread is his flesh which he gives for the life of the world. That he did on the cross so that you and I might have the full and free forgiveness of all our sins.

The Holy Spirit has taught us that when this great I AM, our God, comes to us and says, *"I am the bread of life that has come down from Heaven,"* it is not a fearful and difficult demand, but rather it is a beautiful and gracious promise. *"Those who eat this bread will live forever."*

And so we can say, "We will stay with our Lord Jesus for life." That phrase resonates on three levels. First, "We will stay with our Lord Jesus for life" means that we will cling to Jesus alone as our only source of life. "We will stay with our Lord Jesus for life" means that this will be true for us our entire life long, beginning to end, for life. And "We will stay with our Lord Jesus for life" means that even now, each day, we live our lives in Jesus, in his peace and in his service – because Jesus is the bread of life that came down from Heaven, and that bread is his flesh which he gave for your life, for mine, and for the life of the world.

†

October 2018

What God Starts God Finishes

INI

With mid-term just past, I have an unpleasant question: how are those long-term assignments going? Some of us have a hard time starting things. We've all stared at the computer screen waiting for those first words magically to appear. Some have as hard a time finishing things. We wait till the last minute, we ask for extensions.

We can be thankful that's not the case with God.

God has this important long-term project: **you.** He has another one, me, but let's focus now on Project YOU. God has actually already started the YOU project and he pledges to finish it on time. Here's the promise:

> I thank my God upon every remembrance of you, always in every prayer of mine making request for you all with joy, for your fellowship in the gospel from the first day until now, being confident of this very thing, that He who has begun a good work in you will complete *it* until the day of Jesus Christ. Philippians 1.3-6

Some teachers, as you know, "stage" assignments. Instead of just saying turn in your finished paper on a certain date, they break down the assignment into stages: turn in your **thesis** statement in one week, the **bibliography** in three weeks, next the **outline**, then the first **draft**, and after that the **final paper.** Notice that staging projects is a lot more work for the teacher, who has to read, grade, and offer constructive comments on each stage rather than just waiting for the final paper.

God has staged the YOU Project and note: it's a lot of work for God. In fact, none of this project is what you do. It's all God. We can easily trace the stages of the YOU project through a series of Scripture passages. When did the you project start? You might say, with my Baptism? That answer makes sense, but actually it was way before that. I'm going to name the stages,

Stage 1: PREDESTINED

The YOU project was in God's mind even before he created the world. "*Those God foreknew he also predestined to be conformed to the image of his Son, that he would be the firstborn among many brothers.*" Romans 8.29

Stage 2: PROMISED

Then God made the world. When Adam and Eve messed it up quickly with sin God immediately promised a Savior. God said to the devil, "*And I will put enmity between you and the woman, and between your offspring and hers; he will crush your head, and you will strike his heel."* Genesis 3.15

Stage 3: REDEEMED/ JUSTIFIED

The Savior was sent, Jesus God's Son was born. By now I don't have to tell the story of Jesus' life in which he obeyed God perfectly in our place, then gave his life as payment for our sins. He died in our place; our sins are forgiven. That was God's first great finish: remember Jesus' last words on the cross, words of profound comfort for us, when he said, *"It is finished!"* John 19.30

So far do you see the theme? None of this YOU project is what you do. You haven't even been born yet. **It's all God.**

Up to here you've been only in the mind of God, **already redeemed.** Next you come into the world, again by God's doing.

Stage 4: MADE

"For you created my inner organs. You wove me together in my mother's womb. I praise you because I am fearfully and wonderfully made." Psalm 139.13-16

Before long came

Stage 5: CALLED or FOUND or WASHED

We became children of God by Baptism. *"He saved us – not by righteous works that we did ourselves, but because of his mercy. He saved us through the washing of rebirth (Baptism) and renewal by the Holy Spirit..."* Titus 3:5

And now we have come to where we are living now.

Stage 6: I call EMPOWERED

Here is where we struggle, where through difficulties and challenges we learn to trust God. Here is where we fight sin by remembering our Baptism, and by turning to his Word. Here is where we repent when we fall. Here is where we pray. Here is where we serve others. Here is where we trust. Here is where St. Paul urges us to *"...be strong in the Lord and in his mighty power. Put on the full armor of God, so that you can stand against the schemes of the Devil. ... Stand, then, with the belt of truth buckled around your waist, with the breastplate of righteousness fastened in place, and with the readiness that comes from the gospel of peace tied to your feet like sandals. At all times hold up the shield of faith, with which you will be able to extinguish all the flaming arrows of the Evil One. Also take the helmet of salvation and the sword of the Spirit, which is the word of God."* Ephesians 6.10ff

Now wait a minute, does this stage break the pattern? Is this at last what **we** do, and not all God? Not really. As Paul writes, this is standing firm **in the**

Lord and in the power of **his might**. These are the weapons **he provides us.** *"In fact, it is God who is working in you, both to will and to work, for the sake of his good pleasure."* Philippians 2.13

You know what we can do? Mess it up. After all that God has done, working for us from eternity, we can still throw it all away. Sadly, people do that. That's what makes Jesus weep, as he did over Jerusalem. Luke 13.34 The apostle warns us, *"Do not grieve the Holy Spirit of God, with whom you were sealed for the day of redemption."* Ephesians 4.30

No, instead we pray with the hymnwriter, "Lord keep us steadfast in thy Word," and find comfort in Jesus' own description of us: *"My sheep hear my voice; I know them, and they follow me. I give them eternal life, and they will never perish; no one will snatch them out of my hand. My Father, who has given them to me, is greater than all; no one can snatch them out of my Father's hand."* John 10.27-29

Finally after all the stages in God's YOU Project – predestined, promised, redeemed, made, found, empowered – we come to the final stage: **GLORIFIED.** *"Be faithful unto death, and I will give you the crown of life."* Revelation 2.10

It's all summarized by the Apostle: *"Those God foreknew, he also predestined to be conformed to the image of his Son, so that he would be the firstborn among many brothers. And those he predestined, he also called. Those he called, he also justified: and those he justified, he also glorified."* Romans 8. 29-30

That will be for each of us the Day of Christ, when our redemption is complete, and we are delivered from all effects of sin. When you finally hand in the final draft of your project paper that you have worked on and polished, you've made it your best work. God is good at finishing things; when he finishes his project in each of us he will make us his best work and that will be very good indeed. Love him. Trust him. Thank him.

What God starts God finishes. Thanks be to God!

†

The preceding sermon was presented in Trinity Chapel at Bethany. When I adapted it for use at Resurrection Lutheran Church in Winter Haven during our annual Christmastime visit to Florida, I added the following ending:

That's a promise of God. How sure is it? I'll add one more stage:

Stage 7: CERTIFIED IN CONCRETE

Do you remember Moses' farewell? Just before he died, he assured God's people: "*Be strong and of good courage, do not fear nor be afraid of them; for the LORD your God, He is the One who goes with you. He will not leave you nor forsake you.*" Deuteronomy 31.6 Those very words of promise were echoed by the writer of Hebrews: "*God has said, "Never will I leave you; never will I forsake you.*" Hebrews 13:5

Now let me teach you a little Greek, the original language in which this was written. In Greek there are three words that express the negative, three words for "not." In that passage from Hebrews, "*Never will I leave you; never will I forsake you,*" in the first half, "not" appears twice, in the last half, "not" appears three times. God wants to emphasize his promise so much, the translation should read: "*Not Not will I leave you, Not Not Not will I forsake you!*"

In a moment we'll sing a hymn that captures so well all the stages of God's YOU project. Especially the final stanza captures the firmness of the promise revealed in the Greek words I just spoke of, that wonderful two, and then three-fold **not**. Let me close by reading the last two stanzas of "How Firm a Foundation, Ye Saints of the Lord."

> E'en down to old age all my people shall prove
> My sovereign, eternal, unchangeable love;
> And when hoary hairs shall their temples adorn,
> Like lambs they shall still in My bosom be borne.

> The soul that on Jesus hath leaned for repose
> **I will not, I will not** desert to his foes;
> That soul, though all hell should endeavor to shake,
> **I'll never, no never, no never** forsake!"

God is good at finishing things. Love him. Trust him. Thank him. What God starts God finishes. Thanks be to God!

†

September 12, 2018

God For Us Right Now

INI

Are you a **far-off future Christian** or also a **now Christian**? Are you a Christian just for being in Heaven some day or also for being at Bethany Lutheran College today? Some people think Christianity is only for later and yes, I hope for Heaven after I die – what a wonderful promise! – but what about now? The apostle answers that in today's reading.

> Who shall separate us from the love of Christ? Shall tribulation, or distress, or persecution, or famine, or nakedness, or peril, or sword? As it is written: "For Your sake we are killed all day long; we are accounted as sheep for the slaughter." Yet in all these things we are more than conquerors through Him who loved us. For I am persuaded that neither death nor life, nor angels nor principalities nor powers, nor things present nor things to come, nor height nor depth, nor any other created thing, shall be able to separate us from the love of God which is in Christ Jesus our Lord. Romans 8.35-39

By now you've been in classes for a couple weeks. You know what's expected of you. At first, remember, it might have seemed overwhelming. You got the syllabus, the assignments, the test schedule, the readings laid out, the term papers. It didn't look easy, did it? It shouldn't. If it's too easy, you're not learning what you should. God says in this reading, that's something we should know about our Christian lives – our lives, right now.

Did you hear, in the reading, that for a Christian everything in life would be wonderful? Smooth sailing? All happiness? Not at all. Paul writes about "*tribulation, or distress, or persecution, or famine, or nakedness, or peril, or sword?*" Paul experienced all of these things and he even quotes a psalm from the Old Testament to show it's always been that way. Psalm 44.22 Thank you, God, that these extreme hardships are not coming our way right now. But they could. St. Paul faced them all. Many Christians of his day – many Christians today elsewhere in the world are now facing them all.

But even for us, life is life and we feel pressure, anxiety, disappointment. We can be picked on, ridiculed, bullied. We face dangers, sickness, we feel depression, sometimes not knowing where to turn. Heaven will be the end of it but that's someday. What about now? God tells us here, life may not be easy but it will be good because we have the love of Christ.

Consider every challenge that life can bring. Paul lists here every category of being, highs and lows, the things that happen we have no control over, evil forces that war against soul, **our own sin.** Let's not diminish the power of these foes. They are serious, distressing; bad things happen, and when they do, we may feel angry, afraid, uncertain. There are days, and there are going to be days, when life is not much fun – when **Christian** life is not much fun.

But never hopeless because we're never alone, because in all these things we have the love of God in Jesus. That includes the **forgiveness** of God in Jesus on the cross, the **help** of God in Jesus who lives and walks beside us, who knows what it's like because it all happened to him.

When a friend betrays you, you will be hurt and bewildered – but you have the love of God in Jesus who knew betrayal, who knows exactly how you feel and teaches how to forgive.

When you didn't make the team, or the cast, or choir you will be deeply disappointed – but you have the love of God in Jesus who guides you into how to use your time to serve him.

When that very special relationship ends you will be heartbroken – but you have the love of God in Jesus who knows what special friend you need and can guide you together.

When that sin comes back to snatch you and you even fall again and are disgusted with yourself – you have the love of God in Jesus who came into this world so God could forgive you and who sends you his Spirit to remind you of your Baptism and to make you stronger next time.

And when a dear one dies you will be crushed. You will cry, as Jesus himself did at the tomb of his friend Lazarus. John 11.35 And then in his love for you he went on to his own death on the cross. **There in that awful scene we see the love of God for us most fully.** There he paid the penalty of sin we owed and brought us fully the love of God when he rose again to assure us of a grand and glorious reunion with our loved ones in Heaven.

That's why Paul can say, in **all these things** we are more than conquerors, super victors because Jesus the Victor is with us in every situation.

Let's not forget the times when you aced the test, when your team won, when you enjoy good friends, when you fall in love and are loved back, when you go home for Thanksgiving and everyone is there in good health. These many happy times are gifts of love from God. We give thanks when our Christian lives are pleasant – we have the love of God in Christ! Let's give thanks too when our Christian lives are troubled – we have the love of God in Christ!

If it's too easy, you're not learning what you should. What God wants us to learn is this: *Nothing can separate us from the love of God which is in Christ Jesus our Lord.*

†

December 2019

God Living With Us

INI

You've all seen the look, I know, at one time or another. You approach someone, or maybe a couple of people talking and you get the look that says, stay away, you're not welcome here, you don't fit with us, you're interrupting. Don't come closer, go away! You know the look? Today I'll urge you not to **give** that look to anyone. Especially not to Jesus.

Our assigned subject is the Old Testament book of Zachariah. It's a book of strange images. Look, down in the ravine, a man on a horse – a red horse – behind him red, brown, white horses. What could it mean? Over there, a man with a measuring tape – he's measuring the length and width of the whole city. What could that mean? And up there – a scroll, unrolling till it's 30 feet long, and then it starts flying through the air. What could that mean?

The prophet Zechariah asked an angel, what do these things mean? The angel answered him. Read about these visions in the first few short chapters of the book. Our focus this morning is on one of those meanings which captures the prophet's main message:

> "Shout and be glad, O Daughter of Zion. For I am coming, and I will live among you," declares the LORD. "Many nations will be joined with the LORD in that day and will become my people. I will live among you and you will know that the LORD Almighty has sent me to you. The LORD will inherit Judah as his portion in the holy land and will again choose Jerusalem. Be still before the LORD, all mankind, because he has roused himself from his holy dwelling." Zechariah 2.10-13

When Zechariah wrote, God's people were starting to return from captivity in Babylon, starting to rebuild cities, especially Jerusalem. Circumstances were harsh. Work was hard. Neighbors were hostile. It was very discouraging. Zechariah's message was this: Don't quit, the Lord is with you. The Lord has "*roused himself*" and his commitment is long term. He pledges he is going to live with his people and his people will include all nations. That was Zechariah's encouragement to the people undertaking the hard work of starting to rebuild their land. What's his message for us?

Most of you here are near the beginning of a building project. You are starting to build your lives, deciding and discovering who you will be, what you will do, with whom you will do it. That work isn't easy. The decisions are tough. The world around is hostile. It's a test of character. Let me pull from these verses those same two encouragements Zechariah gave to his people and that are very important to us. The Lord's people will come from all nations, and the Lord will live with us his people.

First, all nations. That's the story of Epiphany when the Lord "*roused himself*" (as Zechariah put it), entered history at the right time. Wise men, non-Jews, came from afar to worship him. We non-Jews take full comfort in that, assured that we are among God's people – as in the hymn, we are among the many who "come from the East and the West to sit at the feast of salvation."

Second, the Lord will live with us. Not visit then go. Not look in from time to time. He is here, with you and me, long term, daily, hourly. Do we take full comfort in that? The Lord God is living with us!

We don't realize it fully if we think of God only in emergencies, if we think of God only when we feel religious, if we think of God only when we say a quick and thoughtless come Lord Jesus at a meal, or if we don't even do those things. Let Zechariah's reminder that our Lord lives with us encourage us to explore more ways of enjoying that wonderful fact. We don't have to display it openly, make a show of it, go around parading our faith – that's not the idea. Just find more ways to keep the Lord's presence close to our minds.

First never put yourself in a situation where you are giving our Lord Jesus that **look** which says, don't come closer, you don't fit in this part of my life, stay away. Set an alarm to go off when that temptation comes.

Then be in constant communication with our Lord who lives with us. Follow Luther's advice. Start your day, first thing in morning, with a prayer. End your day, last thing in evening, with a prayer. Have a prayer in your mind, even on your lips, for everything all day – of thanks when good things happen, for help when we struggle, of care for the friend and for the stranger. Listen to the Lord who speaks to us. Be serious about his Word in church and chapel, as well as in class. Appreciate and seek out the Lord in the sacramental meal where he comes to us with his real body and blood and brings us the forgiveness he won for us on the cross. Remember your Baptism every day, recall how that washing has cleansed us from our sins and joined us to Christ in his death for us, so our death is over, and joined us to Christ in his resurrection, destined for Heaven. Study to live your life more and more as if already in Heaven, the Heaven of which we will sing in a moment.

Zechariah wrote, "'*Shout and be glad, O Daughter of Zion. For I am coming, and I will live among you,*' declares the LORD." As you continue planning and building your life join your heart with Zechariah: Shout and be glad, for the Lord has come and is living with us. Learn how to enjoy that to the fullest.

†

December 29, 2019
Presented first in Trinity Chapel on October 30, the day before the B. W. Teigen Reformation Lectures, then revised for Resurrection Lutheran Church, Winter Haven FL.

Jesus, Always the Same

INI

On this Sunday exactly between our religious celebration of Christmas which reminds us how God entered time, and our secular celebration of New Year which reminds us how quickly time passes, it's good to turn our attention to a crucial fact about time and our Savior. We read:

> Jesus Christ is the same yesterday, today, and forever. Do not be carried about with various and strange doctrines. Hebrews 13.8

I'm going to begin this morning using the words of a great Lutheran missionary, a missionary to – Indiana! 190 years ago (1830s) a great missionary from Germany named Frederich Wyneken travelled by horseback all over Indiana, then mostly Indian country, seeking German immigrants to gather into congregations. Some years later, on New Years Day in 1868, he preached a sermon looking ahead to the new year. His opening questions spoken 151 years ago are exactly the questions in our minds today as we too look ahead to start a new year. So let me begin the sermon by using his words:

> Here we stand once again at the threshold of a new year. It is natural for us to wonder, what will it bring? None of us can answer the question. Only God knows the answer. We might ask, how will it go with your finances and investments? We must answer, God knows. We ask, what good fortune or bad fortune will come upon you? Again, the answer is, God knows. We ask, will you live through this year or die this year? And again, only God knows. So we are in the dark about all this, you say, in darkness and uncertainty, and this bothers me![1]

Those are Missionary Wyneken's questions to his pioneer listeners, questions that haunt us as well. We wonder, what is going to change for me, or for you in this New Year? When you are young change is good; when you get old, not so much. When you were a child, you would meet someone who hadn't seen you in a long time and they would say, "My how you've grown," and that would be good. When you are old and you meet someone who hadn't seen you in a long time, they would say, "You haven't changed a bit," and **that** would be good, but not true.

---

[1] In Harrison, Matthew C. *At Home in the House of My Fathers: Presidential Sermons, Essays, Letters, and Addresses from the Missouri Synod's Great Era of Unity and Growth.* Concordia Publishing House, 2011, pp. 432-3.

When you meet Jesus you can say, "You haven't changed a bit," and that would be good, **and** true. It's in our Scripture reading: *"Jesus Christ is the same yesterday, today, and forever."* Then (you might think, oddly) in the very next verse: *"Do not be carried about with various and strange doctrines."* I say "oddly" because it's easy to wonder: why are these two thoughts next to each other in God's Word? "Jesus never changes" and then "Don't get carried away by false teaching"?

Here is my point for you this morning: **This combination is for us the greatest comfort.**

Note first how true the first half is: Jesus never changes; he is *"the same yesterday, today, and forever."* I'll prove that by citing what first seems a contradiction, the greatest **change** Jesus ever made: **Christmas! His incarnation.** That is, Jesus, never created, always existing God from all eternity – it is impossible for us to comprehend, existing from all eternity, but just as difficult to comprehend is this fact, that this eternally existing Son of God, the second person in the Trinity, "God of God, Light of Light, Very God of Very God,"[1] in what I've called a great change from our human perspective, at a point in history **he became human!** God put on human flesh, was "incarnate," was born, became a man. We celebrated that again just last Wednesday. From our human perspective that seemed a great change.

But does it contradict the passage before us? Not at all. Because in his eternal essence, this was not a change. It was who he is. He did this, entered our world, our flesh, became our human brother to **save us from our sins**. He did it because he was, is, and always will be **our Savior.**

No mere human could live life the way God intended, holy and without sin – certainly you or I don't. The God-Man Savior Jesus did that for us. No mere human's life was so valuable that it could be laid down to suffer the penalty for the entire world's sin. The God-Man Savior Jesus' life was that valuable and he laid it down on the cross to suffer the penalty for your sin, my sin, the sins of all the world. Because of what Jesus did, our sins are forgiven.

Jesus **before the world began** was our Savior. In **his life on this earth** and in his **death on the cross** he was our Savior. Today **coming to us in his Word** he is our Savior. When our **life comes to an end** and on **into eternity** he will be our Savior. *"Jesus Christ is the same yesterday, today, and forever."*

Now what about that next verse? *"Do not be carried about with various and strange doctrines."*

---

[1] Words from the Nicene Creed.

Well, you and I belong to a very special club. Through our faith in this Savior we are members of the Holy Christian Church, that entire assembly of believers now and of all time. When we join a club, we care about its welfare. We want it to succeed and prosper and we'll join in the work to help it do so. What keeps this club, the holy Christian Church, prospering is continuing in the pure and powerful words of Scripture, continuing in the teachings, the doctrines that contain the Gospel, the good news that Jesus was, is, always will be our Savior. So the Bible writer says, Don't get distracted, don't be led astray. *"Do not be carried about with various and strange doctrines."*

Many years ago Martin Luther found himself in a church that had been led astray by various strange doctrines made up by humans and that contradicted God's Word. Luther was convinced that the Devil was especially active in his day, raising up all the heretics, fanatics, threats – Luther knew that against them God alone could be the defense, as he wrote in his most famous hymn, "But for us fights the valiant one whom God himself elected." Luther cited this very passage before us when he wrote:

> God help us as he has helped our ancestors and will also help our descendants to the praise and honor of his divine name throughout eternity. For we are, after all, not the sort of people who could sustain the church. Nor were our forefathers, nor will our descendants be such. But the Lord has done it, is doing it now, and will do it. Jesus Christ is the same, yesterday, today, and forever. He was, he is, he will be.[1]

That Savior God who sustained Luther and the Reformers in those perilous times is the same Savior God who is sustaining his church today. **And we can say the same for each of us.** Missionary Wyneken's questions are still good ones: only God knows what awaits us in this new year. Be we can enter it with utmost trust in our Savior. The Savior who **knew your name** in eternity before the world was created, the Savior who **paid for your sins** on the cross, the Savior who **washed those sins away** in your Baptism, the Savior who **assures you here and now** that your sins are forgiven, the Savior who **strengthens you** to serve him and those around you, the Savior who pledges *"I will never leave you or forsake you,"* Hebrews 13.5 the Savior who began this good work in you **will continue it** throughout your life, and into eternity.

Thanks be to this Savior, Jesus Christ, who is the same yesterday, today, and always. Don't get distracted from him.

†

---

[1] *What Luther Said*, 833.

The Evening Bells Devotions

Bethany Lutheran College's newly constructed video production studio, dedicated in 1999, had gotten on its feet by the end of the current century's first decade. Its major goal, providing students with a quality education, was being achieved, its graduates finding employment in a wide range of relevant professions.

As with its every program, this Lutheran Christian college aimed also to instill in students a sense of their Christian calling, encouraging them to consider how they could use their profession to serve their Lord, particularly in carrying out his Great Commission to bring the Gospel to the world. This same impulse led to the founding of the *Christ in Media Institute* in 2009.

An earlier fruit of this impulse emerged late in the 2000's decade with the production of the "Evening Bells at Bethany" video devotions. For much of its history, Bethany Lutheran College had held chapel services twice each weekday, morning and evening. However, evening chapel attendance had dwindled, largely due to the press of student activities, so evening chapels had been cut to one per week each Wednesday.

Campus residence hall rooms were being wired for cable television in those days, and the Communication Department saw an opportunity: let's revive evening chapel for the remaining four week-evenings in the form of short 5-minute video devotions broadcast over the campus cable system. With the permission of the Madson family, we named the devotions *"Evening Bells"* after the well-known collection of printed evening chapel devotions from years before by Dean Norman Madson, Sr.

The video version of *Evening Bells at Bethany* ran for three years, with some excellent devotions by a variety of college professors and seminary students. The following pages contain a sample of the devotions I taped.

September 2008

Baptism 1

Do you remember some of the great gifts you have received? Maybe a camera, or a doll, or that bicycle, or more lately a car? If you've ever received a really outstanding gift, it's fun to remember it, along with the feeling you had when you first learned of it.

Martin Luther tells us we should remember every day one of the most beautiful gifts the Lord has given us – Baptism. We'll do that tonight on the basis of the words the apostle Peter spoke to the crowd at Pentecost. He had preached a pretty tough sermon to them, and they were moved to ask, what should we do. And we read there:

> Peter replied, "Repent and be baptized, every one of you, in the name of Jesus Christ for the forgiveness of your sins. And you will receive the gift of the Holy Spirit. The promise is for you and your children and for all who are far off – for all whom the Lord our God will call." Acts 2. 38f.

If you who are watching this have never been baptized, this is a direct invitation to you: repent and be baptized. But I think most of us have been baptized, probably when we were babies. And for us, this is an invitation to remember our Baptism, as Luther urges we should do every day. Every day, remember your baptism! In each of the four Evening Bells devotions this week, we will remember our Baptism. The Bible pictures Baptism for us in a number of different ways, and each night we will look at one of those Bible pictures of Baptism, so we can appreciate our own Baptism again in a special way.

The picture of Baptism we will consider tonight is the image of washing, and it is well captured in another passage in the book of Acts where St Paul is recalling his dramatic conversion on the road to Damascus, and how God then sent Ananias to explain to Paul his new God-given role as an apostle and witness to Jesus Christ. Ananias concluded by saying, *"And now what are you waiting for? Get up, be baptized and wash your sins away, calling on his name."* Acts 22.16

Paul, who was then known as Saul, was indeed full of sins. He had made war against Christian believers, and against Jesus himself. When Jesus met him in that blinding light on the roadway to Damascus, his words were *"Saul, why are you persecuting ME?"* Acts 22.7 Yet such awful sin, Ananias promised, would be washed away in Baptism. God gives those who are baptized the gift of being washed clean from sin. That gift became possible, of course, when Jesus lived a clean and sinless life in our place, and in Baptism God transfers Jesus' holiness to us. And how good it feels to be clean! Clean from all sins!

Every one of them washed away. This is a gift God gives to all believers in Jesus, and Baptism is the ceremony by which we officially enter the holy Christian Church, the assembly of all believers. That's why this same apostle Paul could write later, *"Christ loved the Church and gave himself up for her to make her holy, cleansing her by the washing with water through the word."* Ephesians 5.25-26 Since Jesus Christ gave himself up for you and me, we have been washed clean of all our sins. That happened when we were baptized, and it happens again every day when we remember our Baptism. That's Baptism picture number one: **washing away sins.** Tomorrow we'll talk about being born a second time. Meanwhile, go to sleep tonight feeling clean! You were baptized. Your sins are all washed away for Jesus sake.

†

September 2008

Baptism 2

On Evening Bells this week we are inviting you to celebrate your Baptism. If you have studied Lutheran teachings, you know that we call Baptism a "means of grace" – that is, it is one of the means, or vehicles, by which God brings to us his grace, love, and forgiveness. The Word of the Gospel is the primary means of grace, but Baptism and the Lord's supper are also vehicles by which God brings us forgiveness of sins. Unlike the words of the Gospel, which we only hear or read, Baptism and the Lord's Supper are what we call visible means, that is, they contain elements we can see.

Baptism visibly shows us, as with a picture, the gift of forgiveness we have by faith. The Bible gives us a number of pictures to associate with Baptism. Last night we looked at one of them – Baptism as a washing away of sin. Tonight we look at a second – Baptism as birth, as new birth, as being born a second time. This is the picture given us by Titus where we read:

> But when the kindness and love of God our Savior appeared, he saved us, not because of righteous things we had done, but because of his mercy. He saved us through the washing of rebirth and renewal by the Holy Spirit, whom he poured out on us generously through Jesus Christ our Savior, so that, having been justified by his grace, we might become heirs having the hope of eternal life. Titus 3.4-7

Note that phrase, washing of rebirth. And note what rebirth means – a new life, renewal – a life with the Holy Spirit (whom we didn't have before) who we are told is poured out on us **generously**. This is rebirth into an additional family, not just children of our parents, but children of God, and God's heirs.

And what is it we inherit in this new additional family into which we are re-born in Baptism? Eternal life – which starts now as a life of hope and culminates in an endless life of joy in Heaven.

This is the new life poured out on you and me through our rebirth in Baptism. It's the best encouragement possible for us to try to live our new lives in ways that are worthy of what God has made us through the forgiveness of sins won for us by Jesus Christ.

Last night we viewed Baptism as washing away sins, tonight as a new birth into God's family and heirs of Heaven. Remember your Baptism every day.

†

September 2008

Baptism 3

This week on Evening Bells we are celebrating our baptisms by looking at the various pictures Scripture gives us to help us understand this wonderful gift from God. First we considered Baptism as washing sins away. Next we viewed it as a rebirth into God's own family making us heirs of Heaven. To-night we picture Baptism from what at first seems a somber note, but don't worry – it gets much better. This time picture a grave, and picture yourself going down into that grave, dead. That's grim, right? But wait. We don't do it alone, we do it with someone – someone who has the power to raise himself out of the grave, and to bring us with him. Listen to St. Paul describe this:

> Don't you know that all of us who were baptized into Christ Jesus were baptized into his death? We were therefore buried with him through Baptism into death in order that, just as Christ was raised from the dead through the glory of the Father, we too may live a new life. If we have been united with him like this in his death, we will certainly also be united with him in his resurrection. Romans 6.3f.

This, to me, is the most stunning picture of Baptism of all. If you have been baptized, **you have died**. In some forms of Baptism, people actually go under the water, all the way, just like going underground into the grave. We don't need to do it that way – the symbolism is the same; when we sprinkle water we symbolically go under the water. Either way, it signifies death. But then, we come out from under the water again. As Christ rose himself from the grave after dying to pay for our sins, he brings us with him in his resurrec-tion. So there is no need for us to fear death. For us, death is over already, with Christ. If we have been baptized, death is not something we need to look ahead to with dread. It's over. We've died already in our Baptism, with Christ, and he has brought us back from the grave to a new and beautiful life, one we can enjoy now and which will continue for all eternity. That's the third picture of Baptism from the Bible: **buried and raised again with Jesus**. Through Baptism, his victory over death is ours too. Remember your Baptism every day.

†

September 2008

Baptism 4

Tonight ends the week in which we have been inviting you to celebrate your Baptism by looking each night at one of the different pictures of Baptism Scripture provides us. We first saw Baptism as washing away sins, then as a new birth into God's family, and next as dying and being buried with Jesus, and then rising again with his resurrection to eternal life. Dramatic, inspiring pictures, that help us understand and deeply appreciate this wonderful gift of Baptism. Tonight's fourth and final picture sums up the comfort of it all. Let's entitle it "In Jesus' arms." This picture comes from St. Mark's Gospel and, while this passage doesn't mention Baptism, it is often read in our Baptism ceremonies when we baptize children and babies. We read:

> People were bringing little children to Jesus to have him touch them, but the disciples rebuked them. When Jesus saw this, he was indignant. He said to them, "Let the little children come to me, and do not hinder them, for the kingdom of God belongs to such as these. I tell you the truth, anyone who will not receive the kingdom of God like a little child will never enter it." And he took the children in his arms, put his hands on them and blessed them. Mark 10.13-16

This is one of my favorite pictures at a Baptism. Along with the others we described earlier this week, this one always comes to mind when I've conducted a Baptism, and even whenever I witness one. This image especially occurs to me just after I say, "I baptize you in the name of the Father, Son and Holy Spirit." And then I picture… before the baby is returned by the sponsors to the mother, I picture Jesus, for just a moment, takes this baby in **his** arms, puts his hands on the child, and blesses. From then on, moms and dads, that baby is his as well as yours. He loves it, cares for it, watches over it. That baby is precious to him. And as the baby gets older, as you and I are, his care and love continues. As we go through life, Jesus continues walking beside us with his arm around our shoulder. We are still in Jesus' arms.

I love these pictures, don't you? and I love baptisms because they bring all those pictures to mind. Jesus washing our sins away, making us clean – Jesus giving us new birth into his family, as heirs of eternal life – Jesus taking us with him into the grave, with him so we need not fear, with him so we know we will be also a part of his resurrection – and finally, Jesus with us as babies in his arms, with us as older people with his loving caring arm around us all our days to the end of our time on earth, and beyond.

Baptism. What a wonderful gift! Remember your Baptism every day.

†

September 2008

Fortress

All of us have had a chance to show courage already in our lives. Maybe the first time was when you closed your eyes to take that vaccination in the arm when you were 2 or 3 – that took courage, but it was bolstered by the assurance of your parent that it would be OK. Judy, my wife, once confessed that she cried when our kids got shots; of course they didn't see that. But we've all shown courage, perhaps the courage to face a test or even to attend college, maybe to deal with a disability or a health threat.

Many people think that we look inside ourselves for courage. There's a sense in which that's true. But the more important source is outside. To a child it's the assurance of a parent. To us as we grow up we learn it's not **from** parents but **through** them. We learned where our parents got their courage. It was from God who promised to be an ever-present help in trouble. That promise was proved to be reliable when God provided us rescue from the worst possible trouble – the consequences of our own sin and wrongdoing. The work of Jesus Christ demonstrated in the most profound way that in all of our cares we need never let fear overcome us. Jesus showed us that God is our refuge and strength and a reliable and firm source of courage. That's our assurance through the death and resurrection of Jesus Christ.

I suspect that, like a mother, God too cried as his Son died to rescue us and provide us with a reason to trust God, to have courage.

We don't know the future. We don't know when or how you will next be called upon to show courage or even whether that show of courage will be the great moment that defines your entire life. It might be a time when you must stand up for what you believe. It might be at time when you face a tragedy. It might be at a time when you put yourself on the line for someone else, or for your country.

At a time like that, call to mind today's reading as Martin Luther did, Psalm 46, the psalm that inspired him to write what might be the most famous hymn of all time, *A Mighty Fortress is Our God*. Hear these words about the source of real courage.

> God is our refuge and strength, an ever-present help in trouble. Therefore we will not fear, though the earth give way and the mountains fall into the heart of the sea, though its waters roar and foam and the mountains quake with their surging.

> There is a river whose streams make glad the city of God, the holy place where the Most High dwells. God is within her, she will not fall; God will help her at break of day. Nations are in uproar, kingdoms fall; he lifts his voice, the earth melts.

> The LORD Almighty is with us; the God of Jacob is our fortress.

> Come and see the works of the LORD, the desolations he has brought on the earth. He makes wars cease to the ends of the earth; he breaks the bow and shatters the spear, he burns the shields with fire. "Be still and know that I am God; I will be exalted among the nations, I will be exalted in the earth."

> The LORD Almighty is with us; the God of Jacob is our fortress. Psalm 46

†

September 2008

You Know Someone

Time magazine last fall surveyed some of the top ski areas in the country. Along with the basic information – difficulty of slopes, quality of lodges – they furnished hints on possible celebrity sightings. At Vail you might see Brad Pitt, at Aspen Tom Cruise sometimes shows up. Celebrity sighting is a real attraction. If you've ever caught a glimpse of an actual celebrity, or a sports star, or a very important person like the President, you know what a thrill that can be, and if you're like me, you'll never stop boring your friends as you retell the story of it.

More exciting than sighting someone important is actually to **know** someone important. And that can get us things. Want tickets to the big Packer game weekend after next? Hey I know Aaron Rodgers, their new quarterback, I can get us tickets. And you are impressed. I don't really know Aaron Rodgers, unfortunately. But I have an uncle whose brother-in-law once sat next to Aaron's cousin on a bus. For some of us, that's enough to prompt Oh, Wow! That didn't really happen either, but you get the point. Now get the point of this Bible portion before us this evening – be really impressed.

You know God.

You have a connection through God's own Son, Jesus Christ. And as a result, you and I have a very special ticket – one that gives us access to inner peace and joy, a purposeful life, and Heaven itself.

In Old Testament times, the closest person to God in the community was the High Priest. He was the only one authorized to go into the holiest place in the temple and bring the sacrifice of blood that foreshadowed payment for sin. In this passage, Jesus is identified as the great High Priest, who approaches God on our behalf, and brings the ultimate sacrifice for our sin, the most valuable life ever, his own life, the life of God's own Son, which he willingly gave up on the cross to pay the penalty for our sin.

What makes that life so precious is not only that it is God's own life, but that it was lived perfectly, without sin, in complete conformity with God's Law and will. It is the only life ever so lived. That sinless life is now credited to us, so that we can approach God as if holy and sinless. We can without hesitation bring our needs confidently before the throne of grace, certain that God sees us not as sinners but as pure, clean and righteous, as his own Son.

Jesus is the most important person there is to know, and you and I know him. He is the essential connection between humanity and God, and you and I know him. As he turns toward God, he is God's beloved Son, in whom God is well pleased. As he turns toward us, he knows us, he understands, he's been where we are, he knows what we face.

Can you feel the thrill of knowing someone of this importance? Can you appreciate the benefits that knowing him brings us? Can you talk with your friends about this special connection? We know Jesus. Through him we have a connection with God, which invites us to approach God's throne with confidence, so that we may receive mercy and find grace to help us in our time of need. Listen to God's Word:

> Therefore, since we have a great high priest who has gone through the heavens, Jesus the Son of God, let us hold firmly to the faith we profess. For we do not have a high priest who is unable to sympathize with our weaknesses, but we have one who has been tempted in every way, just as we are — yet was without sin. Let us then approach the throne of grace with confidence, so that we may receive mercy and find grace to help us in our time of need. Hebrews 4.14-16

†

November 2008

Thank and Ask

Yes, it's important this Thanksgiving Day to say thank you to God for all the blessings he showers upon us. You will have special moments again this holiday to count your blessings. Perhaps you will do it at church, and then again at home or wherever it is you enjoy your Thanksgiving meal.

But of course we know that giving thanks should not be confined only to Thanksgiving day. We should say thank you to God often, certainly every day, and even more than that, we should **be thankful** always. How can we be assured that we do that? Here is an interesting word from the apostle Paul.

> Do not be anxious about anything, but in everything, by prayer and petition, with thanksgiving, present your requests to God. Philippians 4.6

Notice please the close mixture here of asking and thanking: "*In everything, by prayer and petition, with thanksgiving, present your requests to God.*" It's almost as if they are the same thing; as you are saying thank you to God, you are ready to ask, and by bringing a request we are saying thank you.

There is in fact no better way to show our thanks to God for his blessings than to request more blessings, especially the blessing of faith and trust in him. We show our thanks to God by trusting him more and more to care for us, to continue providing for our needs. And we show him special thanks when we trust him fully for the forgiveness of sins we have through the work of Jesus Christ.

It's a part of our thanksgiving to God that we not worry, but rather trust.

"*Do not be anxious about anything,*" the apostle urges us, "*but in everything, by prayer and petition, with thanksgiving, present your requests to God.*" Then trust his promise, as expressed in the hymn:

> Fear not, I am with you. Oh, be not dismayed
> For I am your God and will still give you aid.
> I'll strengthen you, help you, and cause you to stand
> Upheld by My righteous, omnipotent hand.

†

August 2009

Our Speech of Confidence

Do you think you ever suffer from a lack of confidence? When I teach speech classes, I often find students who at first have no confidence in their ability to give a speech. Maybe it's especially scary when the speech is on an important topic that you dare not get wrong, and when the speech is to an important audience that you dare not offend. Tonight I'd like to bring to you a very short speech that is brimming with confidence – and the best thing about it is that even though the speech is on a **very** important topic, before the most important audience there is, this can be – no I'll put it stronger - this **is your** speech.

These speech, only a few sentences long, was written by one of our most admired church leaders of a century ago, Dr. C. F. W. Walther. He wrote them in response to this Bible passage that is central to all Christianity recording the death of our Savior, Jesus Christ.

> When he had received the drink, Jesus said, "It is finished." With that, he bowed his head and gave up his spirit. John 19.30

It is finished, Jesus said. The work of redemption was finished. What Jesus had accomplished in his life and death had fully and completely, once and for all, forever paid in full all that we owed God because of our sins. Jesus had done it all – there was no uncertainty, nothing left for us to do. Just believe that, and we have the full benefit of it. Here is where Dr. Walther's short speech comes in – and remember, this is our speech too. Listen to what he says and take it to your heart. He says:

> Cling to that word by faith. If I do that, I can confidently meet God on the Last Day; and if He were preparing to condemn me, I could say to Him: "You can not condemn me without making yourself a liar. You have invited me to place my entire confidence in your Word. I have done that, and therefore I cannot be condemned, and I know you will not do it .... it is impossible that we should be sent to perdition. Here is Christ. You will have to acknowledge, O God, the ransom which your Son has given as **payment in full** for our sin and guilt." [1]

These are Dr. Walther's words, brimming with the confidence that God himself invites **us** to feel, confidence in God who through his Son Jesus has finished all that's necessary for our salvation. Enjoy this confidence in your own life and take it to a restful sleep tonight.

†

---

[1] *The Proper Distinction between Law and Gospel*, St. Louis: Concordia Publishing House, 1928, p. 347.

August 2009

The Holy Spirit Loves Me

From time to time speakers on *Evening Bells* encourage you not to forget your prayers. Do you need help with that? We get help with prayer. We get overwhelming help with prayer. Listen to the apostle Paul.

> ... the Spirit helps us in our weakness. We do not know what we ought to pray for, but the Spirit himself intercedes for us with groans that words cannot express. And he who searches our hearts knows the mind of the Spirit, because the Spirit intercedes for the saints in accordance with God's will. And we know that in all things God works for the good of those who love him, who have been called according to his purpose. Romans 8.26-28

We sometimes ask people to help with our prayers. When someone gets sick, or faces trouble, the word goes out: pray for me. We name individuals with special needs in Bethany's chapel and pray for them together. It feels good to know that someone else is joining you in praying for the same thing.

Look who this Bible verse says is joining us in prayer: God himself, God the Holy Spirit.

We don't appreciate the Holy Spirit enough. The primary work for which we thank God the Father, creation, is done. The primary work for which we thank God the Son, redemption, freeing us from our sins, that work was completed when Jesus said "it is finished" on the cross. The work of the Holy Spirit goes on and on with great intensity. The Spirit is the one who comes to us in God's Word, and in Baptism and the Holy Supper, touches our hard hearts, turns them to faith in Jesus, and brings us back to God.

And now we read that the Holy Spirit prays for us intensely. While there's no children's song that goes "The Holy Spirit Loves Me This I Know," the Holy Spirit does love us, and works earnestly and constantly for our good.

It feels good to know someone else is praying for you – grandma, parents, your sponsors, your pastor, your congregation, they all do. But also the Holy Spirit, God himself.

This is the confidence with which you can go to sleep tonight. God has promised to answer **our** prayers. Would he not answer his own? That is why the Apostle can assure us, that all things work together for good to those who love God.

†

August 2009

Stay a Child

People were bringing little children to Jesus to have him touch them, but the disciples rebuked them. When Jesus saw this, he was indignant. He said to them, "Let the little children come to me, and do not hinder them, for the kingdom of God belongs to such as these. I tell you the truth, anyone who will not receive the kingdom of God like a little child will never enter it." And he took the children in his arms, put his hands on them and blessed them. Mark 10.13-16

For many people this is a favorite incident in the life of our Savior. It should be a favorite of every child, to feel in this story the hug of Jesus who loves them and cares for them as the Good Shepherd cares for his lambs and knows each of them by name. It will become your favorite even more when you have children of your own and you have confidence in Jesus' promise that no one will snatch your children out of his hand. For those of you in between being a child and having children of your own, focus on Jesus' words here: *"I tell you the truth, anyone who will not receive the kingdom of God like a little child will never enter it."*

Jesus is talking about childlike faith. College is a time when your world expands quickly. You are away from home, meeting all kinds of new people, learning all kinds of new things, encountering all kinds of new experiences. You are taking the opportunity to re-examine your faith, very likely the faith in which you were baptized when a baby, and in which you grew up through your family and church, your Sunday school, perhaps a Lutheran elementary school. In light of all your new experiences and your studies, your religious beliefs will become more informed, and more sophisticated – really, much more grown up. You'll be dealing with what St. Paul calls theological meat, rather than just milk.

That's all good, healthy, in many ways exciting. But through it all, as you grow in knowledge, don't forget these words of Jesus. Because the essence of belonging to Jesus' kingdom is simple, childlike faith – putting aside doubts, pushing away pride and intellectual arrogance, scuttling any dependence on ourselves and our accomplishments, and instead simply trusting – trusting in the work of salvation Jesus earned for us when he entered the world to serve and please God in our place, and to be our substitute in sin-payment on the cross. At whatever age we are, let this be our song of childlike faith:

Jesus loves me, this I know, for the Bible tells me so.
Little ones to him belong; we are weak but he is strong.
Yes, Jesus loves me, the Bible tells me so.

†

August 2009

Believe and Call

When was the last time you called out to Jesus? Listen to this incident recorded by the Evangelist Mark.

> Then they came to Jericho. As Jesus and his disciples, together with a large crowd, were leaving the city, a blind man, Bartimaeus (that is, the Son of Timaeus), was sitting by the roadside begging. When he heard that it was Jesus of Nazareth, he began to shout, "Jesus, Son of David, have mercy on me!" Many rebuked him and told him to be quiet, but he shouted all the more, "Son of David, have mercy on me!" Jesus stopped and said, "Call him." So they called to the blind man, "Cheer up! On your feet! He's calling you." Throwing his cloak aside, he jumped to his feet and came to Jesus. "What do you want me to do for you?" Jesus asked him. The blind man said, "Rabbi, I want to see." "Go," said Jesus, "your faith has healed you." Immediately he received his sight and followed Jesus along the road. Mark 10.46-52

This bit of history reminds us of a great privilege that we who know Jesus have. We have the privilege of calling out to Jesus in faith. This is a story about prayer. Of course, we know about prayer. But do we pray as we ought? This story should encourage us to do that.

Calling out to Jesus in faith involves two things: faith and calling out. That's what the blind man near Jericho had, and did. He had faith: he knew who Jesus was. He named him when he called out: "Jesus, son of David," he said. This man, whose name was Son of Timaeus, that is Bar-Timaeus, knew his Bible, and he know the prophecies about the coming Messiah, that he would be a descendent of King David. He was confident that this promised one, this Savior, this Son of David, was who was passing by in front of him that very day. This faith prompted him to call out, *"Jesus, Son of David, have mercy on me!"* Despite the discouragement of those around him, he kept calling out, because he knew who Jesus was.

And it worked. Jesus heard him, stopped, and called Bartimaeus to him. Now here is a strange thing. Jesus asked him, *"What do you want me to do for you? How can I help you?"* Now clearly, Jesus knew what the man wanted. It wasn't only from his divine knowledge, but plainly everyone could see that the man was blind. Of course, he wanted to see. But Jesus asked him, made him say it, wanted him to make the request: *"Teacher, I want to see."*

Notice those two things; the man knew who Jesus was, and he called out. Jesus made him ask, wanted him to ask more than once. It was to exercise his faith. And he received what he asked for.

You and I know who Jesus is. He is the Son of David, Son of God, who by his life and death and resurrection has wiped away our sins and set us on the path to eternal life. And he invites us to exercise this faith in prayer, to call out to him in faith, perhaps even repeatedly.

Don't forget your prayers tonight.   †

September 2009

Fishes

We are getting into the first tests of the semester these days. You are used to taking tests by now, but still I know they add stress to your life. They bring you regularly face to face with success or failure. Look at another of Jesus' miracles tonight and see what it teaches us about success and failure. This was one of Jesus' first miracles, which he performed as he was choosing and gathering his special disciples.

> Now Jesus was standing by the Lake of Gennesaret, and the crowd was pressing around him to hear the word of God. He saw two boats by the lake, but the fishermen had gotten out of them and were washing their nets. He got into one of the boats, which was Simon's, and asked him to put out a little way from the shore. Then Jesus sat down and taught the crowds from the boat. When he had finished speaking, he said to Simon, "Put out into the deep water and lower your nets for a catch." Simon answered, "Master, we worked hard all night and caught nothing! But at your word I will lower the nets." When they had done this, they caught so many fish that their nets started to tear. So they motioned to their partners in the other boat to come and help them. And they came and filled both boats, so that they were about to sink. But when Simon Peter saw it, he fell down at Jesus' knees, saying, "Go away from me, Lord, for I am a sinful man!" For Peter and all who were with him were astonished at the catch of fish that they had taken, and so were James and John, Zebedee's sons, who were Simon's business partners. Then Jesus said to Simon, "Do not be afraid; from now on you will be catching people." So when they had brought their boats to shore, they left everything and followed him. Luke 5.1-11

What is the lesson here about success or failure? Well, notice that on this day, Peter and James and John were failures. They had caught nothing. They were professional fishermen, they made their living catching fish, they had worked hard all night – the best time for fishing – and had failed. Even at that, Peter still had pride. When Jesus told him to go out to the deep water and fish some more, Peter's reply indicated that he thought he knew more about fishing than Jesus but would go along with Jesus' suggestion anyway. What followed was tremendous success.

Peter got the main point of the miracle right away, and we do too. He knelt before Jesus and expressed his recognition that Jesus was who he said he was – that was the main point of every miracle Jesus performed: to reinforce his message that he was the Son of God come in the flesh. But alongside that main message we can learn something more about how Jesus came to help us. He is teaching us here that our success and failure are in his hands. It applies to school, and it applies to life. Yes, we are to work hard, but the fruits of our work are gifts from God. Keep that in mind; otherwise if you succeed you risk pride, and if you fail you feel guilt. Do your best, that's important, work hard and do your best, and then let the results rest in God's hands.

Jesus is our Savior. He is also our teacher. He came to please God with his life in our place, and die bearing our sins in our place. Our sins are forgiven. He came to assure us of Heaven. But he also taught us how to depend on him, entirely, not only for our salvation but for every success in life. They are all his gifts and his blessings.

†

September 2009

Pigs

Let me talk with you a few minutes tonight about how much you love your pigs. Yes, I said pigs. Don't own any, you say? What then about the other things you own? How attached are you to your **things**. What's your relation-ship with your car, your computer or iPhone, your wardrobe and fashions, the **stuff** that you own? Are your pigs more important to you than Jesus? What about your other stuff? Some people in Jesus' day faced this question and answered it poorly. Listen to what happened:

> So they came to the other side of the lake, to the region of the Gerase-nes. Just as Jesus was getting out of the boat, a man with an unclean spirit came from the tombs and met him. He lived among the tombs, and no one could bind him anymore, not even with a chain. For his hands and feet had often been bound with chains and shackles, but he had torn the chains apart and broken the shackles in pieces. No one was strong enough to subdue him. Each night and every day among the tombs and in the mountains, he would cry out and cut himself with stones. When he saw Jesus from a distance, he ran and bowed down before him. Then he cried out with a loud voice, "Leave me alone, Jesus,

Son of the Most High God! I implore you by God – do not torment me!" (For Jesus had said to him, "Come out of that man, you unclean spirit!") Jesus asked him, "What is your name?" And he said, "My name is Legion, for we are many." He begged Jesus repeatedly not to send them out of the region. There on the hillside, a great herd of pigs was feeding. And the demonic spirits begged him, "Send us into the pigs. Let us enter them." Jesus gave them permission. So the unclean spirits came out and went into the pigs. Then the herd rushed down the steep slope into the lake, and about two thousand were drowned in the lake. Now the herdsmen ran off and spread the news in the town and countryside, and the people went out to see what had happened. They came to Jesus and saw the demon-possessed man sitting there, clothed and in his right mind – the one who had the "Legion" – and they were afraid. Those who had seen what had happened to the demon-possessed man reported it, and they also told about the pigs. Then they asked Jesus to leave their region. As he was getting into the boat the man who had been demon-possessed asked if he could go with him. But Jesus did not permit him to do so. Instead, he said to him, "Go to your home and to your people and tell them what the Lord has done for you, that he had mercy on you." So he went away and began to proclaim in the Decapolis what Jesus had done for him, and all were amazed. Mark 5.1-20

Rejecting Jesus! It's such a sad and profound loss! What could prompt someone to send Jesus away, out of their lives? In this case, it was the loss of possessions. These people lost their pigs. But they lost much more than that – they lost the presence of Jesus in their lives forever. God has blessed each of us with an abundance of material possessions. We may not appreciate that fact until we travel abroad and see, in other parts of the world, how little people must get along with. That can make us very thankful for the material blessings God has showered on us. But stay focused on the more important spiritual blessings that Jesus brings: the forgiveness of our sins, the sure hope of Heaven, the love and kindness of God that is with us wherever we go – all made possible when Jesus brought us back to God through his sacrifice for us on the cross. Appreciate **all** of God's blessings, including your earthly possessions, but remember that finally they are only pigs. Never let **things** distract you from your deep heartfelt treasuring of Jesus and his gift of our salvation.

†

September 2009

Bold and Humble

How should we pray? First of all, remember that we **should** pray! We have a wonderful privilege to bring our requests and our troubles to God. Since God invites our prayers, we should bring our requests boldly. And yet, at the same time, remembering who we are, we should bring them humbly. Here's a great example.

> After going out from there, Jesus went to the region of Tyre and Sidon. A Canaanite woman from that area came and cried out, "Have mercy on me, Lord, Son of David! My daughter is horribly demon-possessed!" But he did not answer her a word. Then his disciples came and begged him, "Send her away, because she keeps on crying out after us." So he answered, "I was sent only to the lost sheep of the house of Israel." But she came and bowed down before him and said, "Lord, help me!" He said "It is not right to take the children's bread and throw it to the dogs". "Yes, Lord," she replied, "but even the dogs eat the crumbs that fall from their masters' table." Then Jesus answered her, "Woman, your faith is great! Let what you want be done for you." And her daughter was healed from that hour. Matthew 15.21-28

Notice this woman's boldness in bringing her request to Jesus. That came from her faith. She is **sure** Jesus can and will help her, so she doesn't quit, even when discouraged by the disciples, even when seeming to be discouraged by Jesus himself. Jesus wants us to be bold in coming to God with our requests and troubles. But while she is bold, this woman is not proud. When Jesus tells her it isn't right to take bread from the children – that is, the Jews, to whom God's Word came first – and throw it to dogs – that is, to foreigners, to Gentiles like us – she didn't say, can't God have other children? No, she was quick and willing to consider herself among the dogs. And the Lord commended her for her faith.

Our humility in bringing our prayers comes from many directions. We know our sins. We know that as Gentiles we were not the first to whom God's word came. We know we don't deserve anything from God and depend entirely on his grace. But it's that grace that gives us boldness. God showed his love for us by sending his only Son. As St. Paul says, *"He who did not spare his own Son, but gave him up for us all — how will he not also, along with him, graciously give us all things?"* Romans 8.32 That's the source of our boldness, as we humbly bring our prayers before God. Pray boldly and humbly, tonight.

†

September 2009

Thanks

Last night we learned from the example of the foreign woman to bring our prayers and requests and troubles to the Lord boldly, yet humbly. In tonight's reading we learn another important lesson about prayer: don't forget to say thank you. This is a short reading, and it speaks entirely for itself.

> Now on the way to Jerusalem, Jesus was passing along between Samaria and Galilee. As he was entering a village, ten men with leprosy met him. They stood at a distance, raised their voices and said, "Jesus, Master, have mercy on us." When he saw them he said, "Go and show yourselves to the priests." And as they went along, they were cleansed. Then one of them, when he saw he was healed, turned back, praising God with a loud voice. He fell with his face to the ground at Jesus' feet and thanked him. (Now he was a Samaritan.) Then Jesus said, "Were not ten cleansed? Where are the other nine? Was no one found to turn back and give praise to God except this foreigner?" Then he said to the man, "Get up and go your way. Your faith has made you well." Luke 17.11-19

Enough said. Start and end your prayer tonight with a hearty "Thanks be to God!"

†

November 2009

Love as Sign

Do you have any Christian jewelry? Maybe a cross – women wear it on a necklace, guys on a lapel pin. Well, some guys wear it on a necklace too. Maybe you have some clothing with a cross printed on it, or a Christian logo, or even a Bible passage. Good – things like this show you are not ashamed to be identified as a Christian.

God wants us to be obvious Christians. Not that we show it off or parade it. It's not done with pride, or even consciously. It's not something we put on when we choose to, like jewelry or clothing. It's something we **are**.

Listen to Jesus describing what it is about us that shows everyone that we are his followers. Here are his words to his disciples:

> A new command I give you: Love one another. As I have loved you, so you must love one another. By this all men will know that you are my disciples, if you love one another. John 13.34-35

That's the reading, and that's the sign that others should see in us. If we don't show love to others, it makes a mockery of any jewelry or clothing we might wear. If we show love to others, we don't need jewelry or clothing to show we are Christians – our lives are enough. And notice where Jesus says it comes from. *"As I have loved you, so you must love one another."* When we know his love for us, which prompted him to leave his heavenly throne, enter this sad world to live as we should for us, to die paying for our sins in our place, and to rise again to life bringing us with him – that love from Jesus empowers **us** to love him in return, and to obey his new command, that we love one another.

†

November 2009

Radiating Joy

Why does a person stop in the springtime to listen to the song of a bird? I think it's because that's one place we can hear pure joy, and pure joy is such a rare commodity that we notice it – the world notices it. Percy Shelley heard a skylark singing one day and envied the bird's joy and its power to draw the attention of the world. Here is what he wrote:

> Teach me half the gladness that thy brain must know – such harmonious madness from my lips would flow – the world should listen then as I am listening now.

Yes, pure joy is so rare, the world notices. That's why it's good for a Christian to exercise joy at receiving God's goodness and the forgiveness of sins we have through the work of Jesus Christ, as St. Paul urges us in this reading. Because showing our joy is not only a worshipful privilege in itself but it's an important witness of our faith to the world. Listen to the Apostle:

> Rejoice in the Lord always. I will say it again: Rejoice! Let your gentleness be evident to all. The Lord is near. Do not be anxious about anything, but in everything, by prayer and petition, with thanksgiving, present your requests to God. And the peace of God, which transcends all understanding, will guard your hearts and your minds in Christ Jesus. Philippians 4:4

†

November 2009

Thanks for Care

Let's talk birds and flowers. There's a scholarly journal called *Birds of North America* which over past 15 years has published careful detailed profiles of 610 species of birds from the black footed albatross to the sedge wren. You can read all those articles and discover that not one of these bird species has been observed checking the stock market each morning, or the weather report, or their GPA. And God takes care of them just fine.

Do you know lilies? Of course there are the white ones we see and smell at Easter, but have you looked carefully at the other kinds, yellow, apricot, orange, pink, red, multicolored ones – red center blending into yellow petals or yellow centers blending into pink petals or red centers blending into white petals – more than 100 different species, with new hybrids appearing almost daily with even more exquisite colors and patterns.

This thanksgiving we can thank God for a world of beauty, such as we see in birds and flowers. But more than this: Jesus points to birds and flowers as examples for us, examples of **all** of God's loving care and providence. He said,

> Look at the birds of the air; they do not sow or reap or store away in barns, and yet your heavenly Father feeds them. Are you not much more valuable than they? Who of you by worrying can add a single hour to his life? And why do you worry about clothes? See how the lilies of the field grow. They do not labor or spin. Yet I tell you that not even Solomon in all his splendor was dressed like one of these. If that is how God clothes the grass of the field, which is here today and tomorrow is thrown into the fire, will he not much more clothe you, O you of little faith? Matthew 6.26-30

Look, Jesus says, at the grace, the care, the providence of God all around you. See that this is God's way, providing in love for these lesser creatures. And then realize that God didn't send his Son to become a flower or bird but a human being, to become our brother, so he could lead for us the God-pleasing life we couldn't lead; so he could in his death wash away our sin with his own blood; so he could in his resurrection establish us before God's judgment as sinless and righteous.

That's his lesson from the birds and flowers about what we should be truly thankful for this Thanksgiving.

†

April 2010

Fear Love Trust 1

Here's a passage every college student will agree with, whether or not they believe the main message of the Bible which is of course about the salvation God brought to us through his Son Jesus Christ.

> Of making many books there is no end, and much study wearies the body. Ecclesiastes 12.12b

Yes, that's what it says. If ever you need to argue with an unbelieving college student about Scripture as truth, you can start there. But of course don't stop there; go on to the very next verses in Ecclesiastes where it says:

> Now all has been heard; here is the conclusion of the matter: Fear God and keep his commandments, for this is the whole [duty] of man. For God will bring every deed into judgment, including every hidden thing, whether it is good or evil. Ecclesiastes 12.13-14

If you've been through a Lutheran confirmation class, you've memorized all of the Ten Commandments, including Dr. Martin Luther's brief explanation of each of them. Those explanations all start the same way: "We should fear and love God..." and then it goes on to describe the meaning of each commandment. All of our duties to God, as summarized so well in the Ten Commandments, should be based on our fear and love of God. In fact, Luther's entire explanation of the First Commandment, that we should have no other gods, is this: "We should fear, love, and trust in God above all things." That trio: fear, love, and trust, will be the topics of this series of three devotions.

The first of the three is "fear God." It's here clearly in this passage from Ecclesiastes: *"Fear God and keep his commandments, for this is the whole [duty] of man. For God will bring every deed into judgment, including every hidden thing, whether it is good or evil."*

There are two basic meanings of "fear." One is to be afraid of, the other is to revere or seriously respect. We like to emphasize the second since it is more comfortable. We think, God doesn't want us to be afraid of him. But don't rule that out. Every Christian should have seriously considered the reasons we have to be truly afraid of God. He indeed has the power to condemn us to hell for all eternity. For all eternity! And all it takes for us to deserve that is one sin. One little sin, one violation of God's will, and the holy God, who cannot endure sin, must punish it with hell. Our passage says, *"For God will bring every deed into judgment, including every hidden thing, whether it is good or evil."* Next time you are tempted to do something you know is wrong, think about that. For doing that, you can be sent to hell for all eternity. When you fully realize that you start to know about fearing, being afraid of God.

But you know, that kind of fear won't prompt you to avoid that sin. That kind of fear is an appropriate response if all we know is God's Law, his rules for how we should live. Thankfully we know more than that from the Bible. We also know the Gospel – how God in his love for us took that sin that condemns us to hell, and put it instead on his own Son, Jesus Christ, who bore the full punishment for that sin, and for all the sins of the world, on the cross. That's how God can forgive our sins, rescue us from hell, and assure us instead of an eternity with him in Heaven. When we cling to that Gospel in faith we can set aside fear as being afraid of God, and instead fear God in the other sense. Only those who know the Gospel are capable of respecting and revering God, and in gratitude begin to live lives pleasing to God. When we keep in mind what Jesus has done for us, we can start to fulfill what this passage urges us: *"Fear God and keep his commandments, for this is the whole [duty] of man."*

†

April 2010

Fear Love Trust 2

We're talking these nights about Dr. Luther's explanation to the most fundamental of God's commandments, that we should have no other gods. Luther said that means, "We should fear, love, and trust in God above all things." Tonight we consider the second of that triad: love God.

Among the last words Moses the lawgiver spoke to the people before his death, he said this:

> Love the LORD your God and keep his requirements, his decrees, his laws and his commands always. Deuteronomy 11.1

From these words we know that Moses was a Christian, even though he lived many years before Christ was born. Nobody but a Christian could talk in the same breath about loving God and keeping his commands. Great theologians, like Moses, St. Augustine, Martin Luther, C. F. W. Walther, and many others all knew the nature of God's Law, God's commandments, and their effect on those who try to keep them. They all knew that, under the Law by itself, nobody can love God. If God's commands are all we have, there can be no love of God because nobody can keep God's commands. We all fall far, far short of keeping God's commands. When we realize we can't *"keep God's requirements, decrees, laws, and commands always"* (as Moses says), we must hate the God who makes such impossible demands. God's Law, by itself, if understood and taken fully seriously, does not make people better. It makes them worse. It doesn't make them love God – it makes them resent and hate God. Pressure to do the impossible under threat of punishment only increases resentment and anger of God, not love of God.

That's why this passage before us tonight makes me certain that Moses was a Christian. Moses said, love God. He could say that only if he knew the Gospel. Moses knew, as we do, that only the Gospel can prompt love of God. The Gospel teaches us that Jesus by his life and death wiped out our sins in the eyes of God. One who believes in Jesus has no fear of punishment for falling short of God's commands, because God in grace punished his Son Jesus in our place. For that, we can love God.

And only a Gospel-inspired love of God can enable the Christian to embrace the Law of God and try in gratitude to please God by keeping his commands. When Moses said, *"Love the LORD your God and keep his requirements, his decrees, his laws and his commands always,"* he pre-supposed the Gospel, a Gospel Moses knew and believed in just as we do.

Jesus echoed Moses when he said: *"Love the Lord your God with all your heart and with all your soul and with all your mind."* Matthew 22.37 Then Jesus made it possible for us to love God by going to the cross for us. Moved by that love, we keep his commandments.

†

April 2010

Fear Love Trust 3

Jesus, on the night he was betrayed and arrested, said to his disciples,

Do not let your hearts be troubled. Trust in God; trust also in me. John 14.1

We've been talking these evenings about the well-known triad in Dr. Luther's explanation to the most basic of the Ten Commandments, that we should "fear, love, and trust in God above all things." In the verse before us this evening, spoken the night before he was crucified for us, Jesus invited his followers to trust him, just as we trust God.

In social science literature, we find many definitions of trust. This one from Roy Lewicki captures their essence: "Trust," he says, is "someone's belief in, and willingness to act on the basis of the words, actions, and decisions of another." I see two parts in this definition. Last part first: to trust someone, we must first know their words, actions, decisions. And then (first part) we must believe in them to the point of being willing to act on those words, actions, and decisions.

Consider the difficulty of trusting Jesus over the next few hours and days after he spoke these words. He said, trust me and then the disciples would see him arrested, tried, tortured, condemned, killed, and buried. Dark doings indeed. And yet they had heard Jesus say earlier, again and again, that he knew he would have to die and that he would rise again on the third day. Jesus had told them that. Did they trust those words? Did they, according to our definition, believe in Jesus' words that he would rise again, and were they willing to act on them? Apparently not. When Jesus was arrested, they scattered, they denied they knew Jesus, they hid behind locked doors in fright.

Would you and I have done better? It's easy to say we trust our Lord when things are going well. How hard it is to trust the words of our Lord when things are rough, when things seem to be going wrong, when our plans fall apart, when we don't see how things can turn out well. Is that when we scatter, and hide, and in our hearts or our behavior deny that we know Jesus?

Remember that it was at this darkest hour when Jesus urged his disciples, *"Trust in God, trust also in me."* Then he went on to the cross and paid for our sins before God and won us for eternal life. Listen to the words of Jesus again in this passage before us, and then let me read on so you can hear his very next words:

> Do not let your hearts be troubled. Trust in God; trust also in me. In my Father's house are many rooms; if it were not so, I would have told you. I am going there to prepare a place for you. And if I go and prepare a place for you, I will come back and take you to be with me that you also may be where I am." John 14.1-3

Those are words of Jesus that we can trust.

†

April 2010

Fear Love Trust 4

LAW & GOSPEL

We've spoken the past few nights about God's law, the demands and expectations a holy God has for us. We explored the fundamental requirements of the Ten Commandments, as Dr. Luther put it, that we fear, love, and trust in God above all things.

I hope, as you listen to this discussion of God's Law from Bethany Lutheran College, that you fully appreciate that you are hearing a Lutheran discussion. Because Dr. Luther, following in the tradition starting with Moses, and continuing through St. Paul, St. Augustine, and many others including our Lord himself – Dr. Luther understood the role and place of God's Law. Yes, he knew it is wonderful and glorious, because it expresses the perfect will of God. But he also knew what the Law of God does to us: it condemns us. Since we can't keep God's Law perfectly as a holy God must demand, it kills us. Thank God, Dr. Luther (and all those others) knew that besides the Law, there is another great teaching in the Bible, there is another wonderful expression of God's will: God wants everyone to be saved. That's what we call the Gospel. And glorious as the Law is, the Gospel is even more glorious. Listen to St. Paul:

> Now if the ministry that brought death, which was engraved in letters on stone, came with glory, so that the Israelites could not look steadily at the face of Moses because of its glory, fading though it was, will not the ministry of the Spirit be even more glorious? If the ministry that condemns men is glorious, how much more glorious is the ministry that brings righteousness! For what was glorious has no glory now in comparison with the surpassing glory. And if what was fading away came with glory, how much greater is the glory of that which lasts! 2 Corinthians 3.7-11

And so the Gospel unfolded. God's great salvation plan was revealed as Jesus was born in Bethlehem and lived a life sinless and totally pleasing to God – a holiness that was to be transferred to us – and then he died, deserving to die only because our sins had been transferred to him. Jesus fulfilled the Law for us, in our place, and then discharged the debt of our law-breaking by paying its penalty on the cross in our place. So Paul can write, *"If the ministry that condemns men is glorious, how much more glorious is the ministry that brings righteousness!"*

God's Law is precious to us. Yes, it teaches us how we are to live, and that's important to us. But far more important, God's Law is precious to us because it drives us to Jesus Christ in whom alone is our rescue from the Law's condemnation. Jesus is the glory that lasts. Celebrate that every day.

†

September 7, 2010

Time 1 Future

At the beginning of the school year, as we settle down into our Bethany routines, our whole lives, it seems, are oriented to the future, to what the coming year will bring.

Will this or that class be interesting? Will I find my academic passion, and finally decide on a major or a career? Will I make the team, or the choir, or the play cast, or whatever it is you are getting involved in? Will we have a good year? Should I look for an internship? Where? Will any new friendships develop? Will I find that special friend?

All good questions, worth wondering about. In fact, it's God-pleasing to wonder about such things, to pay attention to our future. Our Christian faith makes us very **future oriented**. God in his Word frequently points us to the future, especially inviting us to center our plans and our lives around him. That's the case with the Scripture passage before us this evening from a psalm.

> O Israel, put your hope in the LORD, for with the LORD is unfailing love and with him is full redemption. Psalm 130.7

Put your hope in the Lord! That is, plan your future around God. And if **our** plans don't go as we had hoped, have confidence that what happens to us is still "around God."

The **reason** we can have that confidence is here in this passage too: "*For with the Lord is unfailing love and with him is full redemption.*"

Full redemption. Jesus with his innocent life, his death bearing our sins, his resurrection that brings us too out from under the curse of death – Jesus has brought us full redemption, bought us back from death and destruction, and provides us a real future, one that will go on (as the Bethany Lutheran College slogan proclaims) "beyond a lifetime." That's the Lord's unfailing love.

So we can move into the school year with our hope in the Lord. And in each area of our future orientation – teams, friends, majors, careers, spouses – let our prayer be: Lord thank you for your unfailing love; now, in each of these areas, let me serve you.

Amen.

†

September 8, 2010

Time 2 Present

This is the day the LORD has made; let us rejoice and be glad in it.
Psalm 118.24

Last night we thought about being future oriented. Tonight let's talk about enjoying the present moment.

That's worth doing because, while God out of his great love and grace promises great things for the future of those who believe in his Son, he has also given us the precious gift of **this moment**.

It's too easy to forget about this gift.

We walk to class thinking about what will happen in that class, and we don't enjoy the walk across our beautiful campus.

We make our way through a meal looking forward so much to dessert that we fail to enjoy the meal.

In church we look forward to the sermon while all the beautiful words of the liturgy slip past our consciousness. How much better to be able to concentrate and dwell on the meaning of each word in the confession, and the absolution, and the hymn, and the Lord's Prayer, without our minds slipping ahead to what's next, even to what's going on Sunday afternoon.

If we are always focused on the next thing, we won't appreciate and enjoy this moment.

So the Lord urges us in this psalm: *"This is the day the LORD has made; let us rejoice and be glad in it."*

We might even say, this is the **moment** the Lord has made. Each moment of our lives is blessed by God. Each moment in the life of a Christian steps toward our ultimate goal. As we read in Paul's letter to the Corinthians: *"I tell you, now is the time of God's favor, now is the day of salvation."* 2 Corinthians 6.2 Each blessed moment of our lives, then, can be dedicated to God.

Yes, that includes even the bad moments – and there are some. Even these are moments for rejoicing. As St. Paul wrote to the Philippians, *"Rejoice in the Lord always. I will say it again: Rejoice!"* not just in good times, but always Philippians 4.4. For it shows the utmost trust in God to be joyful in the Lord even in bad times.

This moment is precious, redeemed by Jesus. Notice it and enjoy it.

†

September 10, 2010

Time 3 Past

We've spoken this week about being future oriented, and also about rejoicing in the present moment. Now we speak of appreciating the past.

You are not as old as I. Fewer and fewer people are. But even in your shorter life, you have many highlights to remember – a big date, a big game victory, a family gathering. You know how important those past events were to you – in fact, how important they **are** to you, for they helped shape you into the person you are today.

Tonight let's focus on two past events that did more than any other to shape you into the person you are today. One is reported in St. Paul's first letter to Timothy, where he says:

> Here is a trustworthy saying that deserves full acceptance: Christ Jesus came into the world to save sinners. 1 Timothy 1.15

Of course, that is a past event that makes all the difference for us. Jesus came. He entered history at the first Christmas; God became human, to be our brother, to keep God's holy law in our place since we could not, and to suffer in our place the punishment we owed for our sins. He died for us, and then he rose again from the dead. That historical past event makes all the difference for us. It shapes you into the person you are today: a believer in Jesus.

There is a second historical event that fits perfectly into this first one: your Baptism. St. Paul wrote,

> Or don't you know that all of us who were baptized into Christ Jesus were baptized into his death? We were therefore buried with him through Baptism into death in order that, just as Christ was raised from the dead through the glory of the Father, we too may live a new life. If we have been united with him like this in his death, we will certainly also be united with him in his resurrection." Romans 6.3f

These words illuminate how wonderful for each of us was this second historical event. First Jesus came to save sinners. Then in your Baptism, you were united with Jesus in his death and will join him in his resurrection.

There they are: two events in history, things that really happened, that make you and me what we are today and, more important, they make us what we will be tomorrow and for all eternity.

Thanks be to God!

†

September 11, 2010

Pure Worship

In morning chapel last week I spoke about two verses from Psalm 147,[1] and if you were there you might remember that I promised to bring you back to this psalm in an *Evening Bells* this week. It's an especially attractive psalm because, in a sense, it is pure worship. It doesn't bring any cares before God. It doesn't ask for anything. It is simple joy and gratitude.

Yes, God does invite us to bring our cares to him: he says *"call upon me in the day of trouble, and I will deliver you, and you will glorify me."* Psalm 50.15 Yes, God does urge us to ask him for things: Jesus said: *"Therefore I tell you, whatever you ask for in prayer, believe that you have received it, and it will be yours."* Mark 11.24 So we should not be shy about bringing our cares to God, and about asking him for anything.

But too often our care-burdened prayers and our petition-loaded prayers are too selfish. Too often our prayers take for granted all that God has already done for us and must sound to him like a spoiled little child who has been given everything, and still demands **more more**!

So at times it is good for us to repent of our self-centeredness even in prayer, and come before the Lord as this psalm brings us to him: without expressing cares or needs, without request or petition, but only with an outpouring of thanks for all God has done for us. In that spirit, hear the words of Psalm 147.

> Praise the LORD. How good it is to sing praises to our God, how pleasant and fitting to praise him!
> The LORD builds up Jerusalem; he gathers the exiles of Israel.
> He heals the brokenhearted and binds up their wounds.
> He determines the number of the stars and calls them each by name.
> Great is our Lord and mighty in power; his understanding has no limit.
> The LORD sustains the humble but casts the wicked to the ground.
> Sing to the LORD with thanksgiving; make music to our God on the harp.
> He covers the sky with clouds; he supplies the earth with rain and makes grass grow on the hills.
> He provides food for the cattle and for the young ravens when they call.
> His pleasure is not in the strength of the horse, nor his delight in the legs of a man;
> The LORD delights in those who fear him, who put their hope in his unfailing love.
> Extol the LORD, O Jerusalem; praise your God, O Zion,

---

[1] September 7, 2010, Today, Only Thank You

for he strengthens the bars of your gates and blesses your people within you.

He grants peace to your borders and satisfies you with the finest of wheat.

He sends his command to the earth; his word runs swiftly.

He spreads the snow like wool and scatters the frost like ashes.

He hurls down his hail like pebbles. Who can withstand his icy blast?

He sends his word and melts them; he stirs up his breezes, and the waters flow.

He has revealed his word to Jacob, his laws and decrees to Israel.

He has done this for no other nation; they do not know his laws. Praise the LORD. Psalm 147

†

Index of Bible Texts Referenced

Texts that formed the basis of an entire homily are in **bold italics**